D1551598

Descartes' *Cogito*

Saved from the Great Shipwreck

Perhaps the most famous proposition in the history of philosophy is
Descartes' *cogito*, "I think, therefore I am." Husain Sarkar claims in this
provocative new interpretation of Descartes that the ancient tradition
of reading the *cogito* as an argument is mistaken. It should, he says, be
read as an intuition. Through this new interpretative lens, the author
reconsiders key Cartesian topics: the ideal inquirer; the role of clear
and distinct ideas; the relation of these to the will; memory; the nature
of intuition and deduction; the nature, content, and elusiveness of
'I'; and the tenability of the doctrine of the creation of eternal truths.
Finally, the book demonstrates how Descartes' attempt to prove the
existence of God is foiled by a new Cartesian Circle.

Husain Sarkar is Professor of Philosophy at Louisiana State University.

Descartes' *Cogito*

Saved from the Great Shipwreck

HUSAIN SARKAR

Louisiana State University

CAMBRIDGE
UNIVERSITY PRESS

ST. PHILIP'S COLLEGE LIBRARY

B
1873
S37
2003

PUBLISHED BY THE PRESS SYNDICATE OF THE UNIVERSITY OF CAMBRIDGE
The Pitt Building, Trumpington Street, Cambridge, United Kingdom

CAMBRIDGE UNIVERSITY PRESS
The Edinburgh Building, Cambridge CB2 2RU, UK
40 West 20th Street, New York, NY 10011-4211, USA
477 Williamstown Road, Port Melbourne, VIC 3207, Australia
Ruiz de Alarcón 13, 28014 Madrid, Spain
Dock House, The Waterfront, Cape Town 8001, South Africa

http: // www.cambridge.org

© Husain Sarkar 2003

This book is in copyright. Subject to statutory exception
and to the provisions of relevant collective licensing agreements,
no reproduction of any part may take place without
the written permission of Cambridge University Press.

First published 2003

Printed in the United Kingdom at the University Press, Cambridge

Typeface ITC New Baskerville 10/13.5 pt.   *System* LATEX 2ε   [TB]

A catalog record for this book is available from the British Library.

Library of Congress Cataloging in Publication data
Sarkar, Husain, 1942–
Descartes' *cogito* : saved from the great shipwreck / Husain Sarkar.
p.   cm.
Includes bibliographical references (p.) and indexes.
ISBN 0-521-82166-5
1. Descartes, René, 1596–1650.   I. Title.
B1873 .S37   2003
194–dc21   2002073601

ISBN 0 521 82166 5 hardback

ST. PHILIP'S COLLEGE LIBRARY

For

Ashifa

part ballerina, part lover of children, my daughter

وَجَادِلْهُمْ بِالَّتِيْ هِيَ أَحْسَنُ

Reason with them in the most courteous manner.
(The Koran, Chapter 16, "The Bee," verse 125)

What are you saying? You *know*? Is this certain and beyond all doubt? Is this the sole surviving timber from the great shipwreck that is to be hung up as an offering in the temple of truth?

Pierre Bourdin, "Seventh Set of Objections," in *The Philosophical Writings of Rene Descartes*, Volume 2, 317.

Contents

Preface

Rene Descartes offered an ultimate truth, famously known as the *cogito*. But there have been virtually no takers. Some have thought that it was merely an analytic statement, a statement empty of content; some have thought that he should have begun with a less complex, a less unwarranted statement (but then he could not have derived the *cogito* from it); some have averred that it was an argument that was badly in need of repair (and when repaired, one that could not possibly do what Descartes had wanted it to do); and a distinguished philosopher once argued that the truth of the *cogito*, if that is what it is, is at best odd, "degenerate." This has been the litany for 350 years.

Here is Descartes in *Discourse on the Method*:

But immediately I noticed that while I was trying thus to think everything false, it was necessary that I, who was thinking this, was something. And observing that this truth, "*I am thinking, therefore I exist*" was so firm and sure that all the most extravagant suppositions of the skeptics were incapable of shaking it, I decided that I could accept it without scruple as the first principle of the philosophy I was seeking.

Then, in his "Replies to the Second Set of Objections":

When we observe that we are thinking beings, this is a sort of primary notion, which is not the conclusion of any syllogism; and, moreover, when somebody says: I am thinking, therefore I am or exist, he is not using a syllogism to deduce his existence from his thought, but recognizing this as something self-evident, in a simple mental intuition.

In effect, Descartes is saying both that the *cogito* is an argument (reading the 'therefore' as a conclusion indicator) and that it is not. There is simply no interpretation of Descartes that will not fail to explain at least *some* of the text. One might as well try to square a circle.

Consequently, in this book I have attempted to do the next best thing, to provide an interpretation that will save as much as possible of what is profound and interesting in Descartes. There are two sides to the *cogito* debate: what it is and what it is not. There are novel and fairly conclusive reasons why the *cogito* cannot be construed as an argument. I offer these and thereby show what the *cogito* is not. A great deal of what Descartes has said militates against construing the *cogito* as an argument. It was with some of those reasons that this book was begun.

But if the *cogito* is not an argument, what then is it? It is an experiment. When that experiment is conducted, the mind intuits – learns through an insight – the truth that the *cogito* expresses. The experiment will teach an individual thinker by example what he cannot learn by relying on someone else's experiment, or on that of a collection of individuals, no matter how well conducted the experiment and precise the reporting. However, it is an experiment that can be performed only after the mind has been cleansed and prepared. Now, these two claims are, of course, independent. Whether the view that the *cogito* is an experiment, to be performed by an individual thinker, is true has no implication for whether the *cogito* is an argument. In fact, I think that the negative claim offered here, namely, that the *cogito* is not an argument, is decisive. But that is not so with the positive thesis as to what the *cogito* is.

The investigation into the *cogito*, this first principle, led me to uncover the basic structure of Descartes' method. I wanted to focus not on the details but on the essence of his method. For I was certain that the *cogito* and the method were too intimately linked to be understood one without the other. At any rate, getting the method right was a prerequisite to being right about the *cogito*. The focus on method and *cogito* inevitably led to other issues in Descartes, such as logic and skepticism, will and memory, discovery and explanation, reason and experience, eternal truths and the general rule. I have explored none of these as fully as I might have. I have had a more limited aim: In each instance, the scope of the inquiry was sharply restricted by what it had to contribute to the *cogito* and the method. Thus, I have tried to bring in a sequence of distinct issues in Descartes and to balance and counterbalance them. The result, I trust, is a fresh perspective.

Montaigne wrote an essay entitled, "That Our Happiness Must Not Be Judged until After Our Death." Borrowing the same theme from Ovid, I propose a principle of reconstruction and call it the Sulmo principle, namely, that a philosopher's system must not be reconstructed and judged until after his death. For what he once assumed, he may later radically question (as did Descartes on the certainty of mathematics); what he once sketched, he may in time expand in great detail (as did Descartes on the unity of the sciences); what he once wrote, he may subsequently abrogate (as did Descartes, virtually, on the immortality of the soul); what he once wrote, he may remain silent about for the rest of his life (as did Descartes on the taxonomy of problems). Only after his death can one say that, if he had tied his views together at the end into a single consistent system, he would have done so in this way or that; only then can one judge the worth of the system. When attempting to reconstruct, there are enough avenues to explore, in harmony with the philosopher's general view. This allows for much guesswork. The whole, and only the whole, reconstructed at the end, should be judged for historical plausibility and philosophical soundness. At any rate, it is the principle of Sulmo that I have used in this book.

The ideal author of a book on Descartes would be someone who has mastered all of the French and Latin texts of Descartes as they currently exist in Charles Adams and Paul Tannery, *Oeuvres de Descartes*, and in F. Alquié, *Oeuvres philosophiques de Descartes*. He would be familiar with all of the responses of Descartes' contemporaries, and with the commentaries from the seventeenth century, such as Tepelli's *Historia Philosophiae Cartesiane*; with eighteenth-century works, such as Rousseau's *The Profession of Faith of a Savoyard Priest*; and with items from the nineteenth century, such as Duboux's *La Physique de Descartes*, down to the commentaries of the twentieth century. Not only would he have kept track of all these items, their moorings and interconnections, and how each of them measures up to the original, he would also be familiar with all of the recent work in metaphysics, philosophy of mind, philosophy of religion, philosophy of science, history of physics, and mathematics and logic, so that he could determine how far ahead of Descartes we are in a given field, or how far behind. Then, and only

then, would he write a book on Descartes. I fall miserably short of that
ideal.

This book is not in the same line as the works that sweep over a
vast range of the philosophy of Descartes, such as those of Baker and
Curley; Gaukroger, Kenny, and Kemp Smith; Wilson and Williams. It
is a commentary on Descartes' *Meditations*, which he called "my little
book dealing with First Philosophy." It is, moreover, a commentary
on only the first few pages. Such, I think, is the power of his views.
I have strenuously aimed to be fair to the history of philosophy, and
struggled not to be silly in any anachronistic way: In short, I have tried
to argue with Descartes as if I were his contemporary, not he mine.
This, in part, explains the frequent citation of page and passage from
Descartes. My ultimate aim has been to reconstruct Descartes' ideas in
a manner that demands that we see Descartes' achievement for what it
is: He achieved in his field what Archimedes had only dreamed about
in his.

Baton Rouge, Louisiana
February 1, 2002

Acknowledgments

In the fall of 1989 I went to England with the oldest version of this book, commenced in November or December of the year before, and returned in the spring of the following year with lots of notes and marginalia for the making of a better one. The result of subsequent attempts at doing just that is here. For that result, and the trip across the Atlantic and back, I am grateful to two institutions: Louisiana State University, for granting me sabbatical and other leave, and the University of Cambridge, for electing me a Visiting Scholar for 1989–90. But nearly as much is owed to the commons flanking Victoria Avenue, with a narrow part of the River Cam providing the margin, where I spent long hours, day and night, and did my best thinking, such as it was, under the rarely clear English sky. The second version was completed at the end of September 1992.

Then, for several years, I turned to work on other things (while intermittently thinking about and teaching Descartes). Nine years later, in February 1998, I went to the University of Oxford as a Faculty Visitor for the Hilary Term. I owe a debt not only to the University of Oxford but also, once again, to Louisiana State University for making this possible by granting me sabbatical leave. This time I went with a somewhat better version of the book, in hopes that good things might come from my visit. They did. Anthony Kenny provided written comments; he was encouraging in several details, found the second version better than the skimpy first, but remained steadfast in his belief that the *cogito* is an argument. I mulled a long time over his detailed written comments.

I then rewrote the relevant material to show that his view is confronted by some very serious difficulties. Of my readers, he was the only one to clearly perceive that, among other things, I was trying to show that a continuum can be seen, or forged, between the early and later work of Descartes; he is not entirely convinced by it, although he was kind enough to say that I have made a serious case for it.

Gordon Baker not only proved to be a very kind host but also, through many long conversations on the manuscript, led me happily to believe that perhaps there is something to the central thesis of this book; nevertheless, I reconsidered several of my arguments in light of his remarks and upon reading his own book on Descartes (which he wrote with Katherine J. Morris). In the final analysis, I have always relied on his written, rather than his spoken, word. (Oxford's best gift to me, however, was the discovery of the novels of Jim Crace.)

I am grateful to Katholieke Universiteit Leuven for the invitation to participate in their Thursday Lecture series. In October 1998 I read a paper there entitled "In Defense of Skepticism," an early draft of what now sits as sections II–IV of Chapter 4. I started work on the penultimate version in May 1999, furiously working for about five months, doing minor editing work for several weeks thereafter, and finishing in January 2000. The final version was started in late July 2001 and ended in January 2002.

I am grateful to Richard A. Watson for his generous encouragement. Alas, even what he approved I had to remove for lack of space. Although he agreed substantially with the core thesis, John Compton's trenchant and detailed written criticisms – especially on the self and self-identity – left little doubt about what he thought of Descartes' positive thesis. Had I even fragmentary knowledge of the work of Edumnd Husserl, I know he would have found my responses better informed and my subsidiary theses less objectionable.

Jeffrey Tlumak commented in the margins of the manuscript, virtually on every third page. I refrained from answering every one of his objections, or the book would have been twice as long. I have answered, at least to my own satisfaction, several of his objections; several others have remained unanswered simply because I did not know how to accomplish that within the confines of the allotted space. The force of his other objections I have duly acknowledged. I owe him additional gratitude because he provided me with his painstaking comments at a time when he was passing through an incredible hardship.

Of the anonymous referees for Cambridge University Press, I single out three: for their old-fashioned, easily discernible, Kantian goodwill; and for resonating with the central thesis of this book and saving it from a thousand infelicities, thus making it a better book, both in form and substance – I thank them for that favor, too. Whatever appeal this book may possess by way of artwork and diagrams is owed entirely to my son, Casim Ali. I am grateful as well to Russell Hahn for his superb copyediting. Without the persistence – I almost said protection – of Terence Moore, the editor, this book would have seen the light of day, but under a very different seal.

Last and greatest is my debt to Catherine Wilson. She has been a provider of innumerable corrections, a host of tough philosophical questions, and acute analysis; she has also been a dispenser of encouragement. No doubt this manuscript is far less objectionable than it would have been otherwise, had she not given it her time and expertise. Indeed, the title of the book stands a bit modified, thanks to her.

For my ending I will adapt one of Machiavelli's beginnings and address my benefactors collectively thus: "With this I send you a gift. I have endeavored to embody in it all that long experience and assiduous research have taught me. But you may well complain of my lack of talent when my arguments are poor, and of the fallacies of my judgment on account of the errors into which I have doubtless fallen many times. This being so, however, I know you have a right to complain that I should have written without giving you cause to be satisfied, which, if it bears no proportion to the extent of the obligations that I owe you, is nevertheless the best I am able to offer you."

Abbreviations

AN   Antoine Arnauld and Pierre Nicole, *Logic or the Art of Thinking*. Translated and edited by Jill Vance Buroker. Cambridge: Cambridge University Press, 1996.

AT   Charles Adam and Paul Tannery, editors, *Oeuvres de Descartes*. Volumes 1–12, revised edition. Paris: Vrin/CNRS, 1964–76.

C   Edwin M. Curley, *Descartes against the Skeptics*. Cambridge, Mass.: Harvard University Press, 1978.

CSM   *The Philosophical Writings of Descartes*, Volumes I and II. Translated by John Cottingham, Robert Stoothoff, and Dugald Murdoch. Cambridge: Cambridge University Press, 1984.

CSMK   *The Philosophical Writings of Descartes*, Volume III. *The Correspondence*. Translated by John Cottingham, Robert Stoothoff, Dugald Murdoch, and Anthony Kenny. Cambridge: Cambridge University Press, 1991.

G   Stephen Gaukroger, *Descartes: An Intellectual Biography*. New York: Oxford University Press, 1995.

K   Anthony Kenny, *Descartes: A Study of his Philosophy*. New York: Random House, 1968.

M   Michael de Montaigne, *An Apology for Raymond Sebond*. Translated and edited by M. A. Screech. New York: Penguin, 1987.

R   Genevieve Rodis-Lewis, *Descartes: His Life and Thought*. Translated by Jane Marie Todd. Ithaca, N.Y.: Cornell University Press, 1999.

V   Jack Rochford Vrooman, *Rene Descartes: A Biography*. New York: G. P. Putnam's Sons, 1970.

W   Bernard Williams, *Descartes: The Project of Pure Inquiry*. New York: Penguin, 1978.

WC   Bernard Williams, "The Certainty of the *Cogito.*" In Willis Doney, editor, *Descartes: A Collection of Critical Essays.* London: Macmillan, 1968, pp. 88–107.

WM   Margaret D. Wilson, *Descartes.* New York: Routledge and Kegan Paul, 1986.

Descartes' *Cogito*
Saved from the Great Shipwreck

1

The Prolegomena to Any Future Epistemology

In 1628, Rene Descartes received an invitation to a meeting at the home of Cardinal Bagni, papal nuncio. Descartes brought with him Father Mersenne, a Minim friar, and M. de Ville-Bressieu, a physician of Grenoble. This was no ordinary meeting. It consisted of well-known *honnets gens* of Paris. They had met to hear a famous doctor-chemist by the name of Chandoux. Chandoux was an expert on base metals who three years later was to be executed for peddling fake currency. Chandoux, charming and fluent, was denouncing the verbiage of scholastic philosophy as it was usually taught in the Schools. There was little new in what he said, for it was mostly in the vein of Francis Bacon, Pierre Gassendi, and Thomas Hobbes. Yet he wanted his system of philosophy to appear fresh and novel. Whatever Chandoux said, everyone applauded. That is, everyone save Descartes.

The founder of the oratory, and perhaps the most powerful religious thinker of the Counter-Reformation, Cardinal Berulle, observed this. He asked Descartes what he thought of Chandoux's speech that had so thrilled the audience. Descartes demurred, saying "that he could not speak in opposition to the feeling of the *savants* present."[1] But the Cardinal did not relent. At last, Descartes spoke. He began by praising Chandoux's denunciation of scholastic philosophy. But then he argued against the speaker and "that great and learned company" for

---

[1] Elizabeth S. Haldane, *Descartes: His Life and Times*, 108. The details of the references are given in the bibliography.

taking *probability* as the central notion and not the notion of *truth*. If
one were satisfied with something merely probable, he argued, then
one could easily take false statements to be true and true statements to
be false. As evidence, he asked that someone in the audience propose
what he deemed to be an incontestable truth. Someone volunteered,
and Descartes proceeded to show in twelve arguments, relying on the
notion of probability, that the proposed statement was false.[2] He then
asked that someone propose a statement that he took to be incon-
testably false. Once again, with reasoning by probability as his guide,
he showed the statement to be true. He thus demonstrated that our
minds can become victims of the notion of probability. The audience
was duly stunned, and some openly deserted Chandoux on the spot.

The *savants* begged to know if there was a method, "some infallible
means to avoid these difficulties." Descartes replied that there was his
own method. "I made the whole company recognize what power the
art of right reasoning has over the minds of those who have no learning
beyond the ordinary, and how much better founded, and more true
and natural, my principles are than any of those which are currently
received in the learned world" (CSMK, 32; AT I, 213). Such a method
would be useful not only in metaphysics, but also in mechanics and
medicine. Cardinal Berulle, whom the young philosopher met with
privately shortly afterward, was impressed beyond words. With the full
weight of his ecclesiastical authority, he urged Descartes to write and
publish his views, on the ground that he, Descartes, "was responsible
to God for giving to mankind what had been delivered to him."[3] Thus
was born, some nine years later, *Discourse on the Method* – and with it,
the history of modern philosophy.

[2] On October 5, 1637, Descartes wrote to Father Mersenne, complaining that Fermat
had misunderstood him: "He thought that when I said that something was easy to
believe, I meant that it was no more than probable; but in this he has altogether mistaken my meaning. I consider almost as false whatever is only a matter of probability;
and when I say that something is easy to believe I do not mean that it is only probable,
but that it is so clear and so evident that there is no need for me to stop to prove it."
(CSMK III, 74; AT I, 450–451)

[3] Elizabeth S. Haldane, *Descartes: His Life and Times*, 110. Alas, the private meeting with
Cardinal Berulle – Haldane undoubtedly got it from Adrien Baillet's (1649–1706)
La Vie de Monsieur Descartes, the first biography of Descartes – has been contested by
Genevieve Rodis-Lewis in her marvelous book *Descartes: His Life and Thought*. (See
R, 67–69 and 240, note 21, for further details on this episode.)

Granting the possibility of knowledge, what kind of person can pursue and possess knowledge? Descartes thinks that only a certain kind of person can, or at any rate should, embark on the pursuit of knowledge and come to possess it. Section I of this chapter delineates the making of such an ideal knower, who should be armed with a method in his pursuit, like a traveler who ought to carry a map on his journey. Section II provides just such a rationalist method. Section III presents Descartes' famous tree of philosophy: This is Descartes' view of what the completed structure of science would look like. Finally, section IV presents the moral code a pursuer of knowledge should abide by, and I raise the question of whether Descartes is attempting, in this endeavor, to raise himself by his own bootstraps.

I. The Making of an Ideal Seeker

It is our modern liberal view that anyone, man or woman, of any station in life, can embark on studying any discipline, at any time, and at any place, and that what he or she learns will depend on how hard he or she works. There are no other restrictions. This view was not always held. Descartes, for instance, did not hold it. He thought not only that it was necessary for a person to possess certain intellectual and emotional qualities, but also that he had to undergo an initial period of preparation before he could finally embark on a strenuous philosophical inquiry.

Descartes became aware only very slowly of the problem of the ideal seeker. In *Rules for the Direction of the Mind*, composed around 1628 and published posthumously, Descartes was hardly aware of the problem, even though he had said, "Where knowledge of things is concerned, only two factors need to be considered: ourselves, the knowing subjects, and the things which are the objects of knowledge" (CSM I, 39; AT X, 411). Descartes had scarcely said anything in this work about the knowing subject as an ideal inquirer. But in *Discourse on the Method*, first published anonymously in 1637, he was quite interested in that problem. That issue was shelved, or at best the solution presupposed, when he came to write the *Meditations on First Philosophy*, published in 1641. It was once again in the limelight in the unfinished dialogue *The Search for Truth*, composed, according to one authority, sometime

ST. PHILIP'S COLLEGE LIBRARY

during the last seven years of his life.[4] (There is an interesting parallel in his treatment of mathematics. Descartes assumed the truthfulness of mathematical statements without question in the *Rules for the Direction of the Mind*, but in subsequent works, such as the *Meditations on First Philosophy*, he felt he could no longer make that assumption and tried, as we know, to justify even those truths.)[5]

My aim in discussing this issue is threefold. First, I want to give prominence to a historical issue that has been cast aside, if occasionally noticed. Second, I want to focus afresh on the problem of the reliability of reason. Third, and far more importantly, I hope to show that a proper understanding of the nature of the ideal seeker in Descartes will provide us with one powerful argument, among others, in defense of the central thesis of this book.

From Sextus Empiricus to Michele de Montaigne, the problem of the ideal seeker is hardly in the background. These philosophers had concerned themselves with the problems and pitfalls facing an ordinary seeker. Concerned as he was to respond to the skeptic, it is scarcely surprising that Descartes should have said much that revolved around this topic – although it *is* surprising that he never explicitly discussed the issue, by this name or any other. In what follows, I am clearly offering a reconstruction, namely, a systematic reconstruction of an answer, based on the Cartesian texts, to the question, "How is an ideal seeker made?," as if Descartes had explicitly chosen to ask and answer that question.

An ideal seeker after truth has to pass through four stages.[6] The first stage consists of his "original state of ignorance" (CSM II, 413; AT X,

---

[4] For other conjectures see R, 196–197, note 6.

[5] See C, 35–38. That Curley overstates the case by underplaying the method presented in *Rules for the Direction of the Mind* and overplaying the method presented in the *Discourse on the Method*, and in subsequently published works, does not detract from what he says about Descartes' evolving view of both method and mathematics.

[6] Since this is admittedly a reconstruction, my primary task is to invite the reader to consider not only whether Descartes clearly delineated the four states, but also his thinking that the ideal seeker passes through these states as if they were stages in a progressive order. Descartes did not explicitly develop the notion of an ideal seeker and put it to epistemic use, nor did he take a stand, for or against, on a progressive order of such states, since he did not treat this issue explicitly. However, there is some historical evidence to suggest that the proposed reconstruction is not entirely alien to Descartes' philosophy; indeed, it might be seen to play a vital role in it. See, for example, the final chapter of this book, pages 266–267 and notes 31 and 32.

519).[7] Initially, everyone belongs in this group. Out of this group are sifted those desiring to be seekers after truth from the others who have no such desire; given their dispositions, the nonseekers are unsuited for the philosophical task. This constitutes the second stage. From the group of those desiring to be seekers are distinguished, on the basis of certain right qualities, potentially ideal seekers from those who are not. This is the third stage. These potentially ideal seekers have finally to undergo preparation – study and reflection – in the fourth and last stage, as a way of making them ideal seekers before actually commencing the philosophical task.

The *first* stage, *the original state of ignorance*. "[A]s regards reason or sense," says Descartes, "since it is the only thing that makes us men and distinguishes us from the beasts, I am inclined to believe that it exists whole and complete in each of us" (CSM I, 112; AT VI, 2).[8] Then it would appear that anyone, at the start, is fit for the task of philosophical inquiry; but there are hindrances. Each normal person, at birth, has the senses of taste, smell, touch, sight, and hearing fully and dominantly functioning in him; reason, at this point, plays a small and subservient role. Here commences the growth of "the first obstacle" (CSM II, 406; AT X, 508). For the senses are essentially imperfect: They often deliver false reports about the external world; our inclinations are quite corrupt, our nurses foolish; our appetites and teachers are opposed, our instincts blind. Thus, we are all in the original state of ignorance, and the problem is how to emancipate ourselves from it so that we may become fit truth seekers.

The *second* stage, *the stage of sifting*. There are two types of individuals – "types of minds" – who are clearly unsuited for philosophical inquiry.

First, there are those who, believing themselves cleverer than they are, cannot avoid precipitate judgements and never have the patience to direct all their

---

[7] In the letter of February 27, 1637, to Mersenne, Descartes wrote, "I was afraid that weak minds might avidly embrace the doubts and scruples which I would have had to propound and afterwards be unable to follow as fully the arguments by which I would have endeavoured to remove them. Thus I would have set them on a false path and been unable to bring them back." (CSMK, 53; AT I, 350) Scholars are not agreed on the exact date of this letter.

[8] "[F]ew," wrote Descartes to Mersenne on October 16, 1639, "are capable of understanding metaphysics." (CSMK, 65; AT II, 596) It must follow that the final group of inquirers after truth would be inordinately small.

thoughts in an orderly manner; consequently, if they once took the liberty of doubting the principles they accepted and of straying from the common path, they could never stick to the track that must be taken as a short-cut, and they would remain lost all their lives. Secondly, there are those who have enough reason or modesty to recognize that they are less capable of distinguishing the true from the false than certain others by whom they can be taught; such people should be content to follow the opinions of these others rather than seek better opinions themselves. (CSM I, 118; AT VI, 15)

In short, none of these men are "of a fairly robust intellect" (CSM II, 320; AT VII, 475).

Descartes' fear of losing an individual in the morass of doubt was a genuine one. For him, knowledge was a guide to action, and actions were necessary to the making of a good person. Thus, ignorance and confusion could easily produce poor or evil deeds. Even a good method could produce, in someone incompetent, a bad person. This result must be avoided at all cost. For learning is of secondary importance in comparison to good deeds.

A good man is not required to have read every book or diligently mastered everything taught in the Schools. It would, indeed, be a kind of defect in his education if he had spent too much time on book-learning. Having many other things to do in the course of his life, he must judiciously measure out his time so as to reserve the better part of it for performing good actions – the actions which his own reason would have to teach him if he learned everything from it alone. (CSM II, 400; AT X, 495–496)

The moral risks are plainly too high for anyone who is incompetent to embark on the kind of enterprise Descartes has in mind.

Who, then, is fit for the philosophical task? I am attempting to search for minimal conditions or qualities that a person must possess, in Descartes' view, in order to perform that task; anyone who possesses anything more is more than qualified. In short, I am looking for necessary conditions, jointly adding up to a sufficient condition, that would make a person an ideal seeker.

The *third* stage, *the stage of determining the right qualities*: The ideal seeker must be someone of at least average intelligence, who has reached the age of discretion, whose senses are in good condition, who is blessed with a modicum of insight and has common sense; this eliminates the necessity of having gone to School (and thus having received training in grammar and logic). Peter Ramus, whose logical system Descartes had studied, had defined such a person as a syllogistic reasoner, and not just as a reasoner. So in Ramus' view an ideal seeker would be essentially equipped with syllogistic reasoning. Not so for Descartes; he maintained that he had never presumed his own mind "to be in any way more perfect than that of the ordinary man" (CSM I; 111, AT VI, 2).[9] Descartes would have been quite pleased with John Locke's remark that "God has not been so sparing to men to make them barely two-legged creatures, and left it to Aristotle to make them rational, i.e., those few of them that he could get so to examine the grounds of syllogisms."[10]

The ideal seeker must have a quick wit, a sharp and distinct imagination, ample and prompt memory, and the strongest ability to reason; he must be skilled at ordering his thoughts, troubled by no cares or passions, and capable of seeing clearly into his own actions; he must not be precipitate in his judgments, nor influenced by custom and example; he must allow adequate time in planning his work, and proceed confidently in this life. Only such an ideal seeker will persevere unswervingly in this task and eventually discover the truth, and having

9 This was no mere false modesty. It was typical of the newfound confidence in reason and the belief that reason, whole and complete, was universal in man. Descartes conducted himself accordingly. Thus, he taught his servant, Jean Gillot, and Dirk Rembrandtsz, a cobbler, mathematics; the former became director of an engineering school at Leiden. Noting his talents, Descartes hired Henry Schulter as his manservant, so that Schulter might assist him in his experiments. The captain of a ship on which Descartes had traveled was so impressed with Descartes' vast knowledge of meteorology that when they reached Stockholm, the captain boasted to Christina that Descartes had taught him more in three weeks than he had learned in sixty years at sea. Clearly, Descartes' theory belied his practice: Ordinary people, without any formal learning, can learn difficult and important things. Perhaps this was the net result of his Jesuit education: "The equality the Jesuits established among [the students]," he wrote, "hardly treating the highest born any differently from the most humble, was an extremely good invention" (R, 11; see also vii, 184–186).

The provisional title of *Discourse on the Method* was *Project for a universal science which might raise our nature to its highest degree of perfection. Next the Dioptric, the Meteors, where the most curious matters which the author could find to give proof of the universal science he proposes are explained in such a manner that even those who have never studied can understand them.* He suggested that an ideal seeker should be at least twenty-four years old (CSMK, 120; AT II, 347), because "the younger they are, the less liberty they have," due to the soft nature of their brains (CSMK, 190; AT III, 424), which makes them unfit for learning.

10 John Locke, *An Essay Concerning Human Understanding*, Volume 2, p. 391.

discovered it, be able to persuade others of it. Such seekers will be able to persuade "even if they speak only low Breton and have never learned rhetoric" (CSM I, 114; AT VI, 7).

There might be a conflict of propositions here. In the "Fourth Set of Replies," Descartes had warned that the *Meditations on First Philosophy* should be studied only "by very intelligent and well-educated readers" (CSM II, 172; AT VII, 247). One might conclude that Descartes had not made up his mind whether he wanted his ideal seeker to be just intelligent, like Polyander in *The Search for Truth* (in which Polyander is to Eudoxus what the slave boy was to Socrates in *Meno*), or whether he wanted an ideal seeker who was very intelligent. Again, did Descartes want his ideal seeker to be initially without education, as Polyander was? Or did he want the ideal seeker to be someone initially with a solid education? And yet, says an excited, marveling Eudoxus, who has taken Polyander through the *cogito*, "Would you have thought that an uneducated man who had never bothered to study could reason with such precision, and be so consistent in all his arguments?"[11] (CSM II, 415; AT X, 522) Obviously, being well educated is not a necessary condition for being an ideal seeker. Descartes is concerned, in his "Fourth Set of Replies," to fend off the objection that his method of doubt will engender doubt in the believers, and turn many a person away from the truths of faith. Descartes' counter would have been that such men, if they turned away from their faith, would be precipitate in their judgment and hence would not qualify as ideal seekers.

It is not clear whether the qualities that a person possesses, such as the qualities of quick wit, prompt memory, and sharp imagination, or the qualities of being precipitate in one's judgments and having modest reasoning abilities, are essential properties or accidental ones. If merely accidental, then those eliminated at the stage of sifting can

---

[11] Since this is of some importance later, I cite the historical root of this approach. In the Prologus of Raymond Sebond's *Natural Theology*, written in the 1420s or early 1430s, Sebond wrote: "And there is no need that anyone should refrain from reading it or learning it from lack of other learning: it presupposes no knowledge of Grammar, Logic, nor any other deliberative art or science, nor of Physics nor of Metaphysics. . . ." (Appendix II, in Michele de Montaigne, *An Apology for Raymond Sebond*, xli–xlii) Such was the man Polyander; such was the ideal seeker who could be persuaded of what Descartes was trying to persuade him.

return to the fold by appropriately training themselves, acquiring the necessary prerequisites to be an ideal seeker. If essential, then the set of ideal seekers constitutes a natural class; genuine knowledge seekers would be born, not made. Inasmuch as Descartes maintains that reason exists in each person whole and complete, he must maintain the more realistic doctrine, as follows: All persons are capable of discovering the truth, some more than others. Those who make poor seekers are those in whom reason is clouded by a host of contingent factors over which they have little control.

"Having thus prepared our understanding to make perfect judgments about the truth, we must also learn to control our will by distinguishing good things from bad, and by observing the true difference between virtues and vices" (CSM II, 405; AT X, 506). This is putting the cart before the horse: One cannot prepare the understanding to make perfect judgments without the will; if the will is not in control, it will make poor affirmations or denials. I find it surprising how very little Descartes says about the will in the earlier portions of either the *Meditations on First Philosophy* or the *Discourse on the Method*, given its central importance in his epistemology. For one thing, it is only the will's affirmation that introduces the question of truth or falsity into the discussion. Without the will, such questions cannot arise, and so knowledge seeking cannot proceed apace without the will. Descartes speaks of the intellectual qualities of the seeker, of the morals he should adopt while engaged in his philosophical quest, but there is virtually nothing about the will or the goodness of the will, how it should be controlled and trained, and so on, in order that it may act without error.[12]

The *fourth* stage, *the stage of preparation*: The potentially ideal seeker does not jump into making philosophical inquiries, not yet. He has to prepare himself. He travels and gathers experience of men and the world; he moves in the company of gifted men. (He reads books; and, as a daily routine, he engages in the study of mathematics. These clearly

[12] Why not think, one might ask, that the will is trained through enacting the analytic method of the *Meditations*? I have two reservations: First, there is *no* evidence that Descartes intended that; second, if the will – of a mature individual – is to make appropriate choices as it wades through the *Meditations*, would it not already have to possess goodness, say, if it is not to run afoul and choose erroneously? As an antidote to my reservations, see the splendid Chapter 2, "Descartes: Willful Thinking," in Michael Losonsky, *Enlightenment and Action from Descartes to Kant: Passionate Thought.*

go far beyond the necessary conditions for the making of an ideal seeker. Descartes did these things, but he did not make Polyander, his example of an ideal inquirer, do them.) Thus, the ideal seeker trains his mind, deepens it, makes it more powerful, so that when he finally embarks on his philosophical inquiries he will be a person whose mind is properly balanced between intellectual and emotional matters, and his will will be strong and clear. This, then, is the nature of the ideal seeker, and this is how he is made.

Polyander says, "I am a man who has never engaged in study or accustomed himself to turning his mind so far away from things that are perceivable by the senses" (CSM II, 408; AT X, 512). Epistemon, a bookish man, asserts, "I agree that it is very dangerous to proceed too far in this line of thinking" (CSM II, 408; AT X, 512). Eudoxus (playing the role of Descartes) counters thus: "I confess that it would be dangerous for someone who does not know a ford to venture across it without a guide, and many have lost their lives in doing so. But you have nothing to fear if you follow me." (CSM II, 408; AT X, 512) A strong and bold explorer can lose himself without a guide; a man of common sense and discretion can lose himself, too, without someone to guide him in his search for knowledge. Thus, even the ideal seeker needs a guide, a method.

II. The Method: The Rationalist Thread

If Descartes had been asked, "What is the aim of science?," he no doubt would have replied, quite simply, "The absolute truth." He took truth to be indefinable, but he might have granted the following distinction. There is phenomenal truth, $truth_p$, and there is rational truth, $truth_r$. When we combine $truth_p$ and $truth_r$, we get absolute truth. What, then, are these two species of truth? Descartes wanted our theories of the world to at least match our experiences and experiments. The theories should "enable us to explain all natural phenomena [i.e., the effects that we perceive by means of our senses]" (CSM I, 248; AT VIIIA, 80). Such theories are $true_p$. What cannot explain the deliverances of our sense experiences is, at a minimum, not phenomenally true, and hence not absolutely true.

Now, it is entirely possible for two theories to be $true_p$, that is, phenomenally true, without their being $true_r$, that is, rationally true.

Descartes gives a simple example to illustrate this (what philosophers now call the empirical equivalence of theories).

> However, although this method may enable us to understand how all the things in nature could have arisen, it should not therefore be inferred that they were in fact made in this way. Just as the same craftsman could make two clocks which tell the time equally well and look completely alike from the outside but have completely different assemblies of wheels inside, so the supreme craftsman of the real world could have produced all that we see in several different ways. (CSM I, 289; AT VIIIA, 327)

A theory is determined to be true$_r$ if it appears true when viewed in the natural light of reason. Such, for example, are the truths of logic, mathematics, and metaphysics. The true$_r$ theory will correctly describe how the wheels are assembled within. The true$_p$ theory will correctly describe how the two clocks look and how they tell time. In other words, granting that the supreme Craftsman could have devised various hidden mechanisms to produce the same observable effects, then the true$_p$ theory will explain all of the observable effects, and the true$_r$ theory will capture the veiled internal mechanism of the world that produces these effects, and that truth will be unmistakably exhibited to the natural light of reason. Thus, an absolutely true theory not only will get the phenomena right – it will be true$_p$ –, but also will get the mechanism right – it will be true$_r$.

One might worry that the foregoing is a less-than-exhaustive way of describing Descartes' own problem-situation, because of the problem posed by the micromechanical, that is, that which we do not directly perceive by sense, but which is visualizable. There seems to be a tension in Descartes between the idea that underlying structures are fully determinate and could be perceived with good microscopes, and the idea that they can be approached only by "reason", that is, by model making and intramental model comparison and exclusion. It is still, one might suppose, a very live question whether rational truth just stands in provisionally for the micrographic, or whether subvisible structures are still just phenomenal truth and ultimately have to be supplanted by nonvisualizable rational truth.[13]

---

[13] I owe this objection to Catherine Wilson.

I have no fully satisfactory answer – certainly none that is histori-cally satisfactory – to allay this worry, save this: Drawing on a common antirealist position, I would say that there does not appear to be a third type of truth. Let us say that a model depicts a microphenomenon. Then, the model is to be viewed either as a truth$_p$ or a truth$_r$. If it is not regarded as a truth$_p$, it may for a while have an uncertain status, until it is explained or "approached" by reason. If the model has some sort of truth not characterized by either of these kinds of truth, I am not able to determine what it might be that would cohere with Descartes' method and metaphysics. Finally, if the underlying structures are fully determinate, and we can "approach" them only vis-à-vis our model making, never quite getting at the underlying reality, then this can easily be shown to lead to a kind of skepticism from which Descartes cannot be saved.

For Descartes, science was systematic knowledge: neither a patch-work quilt, nor a mere network, of propositions. It was built on a rational foundation and not on guesswork or conjecture; it was indu-bitable and nothing less. Given the aim of science, there was a method to match. "I formed a method whereby, it seems to me, I can increase my knowledge gradually and raise it little by little to the highest point" (CSM I, 112; AT VI, 3). What was this method?

But first, what exactly did Descartes mean by *method*?

By a 'method' I mean reliable rules which are easy to apply, and such that if one follows them exactly, one will never take what is false to be true or fruitlessly expend one's mental efforts, but will gradually and constantly increase one's knowledge till one arrives at a true understanding of everything within one's capacity. (CSM I, 16; AT X, 371–372)

Descartes was not offering a method whose set of rules could be mechanically applied in order to churn out new and novel truths. If that is what is meant by a method – an algorithm – then Descartes did not offer a method. A truth table is an algorithm used to determine if an argument in propositional logic is valid; a Venn diagram is an algo-rithm used to determine if any of Aristotle's 256 categorical syllogisms is valid. Descartes is not offering anything remotely similar. This does not prevent him, like most current philosophers of science, from being optimistic and claiming that if his method is adopted, then the likeli-hood of discovering more and more scientific truths, the discovery of which lie within the province of human capacity, is far greater than the likelihood of discovering such truths using any alternative method.

These, then, are the four major rules of Descartes' method:

The first was never to accept anything as true if I did not have evident knowledge of its truth: that is, carefully to avoid precipitate conclusions and preconceptions, and to include nothing more in my judgments than what presented itself to my mind so clearly and so distinctly that I had no occasion to doubt it.

The second, to divide each of the difficulties I examined into as many parts as possible and as may be required in order to resolve them better.

The third, to direct my thoughts in an orderly manner, by beginning with the simplest and most easily known objects in order to ascend little by little, step by step, to knowledge of the most complex, and by supposing some order even among objects that have no natural order of precedence.

And the last, throughout to make enumerations so complete, and reviews so comprehensive, that I could be sure of leaving nothing out. (CSM I, 120; AT VI, 18–19)

The first two rules are primarily rules of analysis. Essentially, they maintain the following: (i) Keep doubting a proposition until you have no occasion to doubt it (otherwise, by implication, reject it). Such a method of doubt will lead one to reject not only hasty conclusions but also vague, untested conceptions or preconceptions, such as the notions of vacuum, gravity, and substantial forms. (ii) Divide the given problem into several smaller, yet clearly more manageable, problems. The requisite analysis should be carried *to the limit,* so that the solutions of the smallest and simplest problems can better lead to the solution of the larger problem with which the analysis began. (iii) Accept as true only that which presents itself to the mind as clear and distinct. The combination of (i) and (iii) will yield certain knowledge and not merely probable knowledge.

Perhaps one can now more sympathetically appreciate Descartes' reaction to Galileo. On October 11, 1638, Descartes wrote to Mersenne, "It seems to me that he [Galileo] lacks a great deal in that he is continually digressing and never stops to explain one topic completely, which demonstrates that he has not examined them in an orderly fashion and that, without having considered nature's first causes, he has sought only the reasons for a few particular effects, and thus he has built without foundations" (V, 115). This was no case of sour grapes. In terms of the foregoing, Descartes was complaining that Galileo had proceeded in a disorderly fashion, that he had tried to explain a few particular effects without taking his analysis down to the deepest level. Thus, Galileo had failed to uncover the basic axioms of his science of physics, which would have enabled him to explain not just the particular effects, but all of the facts in the given domain of knowledge.[14] Moreover, it was only the truth and certainty of the axioms of physics that would have given firm anchor to Galileo's science. Galileo had failed in that respect, and hence had "built without foundations". This, then, is the structure of discovery, not just in physics and geometry but in any field of knowledge.

Next, consider rules 3 and 4 of the method. These are primarily the rules of synthesis. Essentially, these rules maintain the following: (i) Assume, even if perhaps contrary to appearance, some natural, not man-made, order among the objects of your investigation. One might ask, "Isn't Descartes saying that one has to impose an order by deciding what to take up first, even if there is no natural order?" Well, Descartes wrote to Mersenne on May 10, 1632, while absorbed in the study of astronomy, "For although [the stars] seem very irregularly distributed in various places in the heavens, I do not doubt that there is a natural

---

[14] Sir Karl Raimund Popper has objected that just such a structure of knowledge as Descartes was proposing was obscurantist in its demand for ultimate explanations in terms of essences; see his *Conjectures and Refutations: The Growth of Scientific Knowledge*, in particular Chapter 3, section 3. Popper states, "Thus my criticism of essentialism does not aim at establishing the non-existence of essences; it merely aims at showing the obscurantist character of the role played by the idea of essences in the Galilean philosophy of science" (105). Popper fears that if essences are postulated, as in Galileo (or in Descartes), useful questions will not be asked (106), and this will prematurely stop the flow of knowledge.

This need not be so. There is nothing inherently wrong in the doctrine of essences; in any event, it is compatible with the doctrine of conjectures and refutations. Thus, no one who postulates essences, described at one level, need claim that he has in fact discovered those essences. He may simply regard himself as being at an earlier level, awaiting further descent into deeper and deeper worlds described at the corresponding levels. In Popper's words, "the world of each of our theories may be explained, in its turn, by further worlds which are described by further theories" (115). Such a philosopher, like Descartes, is simply proposing what the structure of knowledge should look like, *when* there is knowledge at hand. To claim that there *is* knowledge at hand, Descartes proposed a different theory. The former is an ontological claim, the latter an epistemic one, and the two can rest side by side, at ease with each other. Descartes, more than any other philosopher in the history of philosophy – Francis Bacon included, in my view – was the one who determined, for a long time, what was to be regarded as the structure of knowledge.

order among them which is regular and determinate" (CSMK, 38; AT I, 250). I suspect, then, that Descartes' reply to the foregoing question would be twofold: First, there *is* a natural order in the world, and second, often we discover that natural order by starting our search by imposing a conjectured order on the system we are investigating. (ii) Begin with the simplest and most easily known objects that precede the rest of the objects in the order. "[W]e term 'simple' only those things which we know so clearly and distinctly that they cannot be divided by the mind into others which are more distinctly known" (CSM I, 44; AT X, 418). (iii) Ascend to the more complex objects in the order in a slow step-by-step manner, via less complex objects, the steps being dictated by the rules of the subject matter at hand. (iv) Omit nothing by enumerating everything that lies within the domain of your subject matter.[15] Finally, (v) carry out comprehensive reviews and enumeration.

This method of analysis presupposes that we can analyze a problem, break it down into simpler units, like building blocks, without the aid of a theory, a perspective. It presupposes that there is only one unique way of breaking down the problem, that there is a "best order" in which all items can be arranged. But this is quite an implausible assumption, at least as a general statement. There are as many ways of analyzing a problem as there are ways of viewing the objects in a domain, and there are generally quite a few ways of viewing a given set of objects. That this presents a difficulty for Descartes is not hard to see. If the perspective is granted, then the analysis can be carried out. But that leaves the correctness of the perspective in question. For if the

---

[15] "I said also that the enumeration must be well-ordered. . . . if we arrange all the relevant items in the best order, so that for the most part they fall under definite classes, it will be sufficient if we look closely at one class, or at a member of each particular class, or at some classes rather than others. If we do that, we shall at any rate never pointlessly go over the same ground twice, and thanks to our well-devised order, we shall often manage to review quickly and effortlessly a large number of items which at first sight seemed formidably large." (CSM I, 27; AT X, 390–391)

To quote in full rule 5 of *Rules for the Direction of the Mind*: "The whole method consists entirely in the ordering and arranging of the objects on which we must concentrate our mind's eye if we are to discover some truth. We shall be following this method exactly if we first reduce complicated and obscure propositions step by step to simpler ones, and then, starting with the intuition of the simplest ones of all, try to ascend through the same steps to a knowledge of all the rest." (CSM I, 20; AT X, 379)

perspective were false or poor, the analysis would be worthless. On the other hand, if the perspective is not granted, then the analysis cannot even begin. As the dogma has it, there cannot be a theory-neutral observation (or analysis).

III. The Tree of Philosophy

After the *cogito*, these from *Principles of Philosophy* are perhaps the most famous lines in Descartes: "Thus the whole of philosophy is like a tree. The roots are metaphysics, the trunk is physics, and the branches emerging from the trunk are all the other sciences, which may be reduced to three principal ones, namely medicine, mechanics and morals."[16] (CSM I, 186; AT IXB, 14) Descartes' tree of philosophy would look like Figure 1.1. The arrows in the diagram indicate notions such as *dependence, reduction, support, grounded in, resting secure in,* and other such loosely similar ideas, since Descartes did not have a precise conceptual notion of how the sciences at the top of the tree were related to those at the lower levels, or to the one at the bottom. "I will also add," said Descartes to Clerselier, in a letter written in June or July 1646, "that one should not require the first principle to be such that all other propositions can be reduced to it and proved by it. It is enough if it is useful for the discovery of many, and if there is no other proposition on which it *depends*, and none which is easier to discover." (CSMK, 290; AT IV, 444–445; my emphasis) To cover this multitude of concepts, I shall use the colorless term *dependent on*. When he was younger, Descartes had thought that all of the sciences, if their links or derivations were properly established, could be held in the mind's eye quite easily. "The sciences are at present masked, but if the masks were taken off, they would be revealed in all their beauty. If we could see how the sciences are linked together, we would find them no harder to retain in our minds than the series of numbers." (CSM I, 3; AT X, 215) Descartes' tree of philosophy could aid in that cause.

---

[16] The tree analogy is also presented in Francis Bacon's *Advancement of Learning*, II, v.1, v. 3; *De Augumentis*, III, i–ii, quoted in Edwin A. Abbott's *Francis Bacon: An Account of His Life and Works*, 354–355. On November 10, 1619, Descartes had some remarkable dreams, in one of which he dreamed of a dictionary representing all the sciences gathered together; see V, 54–59.

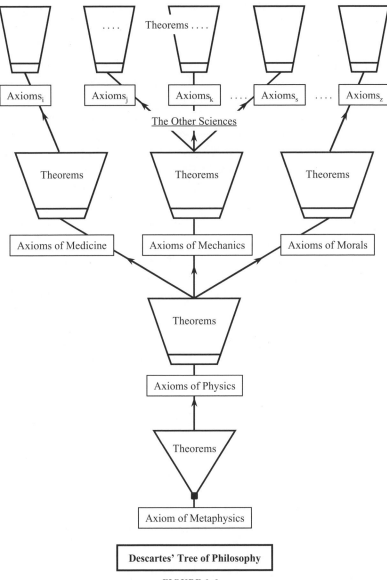

Descartes' Tree of Philosophy

FIGURE 1.1.

To illustrate: Suppose pathology to be one of the sciences defined, say, by $axioms_i$; this field of science can be reasonably regarded as dependent on the science of medicine. Given a theory of how the heart functions – for example, William Harvey's theory of the heart and the circulation of the blood, a theory that Descartes rightly considered important enough to argue with – Descartes approached it in a Hobbes-like manner, but came away less satisfied than Hobbes was with Euclidean geometry.[17] He disagreed with Harvey's explanation, and showed how Harvey's empirical results could eventually be shown to be more satisfactorily dependent on the axioms of medicine, and not on Harvey's outmoded Aristotelianism. Furthermore, the axioms of medicine could be made to be firmly dependent on the theorems, and hence on the axioms, of physics. Finally, the axioms of physics could be made dependent on the theorems and the axiom of metaphysics. Thus, one of the several branches at the top of the tree – pathology – can be shown to be dependent on one of the three principal branches – medicine – below; this latter branch is supported by the trunk – physics – which, in turn, is nourished by the roots – metaphysics. Consequently, pathology is dependent on metaphysics. In a similar vein, everything can be seen to be dependent on metaphysics. The notion of *dependence* allows for knowledge to be increased by experiment; it is not the case that once the metaphysical axiom is discovered the rest of the knowledge can be secured by executing merely logical deduction. Thus, Descartes was in earnest when, at the end of the *Discourse on the Method*, "he had called for the public's help in carrying out all the experiments necessary to 'justify my arguments.' 'It could take several centuries before we have thus deduced from these principles all the truths that can be deduced from them.'" (R, 177–178; AT IX, 2:20)

Now, if metaphysics was the most fundamental discipline, were physics and mathematics dependent on it? Likewise, was morals, for example, dependent on physics and hence in turn on metaphysics? Or were they – physics, mathematics, and morals – just vaguely supported by metaphysics, not dependent on it? In the *Principles of*

---

[17] At forty, yet innocent of mathematics, Thomas Hobbes accepted a nobleman's invitation to travel on the continent and tutor his son. One day, he found a copy of Euclid lying open in the library of his distinguished employer at the page boasting of Pythagoras' theorem. His friend, John Aubrey: "He read the proposition. 'By God,' sayd he, 'this is impossible.' So he reads the demonstration of it, which referred him back to such a proposition; which proposition he read. That referred him back to another, which he also read.*Et sic deniceps* [and so one after another] that at last he was demonstratively convinced of that trueth. This made him in love with geometry." (Quoted in William Kneale and Martha Kneale, *The Development of Logic*, 311.)

Philosophy, Descartes wrote, "medicine and mechanics, and all the other arts . . . can be fully developed with the help of physics" (CSM I, 289; AT VIIIA, 327). What is the nature of this *help*? This leaves unclear, too, whether other principles, besides those of physics, are also required for developing all the other arts. Is physics just necessary for these arts, or is it both necessary and sufficient?

There are, of course, various sciences at the top of the tree, such as (to mention only the ones that Descartes himself acknowledged) transmutation of metals, chemistry, anatomy, virtues of plants, astronomy, botany, meteorology, geography, zoology, psychology, music, and optics. The status of the axioms must be properly understood. The axioms of the other sciences – say, the axioms$_j$ of meteorology – are fundamental relative to their own science, but not fundamental in the whole scheme of knowledge. They are in some ways dependent on at least one of the three sciences below them: For example, the axioms$_j$ of meteorology are dependent on the axioms of mechanics. Again, the axioms of the three sciences of medicine, mechanics, and morals are fundamental relative to their own respective fields, but not in the entire scheme of knowledge. For example, the axioms of mechanics are dependent on the axioms of physics. The latter axioms, in turn, are dependent on the axiom of metaphysics. The axiom of metaphysics is absolute not only within metaphysics, but absolute in the total scheme of knowledge, since ultimately that axiom is not supported by, dependent, derived, or based on anything other than itself.

The relation between the sciences at the top of the tree and those at the bottom is not precisely clear. For example, are the sciences at the top dependent on one of the three principal sciences below (which in turn are dependent on physics and metaphysics)? Or would two or more principal sciences be required? It is understandable if meteorology is dependent on mechanics; which in turn is dependent on physics, and so on. But it is not intuitively plausible to think that pathology would be solely dependent on mechanics; at the very least it may be dependent on mechanics and medicine, which in turn are dependent on physics, and so on. Thus, in *Description of the Human Body*, Descartes says that "it is so important to know the true cause of the heart's movement that without such knowledge it is impossible to know anything which relates to the theory of medicine" (CSM I, 319; AT XI, 245). But the problem of the motion of the heart belongs to physiology, and so clearly physiology, not one of the three branches below, may not be dependent on just medicine, but may be dependent on both mechanics and medicine. Descartes also left open the question of just how independent the three principal sciences were. Indeed, was it essential that they be independent, if conjointly they could serve as the axioms for everything above them?

The various axioms of various disciplines, such as medicine, mechanics, and morals, are in some deeper sense not quite fundamental yet. For as Descartes will show us, they too can be doubted. If so, they must take their nourishment from the roots, namely, metaphysics. But metaphysics itself consists of complex truths about complex disciplines of complex objects, such as the physical world, time, space, numbers, matter, mind, and God. What, if anything, will provide us with the starting point that Descartes is looking for? Will the nature of this philosophical axiom be akin to the other axioms higher up on the tree of knowledge? Or will it be different?

We have arrived at the primary task of philosophy, namely: Is there such a single metaphysical axiom – an axiom that, like the axioms of geometry, cannot be questioned, cannot be argued for, cannot be proved by anything else? An axiom that would support all the axioms and theorems of all the other disciplines, including those of metaphysics? Or are there, after all, *several* metaphysical axioms? If there is just one axiom, then it too would only have to be understood in order to be perceived as clear, distinct, and indubitable, and in such a manner that its truth, says Descartes, would strike home more strongly than the truth of a mathematical axiom when the latter is understood.[18] Descartes' tree of philosophy makes it amply clear that such an axiom would be the foundation of all human knowledge: everything resting on it, *it* resting on nothing else. Were such an axiom to be found, it would be as though a fulcrum had been discovered from which to move the universe.

If we combine the rules of analysis, the rules of synthesis, and the rules of hypothesis making and hypothesis evaluation, we get

---

[18] Such a claim is repeatedly made: See, for example, CSMK, 23, AT I, 144; CSMK, 29, AT I, 182; CSMK, 53, AT I, 350; and CSM II, 416, AT X, 522.

the method Descartes would have advocated to a scientist with the following admonition: "[A]ll the things which can fall under human knowledge are interconnected in the same way. And I thought that, provided we refrain from accepting anything as true which is not, and always keep to the order required for deducing one thing from another, there can be nothing too remote to be reached in the end or too well hidden to be discovered." (CSM I, 120; AT VI, 19)

There are a few central things to be observed. First, there is Leibniz's old saw that Descartes' rules of method were "like the precepts of some chemist; take what you need and do what you should, and you will get what you want."[19] This is not entirely deserved. At no place I am aware of did Descartes give one set of rules for one discipline, and another set of rules for another discipline: say, one method for doing philosophy, and a different method for doing optics. What is truly remarkable is that one method is offered – rightly or wrongly – as sufficient for all of the disciplines. The picture one gets is that of a *unity of method* across disciplines. No matter how different the subject matter under investigation, Descartes' method is supposed to yield the right results.[20] In any event, in the light of Descartes' rules for the making of science, Leibniz's statement is surely suspect.

Given their universal applicability, it is hardly surprising that his rules were of such a general nature; they could not have been otherwise. One might as well complain that Newton's and Descartes' physics were overly general and did not draw nice distinctions between lunar, sublunar, and heavenly phenomena. But if the proof of the physics was in its success, the proof of the method lay no less in its success. Descartes claimed to have used this method in medicine, physics, morals, and a variety of sciences such as optics, geometry, and meteorology. Practice – *practice* – with the method will enable the scientist to learn what the rules mean, and how best to employ them. The rules cannot be understood just formally.

Second, by doubting and digging deeper, Descartes is arriving at axioms that are *simple*. Simplicity is hard to define, but one of the things

---

[19] Leibniz, *Die Philosophischen Schriften von G. W. Leibniz*, Volume 4, 329.

[20] For further details, see L. J. Beck, *The Method of Descartes: A Study of the Regulae*, 287–307. Gerd Buchdahl's *Metaphysics and the Philosophy of Science. The Classical Origins: Descartes To Kant*, Chapter 2, is still a standard reference for anyone doing serious work on Descartes' method.

that Descartes maintains is that it is easier to intellectually apprehend the truth of the respective axioms of a given field of knowledge than it is to understand its more complex theorems. Thus, it is easier to see the truth of a Euclidean axiom, such as "Things that are equal to the same thing are equal to one another," than it is to see the truth of a more complex theorem, such as Pappus' theorem. So, presumably, the axiom of metaphysics will have to be simple, too.

Third, the axioms are of a *general* nature. An axiom of mathematics speaks of the relation between part and whole, not of this particular part and that particular whole, such as a particular cell in a colony of cells. An axiom of passions speaks of wonder generally, not of wonder about this or that, such as wonder about the starry heavens above and the moral law within. An axiom of physics speaks of the motions of objects in general and not of the fixed stars, or the sun, or some particular planet, say, Jupiter. This is an enormously significant point, because eventually we must inquire into the nature of the axiom of metaphysics. Must it too be of a general nature? *Can* it be of a general nature?

Fourth, the direction of the movement of thought between axioms and theorems plays a significant role. As he attempts to move toward the axioms, Descartes is using the method of analysis: His method leads him to *discover* new truths. But once the discoveries have been made, and we attempt to *explain* an old truth or a new one with the help of the axioms, we are using the method of synthesis. Here we might well use the logic of the scholastics, which we would not use in the method of analysis.

The rationalist thread in Descartes' method is vital to the central claim of his metaphysics. It is what concerns me in this book.

IV. Method, Morals, and Bootstraps

"I had to uproot from my mind," says Descartes, "all the wrong opinions I had previously accepted, amass a variety of experiences to serve as the subject-matter of my reasonings, and practice constantly my self-prescribed method in order to strengthen myself more and more in its use." (CSM I, 122; AT VI, 22). Should he now apply his method in every field of endeavor, every science? That would be quite an improper use of the method. For "observing that the principles of these sciences must all be derived from philosophy, in which I had not yet discovered any certain ones, I thought that first of all I had to try to establish some certain principles in philosophy." And, Descartes asserts, "this is the most important task of all" (CSM I, 121–122; AT VI, 21–22).

Here a paradox is in the making. It is crucial that Descartes learn to apply his method in order to strengthen his mind; he cannot just jump into doing philosophy. The practice with the method is important. '[A]s I practised the method I felt my mind gradually become accustomed to conceiving its objects more clearly and distinctly; and since I did not restrict the method to any particular subject-matter, I hoped to apply it as usefully to the problems of the other sciences as I had to those of algebra" (CSM I, 121; AT VI, 21). So I shall call this *the mathematical method.* Indeed, in the *Rules for the Direction of the Mind,* Descartes had declared:

So frequently was I successful in this that eventually I came to realize that I was no longer making my way to the truth of things as others do by way of aimless and blind inquiries, with the aid of luck rather than skill; rather, after many trials I had hit upon some reliable rules of great assistance in finding the truth, and I then used these to devise many more. In this way I carefully elaborated my whole method. (CSM I, 35; AT X, 403–404)

But if he applies the mathematical method elsewhere first, without having discovered a philosophical axiom, a certain principle of philosophy, he is guilty of using this method improperly. If Descartes has not applied the mathematical method elsewhere before using it in his philosophical inquiry, he will neither learn of the efficacy of the method nor strengthen his mind for the epistemic task. Therefore, he will either use the method improperly or use it unjustifiably, without knowing its efficacy. How, then, is he to proceed? He must, I think, raise himself by his own bootstraps.

Let me present this argument differently. With the moral code (by which he will guide his life) provisionally established,[21] Descartes has simply completed the *first* step. He does not feel obliged to commence his philosophical inquiry straightaway.

---

[21] For the influence of Pierre Charron's *Traite de la Sagesse,* which had been on the Index since 1605, on Descartes' view of ethics, see R, 44–48.

As a matter of fact, he tells us, he spent nine years in preparation. This is the *second* step. He read books, met with men of letters, cultivated his reason, and above all solved problems in mathematics, which sharpened his eye for truth and for clear and distinct ideas. He studied mathematics at length because "of the certainty and self-evidence of its reasonings" (CSM I, 114; AT VI, 7) and because "mathematicians alone have been able to find any demonstrations – that is to say, certain and evident reasonings" (CSM I, 120; AT VI, 19). Indeed, in the *Rules for the Direction of the Mind*, Descartes had urged that, at the start, we confine our studies to arithmetic and geometry, for these alone are "free from any taint of falsity or uncertainty" (CSM I, 12; AT VI, 364). What did he hope to gain from this study? "From this, however, the only advantage I hoped to gain was to accustom my mind to nourish itself on truths and not to be satisfied with bad reasoning" (CSM I, 120; AT VI, 19). In short, he believed that he would sharpen his reason.

Now, Descartes says that he was very successful in using the mathematical method in algebra, and since the method was not devised for any particular discipline or subject matter, he felt he would be able to apply it in other fields equally successfully. "Not that I would have dared to try at the outset to examine every problem that might arise, for that would itself have been contrary to the order which the method prescribes" (CSM I, 121; AT VI, 21). The problems to be tackled, in the beginning, would have to be simpler and more manageable problems. There is a necessary order that must be followed when an ideal seeker aims to instruct himself (CSM I, 185; AT IXB, 13). As part of that order, says Descartes – and here comes a crucial bit – the ideal seeker "should study logic" (CSM I, 186; AT IXB, 13).

Not scholastic logic, to be sure, but, continues Descartes,

the kind of logic which teaches us to direct our reason with a view to discovering the truths of which we are ignorant. Since this depends to a great extent on practice, it is good for the student to work for a long time at practicing the rules on very easy and simple questions like those of mathematics. Then, when he has acquired some skill in finding the truth on these questions, he should begin to tackle true philosophy in earnest. (CSM I, 186; AT IXB, 13–14)

Subsequently, he abandoned the study of letters and turned to the practical world of courts and armies, savoring various experiences, meeting people with diverse temperaments and ranks, and reflecting on his experiences that he might derive profit from them. "For it seemed to me that much more truth could be found in the reasonings which a man makes concerning matters that concern him than in those which some scholar makes in his study about speculative matters" (CSM I, 115; AT VI, 9–10). While a scholar can afford to hold any opinion with few if any real consequences, a man of the world has to pay dearly for *his* false beliefs. What he learned through example and custom, he treated lightly, for these were often in conflict even among great communities and nations.[22]

Finally, with his mind sufficiently sharp and clear, Descartes takes the *third* step; he embarks on the strenuous activity of systematic philosophical inquiry.

What, precisely, did Descartes learn prior to his establishing the *cogito* and, with it, the general rule of distinguishing the true from the false? Not yet having established the general rule, how could Descartes have been confident that he was training his mind, stocking it with truths, performing good reasoning, successfully sifting good worldly experiences from bad, profiting from his good experiences, and so on? How could he rely on the truth of mathematics, however simple? How could he trust the rules of logic, old or new? How would he, even as the ideal seeker, know that he had acquired the right and correct skills?

Apparently, a clear mind, a good will, and good sense are not enough; one also requires a good and guaranteed method. For it is the method that will outline the procedure and certify the results. However, not only were his morals based on probability, so was his method. Descartes was aware of the tentativeness of his method: "[P]erhaps

---

[22] Descartes' method, as one distinguished Kantian authority would have it, is to be sharply distinguished from Kant's method: "In Descartes' work the grounding of reason is closely linked to its political impotence. Only the repudiation of politics, and more generally of criticism of action, allows him a meditative perspective from which to discern and deploy the methods without self-stultification. Kant's philosophical enterprise evidently follows quite a different route." (Onora O'Neill, *Constructions of Reason: Explorations of Kant's Practical Philosophy*, 5–6.) The fundamental difference is this: The use and vindication of reason is a public matter, not a private one. "Reason may be (in whole or, in part) 'in' each participant, but it cannot be discovered by introspection: Kant insists that we are opaque, not transparent, to ourselves"(7). In particular, see O'Neill's discussion on the Kantian notion of "the *sensus communis*" (24–27). See also Chapter 2, pp. 40–41, this volume.

what I take for gold and diamonds is nothing but a bit of copper and glass" (CSM I, 112; AT VI, 3). Again:

> It was never my intention to prescribe to anyone the method which he should follow in his search for truth, but simply to describe the method which I used myself: if it should be thought to be defective, it would be rejected; if good and useful, others would use it too.... If someone should now say that it has not got me very far, this is a matter for experience to determine. (CSM II, 419; AT X, 525–526)

In *Discourse on the Method*, he could scarcely have been more tentative about his method. He said that he was presenting that work "only as a history" (CSM I, 112; AT VI, 4).

But then someone might argue – as, indeed, Pierre Gassendi might well have argued – that instead of, say, the mathematical method, the method to follow is the *historical method*.[23] It might be argued that the things to read are just the things that Descartes refused to consider seriously: languages, fables, letters, histories, poetry, morals, theology, and jurisprudence (CSM I, 112–115; AT VI 4–9). *These* will train the inquirer, so a Gassendist might say, in a way in which indulging in mere mathematics would not: indeed, the latter might stunt the natural development and propensities of the human mind. Only after years of intensive study in *this* method should an ideal seeker embark on his philosophical quest, not before. Having embarked, the seeker might discover, say, a stunning moral truth having as much power, clarity, and certainty as the *cogito*, or perhaps having even greater power, clarity, and certainty. And out of this primary moral truth could be recovered an indispensable epistemic rule that would serve to establish other important truths. His physics, medicine, and mechanics would then come to rest on his metaphysics, and his metaphysics on the primary moral truth (and not the other way around).

Is this not topsy-turvy? Surely, someone will point out, Descartes did not approve of the historical method and defended that position. Thus, he claimed that the moral writings of the ancient pagans, although appearing to be magnificent, were nothing but "built only on

---

[23] See, for example, Lynn Sumida Joy's *Gassendi the Atomist: Advocate of History in an Age of Science*. Strictly as an aside, Descartes dreamed on November 10, 1619, that poets, because divinely inspired, often proclaim truths that are not only more profound but better expressed than those of the philosophers.

sand and mud" (CSM I, 114; AT VI, 8). He also showed why, for his purposes, he disvalued poetry and oratory, and so on. In short, we have no reason to rely on the historical method.

But the certain criteria, the general rule, for distinguishing truth from falsity is derived only after the *cogito* has been discovered, not before. If Descartes could certainly distinguish the true from the false at the stage of preparation, then the *cogito* would hardly be important. In fact, the metaphysics of God and soul and the sciences could be constructed with whatever principle or criteria Descartes was working with before he discovered the *cogito*. If discovering the general rule, the criteria for distinguishing the true from the false, is indispensable to claiming certain knowledge, then Descartes' advice to study mathematics – as opposed to, say, history, fables, or poetry – was no more than a mere conjecture about how best to prepare himself for the philosophical task ahead.

Suppose that one is preparing for an elementary calculus exam. One reads George Polya's *How to Solve It*, Richard Courrant's and Herbert Robbins's *What is Mathematics? An Elementary Approach to Ideas and Methods*, and a standard textbook or two on calculus, such as George B. Thomas, Jr.'s *Calculus and Analytic Geometry*. One studies functions, limits, integration, transcendental and hyperbolic functions, vector functions, partial differentiation, multiple integrals, infinite series, differential equations, and so on. One is preparing one's mind for a rigorous examination ahead. One is on the right track in studying these books: They are acknowledged classics in the field; some of them, like Polya's book, deal with heuristics; they deal with important mathematical problems whose solutions are generally acknowledged; these works will teach the accepted general techniques of solving mathematical problems, which will enable the reader to solve new and fresh problems; and in these books, one will encounter problems that are unsolved or unsolvable. The problem here is not the epistemological one of discovering a general rule that will enable us to distinguish, confronted by any proposition, mathematical or otherwise, whether it is true or false. The ability to recognize mathematical truths is taken for granted in such books. It would be irrelevant for an examination in calculus if one studied instead the Book of Job, Petrarca's *On His Own Ignorance and That of Many Others*, or James Baldwin's *Go Tell It on the Mountain* (or Seneca's *On the Happy Life* and Machiavelli's *The Prince*, which Descartes read with Princess Elizabeth) (CSMK, 256; AT IV, 263 and V, 202–203).

But it is begging the question against the historical method if one studied mathematics as a way of preparing for the epistemological exam, so to speak. Why should our epistemic abilities increase when studying mathematics and atrophy when studying history or fable, and not vice versa? It is, I think, that Descartes is here making a choice of method that is solely based on probability. He is implicitly, but forcefully, claiming that there is a higher probability of strengthening his mind, and being successful in the epistemic enterprise, if he uses the mathematical method than there would be if he were to use the historical method. Then he simply argues that the proof is in the pudding: "If someone should now say that it has not got me very far, this is a matter for experience to determine" (CSM II, 419; AT X, 526). He may take a wrong turn and find that it leads nowhere. Alternatively, he may find that he repeatedly makes the right moves – is successful, for example, in algebra – and that this gives him confidence that he is on the right track toward the epistemic goal. Well, was there not a Chandoux to point out to Descartes that resting as it did on probability, his mathematical method could be shown to be false?

One might say in Descartes'defense that one has to begin somewhere. And as we proceed in our task, we shall get a better idea of how effective the method is. There is no other alternative. If one has to fashion tools, one fashions good tools from crude ones, better tools from good ones, and so on. This is, indeed, what Descartes at one point recommends.

If, for example, someone wanted to practice one of these crafts – to become a blacksmith, say – but did not possess any of the tools, he would be forced at first to use a hard stone (or a rough lump of iron) as an anvil, to make a rock do as a hammer, to make a pair of tongs out of wood, and to put together other such tools as the need arose. Thus prepared, he would not immediately attempt to forge swords, helmets, or other iron implements for others to use; rather he would first of all make hammers, an anvil, tongs and other tools for his own use. What this example shows is that, since in these preliminary inquiries we have managed to discover only some rough precepts which appear to be innate in our minds rather than the product of any skill, we should not immediately try to use these precepts to settle philosophical disputes or to solve mathematical problems. Rather, we should use these precepts in the first instance to seek out with extreme care everything else which is more essential in the investigation of truth.[24] (CSM I, 31; AT X, 397)

What Descartes is saying is that we must inevitably begin with some crude concepts of the mathematical method – hence, a nine-year period of apprenticeship. With the help of these crude concepts, we should be able to forge better epistemic tools. However, he might caution, we should not rush into solving mathematical or metaphysical problems with these concepts or tools. With the help of these, we should simply select, with extreme care, whatever is essential to the discovery of fundamental truths. The point is well taken. But could we not have suggested something similar had we begun with the crude concepts of the historical method? *That* is the cardinal question. And had we begun with that method, and its crude concepts, we would have tried to fashion sophisticated concepts as we went along, and we could have been just as cautious in applying those concepts to various other issues and problems. After all, the truth of the *cogito* is independent of the truth of mathematics or morals. Descartes could have arrived at the *cogito* even if he had adopted the historical method. But Descartes, without argument, settles for the mathematical method. This seems plausible, if you accept the pragmatic approach. But Descartes was no pragmatist.[25]

Furthermore, what if the mathematical method is false? What powerful effect would a false idea have on the mind? Once the mind has acquired it, can it go on to acquire any truth whatsoever without hindrance from this idea? If not, then we cannot afford to be unmindful of a false idea in our moral code that we adopt for practical purposes. For who can tell what havoc it would wreak later? The mind might

[24] For a virtually parallel claim, see Benedict de Spinoza, *The Chief Works of Benedict de Spinoza*, Volume 2, "On the Improvement of the Understanding," 12.

[25] Might it be plausible to argue that in studying mathematics the learner's confidence level increases, in studying a humanistic discipline it decreases, leaving the learner baffled and ignorant? Well, this need not always be so. Consider, for example, the Middle Ages: not much of studying mathematics therein, but a great deal of studying the humanities. Was the confidence level generally low? In any society, there will be some discipline that dominates: It may be a practical craft in one society, a theoretical science in another, arts and poetry in a third. The confidence level of the members of each society will to a large extent reflect its history and traditions. In any event, Descartes offers no reason why it is with mathematics that he should *commence* rather than with a humanistic discipline.

be imagined as a flexible storehouse whose capacity to acquire truths increases as it receives and stores more truths, and whose capacity to acquire truths diminishes as it receives and stores more falsehoods. This is not Descartes' analogy, but it is quite close in spirit to what he says: "[E]rrors . . . may obscure our natural light and make us less capable of heeding reason" (CSM I, 116; AT VI 10). Or this: "Someone who . . . is stuffed full of opinions and taken up with any number of preconceptions finds it difficult to submit himself exclusively to the natural light" (CSM II, 416; AT X, 522–523).

The question, then, is this: If the historical method proposes one set of crude notions with which to commence an epistemic inquiry, and Descartes suggests an alternative set of equally crude notions, how can we settle on either in the light of Descartes' doubt? Descartes' claim that his notions are innate settles nothing. Those who propose the historical method may question or doubt Descartes' claim and argue that *their* own crude notions are the ones that are really innate.

It is true that "those who proceed but very slowly can make much greater progress, if they always follow the right path, than those who hurry and stray from it" (CSM I, 111; AT VI, 2). But how is his mathematical method justified as leading to the right path *before* he has used it in philosophy? Descartes might say something like this: "Begin with a method that is conjectured to be probably effective, given its initial success in mathematics. Use this method in philosophy, and one will in all probability get at certain truth. This will enable one to uncover a reliable epistemological principle, the general rule. Henceforth, the procedure can be fully justified without doubt in the following way: Each step after the general rule is justified by appealing to the general rule. Subsequently, the discovered epistemological principle, the general rule, may establish with certainty the correctness of the steps previously taken. That is, the general rule will determine that the moral code as well as the mathematical method were in fact the correct ones to adopt at the start." This is exactly what I meant by the bootstrap approach in Descartes' method.

Let us look at this matter from the point of view of the moral code. Descartes provides himself with four such moral maxims. First, one ought to obey the laws and customs of the country, believe in the religion in which one was raised, and hold moderate opinions. Second, one ought to be firm and decisive in one's actions even when these are based on the most doubtful opinions. Third, one should try to restrain one's wants rather than trying to change the order of the world in order to satisfy one's wants. Fourth, one should review the various tasks and occupations men have in this life in order to choose the best. (CSM I, 122–125; AT VI, 23–28)

There is a problem worth noticing. What is the connection between Descartes' moral code, followed with utter decisiveness, and his epistemology? Suppose the much-maligned Turk,[26] say of the seventh century, were to adopt a different moral code. The Turk, following the faith of *his* fathers, would be a polytheist, practice polygamy, and grant allegiance to different social and market institutions; and Descartes would follow the Christian faith, profess monogamy, and give allegiance to the social, economic, and market institutions prevailing in the France in which he lived a thousand years later.[27] But in other respects, one can imagine the Turk to be like Descartes: The Turk is politically conservative and unwilling to reform institutions built by long custom and tradition; he is at home in what he finds. Question: Would the Turk end up of necessity with *exactly* the same set of principal beliefs as those of Descartes?

There are problems for Descartes on either answer. Suppose the answer is yes, he would end up with exactly the same set of principal beliefs as Descartes. (There is strong evidence to believe that Descartes would have endorsed such an opinion; it would have testified to the belief in the universality of human reason, a commonplace amid the seventeenth century's optimism.) But this answer is undermined by a host of unheeded considerations. The Turk will begin with a different concept of God from that of Descartes: Descartes finds the idea of one good God self-evident; the Turk finds the idea of several gods clear and

---

[26] The Turks "were at the time considered by all Europe to be the major danger" (R, 210). "The sin that Turks and other infidels commit by refusing to embrace the Christian religion does not arise from their unwillingness to assent to obscure matters (for obscure they indeed are), but from their resistance to the impulses of divine grace within them, or from the fact that they make themselves unworthy of grace by their other sins" (CSM II, 105–106; AT VII, 148).

[27] "In traveling through all these countries, Descartes extended his doubt to many customs. Faithfulness to the religion of his childhood set him apart." (R, 62) "I am of the religion of my nurse," said Descartes to the Protestant Revius (R, 208). So might the Turk have traveled and doubted other customs and religions than his own.

indubitable. The Turk will have distinct notions of proof and reason, and Descartes different ones of his own. The Turk may not learn to doubt the reality of the external world simply because his senses have deceived him in the past. The Turk, like some former-day Wittgenstein, or lacking Descartes' skeptical heritage, may not even be able to make sense of that doubt. Indeed, the second moral maxim is so powerful that it admonishes the Turk not to doubt his religious belief, namely, polytheism. How could the second maxim fail to impinge on the subsequent epistemic inquiry? How could a philosophical investigation that led to theism be regarded as satisfactory by the Turk? Thus, so this argument concludes, Descartes' inquiry is merely geared to support his initial beliefs, no more. Clearly, an affirmative answer to the original question – would the Turk end up of necessity with *exactly* the same set of principal beliefs as those of Descartes? – is in need of defense.

If the answer to that question, however, is no, the Turk will not end up with the same set of principal beliefs as Descartes – a more likely response – then Descartes needs an even more substantial argument in favor of his moral code. He needs that argument as no less than a fortress for his epistemology. For an inadequate moral code will condemn him to stray from "the right path," as presumably it did the Turk. But this Descartes cannot, in principle, do: For until Descartes has substantiated his method, which at this point he has not, he will have no adequate means by which to determine the correctness of the moral code. On the other hand, he cannot determine the correctness of his method unless he has a moral code by which he can live. I conclude that in his moral code, as in his method, Descartes is attempting to raise himself by his own bootstraps. That is, he will provisionally accept a moral code as the right one; he will subsequently discover the right method; and then the right method will legitimize the moral code he had initially adopted.[28]

---

[28] For a similar pattern of argument, see, Jeffrey Tlumak, "Certainty and Cartesian Method," and James van Cleve, "Foundationalism, Epistemic Principles, and the Cartesian Circle." Whether these approaches are susceptible to the kind of objection I level against Descartes, I leave to the reader to decide.

2

The Problem of Epistemology

In the structure of a philosophical system, the form is at least as important as the content. Part of what I wish to demonstrate, but only by implication, is that Descartes' hold on later philosophy has a great deal to do with its form, and perhaps less with its content. One can quibble, for instance, about whether Descartes has given us an adequate proof of the existence of God, or even of the existence of the external world. One can doubt that his reasoning is sound about the mind being a distinct and unique substance in its own right as matter, or doubt that he is right about their essential properties being thought and extension, respectively. But it would not follow that therefore his way of doing philosophy is inadequate. Descartes has provided a form, a way, a mode of doing philosophy that has not yet disappeared even if no one takes seriously, for example, the idea that the pineal gland in the brain is the meeting place of mind and matter. This chapter is as much about the form of that kind of philosophizing as it is about the specific issues in Descartes' philosophy.

Let me, at least once, draw an explicit parallel between the form of philosophy in Descartes and the form of philosophy employed by some twentieth century philosophers of science: Descartes was after not only truth, but also certainty; contemporary philosophers of science are after truth or probable truth. Descartes used the method of doubt to get rid of uncertain propositions; contemporary philosophers of science recommend the use of experimental falsification to reject scientific hypotheses. Descartes invoked a fundamental experience as a starting point; contemporary philosophers of science suggest invoking paradigms and standard cases in the sciences as the point of departure. Descartes laid down, in the light of that fundamental experience, a strong and sweeping epistemic principle; contemporary philosophers of science invoke a theory of corroboration in the light of paradigms and standard examples. And finally, Descartes was after a deductive system of knowledge; contemporary philosophers of science want something structurally quite similar, say, an inductive system of knowledge.

Descartes was among the first to provide us with a taxonomy of problems – not just scientific problems, but philosophical problems as well. Furthermore, he provided the conditions under which, for instance, a solution is adequate and well understood. He argued that the failure to solve a philosophical problem was oftentimes, in large measure, due to the failure to characterize the problem properly. Those issues define the task of section I. In the next section, I distinguish between mental states and mental processes, as well as between first- and second-order states and processes, the better to understand Descartes' directive to dismantle what hitherto had stood as the structure of knowledge. In section III, two models of doubt – the ordinary-doubt model and the extraordinary-doubt model – are provided, and their rationales underscored. In section IV, I make explicit the various steps in the process of doubt, and argue against recent empiricist and causal theories that purport to explain what Descartes was about in the First Meditation.

I. Types of Problems

Let us begin somewhere in the back alley. I refer to rule 13 of *Rules for the Direction of the Mind*. Here Descartes is focusing on the nature of problems, the constraints on their solution, and the things that one should do in order to have the best chance of solving them. Descartes claims that, first, in every problem there must be something unknown. Second, this unknown must be characterized in some way; such a characterization will point us in one direction rather than in another. Thus, the characterization is crucial, since a false characterization can put us on a dead-end path. Third, the unknown can be characterized only in terms of what is known, otherwise the problem could not even be formulated or understood.

These conditions hold for both perfect and imperfect problems. For a problem to be a perfect problem, it must be determinate in every respect. Its terms must be perfectly understood. Descartes offers as an illustration the following: Suppose that someone raises the problem, "[W]hat conclusions are to be drawn about the nature of the magnet simply from the experiments which Gilbert claims to have performed, be they true or false?" (CSM I, 52; AT X, 431) The point is not to question the veracity or the reliability of the experiments, but simply to deduce whatever we can from the knowledge of these experiments. The three characteristics of every problem appear: First, some of the properties of the magnet are unknown; second, the unknown is characterized in some way (depending on how we understand "nature"); and third, the unknown is constrained by the experimental results.

In the previous rule, dealing with the same problem, Descartes says,

But take someone who thinks that nothing in the magnet can be known which does not consist of certain self-evident, simple natures: he is in no doubt about how he should proceed. First he carefully gathers together all the available observations [i.e., results of experiments] concerning the stone in question; then he tries to deduce from this what sort of mixture of simple natures is necessary for producing all the effects which the magnet is found to have. Once he has discovered this mixture, he is in a position to make the bold claim that he has grasped the true nature of the magnet, so far as it is humanly possible to discover it on the basis of given observations. (CSM I, 49–50; AT X, 427)

It is clear from the foregoing that Descartes believes that a perfect problem must have a unique solution. He seems to suggest that in this work, but his examples leave the matter open. The magnet case does not have a unique solution. One might have a variety of characterizations of the unknown properties of the magnet, given the observations, the data. Not that Descartes himself was unaware, as we have already seen, of the problem of underdetermination by the data. What Descartes is more likely to have had in mind here is a problem in mathematics that does have a unique solution, such as, "What is the sum of the interior angles of a triangle in a Euclidean plane?" Given the nature of triangles, there is only one correct answer, namely, "It is equal to two right angles."

On the other hand, the problem is imperfect if we are simply asked, "What is the nature of a magnet?" Here the solution to the problem is not conditioned in any respect. The terms are not perfectly understood. Once again the three conditions of every problem are satisfied. Note Descartes' remark, "[W]e already understand what is meant by the words 'magnet' and 'nature', and it is this knowledge which determines us to adopt one line of inquiry rather than another" (CSM I, 52; AT X, 431). Presumably, a change in the meanings of the words, due to the growth of scientific knowledge, would change the problem as well as the line of inquiry. (Descartes thought that all imperfect problems could be reduced to perfect problems, but he never completed that part of his work. A conjecture on his behalf: If we let any imperfect problem have as constraints any subset of the existing knowledge relating to the thing we are investigating, then the imperfect problem turns itself into a perfect problem.)

There is another demarcation of the class of problems. This is the division between perfectly understood problems and those that are imperfectly understood. One should not suppose that a perfect problem is simply a perfectly understood problem. There is more in the characterization of the latter class of problems than in the characterization of the former class. Thus,

We must note that a problem is to be counted as perfectly understood only if we have a distinct perception of the following three points: first, what the criteria are which enable us to recognize what we are looking for when we come upon it; second, what exactly is the basis from which we ought to deduce it; third, how it is to be proved that the two are so mutually dependent that the one cannot alter in any respect without there being a corresponding alteration in the other. (CSM I, 51; AT X, 429)

How do problems arise? They may arise due to the obscurity and obfuscation of our language. Riddles belong to this class, such as the riddle of the Sphinx, as well as those problems that turn on ambiguity and vagueness of terms, such as the one about the anglers on the shore who maintain, while holding the rod and line, that they no longer have the fish they have caught but have the ones they have not caught. The dispute of the learned is not infrequently about words, such as the one about the definition of 'space.' Indeed, Descartes declares that "[t]hese questions about words arise so frequently that, if philosophers always agreed about the meanings of words, their controversies would almost all be at an end" (CSM I, 54; AT X, 434).

Almost all, but not all. There are genuine problems that are not the result of careless use of language, or due to some inherent ambiguity in the language. These are the problems in which one is asking if something exists or, if it does exist, asking what is its nature, as in the case of the problem of perpetual motion, or the problem of stellar motion. Take the simpler problem posed by the statue of Tantalus that Descartes once saw. The statue has a column at the top of which is a figure of Tantalus. In this statue, water keeps pouring out of a spout, but as soon as the fountain reaches Tantalus' mouth, it runs out. Descartes states that the important thing is to get to the essence of the problem rather than to get bogged down in inessentials, such as, how is the figure of Tantalus constructed? This, says Descartes, is just a "coincidental feature" of the problem. Rather, "The whole difficulty is this: how must the bowl be constructed if it lets out all the water as soon as, but not before, it reaches a fixed height?" (CSM I, 55; AT X, 436) Thus, "no matter what the problem is, we must above all strive to understand distinctly what is being sought" (CSM I, 54; AT X, 434).

"[T]hree different sorts of questions," says Descartes, should be distinguished.

First, some things are believed through faith alone – such as the mystery of the Incarnation, the Trinity, and the like. Secondly, other questions, while having to do with faith, can also be investigated by natural reason: among the latter, orthodox theologians usually count the questions of the existence of God, and the distinction between the human soul and the human body. Thirdly, there are questions which have nothing whatever to do with faith, and which are the concern solely of human reasoning, such as the problem of squaring the circle, or of making gold by the techniques of alchemy, and the like. Just as it is an abuse of Scripture to presume to solve problems of the third sort on the basis of some mistaken interpretation of the Bible, so it diminishes the authority of Scripture to undertake to demonstrate questions of the first kind by means of arguments derived solely from philosophy. (CSM I, 300; AT VIIIB, 353)

Thus, on Descartes' view there are problems that have genuine rational solutions, and there are some that have none, problems that are solely the province of faith. As an example of the latter: "As for the

question whether it is in accord with the goodness of God to damn
men for eternity, that is a theological question: so if you please you
will allow me to say nothing about it. . . . when truths depend on faith
and cannot be proved by natural argument, it degrades them if one
tries to support them by human reasoning and mere probabilities."
(CSMK, 26; AT I, 153) But some problems of faith do have rational
solutions, such as the problem pertaining to the existence of God
and, against the Calvinists, the problem of understanding transubstantiation (CSMK, 88; AT I, 564). Finally, there are problems that
fall solely in the province of reason, where faith or scripture is invoked only mistakenly. "It is true," – of course – "that we are obliged
to take care that our reasonings do not lead us to any conclusions
which contradict what God has commanded us to believe" (CSMK, 120;
AT II, 348).

My purpose in detailing this brief on the type of problems is to
ask, would Descartes have argued that a comparable situation prevails
in philosophy? That is, are there perfect and imperfect problems in
philosophy as well? Consider the philosophical problem, does God
exist? Is this a perfect problem? The term *existence* may be perfectly
understood. But is the term *God* clearly understood? Indeed, some
may argue that this problem may not be a genuine problem, for it
may conceal inherent contradictions.[1] This gives rise to the possibility,
as in the case of mathematics, that some problems hitherto regarded
as genuine problems may later be shown to be unsolvable. Are there
unsolvable problems also in philosophy? Or are philosophical problems unsolvable only when they are couched in vague language?
(CSMK, 10–13; AT I, 76–82) How should philosophical problems
be characterized? What constraints should operate on them? By
what known factors should the philosophical unknown be characterized? Which philosophical problems, if any, are perfectly understood?
Which ones are imperfectly understood, and why? Finally, how will the
meanings of terms, or the conditions on the solution, direct the line
of philosophical inquiry? Interestingly enough, it was the particular
way in which the problem, can I know anything that I cannot doubt?,
was formulated that determined Descartes' *line of inquiry*. Thus, he
doubted.

---

[1] This was Leibniz's well-known concern; see K, 128–131.

II. Directive to Dismantle

The motto of this section could well be, "*The seeker after truth must, once in the course of his life, doubt everything, as far as is possible*" (CSM I, 193; AT VIIIA, 5). To begin to explain the nature and purpose of this doubt, I resort to the frequent analogy in Descartes between rejecting old, uncertain opinions in order to establish new ones or to secure old ones on a firmer basis, and the dismantling of an old house in order to build a new one:

And, just as in pulling down an old house we usually keep the remnants for use in building a new one, so in destroying all those opinions of mine that I judged ill-founded I made various observations and acquired many experiences which I have since used in establishing more certain opinions. (CSM I, 125; AT VI, 29)

And again:

For, since this knowledge is not enough to satisfy him, it must be faulty: I would compare it to a badly constructed house, whose foundations are not firm. I know of no better way to repair it than to knock it all down, and build a new one in its place. For I do not wish to be one of those jobbing builders who devote themselves solely to refurbishing old buildings because they consider themselves incapable of undertaking the construction of new ones. But, Polyander, while engaged upon this work of demolition we can use the same method to dig the foundations which ought to serve our purpose, and to prepare the best and most solid materials which will be needed for building up these foundations. (CSM II, 407; AT X, 509)

The image that is conjured up is that of an architect who demolishes a house by taking every part of the house – bricks and walls, doors and window frames, tiles and roof, beams and stones – apart, whether or not the parts are good and functional. The architect lays the new foundation and then scrounges in the pile of dismantled things, which once belonged to the house, to determine whether anything in it is usable in the construction of the new house. Consequently, one of three things can happen: The architect may find, first, that no object is usable – they are all cracked, corroded, or damaged; second, that some objects are usable and some not; or finally, that everything is usable. In the last case, they would all be used to reconstruct the new house, lie in equilibrium with one another, and rest

on a fresh and solid foundation, a foundation that will be known
not to give way. As it turns out, it is the second possibility that is
eventually realized.

Here is a perceptive contrast with Kant's invoking of the building
analogy.

Like Descartes, Kant uses metaphors of construction to explain his view
of philosophical method; but he starts with a more down-to-earth view of
building projects. The result is a quite different vision of philosophical pro-
cedures. We are to look back on what has been done in "Transcendental
Doctrine of Elements" as an *estimate* or *inventory* of our building materials,
which has instructed us about some constraints on what we can build. The
result is in some ways disappointing, especially when matched against the
rationalist ambition to build "a tower that would reach the heavens." However, rationalism failed because it took no account either of the paucity of
materials or of the disagreements about the plan among the fellow workers.
It relied on the fiction of a unitary and authoritative architect, whose innate
ideas correspond to their real archetypes, to construct the edifice of human
knowledge.[2]

A full Cartesian response is still awaited. But, I venture, Descartes
would have asked of Kant the following questions: What makes for the
paucity of the inventory, namely, the human material? What leads to
the disagreement about the plan? Is the low estimate of the material
due to an inherent defect in the material or to an essentially eradicable
defect? If the former, then there is no way to resolve conflicts over a
plan, no matter how long, elaborate, or frequent the public use of
reason. If the latter, what makes the eradication of the defect possible,
other than the inherent nature of the individual reasoner and his
ability to make a correct decision? Then, in what way is that inherent
nature or ability to be described in non-Cartesian terms? Or, how can
this possibility rest on a non-Cartesian method? Must not the reasoning
parties ultimately share something in common if they are to arrive at
an agreement?

If the Kantian argument is that Descartes was guilty of not allowing public use of reason in building his project because it would have
hastened that project, Descartes might have conceded the point. But he
might still have insisted that something like a community of Cartesian

---

[2] Onora O'Neill, *Constructions of Reason: Explorations of Kant's Practical Philosophy*, 11–12.

reasoners would be required if a final agreement is to be reached. Perhaps we might profitably combine the two views. Here is an oft-quoted remark from the *Critique of Pure Reason*: "The very existence of reason depends upon this freedom, which has no dictatorial authority, but whose claim is never anything more than the agreement of free citizens, each of whom must be able to express his reservations, indeed even his *veto*, without holding back"(A738–739/B7667–767). The free citizen would profit from the Kantian idea of the public use of reason – freely and openly conducted – no less than from the Cartesian idea of exercising reason in private. Both are necessary, perhaps, in the final analysis.

How he arrives at the foundation stone, we shall see later. What we now need to do is to see how the architect examines the various objects and determines their fitness for the construction of a new house. The house corresponds to the system of beliefs; the various objects in the house correspond to the various beliefs; and the design and structure of the house correspond to the structure of, and the relationships among, the beliefs. It is these particular beliefs, and the relationships among the beliefs, that a system builder needs to examine.

Examine, then, the following propositions:

[1] Placebos can prevent pregnancy.
[2] Mount Everest is not the highest mountain in the world.
[3] Phenotypic variance is composed of three main sources of variation: genotypic, environmental, and interaction.
[4] There is a piece of paper in front of me.
[5] $2 + 9 = 11$

With respect to the foregoing propositions, if the reader is anything like me, he will harbor extreme doubt about [1]. He will have some doubt about [2], a doubt that can be settled by consulting a book of maps. Of [3] he will be unsure rather than doubtful, and would have to reread a book on genetics in order to determine its truth-value (incidentally, it is true). Of [4] he will be quite sure. Of [5] he will be absolutely certain. These propositions are arranged in a sequence beginning with utter doubt about a certain proposition and ending with utter certainty about another. In other words, the sequence of propositions moves from one about which we have grave and genuine doubts, to ones about which we have weak doubts, and finally to one about which we have no doubt at all. As Descartes will show us, there is room for one more kind of doubt: exaggerated, pretend, hyperbolic, or metaphysical doubt. This kind of doubt, its purpose served, he will laugh about later. This style of doubt is meant to cast [4] and [5] in a different light.

The following diagram corresponding to our beliefs represents degrees of doubt by the number of lines in each circle:

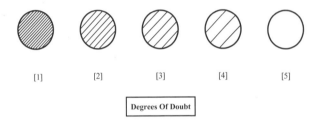

Degrees Of Doubt

Next, let us distinguish a *mental state* from a *mental process*. I shall assume the term "mental state" to be a simple, undefined term. A mental process is a collection of mental states. There are, of course, myriad mental states, states that we are in when we command, desire, compel, ask a question, are happy, or are in pain or deep sorrow, as King Lear was when he said, "Never, never, never, never, never." However, I shall confine myself to those mental states that a thinker is in when he is entertaining a declarative proposition, that is, a proposition that is either true or false. Such propositions may range from "There is salt on the table" to the recent pronouncements in high-energy physics. Some mental processes are more coherent than other mental processes. There is a more rational sequence of mental states in some mental processes, a less rational sequence in others, as when one is free-associating, daydreaming, or in a reverie. I shall deal with more or less coherent processes. Thus:

[6]   All white dwarfs are neutron stars.
[7]   All collapsed stars are white dwarfs.
       Therefore,

[8]   All collapsed stars are neutron stars.

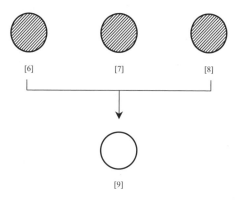

[9]   The argument is valid.

My believing proposition [6], All white dwarfs are neutron stars, is a mental state; on the other hand, my mental process is one consisting of three mental states, namely, beliefs in [6], [7], and [8], respectively. There is an argument, and corresponding to it is a mental process. One might be doubtful when in a mental state corresponding to propositions [6], [7], and [8], respectively, and yet have no doubt when in a mental state corresponding to proposition [9]. In fact, the premises are all false, and so presumably one can be in a state of doubt with respect to each of these three propositions. But the argument is a simple one, a categorical syllogism, which the logicians call *Barbara*, and it is valid: If the premises are true, the conclusion cannot be false.

Finally, we must distinguish between *first-order* mental states and processes and *second-order* mental states and processes. My second-order mental state is one in which I believe the proposition

[9]   The argument is valid.

which is about my first order mental process. It is entirely possible that first-order states may be unclear and confused while the second-order state, which is about the first-order state, is perfectly clear and beyond doubt. Thus, [3] is dubious to me; but my second-order mental state, namely, the belief that I do not know the truth-value of [3], seems quite clear. So we have several possibilities if we commute a first-order mental state (or process) with a second-order mental state (or process), defining each state (or process) as either clear or doubtful. For instance, a first-order mental process may be doubtful, but a second-order mental process about that first-order mental process may be clear; a first-order mental state may be clear, but a second-order mental state about that first-order mental state may be doubtful, and so on.

Now, Descartes' enterprise can be described in terms of the foregoing as follows. When an ideal investigator searches for truth, is there any mental state or mental process in which he has *no* doubt[3] – that is, speaking pictorially, in which there are no lines in the diagram of that mental state (or process) at all? Beliefs about [1] and [3] clearly could not serve as candidates, since they are infected by doubts. Could beliefs in [4] and [5] serve as candidates? One would be hard put to find clearer or more cogent beliefs. Descartes suggests that we should not just rely on ordinary doubts to reach indubitability, but that we should strive, as far as the human mind can be bent and stretched, to *induce* doubts in ourselves by hook or by crook until we can doubt no more. The task is to ensure that our doubt is sufficiently sweeping, that the mind actually *feels* the pressure of doubt; the doubt should extend to anything and everything until it arrives at a point that it cannot touch or infect with doubt.

---

[3] One might object to this formulation on the grounds that Descartes is not so much after indubitable mental states (of whatever order) as he is after indubitable propositions. However, this objection overlooks the Cartesian view that language is merely an instrument for dressing up one's thought. What is primary is thought. Jill Vance Buroker makes the point pithily: In Descartes, "thought is prior to language, that words are merely external, conventional signs of independent, private mental states. On this view, strictly speaking, linguistic utterances signify the thoughts occurring in the speaker's mind. Although the association between words and ideas is conventional and thus arbitrary, language can signify thought insofar as both are articulated systems: there is a correlation between the structure of a complex linguistic expression and the natural structure of the ideas it expresses." Introduction, xxiii.

Given the correlation between the structure of a complex linguistic expression and the natural structure of the ideas it expresses, one might say that given any mental state (of whatever order) one can formulate a corresponding proposition. Having arrived at one, one can easily arrive at the other. But the objection raises some nice issues. For example, to what extent is the truth of the *cogito* language-dependent? Could a speaker of the most rudimentary language – a language sans science, logic, mathematics, or metaphysics – come to recognize the truth of the *cogito*? What minimum linguistic resources would be needed for such a recognition?

This is not overstated. Descartes admonishes himself thus:

My habitual opinions keep coming back, and, despite my wishes, they capture my belief, which is as it were bound over to them as a result of long occupation and the law of custom. I shall never get out of the habit of confidently assenting to these opinions, so long as I suppose them to be what in fact they are, namely highly probable opinions. . . . I think it will be a good plan to turn my will in completely the opposite direction and deceive myself, by pretending for a time that these former opinions are utterly false and imaginary. I shall do this until the weight of preconceived opinion is counter-balanced and the distorting influence of habit no longer prevents my judgement from perceiving things correctly. (CSM II, 15; AT VII, 22)

Three remarks are in order. First, either his doubts are real or his doubts are hyperbolic, a mishmash of these two kinds of doubt not being possible. Now, he has certainly not demonstrated the former. But only if his doubts are real can he lose confidence in assenting to his customary opinions and genuinely tilt his will in the direction he wants. If his doubts are hyperbolic, as he avers, then the weight of preconceived opinion cannot, or will not, be counterbalanced and the distorting influence of habit cannot, or will not, be set aside. Second, the preconceived opinion cannot both be distorting, preventing correct judgment, *and* be highly probable. Third, it is not necessary that he turn his will in completely the opposite direction and deceive himself. It is enough for his epistemic enterprise if he can keep clearly distinguished in his mind real doubts and hyperbolic doubts, but keep enlarging the domain of hyperbolic doubts until their domain can be increased no further. With each piece of certain knowledge gained, that domain will shrink proportionally; or, he will discover that the domain of hyperbolic doubts is simply here to stay.

III. Two Models of Doubt

Let me explain the structure of what I shall call the *ordinary-doubt model*. Consider again

[1]   Placebos can prevent pregnancy.

What does it mean to say that I doubt it? It means that my knowledge of the causal lines that constitute the world's make-up, in particular, the

causal lines that are responsible for conception, contravenes claim [1].
Essential to conception is the process of ovulation in women and the
entry of the sperm into the ovum. Ovulation is controlled by hormones
that are secreted by the pituitary gland. Sperm cells are produced in the
testes, stored in the epididymis, and passed through ejaculatory ducts.
Conception occurs in the oviduct, and if fertilization occurs, then the
egg becomes embedded in the uterine wall. Thus, if the fallopian tubes
or the oviducts are blocked, conception will not occur. If the passage to
the ovum is not blocked in any manner, then a sperm cell can find its
way there; often it will. Then it may fertilize the ovum, and conception
will occur. But a placebo has no known causal property, as do some
contraceptives, by which it can block that passage. Therefore, I doubt
that [1] is true.[4]

This model of ordinary doubt presupposes the correctness or
the reliability of several things about human sexuality mentioned in
the foregoing paragraph. For example, it presupposes the truth of
the following: Ovulation occurs; sperm are produced in the testes;
fallopian tubes are not blocked; and ejaculatory ducts are not blocked.
If these propositions too were questionable, and no reliance could be
placed on them, *then* I could not properly doubt in the ordinary way.
The denial of [1] would be just as much open to doubt as its affirmation. Should we conclude, then, that a model of ordinary doubt
consists of a doubted proposition that necessarily *presupposes a framework of propositions believed to be certain*? Can a proposition be doubted
with no certain propositions to rely upon at all?[5]

---

4 I am not drawing any sharp distinction between doubt and disbelief. If disbelief is
   a stronger notion than doubt – so that what is disbelieved is doubted, while what is
   doubted may not necessarily be disbelieved – then I am dealing here only with doubt.
   I proceed to show how genuine doubt leads by stages to hyperbolic doubt, and it is
   by no means obvious, nor is it my task to show, that they lie on the same continuum.
   This I take to be precisely Descartes' enterprise.
5 "However, the menace of universal shamming is an empty menace" – Gilbert Ryle,
   The Concept of Mind, 166. H. A. Prichard claimed, "We can only be uncertain of one
   thing because we are certain of something else" ("Descartes's *Meditations*"). Ludwig
   Wittgenstein proclaimed, "The game of doubt presupposes certainty. If you tried
   to doubt everything, you would not get as far as doubting anything" (*On Certainty*,
   section 115). The last two are quoted in James van Cleve's "Foundationalism, Epistemic
   Principles, and the Cartesian Circle," 108. Van Cleve's own reaction to these assertions
   is to argue that one must distinguish between the *ground* for certainty and the *source* of
   certainty. "We may sum things up thus: doubt presupposes that *something* is certain; so

The answer to the last question – in the ordinary, practical context – is no, it cannot. Each doubt must be supported, in that context; indeed, the author of the "Seventh Set of Objections" insisted that any doubt in any context must be so supported. But that is not what Descartes was after. Descartes simply contended that if a mere possibility can be established that a proposition is false, then it is, for the epistemological purpose at hand, to be regarded as false. Thus, a doubt may be a metaphysical doubt, yet it serves this purpose: to "reject as if absolutely false everything in which I could imagine the least doubt, in order to see if I was left believing anything that was entirely indubitable" (CSM I, 127; AT VI 31–32). I am unsure what precisely Descartes means by *absolutely false* – or *wholly false*, as he says elsewhere – that is not captured by *false*. One might say that Descartes was fashioning an *extraordinary-doubt model*. This is a doubt that presupposes no true propositions. "There may be reasons," says Descartes, "which are strong enough to compel us to doubt, even though these reasons are themselves doubtful, and hence are not to be retained later on" (CSM II, 319; AT VII, 473–474).

Let me illustrate the nature of this extraordinary doubt by considering three distinct cases: (a) the probabilistic case, (b) the deterministic case, and (c) the mathematical case. (a) Suppose we wish to determine what effect high blood pressure has on the human heart. More specifically, we wish to determine if high blood pressure is the cause of cardiac arrest. We take a sample of 5,000 (in routine cases, sample sizes are much smaller) individuals varying in age, traditions of eating, habits of exercise, profession, culture, social status, sex, and religion. This guarantees sufficient diversity and ensures that there is no bias in our sample; in short, our sample is a random sample. But individuals in the sample have one thing in common, namely, they all suffer from high blood pressure. These individuals, the control group, are not treated for that disease. We take another similar group of 5,000 individuals, except these individuals are treated for high blood pressure. We trace the life histories of the individuals in the

far, Prichard and Wittgenstein are right. But the *ground* on which one bases a doubt need not be certain; on this point Descartes was right." (110) This is, in fact, quite a concession, as will become clear as this book unfolds; in any event, it does scant justice to Descartes: For the details of my argument against van Cleve, see Chapter 4.

two respective samples. In the first group, 650 individuals experience cardiac arrest; in the second group, 150. Thus, the difference between the two random samples is $650 - 150 = 500$. If we want our test results to be significant at three standard deviations (most investigations make do with only two standard deviations), then we require the difference between the two samples to be 500 (plus or minus 150). As a matter of fact, the difference between our two samples is 500. Consequently, our hypothesis is corroborated at a 99.7 percent level of confidence.

Would this satisfy Descartes? No, it would not, because there is a clear, but extremely small, probability that this was a chance occurrence, and that high blood pressure has no bearing on a person's suffering cardiac arrest. Even very, very high probability is not the same thing as absolute certainty. And that is what Descartes is seeking.

(b) Consider the deterministic case: Suppose that Newton's three laws of motion (or Descartes' own version of them) plus the gravitational law entirely determined the observable, physical world. Suppose further that no observation yet known to man falsified the theory. Would this satisfy Descartes? No, because an alternative to Newton's first law can be conceived. As it stands, the first law (in the modern version) states: If an object is at rest, it will continue to stay at rest, or if it is in motion, it will continue to move in a straight line, if unhampered by any external force. But to cast a mere minimal doubt on this proposition, we need only to conceive the possibility of an object moving in a circular motion when unhampered by any physical object. In the days of Ptolemy, astronomers believed that the natural motion of celestial objects was circular. So even the complete empirical adequacy and success of a theory of a deterministic system is not the same thing as certain knowledge.

Consider, finally, (c) the mathematical case. Here is the proof of a simple mathematical theorem, namely, that in an equiangular triangle, all the sides are equal:

[1A] $\angle B = \angle C$, by hypothesis
[2A]   AD is the common side
[3A] $BD = DC$, by construction
[4A] $\therefore \triangle ABD = \triangle ADC$

[5A] $\therefore AB = AC$

[6A] Similarly, $AB = BC$
[7A] $\therefore AB = AC = BC$

Would *this* satisfy Descartes (*before* the discovery of the *cogito*)? No, because there might be a slip on our part unbeknownst to us. Or there might be a deceiver who makes us think that we have a proof, when in fact we do not. For example, we have invoked in this proof the principle that when two things are equal to a third, they are equal to one another. It was this principle that enabled us to infer [7A] from [5A] and [6A]. But perhaps that principle, no matter how perspicuous, may be false. Descartes says explicitly in the *Discourse on the Method*: "And since there are men who make mistakes in reasoning, committing logical fallacies concerning the simplest questions in geometry, and because I judged that I was as prone to error as anyone else, I rejected as unsound all the arguments I had previously taken as demonstrative proofs"[6] (CSM I,127; AT VI, 32). In *Principles of Philosophy*, in paragraph five, entitled *The reasons for doubting even mathematical demonstrations*, Descartes says, "Our doubt will also apply to other matters which we previously regarded as most certain – even the demonstrations of mathematics and even the principles which we hitherto considered to be self-evident" (CSM I, 194; AT IXB 6).

---

[6] In parodying the Second Meditation, Hyperaspistes (an assumed name of one of Descartes' correspondents) had said that a sceptic could say, "Let the evil demon deceive me as much as he can, he will never deceive me about this geometrical proposition," to which Descartes had responded that "anyone who says this is by that token not a sceptic, since he does not doubt everything" (CSMK, 196, note 5; AT III, 433–434). Presumably, then, the doubting of mathematical proofs is very much in order if one is to be a Cartesian skeptic in search of the indubitable. To be fair, however, the context in which Descartes writes this to Hyperaspistes is different; but that does not affect my purposes, or Descartes' intentions, here.

IV. Doubt and Principles

In light of the foregoing, we can see the structure of Descartes' own doubt. It is this. It is impossible – or, as he puts it, "an endless task" (CSM II, 12; AT VII, 18) – to examine each of his beliefs and determine if he can find reasons to induce even the least doubt about those beliefs. There are just far too many beliefs. But the beliefs rest on certain basic principles, and if these principles can be undermined, then all of the beliefs that rest on the principles can be made to collapse; they can be "demolished." Note that Descartes assumes without argument that these so-called principles are finite. It appears that these principles are associated with sense experiences and reason, and since the latter are finite, it is tacitly assumed that the principles are finite.

What, in this context, did Descartes mean by *principles?* He must have meant the five senses and the intellect. There are, so to speak, the sight principle, the smell principle, the sound principle, the touch principle, the taste principle, and the intellect principle. (I distinguish between the intellect principle and the principle of intuition.) Otherwise, it is difficult to see how Descartes could have avoided an endless task. For let us suppose that numbers are the principles of arithmetic; lines, the basic principles of geometry (prior to the Cartesian analytic geometry); humors, the basic principles of medicine; earth, air, water, and fire, the basic principles of geology; and we can easily extend the list. We doubt the numbers, so arithmetic collapses; we doubt the humors, so medicine collapses. If such a list of basic principles is not finite, then the task is just as endless. But the knowledge of these basic principles is derived from the sense organs or from the intellect. Consequently, if the occasional testimony of these organs or of the intellect could be impugned, the task would be finite and manageable. This is exactly what Descartes attempts to do: to impugn the testimony of the five senses and the intellect.

He now commences his doubt. The least, or minimal, doubt of which Descartes speaks can be established in a variety of ways. *First step.* Many of his beliefs – say, about far and near objects, or objects that are big or small – are "acquired either from the senses or through the senses" (CSM II, 12; AT VII, 18). But the senses have sometimes patently deceived: For example, square towers, at a distance, have been judged to be round. Thus, the sight-principle is impugned. Consider once again the proposition

[4] There is a piece of paper in front of me.

How can I doubt *it*? By challenging the testimony of the witnesses. In this case, the witnesses are my five senses. These witnesses report that the object before me looks like paper, smells like paper, feels like paper, and so on. How can I challenge these witnesses? By pointing out that they have frequently been unreliable; and since they have perjured themselves in the past, so to speak, their testimony should be scratched from the books. Indeed, "it is prudent never to trust completely those who have deceived us even once" (CSM II, 12; AT VII 18). Thus it is that the sound-principle, the taste-principle, the smell-principle, and the touch-principle are impugned, too. Descartes did not aim to establish that propositions like [4] are in fact false, but rather that they are to be presumed false, if not proved true. If they are not proved true, he would withhold assent to them.

Second step. Some beliefs seem too stable and solid to deny, even though they are "derived from" the senses. For example, the belief that I am awake, wearing sandals, sitting on the lawn, and looking at an orange tree. Or that I have ears, eyes, hands, and a body. To deny these claims is to border on insanity. At this point comes the argument from dreams. My dream experience cannot be distinguished from my waking experience with certainty: "I see plainly that there are never any sure signs by means of which being awake can be distinguished from being asleep" (CSM II, 13; AT VII, 19). (What if waking experiences were always colored and dream experiences were always noncolored, and each possessed the usual properties of clarity, coherence, and continuity? Would we then be able to distinguish waking experiences from dream experiences?) But if we demolish the distinction between dream experiences and waking experiences, then it is possible that my experiences of my body, physical objects, and physical states are nonveridical. It is possible that I am all – and nothing but – mind or mental states, and have no body or bodily states.[7]

Third step. Can anything be salvaged? My dream experiences are like paintings. Now, an artist can paint or create "sirens and satyrs with

---

[7] Of the very many expositions of the dream argument in the literature, none supersedes Edwin M. Curley's in *Descartes against the Skeptics*, Chapter 3, "Dreaming."

the most extraordinary bodies" (CSM II, 13; AT VII, 20), but there are some things in the paintings that are not, and cannot be, the creation of the artist, namely, colors, corporeal nature in general, its extension, quantity, size, number, place, and time. Thus, an artist can create an image of an animal that has the trunk of an elephant, the feet of an ostrich, the head of a crocodile, the tail of a polar bear, and the ears of a poodle. He can create composite objects, such as the idea of the head, ears, and feet, but he cannot create simple things, such as the idea of size, time, quantity, or place. These are called simple, general, and universal things. Here Descartes relies on the (causal?) principle that what is imagined ultimately "must have been fashioned in the likeness of things that are real" (CSM II, 13; AT VII, 19). He never questioned the causal principle, which would have given him a natural entry to doubting these things as well. In those pre-Humean days, that was perhaps too much to question. "So a reasonable conclusion from this," says Descartes, "might be that physics, astronomy, medicine, and all other disciplines which depend on the study of composite things, are doubtful; while arithmetic, geometry and other subjects of this kind, which deal only with the simplest and most general things, regardless of whether they really exist in nature or not, contain something certain and indubitable" (CSM II, 14; AT VII, 20). Perhaps these are salvaged?

Fourth, and final, step. Whether in my dream experiences or in waking experiences, the truths of arithmetic, such as [5], always hold, as do the propositions of algebra and geometry. These propositions about the simplest and most general things do not make any existential claims, and are not dubious in a way in which propositions are that make existential claims. Has Descartes, at last, found something certain? Not quite. It is the model of extraordinary doubt that drives Descartes to invent the hypothesis of an evil demon. Here, then, is that (in)famous hypothesis:

I will suppose therefore that . . . some malicious demon of the utmost power and cunning has employed all his energies in order to deceive me. I shall think that the sky, the air, the earth, colours, shapes, sounds and all external things are merely the delusions of dreams which he has devised to ensnare my judgment. I shall consider myself as not having hands or eyes, or flesh, or blood or senses, but as falsely believing that I have all these things. (CSM II, 15; AT VII, 23)

The demon's powers of deception are fantastic. This hypothesis in hand, Descartes can now contest [5] and its ilk.

Descartes first postulated the existence of an omnipotent God, his Maker, who has "brought it about that there is no earth, no sky, no extended thing, no shape, no size, no place, while at the same time ensuring that all these things appear to me to exist just as they do now" (CSM II, 14; AT VII, 21). Yet how could a good God even occasionally deceive, let alone often or continually deceive? But we *are* deceived, and this requires an account. Consequently, second, Descartes supposed that he was created "by fate or chance or continuous chain of events, or by some other means" (CSM II, 14; AT VII, 21). However, the less powerful and random the cause of his existence, Descartes concluded, the more, not less, liable he would be to error. Descartes, third, supposed that he was being manipulated by some "malicious demon of the utmost power and cunning," and that this demon can actually lead Descartes to believe that $2 + 9 = 11$ when in fact it does not add up to 11.

One can see that this is an extraordinary doubt. There is no presupposition of a framework of true propositions. There is no argument to establish the evil demon; there is no argument to establish that he is bent on deceiving us; thus, there is no argument to establish that one could believe propositions that are negations of the laws of mathematics as we know them. There is simply a fiat: There is a malicious demon, and he can deceive a person about the laws of mathematics. Such a stipulation would cast doubt on proposition [5]. But truths such as [5] or the propositions of arithmetic, algebra, geometry, and the like are known by the intellect. Consequently, the intellect principle is impugned. The demon hypothesis has taken Descartes to the outermost limit of human doubt.

I am unsympathetic to Sir Karl Raimund Popper's criticism that if we eliminate all of our existing knowledge in order to start afresh, there is no reason why we would advance any further than did Adam and Eve. Thus, in *Conjectures and Refutations: The Growth of Scientific Knowledge*, Popper says,

Some people say that ... it is their greatest wish to clean the canvas thoroughly – to create a social *tabula rasa* and to begin afresh by painting on it a brand new social system. But they should not be surprised if they find that once they destroy tradition, civilization disappears with it. They will find

that mankind have returned to the position in which Adam and Eve began –
or, using less biblical language, that they have returned to the beasts. (344)

Nor is this just a social hypothesis; it is also an epistemological one:

In other words, you should study the *problem situation* of the day. This means
that you pick up, and try to continue, a line of inquiry which has the whole
background of the earlier development of science behind it; you fall in with
the tradition of science. It is a very simple and a decisive point, but nevertheless
one that is often not sufficiently realized by rationalists – that we cannot start
afresh; that we must make use of what people before us have done in science.
If we start afresh, then, when we die, we shall be about as far as Adam and Eve
were when they died (or, if you prefer, as far as Neanderthal man). (219)

Descartes wants to wipe the epistemic slate clean in order for us to write
on it again properly. This time we are to write on it, not just a medley of
conjectures and refutations, but rather systematic, certain truths. But
any attempt to get rid of existing knowledge – by the method of doubt,
for instance – would prove injurious to science and knowledge. Thus
far, Popper. Descartes' response to Popper's objection would be that
if a given scientific society were to start in the way in which Descartes
recommends that an ideal seeker should proceed, then, of course, in
the beginning such a society might do only as well as, or slightly better
than, our ancestors. But in the long run, with each such successive
society running on the Cartesian principles and bequeathing certain
truths to the next – truths determined by the criteria of certainty –
there would be no necessity for each society to start afresh. Descartes
would argue that each scientist in each society should, *in principle*,
be able to start afresh in order to see clearly and distinctly that the
principles of his science are well founded. Such certainty the scientist
cannot have unless he proceeds in a Cartesian fashion. This, of course,
does not diminish Popper's central point against rationalists such as
Descartes: that seeking certain knowledge in the empirical sciences is
a pied piper's dream.

   Harry Frankfurt has argued, in *Demons, Dreamers, and Madmen:
The Defense of Reason in Descartes'* Meditations, that the "principles"
Descartes was attacking were simply epistemic policies "to be followed
in determining whether or not to accept a belief" (33–34). Descartes'
skepticism in the First Meditation, said Frankfurt, lead him to formulate more and more precise epistemic policies; however, since
these policies ultimately relied on sensory evidence, they could be

regarded as falling essentially under a single principle. Thus, what I call the sight-principle, the smell-principle, the sound-principle, the touch-principle, and the taste-principle fall essentially under a single principle, the sensory principle. (Presumably the intellect-principle falls under it as well? Or not?) Given this single sensory principle, Frankfurt must inevitably adopt the position that mathematical statements, discussed at least in the opening meditation, are to be construed as empirical statements. Descartes' final goal in the First Meditation, as Frankfurt sees it, was to demonstrate the untenability of any such epistemic sensory principle, however precisely formulated.

Margaret Wilson found Frankfurt's view inadequate, especially past the dreaming argument; but she was not quite happy either with the way Frankfurt handled the arguments preceding the dreaming argument. She offered an alternative account of what Descartes meant by "principles" (WM, 5–6, 38–42). Wilson's causal account is specifically offered as a rival to Frankfurt's account of principles as rules of sensory evidence. Her one significant reservation, for example, is that "Descartes' view is not merely that sensations provide us with an inadequate basis for distinguishing true perceptions from false. Rather, Descartes thinks the senses actually mislead us concerning what the world is really like." (WM, 39) Furthermore, she says, there is no adequate textual support for the suppositions of Frankfurt: namely, (a) that simple natures are regarded as derived from the senses, and (b) that mathematical knowledge is dependent on existence in nature and on our sensory apparatus. Descartes, she maintained, was just simply noncommittal on these issues, at least in the First Meditation (WM, 40).

Consequently, she offered her own causal account of principles and said of it:

> If this perspective is valid, the arguments of Meditation I are indeed directed against different versions of one principle, but the 'foundation' attacked is not, as Frankfurt holds, faith in the senses specifically; it is rather faith in the truth-conferring nature of the immediate causes of our beliefs.... Descartes does not need specifically to suppose that the cause of the belief in simple natures or mathematical propositions is *sensory* in order to question that they are founded on a truth-conferring causal process. (WM, 42–43)

There are three fundamental difficulties in Wilson's approach. First, her causal theory is an ontological theory, not an epistemic one. It is not inappropriate to ask, what is the *basis* for questioning our faith in the truth-conferring nature of the immediate causes of our beliefs? To answer *that* question, it is difficult to imagine Wilson, while staying within the Cartesian strictures, falling upon an approach, that is distinct from the Frankfurt, or Frankfurt-like, approach. One must perforce fall back upon sensory evidence, at least up to the dreaming argument.

Second, if one is to doubt mathematical knowledge, then one must – despite Wilson's remarks to the contrary quoted earlier – assume that Descartes was not noncommittal, but rather distinctly empiricist in his views about mathematical knowledge. If not, it is difficult to see – even on minimalist assumptions – to *what* mathematical knowledge is causally hooked. Paying close attention to analogous passages in similar places in the *Discourse on Method* also reinforces one's belief that Descartes did not hold an empiricist view of mathematics in the First Meditation. This is a view for which I have also heard Gordon Baker argue. Perusing *Descartes' Dualism*, the basis of his and Katherine Morris's claim becomes clearer. The authors write:

Descartes repeatedly tackled the common error of confusing modes and substances, i.e., of failing to distinguish what is "modally distinct". He [Descartes] suggested that mathematicians had misconceived what they investigated through taking numbers or shapes to be substances. They will achieve a clear and distinct understanding of these things provided they scrupulously avoid "tack[ing] on to them any concept of substance" and "do not regard order or number as anything separate from the things which are ordered or numbered" [CSM I, 211; AT VIIIA, 26]. (68–69)

Arguably, when Descartes speaks of $2 + 3 = 5$, in the First Meditation, he must mean two birds (or stones, or trees), added to three birds (or stones or trees), yields five birds (or stones or trees) (CSM I, 212; AT VIIIA, 27–28).

Let us ignore Frege's devastating arguments against reading arithmetical truths in this way; let us simply concentrate on what Descartes himself says, for example, in the Fifth Meditation:

But I think the most important consideration at this point is that I find within me countless ideas of things which even though they may not exist anywhere outside me still cannot be called nothing; for although in a sense they can be thought of at will, they are not my invention but have their own true and immutable natures. When, for example, I imagine a triangle, even if perhaps no such figure exists, or has ever existed, anywhere outside my thought, there is still a determinate nature, or essence, or form of the triangle which is immutable and eternal, and not invented by me or dependent on my mind. (CSM II, 44–45; AT VII, 64)

These are the truths – not merely empirical ones – that Descartes set out to demolish with the help of the evil genius, the better to show how the latter would be rendered helpless in the face of the *cogito*, thereby demonstrating the power of the truth of the *cogito*. Otherwise, Descartes' skepticism in the First Meditation would have been a rather limited thing. (There remains the task, of course, of showing how the *Meditations on First Philosophy* dovetails with *Principles of Philosophy*.)

Third, it is not clear how either Frankfurt or Wilson would be able to account for Descartes' challenging the principles of logic, explicitly referred to in the *Discourse on Method* (for example, at CSM I, 119–120; AT VI, 17–18) and strongly implied in the First Meditation by the phrase "and other subjects of this kind" (CSM II, 14; AT VII, 20) – "this kind" presumably referring to arithmetic and geometry.[8] Perhaps what I call the intellect principle might be considered an important principle, too, that Descartes was just as much concerned to challenge; and perhaps this might raise afresh the issue concerning the validation of reason.[9] It is true that the view I offer does not have the nice unity that is to be found on either Frankfurt's or Wilson's approach. I call for at least two distinct kinds of principles – a sensory principle and an intellect principle; they can make do with just one. But that is Descartes' problem, not mine (although, I confess, I do not know what this lack of unity destroys in substance).

Doubting seems to lead nowhere. The building has been dismantled, and nothing salvageable is in sight. This led the Jesuit Pierre Bourdin (1595–1653) to ask despairingly, "Is there no sole surviving timber from the great shipwreck that is to be hung up as an offering in the temple of truth?" (CSM II, 317) There is.

[8] I owe this citation to my student Truitt Richter.
[9] See Chapter 4 of this volume.

3

The Solution: *Cogito*

No one has portrayed better the deep and powerful skepticism that prevailed during the sixteenth and seventeenth centuries, especially in France, in the fields of science, mathematics, and religion than Richard Popkin. Religious persecution was rampant, and epistemology was "a new machine of war."[1] Given the extreme doubt regarding so many matters, confidence in the possibility of knowledge was low, at best. This was the skepticism that Descartes tried desperately to combat. He wanted to combat it by showing that there was, at least, one certainty on which an entire edifice of knowledge could be constructed. That certainty was such that it could not be doubted, no matter how deep and sweeping the doubt that the human mind could invent. On that certainty, the confidence in human reason could be regenerated. So Descartes thought.

In this matter, Descartes nicely contrasts with Saint Augustine. Here is Saint Augustine in *De Utilitate Credendi*: "I could produce many arguments to show that absolutely nothing in human society will be safe if we decide to believe only what we can regard as having been clearly perceived"[2] (CSM II, 152; AT VII, 217). By contrast, Descartes'

---

[1] Richard H. Popkin, *The History of Scepticism: From Erasmus to Descartes*, 69; see especially Chapters 4–8.

[2] John Compton suggests that the cited passage from Saint Augustine contrasts sharply with what he says elsewhere, for example, in *On the Free Choice of the Will*. Among the endlessly fascinating parallels between Saint Augustine and Descartes, he thinks, may be this one: In the last-mentioned book, Augustine anticipates Descartes' own

revolution of reason was designed to show that nothing would be safe if we decided otherwise – neither society, nor knowledge, nor for that matter faith. "I am vain enough to think," he said, "that the faith has never been so strongly supported by human arguments as it may be if my principles are adopted" (CSMK, 88; AT I, 564). What was that certainty on which Descartes staked so much? That is the subject matter of this chapter.

Now, if he is searching for at least one solid certainty, the seeker after that certainty must know the characteristics of a certainty in order for him to recognize that he has stumbled onto the real thing, and not its fake surrogate. Thus, in section I, I list six criteria that that which is certain must satisfy. In section II, a famous experiment in thought is described in order to discover the sought-after certainty. In section III, in light of Descartes' taxonomy of problems and solutions, that thought experiment is evaluated. Section IV raises a philosophical objection on the basis of a claim made by Descartes in a theological context. Section V illustrates the scope and mode of doubt in the case of the *cogito* by highlighting the use of doubt in other cases. In the sixth and final section, from the experience of certainty, an epistemic rule of cardinal importance is elicited.

reasonings about the certainty of the existence of thought, and with it the existence of truth, and with this the existence of "The Truth." Granting this, for the sake of argument, I am left wondering how an Augustinian reconciliation might be effected between the two works.

Stephen Menn, for example, has argued (*Descartes and Augustine*, especially 185–194) that Augustine distinguished between understanding, belief, and opinion; having faith in the correctness of the scriptures and struggling with them were necessary conditions, but neither singly nor jointly constituted sufficient condition(s) – the grace of God was also necessary (but not sufficient?) – for achieving understanding. While ignorant, one ought to seek understanding from authority (as Augustine did from Saint Ambrose, especially seeking the latter's allegorical reading of the scriptures), and thence one would be led to understanding. As Menn notes, this leaves open the question concerning which authority one should follow – or, for that matter, I should think, which revealed scripture. Moreover, if the authority relied upon received his understanding as a result of God's grace, might not the learner receive it similarly? Or isn't God's grace necessary for understanding what the authority instructs, given that one has picked the right authority? If necessary, then why couldn't that grace work on that individual without any authority? If not necessary, what need of an authority? Descartes seems to escape these problems. Or he at least seems to make the tension between faith and reason vivid (and so the tension between himself and Saint Augustine), with reason having a slight edge over faith.

I. The Nature of the First Principle

But first, and briefly, we need to ask, what properties should that thing that Descartes is looking for possess? In short, does Descartes have any criterion or criteria for recognizing what he is after? I should warn that Descartes himself does not proceed in this way. What I am immediately interested in, in this section, is not so much a historical report of Descartes' intention as a philosophical reconstruction of his ideas and what he ought to have said. Something, I think, of philosophical interest emerges.

In fact, Descartes does list a few criteria. For example, he says that the thing must be "transparently clear" (CSM II, 104; AT VII, 145); it must be a "first principle" (CSM, II, 415; AT X, 521) or the "first item of knowledge" (CSM II, 24; AT VII, 35); it must be "easiest to become acquainted with" (CSM II, 407; AT X, 509–510); and it must be the most easily known and "the simplest" (CSM II, 400–401; AT X, 496–497). These are some of the characterizations of what is the "first thing we come to know if we philosophize in an orderly way" (CSM I, 194; AT VIII A, 6). There is a question about how far Descartes listed these criteria *prior* to his discovery of the central truth of his philosophical inquiry and the extent to which he listed them *after* his discovery. The answer is that some of the criteria he listed prior to, and some after, the discovery; and not all of the criteria were listed with that first item of knowledge in mind. But it is arguable that all of them *could*, and should, have been listed before he made his discovery. If Descartes had not listed the criteria, how would he have recognized the thing he was looking for, if and when he stumbled onto it? As we have already seen, Descartes himself said in characterizing a perfectly understood problem that "[a] problem is to be counted as perfectly understood only if we have a distinct perception of the following three points: first, what the criteria are which enable us to recognize what we are looking for when we come upon it" (CSM I, 51; AT X, 429). Consequently, if searching for an absolute certainty is to be characterized as a perfectly understood problem, we must at least have criteria for distinguishing or recognizing "what we are looking for."

Let us then, at least tersely, state these criteria, cast in their proper contexts, and explain their virtues. In *The Search for Truth,*

Descartes said:

Go on, then, Polyander, and show him how far we can get with good sense, and also what conclusions can be derived from our *first principle*. (CSM II, 415; AT X, 521; my italics)

Whatever is the truth to be discovered, the *first* criterion is that it must be a *first principle*, a first item of knowledge. Not necessarily first in the way things are, but necessarily first in the way things come to be known. The first principle will help in the derivation of other truths, and it will not be one that is derived from another truth, or from some other truths.[3] The primacy of this truth – hereinafter called the first principle – should be unquestionable, or the epistemic enterprise will not succeed. Descartes is insistent, as for example in *Principles of Philosophy*, that we "*philosophize in an orderly way*" and that when we do so, "*the first thing we come to know*" (CSM I, 194; AT VIII A, 6; my italics) is the first principle. There *is* something that we know first. There is a hierarchy, at least in the order in which we come to know with certainty, the order in which one item of knowledge takes precedence over others, and necessarily so.

The *second* criterion of the first principle is that it should be a *clear and distinct notion*. Here is Descartes in *Meditations on First Philosophy*:

Do I not therefore also know what is required for my being certain about anything? In this first item of knowledge there is simply a *clear and distinct perception* of what I am asserting. (CSM II, 24; AT VII, 35; my italics)

Again, in *The Search for Truth*:

All the mistakes made in the sciences happen, in my view, simply because at the beginning we make judgements too hastily, and accept as our first principles matters which are obscure and of which we do not have a *clear and distinct notion*. That this is true is shown by the slight progress we have made in the sciences whose first principles are certain and known by everyone. (CSM II, 419; AT X, 526; my italics)

---

[3] Using 'derivation' broadly in the sense of being dependent on; see Chapter 1, section III.

Finally, in the "Second Set of Replies":

> Now some of these perceptions are so transparently clear and at the same time so simple that we cannot ever think of them without believing them to be true. (CSM II, 104; AT VII, 145)

The virtues of clarity and distinctness of the first principle are stated directly in the former passage, by implication in the latter.[4] The second passage also indirectly supports the claim that the first principle should be the easiest to be acquainted with, since if it were not, it could not surely be known by everyone. By *everyone*, Descartes means persons who are intelligent and mature, with or without any paraphernalia of special, acquired knowledge – in short, ideal seekers.[5]

We arrive at the next two criteria:

> But, Polyander, while engaged upon this work of demolition we can use the same method to dig the foundations which ought to serve our purpose, and to prepare the best and most solid materials which will be needed for building up these foundations. So please join me in considering which, of all the truths men can know, are *the most certain* and *the easiest to become acquainted with.* (CSM II, 407; AT X, 509–510; my italics)

The *third* criterion the first principle must satisfy is that it must be *the most certain.* This criterion virtually defines this epistemic enterprise. In fact, so strong is this requirement that Descartes thinks that when we finally come to know the first principle, we shall find that it is even more certain than an instance of the law of noncontradiction. He says,

> [I]f you simply know how to make proper use of your own doubt, you can use it to deduce facts which are known with complete certainty – facts which are even more certain and more useful than those which we commonly build upon the great principle, as the basis to which they are all reduced, the fixed point on which they all terminate, namely, "It is impossible that one and the same thing should exist and at the same time not exist."[6] (CSM II, 415–416; AT X, 522)

---

4 Gaukroger offers an interesting conjecture of the connections – "striking parallels," he calls them – between Descartes' theory of clear and distinct grasp of an idea and the psychological theory of cognitive grasp as found especially in the work of Quintilian, a psychological theory whose origin lay in Aristotle and which had its early development in the Stoics (G, 118–123).

5 See Chapter 1, section I, this volume.

6 To Mersenne he wrote on April 15, 1630: "At least I think that I have found how to prove metaphysical truths in a manner which is more evident than the proofs of geometry" (CSMK 22; AT I, 144). He made elsewhere similar claims: see CSMK,

The first principle should also satisfy the *fourth* criterion, that of being *the easiest to become acquainted with.* If the first principle is difficult to get to know, we cannot rely on its certitude. The entire edifice of knowledge would be shaky and could collapse. Descartes claimed, in fact, that an ordinary inquirer after truth, who has reached the age of discretion (CSM II, 406; AT X, 508) and has a modicum of insight (CSM II, 409; AT X, 514), would be able to know the first principle. Such an inquirer, an ideal seeker, would not require the resources of learning preached in the Schools. So: The first principle must be the easiest to be acquainted with.

Here is Descartes' *fifth* criterion:

For the items of knowledge that lie within reach of the human mind are all linked together by a bond so marvelous, and can be derived from each other by means of inferences so necessary, that their discovery does not require much skill or intelligence – provided we begin with the *simplest* and know how to move stage by stage to the most sublime. (CSM II, 400–401; AT X, 496–497; my italics)

This passage lists another criterion, namely, that the first principle should be the *simplest,* a virtue hard to define. For the moment, I wish to express a puzzle. If Descartes is to be taken literally, then the first principle is an item of knowledge on a par with other items of knowledge. Descartes is claiming that the first principle is hooked by a proper inference to those other items of knowledge just as surely as those other items are hooked to the first principle. They can be "derived from each other." If this is true, then calling anything *the* first principle is moot, since it can be derived from some other item of knowledge. Any such item of knowledge could serve as the starting point from which all other items of knowledge could be derived.

Of rule 6 in *Rules for the Direction of the Mind,* Descartes said that it contained "the main secret of my method." Here is the rule's caption:

In order to distinguish the simplest things from those that are complicated and to set them out in an orderly manner, we should attend to what is

29; AT I, 181–182 and CSMK, 53; AT I, 350, although in the latter he was talking about his proof of the existence of God. But since that metaphysical truth is dependent on the *cogito*, it could not be more certain than the *cogito*. Consequently, it is arguable that the *cogito* is known with greater certainty than the truths of mathematics, which is precisely what Descartes maintains.

most simple in each series of things in which we have directly deduced some truths from others, and should observe how all the rest are more, or less, or equally removed from the simplest. (CSM I, 21; AT X, 381; italics omitted)

This rule "instructs us that all things can be arranged serially in various groups, not in so far as they can be referred to some ontological genus (such as the categories [e.g., the Aristotelian categories of substance, quality, quantity, relation, etc.] into which philosophers divide things), but in so far as some things can be known on the basis of others" (CSM I, 21; AT X, 381). By parity of reasoning, Descartes, I conjecture, would have asserted the following: All items of knowledge can be arranged serially, and that arrangement will reflect the order in which things can be known on the basis of others. The first item in the series will be the simplest, and it will not be known, *ex hypothesi*, on the basis of anything else. However, it will serve as a basis on which succeeding items of knowledge in the series can be known.

Now, all things can be divided into the *absolute* and the *relative*. The absolute is pure, simple, and independent. "I call this the simplest and the easiest thing when we can make use of it in solving problems" (CSM I, 21; AT X, 381). The relative shares its nature, and so it can be related, and deduced, from the absolute. But the distinction between absolute and relative depends on a point of view. "For some things are more absolute than others from one point of view, yet more relative from a different point of view" (CSM I, 22; AT X, 382). For example, from the point of view of simplicity, a universal is more absolute than a particular; but from the point of view of dependency, a particular is more absolute than a universal, since the latter depends for its existence on the particular. Descartes offers a different example: Species is absolute relative to the individual, but relative with respect to the genus.

Descartes could have effectively argued, then, that from an epistemic point of view, the first principle should be not only the simplest but also more easily known than the rest of the items in the series. Consequently, if a particular is more easily known than a universal, then the first principle will have the character of being a *particular*. If knowledge of a universal is dependent on knowledge of a particular, then, too, the first principle cannot be a universal. In short, the first principle *cannot* be a universal. This is the *sixth* criterion for something serving as the first principle. This will later prove to be very important.

There is a potential conflict between the requirements of simplicity and particularity. The first principle must be simple, so it must be universal; the first principle must be particular, so it cannot be universal. I resolve this conflict by suggesting that simplicity is a relative term. What Descartes calls the simplest is that which we can make use of in solving problems. Thus, I infer that for the problem at hand, if the first principle is a particular, it will aid in solving problems in a manner in which a universal first principle cannot.

To say the least, none of these criteria or properties is precise. For example, what constitutes simplicity? Is the law of noncontradiction simple? Is utmost simplicity a property possessed by only one object, or by a host of objects? What is "easiest to become acquainted with" (acquaintance not through the senses, but presumably by reason or intuition)? Is anything known by discursive reasoning either simplest or easiest? Will only an intuition do for that? What is the argument, if there is one, for the possibility that an object can simultaneously possess two or more properties, such as that of being the simplest and that of being known most easily? What is a principle: Is it a proposition or a perception? Most significantly, can any of this be known *prior* to stumbling onto the first item of knowledge? Are these properties not discerned *after* the discovery of the object, and upon subsequently examining and reflecting on it?

It is useful to keep these cues and questions in mind as Descartes now approaches the climax.

II. The Thought Experiment

Descartes did not plan to draw any practical consequences from his doubt. He was not going to let his daily life be interrupted or interfered with on the basis of his doubts. But he did want these metaphysical doubts to be treated seriously, in the hope that they might point to something that is not susceptible to such doubts. If there is no such thing, then at least he would know that there is nothing that can be known for certain. "I will proceed in this way until I recognize something certain, or, if nothing else, until I at least recognize for certain that there is no certainty"7 (CSM II, 16; AT VII, 24). Now, Descartes took these doubts seriously, hyperbolic though they were.

So serious are the doubts into which I have been thrown as a result of yesterday's meditations that I can neither put them out of my mind nor see any way of resolving them. It feels as if I have fallen unexpectedly into a deep whirlpool which tumbles me around so that I can neither stand on the bottom nor swim up to the top. (CSM II, 16; AT VII, 23–24)

Descartes believed that such mental states of doubt were essential to the proper reception of that sought-after proposition – or argument – that cannot be doubted. It is essential that one also feel the psychological pressure involved in actually coming to *believe* that one's beliefs, or one's system of beliefs, are without foundation or justification. It is not enough to have intellectually established these doubts, at a distance, disinterestedly, as it were. As he says, "it is not enough merely to have noticed this" (CSM II, 15; AT VII, 22). Descartes claims that he must remember these doubts, goad his mind in the direction of these doubts when the mind slips back into its habitual ways of thinking and feeling. The pressure of commonplace thoughts, due to repetition, law, and custom, is not to be underestimated, because the mind will continue to believe such thoughts to be "highly probable opinions," which is "what in fact they are" (CSM II, 15; AT VII, 22). There is an inherent "laziness" in us. Thus, he must undertake an arduous task: The will must be turned in the opposite direction, and Descartes must attempt to deceive himself "until the weight of preconceived opinions is counterbalanced and the distorting influence of habit no longer prevents my judgement from perceiving things correctly"(CSM II, 15; AT VII, 22).

Descartes thinks that unless there is this strong initial intellectual discomfort brought about by a pervasive doubt, a would-be knower will never come to know certain truth. Or at least, his grasp of that truth will not be what it could be. *How* he grasps that truth is as important as *what* he comes to grasp.

---

7 There is nothing paradoxical in that remark. Descartes is merely saying that his lack of certainty about an nth-order proposition is compatible with his having certainty about an $n+1$th-order proposition. Thus, his recognizing for certain that there is no certainty in any nth-order proposition is simply a certainty about an $n+1$th-order proposition. Either Descartes hits upon a proposition like the *cogito*, or he comes up empty-handed. In either case, he has at least one certainty.

Here, then, in the *Meditations on First Philosophy* of 1641, comes the heart of the *cogito* claim:

But I have convinced myself that there is absolutely nothing in the world, no sky, no earth, no minds, no bodies. Does it now follow that I too do not exist? No: if I convinced myself of something, then I certainly existed. But there is a deceiver of supreme power and cunning who is deliberately and constantly deceiving me. In that case I too undoubtedly exist, if he is deceiving me; and let him deceive me as much as he can, he will never bring it about that I am nothing so long as I think that I am something. So after considering everything thoroughly, I must finally conclude that this proposition, *I am, I exist*, is necessarily true whenever it is put forward by me or conceived in my mind. (CSM II, 16–17; AT VII, 25)

Four years earlier, in *Discourse on the Method*, a similar passage, at a similar juncture in the argument, had read:

I resolved to pretend that all the things that had ever entered my mind were no more true than the illusions of my dreams. But immediately I noticed that while I was trying thus to think everything false, it was necessary that I, who was thinking this, was something. And observing this truth, "*I am thinking, therefore I exist*" was so firm and sure that all the most extravagant suppositions of the sceptics were incapable of shaking it, I decided that I could accept it without scruple as the first principle of the philosophy I was seeking. (CSM I, 127; AT VI, 32)

While three years later, in *Principles of Philosophy*, published in 1644, the corresponding passage was formulated thus:

In rejecting – and even imagining to be false – everything which we can in any way doubt, it is easy for us to suppose that there is no God and no heaven, and that there are no bodies, and even that we ourselves have no hands or feet, or indeed any body at all. But we cannot for all that suppose that we, who are having such thoughts, are nothing. For it is a contradiction to suppose that what thinks does not, at the very time when it is thinking, exist. Accordingly, this piece of knowledge – *I am thinking, therefore I exist* – is the first and most certain of all to occur to anyone who philosophizes in an orderly way. (CSM I, 194–195; AT VIIIA, 7)

And in each case, without further ado, Descartes sets about to discover the properties of this 'I'.

How are these passages to be understood? Let us draw on our distinctions. Are the passages susceptible to the ordinary-doubt model

analysis, or will only the extraordinary-doubt model do? Is the *cogito –
I am thinking, therefore I exist* – a mental state or a mental process? Is it
a first-order or a second-order type of thought? Finally, does the *cogito*
satisfy the six criteria in virtue of which it is to be accorded the status
of the first principle of the philosophy that Descartes was seeking? Is
it a perfect solution to a perfect problem? The answers to all of these
questions will not be finally settled here; but we must begin to answer
them now.

The cited passages cannot be susceptible to the ordinary-doubt
model, since to doubt a proposition, according to that model, is to
presuppose the truth of some other propositions. Descartes explicitly vows to doubt everything that can be doubted: the existence of
such things as the sky, earth, minds, and bodies. Thus, extraordinary-
doubt is involved, but in this case it has a curious feature. At this
point, I need you, the reader, to conduct the thought experiment that
Descartes is urging. Attempt to carry out the extraordinary doubt,
no matter how silly it seems to you. Well, then: Commence doubting
that the sky exists, that numbers exist, that there are mathematical
demonstrations, and so on. Provide yourself with reasons for raising
minimal doubts, reasons for rejecting the proposition that the sky exists or that there are mathematical proofs and propositions. If you
are unable to find reasons for rejecting a proposition, then do what
Descartes did: Raise the specter of an evil genius who is bent on deceiving you. Carefully notice and register the properties of your mental
states, whether they are doubtful or certain, clear or confused, distinct
or otherwise, and note as well the intensity, quality, and character of
these properties.

Now, either at the various stages in your attempting to give reasons,
or at the stage where you have arrived at that about which you have
reasoned, attempt to question your own existence. Attempt to doubt
your own existence, giving yourself reasons parallel to those you gave
yourself for doubting other things. "I do not exist," say to your*self,*
"because ——." Inquire *why* no reason is sufficient. You will find that
any attempt, *at any stage,* at providing even a solitary reason for the
least conceivable amount of doubt regarding any proposition, about
either yourself or anything else, will confront you with your own existence, thus notarizing – with *you* as the notary – the proposition that

you exist. You will "notice" the ineluctable truth of the proposition, namely, that you, the doubter, exist. "I am thinking, therefore I exist" will come home to you as no other truth does. It is the coming home of this truth that I need for you to latch onto, with whatever properties are attendant upon it. The extraordinary doubt ruins each belief, presupposing no other truth, and yet constantly and inevitably leads to the *cogito.*

The focus should be on the *doubting* of the proofs or propositions, rather than on the proofs or propositions themselves, because clearly which proofs or propositions are doubted is quite irrelevant to establishing the truth of the proposition that you exist. The method of doubt is meant as a purge, purification, and preparation: The doubt's "greatest benefit lies in freeing us from all our preconceived opinions, and providing the easiest route by which the mind may be led away from the senses. The eventual result of this doubt is to make it impossible for us to have any further doubts about what we subsequently discover to be true." (CSM II, 9; AT VII, 12) The doubt is certainly meant as a purge, to rid the mind of any beliefs that can be doubted. The doubting process will purify the mind and rid it of the intrusion of the senses. To speak metaphorically, the doubt enables Descartes to eliminate the background noise produced by the senses, by withdrawing the senses, the better to hear the voice of reason. Thus completely unencumbered, reason will perceive clearly what it could not otherwise perceive. Finally, the doubt will prepare the mind to witness, or notice, that in the act of doubting, it cannot – cannot in principle – purge the belief in the doubter's own existence.

This should also answer the question, is the *cogito* a mental state or a mental process? It is, in the final analysis, a mental state. It is a mental state in which the truth of the *cogito* is intuitively perceived. But it is a final state that is linked to a mental process. The final mental state can come about as the culmination of a variety of mental processes, none of which is essential. If the *cogito* were a mental process, would it be some definite process? That is, is there one and only one route to recognizing the truth of the *cogito*? There is not. From Descartes' perspective, no particular mental process is essential, but it does not follow that one could do without any of them. There are three streets leading to my house: It is not essential to take any one particular street, but it does not follow that one could do without taking any one of them. Similarly, there are several mental processes leading up to the *cogito*: It is not essential to take any one particular mental process, but it does not follow that one could do without taking any one of those mental processes. Any such mental process is simply a matter of preparing the mind to receive the first truth, as it were.

The point can be illustrated by imagining possible worlds based on the following propositions expressed in a mental state. M_1 *There is an earth* is *The Thought$_1$: There is an earth*. M stands for a mental state, the subscript numbers the thought,[8] and the remainder is the proposition.

M_1 There is an earth.
M_2 There is a sky.
M_3 There are numbers.
M_4 There are human bodies.
M_5 There is a heaven.
M_6 There are minds.
          $\vdots$
M_n There is a God.
M_o I am thinking, therefore I exist.

We can now imagine the following possible worlds (using the '$-$' as a sign for *it is not the case that*; thus, $-M_2$ is *The Thought$_2$: It is not the case that there is a sky.*).

---

[8] "[M]oreover I have various thoughts which I can count" (CSM II, 30; AT VII, 44). This is from the Third Meditation, where Descartes is trying to give an account of how all of his ideas (ideas of "corporeal and inanimate things, angels, animals and finally other men like myself" [CSM II, 29; AT VII, 43]) – save the idea of God – can be explained in terms of ideas that give him a representation of himself. This line is rarely cited, if ever, but it raises an interesting question: If Descartes can assume that he can count his thoughts, is he then not able also to count how many total thoughts he has? If that is the case, is he not assured of at least some simple truths of arithmetic? But the existence of God has not yet been demonstrated, and the truths of arithmetic have already been questioned in the First Meditation. This would leave mysterious his ability to successfully count his thoughts.

$$w_1: \quad \{M_1, M_2, M_3, \ldots\ldots\ldots, M_n\} \quad\quad \rightarrow \quad M_0$$
$$w_2: \quad \{-M_1, M_2, M_3, \ldots\ldots\ldots, M_n\} \quad\quad \rightarrow \quad M_0$$
$$w_3: \quad \{M_1, -M_2, M_3, \ldots\ldots\ldots, M_n\} \quad\quad \rightarrow \quad M_0$$
$$w_4: \quad \{M_1, M_2, -M_3, \ldots\ldots\ldots, M_n\} \quad\quad \rightarrow \quad M_0$$

$$\vdots$$

$$w_i: \quad \{M_1, -M_2, -M_3, \ldots\ldots\ldots, M_n\} \quad\quad \rightarrow \quad M_0$$

$$\vdots$$

$$w_k: \quad \{-M_1, -M_2, M_3, \ldots\ldots\ldots, M_n\} \quad\quad \rightarrow \quad M_0$$

$$\vdots$$

$$w_n: \quad \{-M_1, -M_2, -M_3, \ldots\ldots\ldots, -M_n\} \quad \rightarrow \quad M_0$$

If one worked with just n propositions, one would have 2^n possibilities. One can increase the possibilities by introducing new propositions without limit, or one can decrease the possibilities by eliminating the propositions without limit, so long as there is at least one proposition. Each possibility would lead to M_0. The symbol '$\rightarrow$' is simply a sign that vaguely means *leading up to*, and could, depending on the discussion, take on a more definite meaning later. Notice, too, that *I think* in M_0, namely, *The Thought$_0$: I am thinking, therefore I exist*, is quite redundant, since it is some thought, a mental state, that expresses it; thus, *The Thought$_0$: I exist* could do just as well.

Now, imagine a doubter, D_1, living in world, w_1. The earth, sky, bodies, minds, and numbers exist; in short, it is our world as we ordinarily know it. D_1's ordinary life is geared in the belief that the propositions M_1 through M_n are true. His thought and talk, act and will, and beliefs and performances make that clear. But D_1 succumbs to Descartes' advice and invents reasons to doubt the propositions that he normally believes in. He discovers that in the very act of doubt, he discovers the truth of the *cogito*. By contrast, in another world, w_k, say, there is a doubter D_k: In this possible world, nothing is true save the following three propositions (and whatever is implied by them) – *numbers exist, the doubter exists,* and *God exists.*[9] The doubter's ordinary life

---

[9] In a letter of August 1641, written to Hyperaspistes, Descartes had speculated, "I have no doubt that if [the soul] were released from the prison of the body, it would find [the ideas of God, itself, and self-evident truths] within itself" (CSMK, 190; AT III, 424).

(whatever is ordinary in such a possible world!) is lived out in accordance with his belief in those propositions. Once again, his thought and talk, act and will, and beliefs and performances make that clear, although it may be extremely difficult for us to imagine what these would be like, since D_k lacks a physical body, and hence our form of life. Now, D_k too succumbs to Descartes' advice about engaging in doubt at least once in one's life and invents reasons to doubt the propositions that *he* normally believes in. Yet, as a doubter, he finds reasons that give him minimal doubt about whether numbers and God exist. (Of course, he could not doubt the proposition that he, the doubter, exists, without guaranteeing his existence.)

And so on for other doubters in other possible worlds.

If we trace the mental histories of the doubts of the individuals in various possible worlds, and the reasons that they give for these doubts, we shall surely find them to be quite different. For one thing, unlike D_1, an individual of our world, D_k, will have no concept of the *external* world, and no concept of *place, color,* or *shape.* Yet, in each case, the doubter in each possible world will arrive at the same final *cogito*-state, namely, M_o. Qualitatively, and in every relevant way, if Descartes is right, there should be no difference between the *cogito*-state of any two possible worlds. M_o is true in every possible world, it is a necessary truth.

One might wonder: How can the *cogito* be foundational for knowledge of our actual, determinate world, if it is certain in such a wide variety of worlds (not that Descartes has any positive theory of possible worlds)? It does not seem to be slanted, in other words, toward our world and our knowledge problems, so how can it be helpful?

There is also this from Pierre Gassendi (1592–1655), the author of the "Fifth Set of Objections": "For I ask you, what progress do you think you would have made if, since being implanted in the body, you had remained within it with your eyes closed and your ears stopped and, in short, with no external senses to enable you to perceive this universe of objects or anything outside you" (CSM II, 217; AT VII, 310). Descartes replied thus: "I do not doubt that the mind – provided we suppose that in thinking it received not just no assistance from the body but also that it received no interference from it – would have had exactly the same ideas of God and itself it now has, with the sole difference that they would have been much purer and clearer" (CSM II, 258; AT VII, 375). Consequently, the example imagined here is quite in keeping with the Cartesian spirit.

Therein, precisely, lies the beauty and power of the *cogito*. One might say that it is an empirical necessary truth, a first truth in all possible worlds (in which there are truth seekers). But the common starting point of the inquirers in all of these possible worlds notwithstanding, what they know about their respective worlds will eventually diverge. One will claim that his physical world is informed by a gravitational law, another that his world is informed by a gravitational law but of a different order of magnitude, a third that there is no gravitational law at all in his world. What is so incredibly fascinating is that the knowledge of such remarkably different worlds can begin on so slender a basis.

This way of viewing the matter may be an answer to just the kind of query that Montaigne might be thought of as constructing. Thus: "Now if there are several worlds, as Democritus, Epicurus and almost the whole of philosophy have opined, how do we know whether the principles and laws which apply to this world apply equally to the others? Other worlds may present different features and be differently governed" (M, 96). Much later, this is followed by the following challenge: "For whatever Nature truly ordained, we would, without any doubt, all perform, by common consent: not only all nations but all human beings individually would be deeply aware of force or compulsion when anyone tried to make them violate it. Let them show me just one law with such characteristics: I would like to see it." (M, 161) Descartes' *cogito* would be such a "law": applicable, I have argued, not only among all men, in all nations, at all times, but in every world – even in an inconceivable world that defied our laws of logic? "Or, had I not been such a commonsensical chap," says David Lewis, "I might be defending not only a plurality of possible worlds, but also a plurality of impossible worlds, whereof you speak truly by contradicting yourself."[10] While I quite prefer Lewis' common sense, it would be enormously interesting to see *how* the denial of the *cogito* would be true in an impossible world, not just simply claimed to be true by fiat or stipulation. I am not unmindful of the fact that Montaigne is speaking here of a moral rule as a Natural Law. The generalization is very much in keeping with the spirit of Montaigne's point.

[10] David Lewis, *On The Plurality of Worlds*, 1.

Now Descartes takes these doubts seriously. That is, he thinks that he should compel his mind to concede the soundness of the reasoning that leads to utter skepticism, a concession that leads him to intellectual despair and to an understandable desire to find a way out. But it is difficult to see why this is necessary. May I not casually entertain the possibility that each proposition put before me is false? As nearly as I can judge, the process of serious doubt is not essential to establishing the truth, even the necessary truth, of the *cogito*. But Descartes is after bigger things. He wants to establish not only that the *cogito* is necessarily true every time he conceives it, but also that it is the *only* truth of which Descartes could be certain at the start. Whereas, if I am right, an individual can correctly perceive the truth of the *cogito* and yet leave open the possibility that there might be other propositions of which he could be equally, or even more, certain. Or again, he might believe that there is no other such proposition.

Is the *cogito* a first-order or a second-order mental state? Is it a first-order or second-order mental process? If we map the propositional content of each distinct mental state (represented by a circle, with or without shading) onto a proposition, then we might formulate some of the questions as follows: Is the *cogito* a proposition? Is it an argument? Is it valid? Is it sound? For now, I continue to speak in terms of mental states and mental processes. Consider, then, the following few possibilities:

Case 1. First-order mental state

s_1 s_2 s_3 .... s_n .... s_c

Case 1 represents the possibility where the thinker goes through a series of mental states, $s_1, s_2, s_3, \ldots, s_n$, and is lead to s_c, where s_c is the state in which he, the thinker, acknowledges the truth of the *cogito*. As before, a circle shaded with lines expresses a mental state in doubt about the proposition it is entertaining. In this case, all of the mental states prior to the *cogito*-state are represented by circles shaded with lines. The propositions entertained by these mental states are doubted, as did Descartes in his hyperbolic doubt: the model of extraordinary doubt. The earlier mental states simply lead up to the *cogito*-state; they are a preliminary to, a framework for, the *cogito*-state. The earlier mental states have no essential hook-up with the final *cogito*-state. The mental state s_c is free of doubt; the other mental states are infected by at least a minimal doubt. In the state s_c, the thinker is compelled[11] to recognize and assent to the truth of the *cogito*; but in the other mental states, he is free to withhold assent.

Case 2. First-order mental process

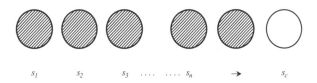

s_1 s_2 s_3 .... s_n → s_c

Case 2 represents the possibility where a series of mental states leads up to the *cogito*-state, but the earlier states are essential to that state. That is, the earlier mental states ineluctably lead to the final *cogito*-state. What precisely is the nature of this ineluctability, this compulsion, is as yet left undefined or undetermined, and is represented by the symbol '→'.

Case 3. First-order mental process

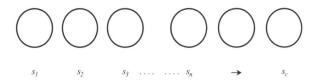

s_1 s_2 s_3 .... s_n → s_c

Case 3 is similar to Case 2 in all respects, except that the earlier mental-states are all free from doubt, too.

---

[11] To read this compulsion as no more than psychological, although it is at least that, is a serious mistake; see also Chapter 4, especially 127 and note 24. For further support of the idea that "certainty is always at least partially an evidentiary notion, and never a purely psychological or purely a semantic one," see Jeffrey Tlumak, "Certainty and Cartesian Method," 40, 43–44.

Case 4. Second-order mental state

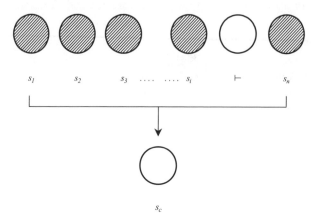

Case 4 represents the possibility in which the earlier mental states, $s_1, s_2, s_3, \ldots, s_i$ are related to s_n as premises are related to the conclusion of an argument. Here, s_c, the final *cogito*-state, is a second-order mental state of a first-order mental process, $s_1, s_2, s_3, \ldots, s_i \vdash s_n$. The symbol '$\vdash$' is a sign for a mental state acknowledging valid inference. In this case, it signifies that s_n is acknowledged to be validly inferred from $s_1, s_2, s_3, \ldots, s_i$. In the second-order mental state, s_c, the thinker recognizes in a compulsive way that the inference from $s_1, s_2, s_3, \ldots, s_i$ to s_n is valid. In short, it is in s_c that the thinker recognizes the truth, the absolute certainty, of the *cogito*.

Case 5. Second-order mental state

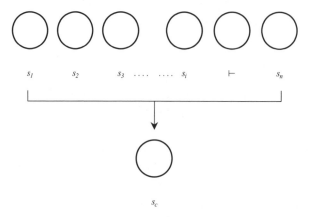

Case 5 is identical in all respects to Case 4, save in one. In Case 4, there was some element of doubt in all the earlier states; only the final *cogito*-state was indubitable, without shading. In the present case, Case 5, all the earlier states leading up to the *cogito*-state are indubitable too; they are all represented by circles without shading. Alternatively, only those earlier mental states, which are without shading, lead up to the *cogito*-state in a way in which the shaded earlier states could not.

There are, of course, other possibilities,[12] and the question is, how can we best understand the *cogito* that represents Descartes' view and is also the least objectionable?

Descartes' view is as follows. The *cogito*-state is a first-order state. It is not about any other state. The individual doubter recognizes, *in* the first-order state, the truth of the *cogito*. This is extremely difficult to express, and once again I need to beg the reader to conduct the thought experiment. Descartes says that the notions of *truth, doubt, thought,* and *existence* are primitive notions, that is, notions that are not definable in terms of other notions. (Another primitive notion that Descartes needs, but that he never separately lists in this context, is the notion of the indexical 'I'.) They are also clearly understood by us.[13]

Thus in *The Search for Truth* he writes: "But someone who wants to examine things for himself, and to base his judgements about them on his own conceptions, must surely have enough mental capacity to have adequate knowledge of what doubt, thought and existence are, whenever he attends to the question, without having to be taught the difference between them" (CSM II, 417; AT X, 523). He makes a similar claim with respect to the notion of truth. On October 16, 1639, he wrote to Father Mersenne that truth is

a notion so transcendentally clear that nobody can be ignorant of it. There are many ways of examining a balance before using it, but there is no way to learn what truth is, if one does not know it by nature. What reason would we have for accepting anything which could teach us the nature of truth if we did not know that it was true, that is to say, if we did not know truth? (CSMK, 139; AT II, 597)

---

[12] For example, substitute '⊢' for '→' in *Case 1* and *Case 2*.
[13] CSMK, 218; AT III, 665–666 provides a very useful backdrop to this paragraph and for what immediately follows. See also CSMK, 191–192; AT III, 426–427 together with the corresponding note 5.

Armed with the meaning of these four terms, notions that are in-nate in us, the doubter in the *cogito*-state learns to *join* the particular doubting thought with his particular existence. He must try to rear-range the four innate concepts, linking them to his thoughts, in order to formulate a proposition that he cannot doubt. Now, the doubter cannot say that he knows even the following truth of identity, namely, the concept of thought is the concept of thought, nor can he assert the following logical truth, namely, the concept of doubt is included in the concept of thought. For the thinker can invoke the demon who will make Descartes doubt the truth of these statements, as the demon made him doubt the truths of mathematics. At any rate, second, such truths do not give him what he is looking for, if he is looking for the first existential truth.[14] The first truth then suddenly dawns on him. He sees – notices, perceives, intuits, witnesses – that it is true that in this particular case, his doubting now ensures his existence now. "You will surely admit that you are less certain of the presence of the objects you see than of the truth of the proposition 'I am thinking, therefore I exist.' Now this knowledge is not the work of your reasoning or infor-mation passed on to you by teachers; it is something that your mind sees, feels, and handles." (CSMK, 331; AT V, 137–138)

One might suggest that this experiment idea be explored in terms of falsification.[15] Maybe the *cogito* is not an argument or even an insight, but a challenge to falsify. It says something like, "Falsify this!: I exist – exclusively as a consciousness." The experiment surrounding the *cogito* shows that the "information" that would falsify all other propositions cannot falsify this one. The *cogito* proper – the various I think, I exist ensembles, with or without connecting therefores – might be just an el-ement in this experiment that really cannot be understood separately.

[14] "But because these are very simple notions [the notions of thought, existence, cer-tainty, it is impossible that that which thinks should not exist, and so on], and ones which on their own provide us with no knowledge of anything that exists, I did not think they needed to be listed" (CSM I, 196; AT VIIIA, 8). Some scholars think that therefore Descartes was searching for the first existential truth, and in that search for the first truth, as well as in its substantiation, Descartes could have used any of these "very simple notions." This must be mistaken. Descartes proclaims to know *no* truth at the end of the First Meditation, and not merely that he has no knowledge of an existential truth. Descartes would have been pleased, at this stage of the in-quiry, if he could have assured himself of a conceptual truth or two. His doubting of nonexistential truth makes very little sense, if he was not concerned with these.

[15] Following a cue from Catherine Wilson.

This is, indeed, a happy suggestion and would at least in significant part capture Descartes' intentions. After all, the First Meditation is a skeptical challenge and attempts to show that all other propositions can be "falsified." The Second Meditation proposes the *cogito* experiment; the *cogito* proposition is put severely to the test by the very skeptical arguments of the First Meditation and is shown to be unfalsified – indeed, Descartes would claim it to be unfalsifiable. Here we run into problems that would suggest caution: First, a proposition thus far unfalsified, from a purely Popperian angle, is not a guarantor even of probable truth, let alone of truth. Consequently, even the most severe testing of the *cogito* statement, leading to nonfalsification, would not start the Cartesian enterprise. Second, Descartes would need the *cogito* to be at least an insight, an intuition, if not an argument. Third, there is an interesting asymmetry: On the one hand, several propositions are demonstrated to be false or purported to be false, *without* invoking the *cogito*; on the other hand, the *cogito* experiment is meant to verify one truth, without showing *why* particular propositions are, or may be, false.

Finally, what about the claim that the *cogito*-state is a first-order state? Here is a counterclaim: "It is not true that the *cogito*-state is a first order-state; it is a second-order state. Recognizing that I am thinking is a second-order-state: I have a propositional attitude to the proposition that I am thinking, which involves a first-order state. For example, when I believe that 2 + 2 = 4, I am thinking that 2 + 2 = 4. Here my belief is a first-order state. When I believe that I am thinking that 2 + 2 = 4, my belief is a second-order state. Correspondingly, when I am thinking that 'I am thinking, therefore I am', clearly my thinking that is a second-order state." But this will not do, for a variety of reasons. First, let us clearly identify the distinct states. The first-order *cogito*-state is, "I am thinking, therefore I am." The second-order state is, "I am thinking that 'I am thinking, therefore I am.' " But the latter is not Descartes' *cogito*; it is something else: it is *about* the *cogito*. Second, the objector might contend that our formulation is mistaken. He might argue that "I am, I exist," is the first-order state; the second-order state is the *cogito*, namely, " 'I am, I exist,' is necessarily true." However, the latter does not capture the exact formulation of the *cogito* in the Second Meditation; the key phrase –"whenever it is put forward by me or conceived in my mind" – is missing. That phrase indicates Descartes' knowing something in the very *act* of conceiving it. Take the analogy with mathematics: When I have clearly intuited 2 + 2 = 4 – recall the "self-evidence and certainty of intuition" (CSM I, 14; AT X, 369) – am I in the second-order state? If I am not in the state of certainty while in the first-order-state, what element confers that certainty while in the second-order state? It is difficult to provide a satisfactory Cartesian answer to that question.[16] Third, if we allow the *cogito* to be a second-order state, do we open up the possibility of the mind making a mistake – however slender the possibility – as to what it is claiming its state to be *about?* If so, we shall rob the *cogito* of the certainty that Descartes was after. Fourth, and importantly, whether the *cogito* is first-order or second-order, it is still claimed to be a state (not a process), a state to which there corresponds a proposition.

III. The Experiment Evaluated

At this juncture, I should like to bring in the resources of the first section and raise some pertinent questions. Descartes, as we saw, had defined a problem, a perfect problem, and a perfectly understood problem. Let us call the problem – can I know anything for certain? – *the epistemic problem.* I shall argue that the epistemic problem of Descartes is a problem, a perfect problem, and a perfectly understood problem. Descartes had maintained that every problem must be about something hitherto unknown. The unknown should be characterized in some way. The characterization must be cast only in terms of what is known. Thus, one might now argue on Descartes' behalf that the problem, can I know anything for certain?, is a problem because it possesses the three necessary features: First, something is unknown at the start, namely, a certain truth. Second, the solution to the epistemic problem is characterized in terms of several properties, such as *simplest, can be easily known, particular,* and *most certain.* Third, characterization of these properties is set in terms that are known. Thus, the epistemic problem is a problem.

Next, the epistemic problem is a perfect problem. Descartes would have argued it so. A perfect problem is determinate in every respect. Its terms must be perfectly understood. The epistemic problem is determinate in every respect, and its terms are perfectly understood.

[16] The last section of Chapter 7 may prove relevant here.

The central concepts are the concepts of *truth, doubt, certainty,* and *existence.* Descartes claims to understand them. Furthermore, Descartes would have claimed that given the boundary conditions on the epistemic problem, the solution – Descartes' solution – is a unique one. The boundary conditions on the epistemic problem are defined by the six criteria that the first principle must possess. There cannot be any other solution; if there were, then the problem would be an imperfect problem. As Descartes put it in the *Discourse on the Method,* "[T]here is only one truth concerning any matter, whoever discovers this truth knows as much about it as can be known" (CSM, I, 121; AT VI, 21). Whatever may be the truth of that statement as a general statement, it is surely true that Descartes would have argued that the *cogito* is a unique solution to a perfect problem.[17] There is no other proposition that could have served as a solution. This is shown by the exhaustive list of propositions considered and doubted. Each proposition in the system of belief has been doubted; each part of the building has been dismantled. Only the foundation stone, the *cogito,* remained unscathed.

Finally, Descartes would have argued that the epistemic problem is a perfectly understood problem, not an imperfectly understood one. I quote again the relevant passage:

[A] problem is to be counted as perfectly understood only if we have a distinct perception of the following three points: first, what the criteria are which enable us to recognize what we are looking for when we come upon it; second, what exactly is the basis from which we ought to deduce it; third, how it is to be proved that the two are so mutually dependent that the one cannot alter in any respect without there being a corresponding alteration in the other. (CSM I, 51; AT, 429)

One can now appreciate why it was important to lay down the criteria by which one could recognize the first principle. It would "enable us to recognize what we are looking for when we come upon it." The universal doubt will be the basis from which we will deduce it. As

---

[17] To be sure, Descartes has offered diverse formulations of the *cogito;* look no further than *Discourse on the Method* and *Meditations on First Philosophy.* This, however, does not detract from the claim about uniqueness. For Descartes offers no argument to suggest that one formulation is inherently better, or captures his intentions better, than another formulation. Where formulations are different, their differences are insignificant; and where the differences are marginally significant, they should be tidied up in order to bring them in line with one another.

Descartes said, "if you simply know how to make proper use of your own doubt, you can use it to deduce facts which are known with complete certainty" (CSM II, 415–416; AT X, 522). When Descartes speaks here of 'deducing' a fact, he is speaking loosely, and not using 'deducing' in the sense used in formal logic. We need to show, of course, that if we alter the criteria by which we recognize the first principle, our first principle will no longer appear to be the first. Quite simply, let the criterion of certainty be replaced by the criterion of high probability. Then the first principle will be quite different, the epistemic problem will not be a perfect problem, and the solution will not be a unique one.

The *cogito* is a perfect solution to a perfect problem. The six criteria enable Descartes to recognize that the *cogito* is indeed the solution he was looking for. First, his survey of the prospective claimants to the first principle has been exhaustive and complete. It is the sought-after first principle because "after considering everything thoroughly," Descartes could not find any proposition that he could not doubt save the *cogito*. Second, the *cogito* is the most certain. Given that certainty and minimal doubt are contradictory notions – the absence of one entails the presence of the other – Descartes has shown that in the *cogito*, any attempt to establish minimal doubt fails and hence leads to certainty. Third, the *cogito* is also a clear and distinct notion. Both of these properties are noticed when the doubter is in the *cogito*-state. Fourth, the *cogito* is the easiest to become acquainted with. It presupposes no special knowledge; the terms of understanding it, or coming to recognize it, are common currency. The doubts and dismantling that precede the *cogito* may involve special fields – such as history and mechanics, morals and mathematics – but the doubting itself does not rest on any special knowledge of these fields. Thus an ordinary, but ideal, seeker can easily become acquainted with it. Fifth, it is the simplest. Essentially, only the grasp of simple notions – such as, truth, doubt, certainty, and existence – are presupposed, together with the ability to join them. But the joining takes place in a simple, single mental state and does not involve a complex mental process. Finally, it is a particular: That is, it does not rest on some deep and general propositions about time, thinkers, and existence; it is rather about *this* thinker in *this* mode of doubt and of his existence in *that* moment. The *cogito* satisfies all six criteria, and hence it is the first principle that Descartes was seeking.

In June or July 1646, Descartes wrote to Clerselier that

the word "principle" can be taken in several senses. . . . In the first sense, it can be said that "It is impossible for the same thing both to be and not to be at the same time" is a principle which can serve in general, not properly speaking to make known the existence of anything, but simply to confirm its truth once known. . . . This is of very little importance, and makes us no better informed. In the second sense, the first principle is *that our soul exists,* because there is nothing whose existence is better known to us. (CSMK, 290; AT IV, 444)

This reinforces the point of particularity in the last criterion, which will prove significant later.

There is an inevitable paradox. At the start of his inquiry, Descartes does not have a criterion – indeed, by the nature of the case, he cannot have one, let alone have six – whereby he can judge whether he has stumbled onto the right answer to the epistemic problem. For if he has any criterion, he must be certain about it. If he is certain about any criterion, such as the criterion of simplicity, then he need look no further, for that criterion can serve as the first item of knowledge, the first truth of his philosophy. On the other hand, if he does not have a criterion, then by his own admission he will not know when he has encountered the first principle, the first truth, if he should encounter it. Perhaps Descartes is once again trying to raise himself by his own bootstraps: He provisionally accepts the six criteria at the start, with no certainty as to where he will be led by them. He is, in fact, led to the *cogito.* In that state, and in that state alone, he is certain of its truth. Thence, he is led to believe with certainty in the veracity of the criteria with which he began his inquiry.

IV. The Eucharist Objection

There is an objection that is devastating for the *cogito.* The source of the objection has to do not with the *cogito* but rather with Descartes' view on the doctrine of the Eucharist. In the "Fourth Set of Objections," Antoine Arnauld (1612–1694), the French logician and theologian, wrote:

But what I see as likely to give the greatest offence to theologians is that according to the author's doctrines it seems that the Church's teaching concerning the sacred mysteries of the Eucharist cannot remain completely intact. We believe on faith that the substance of the bread is taken away from the bread of the Eucharist and only the accidents remain. These are extension, shape, colour, smell, taste, and other qualities perceived by the senses.

By contrast, said Arnauld, Descartes "denies that these powers are intelligible apart from some substance for them to inhere in, and hence he holds that they cannot exist without such a substance" (CSM II, 152–153; AT VII, 217–218).

What was Descartes' reply? First, "[M]y saying that the modes are not intelligible apart from some substance for them to inhere in should not be taken to imply any denial that they can be separated from a substance by the power of God; for I firmly insist and believe that many things can be brought about by God which we are incapable of understanding" (CSM II, 173; AT VII, 249). In short, God could have created an attribute, a mode, or an accident (powers, to use Arnauld's word) that did not inhere in any substance. Second, God could have created a new substance in place of the old. Specifically, in the case of the Eucharist, the substances of the bread and wine could be transformed into another substance in such a way that this latter substance affects all of our senses in "exactly the same way as that in which the bread and wine would be affecting them if no transubstantiation had occurred"[18] (CSM II, 175; AT VII, 251).

Now consider the *cogito*. A thought is an attribute that inheres in the mind or soul of the person thinking that thought. Thus from the existence of the thought, the thinker infers his own existence. The thought of the thinker is an attribute, an accident, a mode; the 'I' of that thinker is the substance. But if the foregoing about the Eucharist is correct, then there are two possibilities: First, the attribute of thought could exist without the substance, 'I'. Second, in place of the 'I' there could be another substance. Indeed, such a possibility was touted by Hyperaspistes, an unknown supporter of Gassendi, in August 1641: "Moreover," he said, "you do not know whether it is you yourself

---

[18] Elsewhere Descartes says, "[T]here is nothing incomprehensible or difficult in the supposition that God, the creator of all things, is able to change one substance into another, or in the supposition that the latter substance remains within the same surface that contained the former one.... It clearly follows from this that any given surface must always act and react in the same way, even though the substance which is beneath it is changed." (CSM II, 177; AT VII, 255) For further interesting details, see R, 136–137, 160, 213–214, 246 note 7.

who think or whether the world-soul in you does the thinking, as the Platonists believe" (CSMK 192, note 1; AT III, 403). This was no wild conjecture, but rather had solid historical roots. "Augustine's work on the Trinity," writes an eminent scholar of Saint Augustine,

had profound influence on subsequent western concepts of personality. Porphyry had thought that all souls had a share in the "world-soul," source of all energy and vitality in the physical universe. The early Augustine used the notion of a world-soul. The late Augustine never said there was no such entity, but thought the young Augustine rash to assume that there was: "For us God is not this world, whether or not there is a world-soul. If there is, God created it. If not, the world cannot be anyone's god, *a fortiori* not ours. But even if there is not a world-soul there is a life-force obeying God working through the angels."[19]

Parroting Descartes, one could say that this new substance (the world-soul) affects all of our senses in the same way that the old substance – the 'I' – would be affecting them if no change or transubstantiation had occurred. In either case, the inference to *sum* is mistaken or invalid. In the first case, that 'I' does not exist, and so the conclusion is false; in the second case, there is blatant ambiguity of terms. The *cogito* collapses.[20]

Add other operating assumptions and we have the following possibilities and consequences:

[1]   There exists the thought, "I think," but there is no 'I,' no thinker, thinking that thought. An attribute exists independent of any

---

[19] Henry Chadwick, *Augustine*, 94.

[20] I have encountered the following intriguing objection: Descartes is arguing to the existence of his self, and not necessarily to the necessary existence of a substance underlying some attributes. There is no ontology of the self presumed yet at this point. And thus to argue that Descartes cannot legitimately conclude to the existence of a substance is irrelevant. This defense of Descartes can be squarely met on several grounds. First, such a response to Arnauld would be odd, since Descartes himself in his reply invokes the notion of substance. Second, Descartes would have questioned the first sentence of the objection, given his 1648 reply to Henri de Roy (Henricus Regius), *Comments on a Certain Broadsheet*: "I wrote that we cannot doubt that our mind exists, because from the very fact that we are doubting, it follows that our mind exists.... From this I concluded and demonstrated that we clearly perceive the mind as an existing thing, or substance" (CSM, 301; AT VIIIB, 354; see also CSM, 300; AT, VIIIB 352). Third, nowhere, either before or after the *Meditations*, did Descartes ever regard a self as anything other than a substance. Finally, the Eucharist objection could be read as if it made no overt assumption about the nature of the self. It could be interpreted simply as making a claim about the 'I' parallel to the one that Descartes makes about the substance, relying on Descartes' assertion that "many things can be brought about by God which we are incapable of understanding."

substance. In this case, the *ergo* of the *cogito* cannot possibly lead
to the conclusion that the 'I,' or the thinker of that thought,
exists. The argument is invalid, and God is a deceiver.

[2]   God is not a deceiver. The thought, "I think" *must* inhere in the
'I,' or the thinker thinking that thought. An attribute inheres of
necessity in a substance. God could not have done otherwise. In
this case, the argument is valid, but God is not omnipotent: He
could not alter at least one eternal truth. Moreover, Arnauld's
objection, in view of the Eucharist, rises anew in full force.

[3]   God is not a deceiver. He could have altered the eternal truth
that an attribute does not exist independent of a substance. The
thought "I think" contingently inheres in the 'I,' or in the thinker
of that thought. An attribute inheres contingently in a substance.
In this case, the *cogito* is a contingent truth and not a necessary
one, and the argument is invalid.[21]

I conclude: Either Descartes accepted the theological doctrine of
the Eucharist and in private cast aside the necessity of the truth of the
cogito, or Descartes retained the *cogito* as a necessary truth and espoused
the doctrine of the Eucharist only in public.

V. Doubt and the *Cogito*

That doubt plays a significant role in Descartes' metaphysics is generally appreciated. But what specific role does it play in the case of the
cogito? Hitherto I have argued that the systematic doubt of the First
Meditation was meant to accomplish four things: first, to undermine
current beliefs; second, to underscore the correlation between the degree of doubt required and the degree of simplicity of the proposition
to be doubted; third, to provide the ideal seeker with an arsenal for
challenging substantial claims when they are subsequently made; and
fourth and finally, to provide an indirect way of establishing the first
truth. I now want to bring these claims into the foreground and to show
how they highlight my interpretation of the *cogito*, and how they enable us to correctly understand a solitary, but outstandingly important,
passage.

[21] I am grateful to Anthony Kenny for his encouragement on the Eucharist counter-
argument against Descartes provided in this section.

The first claim, about undermining current beliefs, is simple enough, so I let it pass without comment. The last claim is simple enough, too, so I let it pass, with the comment that when all of our current beliefs are shown to be false, then *ex hypothesi* any truth that is established after that is the first truth, or the first principle for which Descartes has been looking. The second point I save for later. I begin now with the crucial third point and show how, in fact, doubt is used in cases other than the *cogito.*

Having just established the truth of the *cogito,* in the Second Meditation, Descartes says that "I do not yet have a sufficient understanding of what this 'I' is" (CSM II, 17; AT VII, 25). As we know, Descartes establishes that the essence of this 'I' is to think. But the pattern of reasoning that leads him to that conclusion is important. He lists a variety of hypotheses:

(h_1) I am a man.
(h_2) I am a rational animal.
(h_3) I am a body (consisting of hands, face, arms, and the whole mechanical structure of limbs).
(h_4) I am a thing that is nourished, moves about, and is engaged in sense perception and thinking ("and these actions I attributed to the soul").
(h_5) I am a soul (that is, a soul that is imagined to be tenuous, like wind, fire, or ether).
(h_6) I am a thing that thinks.

Having listed these hypotheses, how does Descartes proceed? Descartes' announced strategy is this: "I will then subtract anything *capable of being weakened, even minimally, by the arguments now introduced,* so that what is left at the end may be exactly and only what is certain and unshakable" (CSM II, 17; AT VII, 25). The emphasis is mine. The "arguments now introduced" are none other than the skeptical arguments of the First Meditation, and these skeptical arguments are precisely the ones invoked in rejecting various hypotheses concerning the nature of this 'I'. There is an exception, though. Hypotheses (h_1) and (h_2) are rejected based on a bold assertion not even mentioned, to my knowledge, elsewhere in the *Meditations on First Philosophy,* save in a single sentence in the Second Meditation. The assertion is developed and substantiated, however, in *The Search for Truth*

(CSM II, 410–412; AT X, 515–518). It expresses the argument against the scholastic way of solving problems by defining terms, à la Porphyry; and consequently Descartes dismisses the first two hypotheses as relying on scholastic subtleties on which he does not wish to waste time. The point, however, is that this can be rightly construed as a skeptical argument, part of the general strategy. That is, no real solution is possible based on the definition of terms that in turn have to be further defined. The explicitly developed skeptical arguments of the First Meditation, then, enable him to undermine, even if these are undermined only minimally, such hypotheses as (h_3), (h_4), and (h_5). For example, he rejects the hypothesis that the soul has nutrition or movement on the ground that these attributes cannot occur without the body, and that there are already "powerful and well thought-out reasons" for being skeptical about the existence of the body or any corporeal thing.

When, in the Sixth Meditation, Descartes sets out to prove the existence of the external world, or "that corporeal things exist," his strategy is not one whit different. He says, "To begin with, I will go back over all the things which I previously took to be perceived by the senses, and reckoned to be true; and I will go over my reasons for thinking this. Next, I will set out my reasons for subsequently calling these things into doubt. And finally I will consider what I should now believe about them" (CSM II, 51; AT VII, 74). Once again, there is the listing of hypotheses, eliminating some of them in the light of the skeptical arguments of the First Meditation, and espousing the remainder as true.

So I submit that the method of doubt proposed in the First Meditation is not just a way to undermine current beliefs. It is much more. The function of the skeptical arguments is to provide the most powerful weapons that can be devised to undermine proposed knowledge claims. A proposed knowledge claim is a proper knowledge claim when, and only when, it withstands the onslaught of the skeptical arguments. If Descartes does not use some of these arguments in the Third and Fifth Meditations, it is because there he is proving the existence of God, and there is no traditional hypothesis that regards God as a bodily being. Nor is there any occasion to doubt the truths of mathematics, or any like truths, since they are created by God. In the Fourth Meditation, no existential claim is proved. So it is that Descartes' strategy is prominent mostly in the Second and Sixth Meditations.

We are now prepared to examine the passage in the Second Medi-tation that contains the *cogito.* I shall divide this long passage into four parts. I divide it differently than the recent tradition does, in order to exhibit that Descartes' strategy is at work here just as well and just as much as it was in the two other cases (where he concluded that his essence is to think and that corporeal things exist).

(h'_1) Is there not a God, or whatever I may call him, who puts into me the thoughts that I am now having? But why do I think this, since I myself may perhaps be the author of these thoughts? In that case am I not, at least, something?[22]

(h'_2) But I have just said that I have no senses and no body. This is the sticking point: What follows from this? Am I not so bound up with a body and with senses that I cannot exist without them? But I have convinced myself that there is absolutely nothing in the world, no sky, no earth, no minds, no bodies. Does it now follow that I too do not exist? No: If I have convinced myself of something, then I certainly exist.

(h'_3) But there is a deceiver of supreme power and cunning who is deliber-ately and constantly deceiving me. In that case too I undoubtedly exist, if he is deceiving me; and let him deceive me as much as he can, he will never bring it about that I am nothing so long as I think that I am something.

(h'_4) So after considering everything thoroughly, I must finally conclude that this proposition, *I am, I exist,* is necessarily true whenever it is put forward by me or conceived in my mind. (CSM II, 16–17; AT VII, 24–25)

Descartes is offering us the truth of the *cogito,* and that truth is reached as a climax in (h'_4). It is only when each hypothesis – (h'_1), (h'_2), and (h'_3), respectively – is offered and refuted that we arrive at the unrefuted – indeed, irrefutable – claim of the *cogito.*

Descartes' procedure is worthy of close examination. Descartes is *not* offering a single claim supported by different arguments. He is doing here tacitly what he does explicitly elsewhere. As in the other two cases, he is offering different claims supported by different arguments; each claim is falsified until he reaches (h'_4). Thus, he offers (h'_1). Some think that Descartes is only asking questions, not making any claims (C, 82). On the contrary, he is making the strong and clear, but implicit, claim that I (Descartes) am something, namely, the author of my thoughts. His reason for making this claim is that he is now having some thoughts.

[22] There is a clear implication: I am something.

He makes the assumption that nothing comes from nothing, and rejects the conjecture that God is the author of his thoughts in favor of the conjecture that he is himself their author. If he is the author, then he is something. This is the first step. Perhaps it is best not to regard this part of the passage as proposing a distinct hypothesis, but rather to read it as a preliminary to what is immediately to follow.

This step is subjected to a doubt using the kind of skeptical doubt presented in the First Meditation. If I am to exist as an author, I must have senses and a body. (This is clearly implied by the following conjunction of statements: "...am not I, at least, something? But I have just said that I have no senses and no body.") So a skeptical argument of the second degree is introduced, an argument that challenges the existence of senses and body. (The skeptical argument of the first degree is the argument against solving problems by defining terms.) Notice here the second point of the systematic doubt, namely, the degree of doubt needed to cast an epistemic shadow on a proposition depends on the simplicity of the proposition in question. The proposition challenged is a complex proposition: "I am an embodied author." If (h'_2) is regarded as one of the arguments, among four, establishing the *cogito*, as some have claimed (K, 56–58), then it is a poor argument. The premises can be, and are, questioned or doubted. Thus even if the argument is valid, we do not know it to be a sound one.

This leads to the next step: I do not have to have senses or a body. I would still exist, so long as I have convinced myself of something. The proposition to be questioned here – "I have convinced myself of something" – is even simpler than the foregoing. So, now a third degree of doubt is introduced, and it is induced in me by "a deceiver of supreme power and cunning who is deliberately and constantly deceiving me." This deceiver can falsify that which I have "convinced myself of." For example, I may have convinced myself that there is nothing in the world: no mind, no earth, no sky, and so on. Once again, if (h'_3) is regarded as one of the arguments, among four, establishing the *cogito*, then it is an inadequate argument.

And then there is the final step. But first note the difference between the two following claims:

(*a*)   If I have convinced myself of something, then I certainly exist.
(*b*)   I am [not] nothing so long as I think that I am something.
     I paraphrase (*b*) as

(b')   If I think that I am something, then I am not nothing.[23]

The antecedents of the two conditionals are quite different. So we have reason to think that (h'_2) and (h'_3) are different. The proposition to be doubted – "I think that I am something" – is the simplest, and hence calls for extreme doubt, the fourth degree of doubt. When this supreme doubt is allayed, then the *cogito* is established, and not before. It is for this reason that Descartes says, "So after considering everything thoroughly . . . " He intends to say that when the *cogito* has been subjected to each and every degree of doubt, and emerges unscathed at the end of the most powerful doubt devised by Descartes, then the first truth has been discovered, and not before. This first truth, as we have seen, is elicited from performing a thought experiment: an experiment in which the 'I,' through a thought, comes to realize that in the very act of performing an experiment, devised to show that it, the 'I,' does not exist, it, the 'I,' is inevitably assured of its existence.

VI. The General Rule and Truth

Why is the *cogito* important, even if we grant that it serves as the starting point, the foundation, of Descartes' philosophy? What other truths, if any, will it yield? Or what other *types* of truth will it yield, which, in turn, will yield truths of the *cogito type?* The *cogito* is the first existential truth, that is, the first truth about what exists in the universe. The *cogito* is thus an ontological claim. Descartes' next step is not to establish other ontological claims on the basis of this one, but something else. His next step is to establish the first epistemological truth. This epistemological truth will henceforth serve as an insignia of truth. When ideas bear this insignia, then Descartes can confidently assert them to be true. For example, using this insignia Descartes will arrive at the second existential truth, namely, God exists. Using this insignia, henceforth, he will prove the distinction between

[23] Let me defend my reading. I have rendered 'so long as' as 'if' – everything else remaining the same. It is obvious that 'if' does not capture the nuances of 'so long as': for one thing, 'so long as' has the idea of something continually present, while something else is occurring, and to that extent (b) and (b') are different. Granting the difference, then, two remarks are in order: First, how crucial is the difference for the point that is being made? Second, can (b) or (b') be made the same as (a)? If not, the conclusion of the argument is not seriously affected.

mind and body, discover their respective essences, demonstrate the existence of the external world, and so on. Without the insignia, he is not in a position to assert or know anything to be true, even if it is true.

With the appropriate context, the epistemological truth reads as follows:

I am certain that I am a thinking thing. Do I not therefore also know what is required for my being certain about anything? In this first item of knowledge there is simply a clear and distinct perception of what I am asserting; this would not be enough to make me certain of the truth of the matter if it could ever turn out that something which I perceived with such clarity and distinctness was false. *So I now seem to be able to lay it down as a general rule that whatever I perceive very clearly and distinctly is true.* (CSM II, 24; AT VII, 35; my emphasis)

There is a stronger version of the principle, which I prefer, for it better captures Descartes' position. It reads:

I have drawn the conclusion that everything which I clearly and distinctly perceive is of necessity true. (CSM II, 48; AT VII, 70)

But why of necessity? Because, says Descartes, of his nature. He is so constituted that he cannot help believing what is clear and distinct to be true. "Admittedly my nature is such that so long as I perceive something very clearly and distinctly I cannot but believe it to be true" (CSM II, 48; AT VII, 69). This must be of his essence. If he were not so constituted, then he could not ever possess any knowledge, any certainty. If it were just an accidental feature of Descartes, and of man in general, that he just happened to believe to be true what is clear and distinct, then there could be circumstances in which he had a clear and distinct idea, but in which the accidental feature or property of believing that idea to be true was absent, so that, in those circumstances, he would either regard the idea as false or be indifferent to the truth-value of the idea. There would be no insignia with which to mark his perceptions or ideas. Thus, there would be no escape from doubt. One need not fear that this would commit Descartes to idealism: It is not saying that Descartes' mind or thought makes the clear and distinct propositions true. Thanks to God, he cannot help believing clear and distinct propositions to be true, where truth is defined independent of Descartes', or anyone else's, mind.

Notice that in the general rule the epistemic and the ontological converge: *Ontologically,* clear and distinct ideas are *true,* and *epistemically,* clear and distinct ideas are *known* to be true. (This is the point in Descartes' thought that has determined much of the subsequent development of the history of philosophy. Some have reinforced this convergence; others have denied it. Those who have denied it are legion; they have claimed that no amount of piling up of evidence [epistemic talk] can ineluctably lead to the truth [ontological talk], the gulf between the two – evidence and truth – being what it is.) If it were not of his essence, Descartes would have had no insignia of truth, and yet unbeknownst to him his ideas may have been true. Alternatively, his clear and distinct ideas may have been false, yet he could have been so constituted, his essence could have been such, that he could have mistakenly taken his clear and distinct ideas to be true; in short, the general rule would have been false. The *cogito* serves as a powerful anchor that holds these two claims, the ontological and the epistemic, together in a fascinating way: First, whatever the insignia of truth, the *cogito* cannot be false; and second, so clear and distinct is the idea of the *cogito* that nothing else could serve, for a human being, as *the* epistemic criteria.

When you go to solve a problem, says Descartes, do not forget your yardstick.

Frequently people are in such a hurry in their investigation of problems that they set about solving them with their minds blank – without first taking account of the criteria which will enable them to recognize distinctly the thing they are seeking, should they come across it. They are thus behaving like a foolish servant who, sent on some errand by his master, is so eager to obey that he dashes off without instructions and without knowing where he is to go. (CSM I, 54; AT X, 434)

Someone looking for an epistemic criterion, such as the general rule, might easily be puzzled by this advice: If he already has the criterion, the yardstick, he does not have to look for it; if he does not have the criterion, how will he know that he has the right one if he should stumble upon it? Perhaps Plato's Socrates in the *Meno* could not escape from this problem; but Descartes thinks he can. The *cogito* is not established by any antecedent epistemic criterion; the criterion, the general rule, emerges only later *from* the *cogito.*

What it is vital to recognize, the *therefore* and *conclusion* in the passages quoted earlier notwithstanding, is that Descartes is not explaining or offering an argument – and rightly so – for the epistemological truth. He is not grounding this epistemological truth on some other epistemological truth, or on anything else, save the *cogito.* Indeed, Father Mersenne had demanded that Descartes do just that:

> Why should it not be in your nature to be subject to constant – or at least very frequent – deception? How can you establish with certainty that you are not deceived, or capable of being deceived, in matters which you think you know clearly and distinctly? Have we not often seen people turn out to have been deceived in matters where they thought their knowledge was as clear as the sunlight? Your principle of clear and distinct knowledge thus requires a clear and distinct explanation, in such a way as to rule out the possibility that anyone of sound mind may be deceived on matters which he thinks he knows clearly and distinctly. Failing this, we do not see that any degree of certainty can possibly be within your reach or that of mankind in general. (CSM II, 90; AT VII, 126; see also CSMK, 201–203; AT III, 474–479)

Mersenne had failed to see the fundamental nature of the general rule, the epistemic truth. He had failed to recognize that the ideal seeker after truth must see, intuit, the general rule as *emerging* from the *cogito,* or else nothing could induce him to believe in the veracity of the general rule. An attempt to explain the general rule would result in either an infinite regress or a vicious circle. Let us suppose that the general rule was explained by "a clear and distinct explanation," E. Now, the legitimacy of E can be questioned in just the same way as the general rule was. Either E itself proposes a different insignia of truth, S, or it proposes the insignia of the general rule of clear and distinct ideas. In the latter case, we would be arguing in circles. In the former case, we will require "a clear and distinct explanation" for S. Then one questions the legitimacy of S, and so we offer a "clear and distinct explanation," T, for S's legitimacy. Then T is questioned, and so on. The infinite regress is unavoidable. Mersenne's demand cannot be met in principle.

Descartes probably foresaw that. When a person suffers from dropsy, says Descartes, he feels thirsty, but a drink of water would be quite harmful; here following an instinct implanted in us would lead to disastrous consequences. "[I]t does appear that we are really deceived by the natural instinct which God gave us" (CSM II, 102; AT VII, 143).

But in the Sixth Meditation, Descartes did explain why this would not reflect poorly on God, who is all-good. Now, could not God have similarly implanted in us a faculty of judgment that occasionally leads us astray, in the same way in which the feeling of thirst occasionally leads us to do a harmful thing? Or is there a parallel story that preserves the idea of an all-good God? Descartes answers: "In the case of our clearest and most careful judgements, however, this kind of explanation would not be possible, for if such judgements were false they could not be corrected by any clearer judgements or by means of any other natural faculty" (CSM II, 102–103; AT VII, 143–144). We can prevent harming ourselves in the state of dropsy by not drinking water, by a clearer judgment about our sick condition and about the consequences of drinking water for our body. But what explanation could be clearer than the clearest and most distinct ideas of which we are capable?

The beauty of the *cogito* is that it does not fall prey to the vicious circle or infinite regress argument. The *cogito* is not justified by the general rule. This is why the actual thought experiment and the undergoing of the doubt by the ideal investigator are so crucial to Descartes' method. Descartes is not arguing that the *cogito*-argument is sound or the *cogito*-statement true *because* it instantiates the general rule. This would put the cart before the horse. Rather, the ideal investigator finds himself first in the *cogito*-state (or *cogito*-process) and only subsequently recognizes, while still in that state, that the general rule is true. If he does not come to see it in that state, nothing will induce him to espouse the general rule. If he does not espouse the general rule, he will not be certain that he can, henceforth, know any truth.[24]

What, then, is the notion of truth that Descartes was after? There is a tension in Descartes' views. Let us call absolute truth, truth$_1$, the God's-eye view. Then there are relative truths, let us call them truth$_2$, the angel's-eye view; and truth$_3$, the man's-eye view. By parity of reasoning, there is truth$_4$, say, the horse's-eye view; truth$_5$, the bird's-eye view; truth$_6$, the serpent's-eye view, and so on. Descartes set out to discover truth$_1$, but sometimes spoke as if he was interested only in truth$_3$. A proposition may be true$_3$ but not true$_1$. We may think that the proposition "The blue bells are blue," is true$_1$. But we would be

[24] See also Chapter 4, section IV, and Chapter 8, section III.

mistaken; it is only $true_3$, not $true_1$, for material objects do not possess the property of being colored. It requires strenuous thought to recognize, as did Descartes, that while the material world exists, a truth of type 1, it is not $true_1$ that they are colored; they only possess properties, such as length, breadth, width, and duration, that can be mathematized.

There is every reason to think that Descartes was after the God's-eye view, $truth_1$, insofar as he, a finite being, could attain it. That is, he wanted to discover as many $truth_3$s as he could that were also $truth_1$s. Yet, this is also what he said:

[A]s soon as we think that we correctly perceive something, we are spontaneously convinced that it is true. Now if this conviction is so firm that it is impossible for us ever to have any reason for doubting what we are convinced of, then there are no further questions for us to ask: we have everything that we could reasonably want. What is it to us that someone may make out that the perception whose truth we are so firmly convinced of may appear false to God or an angel, so that it is, absolutely speaking, false? Why should this alleged "absolute falsity" bother us, since we neither believe in it nor have even the smallest suspicion of it? (CSM II, 103; AT VII, 144–145)

First, even granting the distinction between absolute and relative truth, there must be some truths that are absolute even on Descartes' view and not just relative ones, such as the proposition, "God exists." And what about the *cogito*? Is it not an absolute truth, too?

Second, inasmuch as Descartes talks about degrees of clarity and distinctness, we can imagine the following possibilities. Let us range these in the following order: $C_1, C_2, C_3, \ldots, C_n$. Let us suppose that God has created sentient creatures of n orders.[25] The first-order creatures (say, the serpents) have the lowest degree of clear and distinct ideas, namely, ideas of type C_1. The second-order creatures (say, birds) have a slightly higher degree of clear and distinct ideas, namely, ideas of type C_2; the third-order of creatures (say, horses) have a slightly higher degree of clear and distinct ideas, namely, ideas of type C_3, and so on. (If the reader should properly object that since, for Descartes, these creatures are mechanical objects and have no mind, they could not have any ideas at all, then he should imagine

---

[25] "For an infinite number of other creatures far superior to us may exist elsewhere" (CSMK, 349; AT V, 168).

that God created n varieties of *Homo sapiens*, and that He gifted each variety with a different unique degree of clear and distinct ideas.) These creatures are endowed with a nature such that when considering an idea of the highest degree of clarity and distinctness for their order, they cannot help but assent spontaneously to that idea. If Descartes were interested solely in relative truth, then he could claim only that, given his nature, he cannot help believing that certain ideas that are clear and distinct are $true_3$, but not $true_1$. This is innocuous enough, and all creatures in each order can make a similar claim, relying on a similar general rule of their own, namely, that whenever ideas of clarity and distinctness of order i appear to them (creatures of order i) they shall regard them as $true_i$. This would seem to be Descartes' position, duly generalized, if one relied on the last quoted passage.

If Descartes is interested in absolute truth, then of course he has to show why the general rule that he relies upon should tell him anything more than $truth_3$, rather than $truth_1$. Descartes, I think, is interested in absolute truth. The notions of truth and falsity are implanted in us, says Descartes; he does not say that the notions of relative truth and falsity are implanted in us. Thus, it is natural to conclude that the human mind cannot be deceived in taking certain ideas to be true when these ideas are perceived to be clear and distinct. Could it be that Descartes thinks that we need to know the existence of God – an example of absolute truth – so that we are not deceived even about relative truth?

But third, there is an interesting query to be raised even if Descartes were interested only in relative truth. Suppose that each order of creatures in God's creation possessed the ability to have clear and distinct ideas of all *the degrees possessed by all the lower orders*. For example, creatures of order j would possess the clarity and distinctness of ideas of orders 1 through j, and those of order i would possess the clarity and distinctness of ideas of orders 1 through i, but not that of j. (I limit myself to a single modality.) Each order of creatures, then, would have its own outermost limit of clarity and distinctness. The serpent perceives less clearly and distinctly than the bird, the bird less than the horse, the horse less than man. I wonder: Will each order have its own unique paradigm that displays the outermost limit to it, as the *cogito* displays our outermost limit of clarity and distinctness to us? For example, while a person pursues truth$_3$, the angels pursue truth$_2$. Will the *cogito* also serve as a paradigm for the angels – will it also be the first existential truth that *they* know?

Now, how could Descartes justify the claim that he has successfully reached the outermost limit for the human order? We can imagine the community of creatures of j order making do with only i degree of clarity and distinctness, until a Descartes in their community comes along and shows them what they can in principle achieve, namely, j degree of clarity and distinctness. Indeed, for a long time we took the deliverance of our senses as giving us true reports, until Descartes showed us better. Will there arise another Descartes among us who will take us one step forward toward a higher degree of distinctness and clarity, as Descartes took us a step forward from what we were used to before? Failure to demonstrate that the general rule takes us to the outermost limit of which we as human beings are capable would mean that we have no reason to be certain even of the relative truth, let alone of the absolute truth. For we can be certain of the relative truth only if we are at the outermost limit of what we can clearly and distinctly perceive. Descartes, therefore, must claim that in the *cogito*-state we have arrived at the outermost limit. My question is, has Descartes shown that?

Fourth and finally, what about the criteria of clear and distinct ideas themselves? There are plenty of people who go about their entire lives, says Descartes, without perceiving anything sufficiently clearly and distinctly to warrant a sound and certain judgment about it. A judgment based on anything else would surely not do. Hence, it is essential to understand what Descartes means by *clear* and *distinct.*

A perception which can serve as the basis for a certain and indubitable judgement needs to be not merely clear but also distinct. I call a perception 'clear' when it is present and accessible to the attentive mind – just as we say that we see something clearly when it is present to the eye's gaze and stimulates it with a sufficient degree of strength and accessibility. I call a perception 'distinct' if, as well as being clear, it is so sharply separated from all other perceptions that it contains within itself only what is clear. (CSM I, 207–208; AT VIIIA, 22)

What is at work here is more an analogy than a close-knit argument. Imagine a simple object, such as a piece of wax, present to the eye's gaze under normal circumstances, such as ordinary daylight, normal eyesight of the viewer, and so on. The wax, under those conditions, stimulates the eye with a sufficient degree of strength and accessibility. The eye "distinctly" perceives the wax, perceives it as distinct from surrounding objects. In a similar way, when the senses are withdrawn – or, so to speak, cast off – and the mind is to itself and fully attentive, then a 'distinct' perception will stimulate it with a sufficient degree of strength and accessibility. This is the case, for example, when the wax is "not strictly perceived by the senses or the faculty of imagination but by the intellect alone" (CSM II, 22; AT VII, 34). Descartes has an even more distinct perception of himself upon having a more distinct perception of the wax. As he states it in the Second Meditation: "Moreover, if my perception of the wax seemed more distinct after it was established not just by sight or touch but by many other considerations, it must be admitted that I now know myself even more distinctly" (CSM II, 22; AT VII, 33).

In this passage, Descartes speaks only of distinctness, and not of clarity. "Clarity" and "distinctness" are not the same thing. Descartes offers an example of a perception – pain – that can be clear without being distinct. When someone suffers a pain in the foot, he has a very clear perception of the pain, but he may sometimes confuse it with "an obscure judgement [he makes] concerning the nature of something which [he thinks] exists in the painful spot" (CSM I, 208; AT VIIIA, 22). Thus, running distinct perceptions together, or mixing up a perception with a judgment about another perception, is not conducive to having a distinct perception. Now, whereas what is clear may not be distinct, what is distinct must be clear (CSM I, 208; AT VIIIA, 22). Hence, the perception of the wax, and of himself, while referred to only as being distinct, implies that such a perception is clear, too.

Evidently, then, the *cogito* must be both clear and distinct. It must be, first, a perception that will serve as a basis for a certain and indubitable judgment. This perception is unique in this respect: It will be present and accessible to the attentive mind and will stimulate it with the highest degree of strength and accessibility of which a human mind is capable; in short, it will take the mind to the outermost limit of its epistemic abilities. This supports, too, the psychological casting of the *cogito* in the present chapter. Second, it must be "sharply separated from all other perceptions." This lends at least preliminary support to

the hypothesis that the *cogito* is a mental state rather than a mental process, and a first-order mental state rather than a second-order mental
state, since the latter cannot be sharply separated from the first-order
perception that it is about. Third and finally, the *cogito* must contain
"within itself only what is clear."

4

A Skeptic against Reason

The defense of reason has had a long history. Descartes played a pivotal role in it, if for no other reason than that he sharply focused on the problem (look no further than the start of the *Meditations on First Philosophy*), firmly etched the separate domains of reason and religion, and believed that his work would quietly, but firmly, restore reason to its rightful place, not at the periphery of human thought but at its very epicenter. This chapter attempts to construct a sequence of arguments that a skeptic might pose against Descartes' defense of reason.

I begin, in section I, with a brief look at another player in this history, not given much attention by philosophers: Michel de Montaigne. Montaigne was Descartes' precursor, with views on reason that have much bearing on the work of his successor in France.[1] In his book *Descartes against the Skeptics*, Edwin M. Curley argues that the proof of the existence of God is interlocked with the argument of the *cogito* in this way: "Descartes would hold that even the proposition 'I exist' is fully certain only if the rest of the argument of the Meditations goes through. We must buy all or nothing." (C, 95) Section II is designed to demonstrate that Curley's view would land Descartes in a paradox from which it would be impossible for him to escape, and would thereby wreck his entire system. But arguing against Curley is not the primary purpose of this section. In it, I show that there is a new

[1] Montaigne died on September 13, 1592; Descartes was born three and a half years later, on March 31, 1596.

Cartesian Circle, more devastating than the old one made famous by Descartes' contemporary Antoine Arnauld. One needs to confront this new Cartesian Circle; it is, I think, of intrinsic interest. But more: The new Cartesian Circle will be needed as a constant reminder later, when various ways of understanding the *cogito* as an argument are dismantled. It should also become amply clear why the Cartesian Circle argument, usually discussed in relation to the Third Meditation, is discussed here when dealing with issues prominent in the Second.

Sections III and IV are devoted to examining the common allegation that Descartes committed an egregious error at the heart of his system, infamously known as the Cartesian Circle. (He did not, in my view. But I shall not argue that here.) Here I am concerned with refuting an interesting proposal by Curley intended to free Descartes from that objection. The virtue of my argument is its generality. If my argument is right, a skeptic can be defended against Curley – or at least against Curley's Descartes. Section V presents an argument against James van Cleve's well-known way of escaping from the Cartesian Circle. The final section shows how a skeptic might argue against a recent conjecture of Stephen Gaukroger in answer to the question, "What was the method Descartes adopted in his deductive demonstrations in the *Meditations*?" Whatever the historical worth of this conjecture, a skeptic could show that it would have been something of an embarrassment for Descartes.

I. Why *Natural* Reason?

Michel de Montaigne:

> God in his mercy may perhaps have deigned to protect those tender principles of rough-and-ready knowledge of Himself which Natural Reason affords us, amid the false imaginings of our dreams. But there are religions Man has forged entirely on his own: they are not only false but impious and harmful. (M, 82)

Natural Reason is taught by philosophers to be "the Comptroller-General of everything within and without the vault of heaven; they themselves say that it can embrace everything, do everything, and is means by which anything is known or understood" (M, 116). But Natural Reason is not to be trusted: It is an imbecile; it is sickly; it is so inadequate, so blind; it is full of falsehood, error, defects, and feebleness; it hobbles, limps, and walks askew (M, 86, 12, 13, 117, and

144). Nor was this merely notes for a program. Montaigne offered at least two arguments: one remarkably Cartesian in its design, the other more modern.[2]

The first argument: "Our discursive reasoning," says Montaigne, "is driven and shaken at the mercy of [the] influence" of the sun, moon, and stars (M, 14). They "govern us by silent laws." As a result of their influence, not just one man or one king, but monarchies and empires reel and collapse, and our discourse on virtues and vices, knowledge and competencies is (mis?)guided. "If we are dependent upon the disposition of the heavens for such little rationality as we have, how can our reason make us equal to the Heavens? How can their essence, or the principles on which they are founded, be subjects of human knowledge?" (M, 15) So I infer: If the influence of the heavenly bodies is baneful on us, it will make us think that reason is thus-and-so in essence when reason is no such thing; if their influence is pernicious, they may thwart our reason as easily as they engineer the collapse of a king. How can we tell? Perhaps our reason is ill-structured, let alone equal to the reason of the heavens. Descartes cannot counterargue that the astrological hypothesis – namely, that the heavenly bodies determinately influence the behavior of a person – is quaint, at best. Like the improbable hypothesis of the evil genius that is designed to cast doubt on the truths of mathematics, the former hypothesis is offered to cast doubt on reason's trustworthiness.

The second argument: "The senses themselves being full of uncertainty cannot decide the issue of our dispute. It will have to be Reason, then. But no Reason can be established except by another Reason. We retreat into infinity." (M, 185) A reason cannot establish itself; it has to be established by another. No unestablished reason is reliable. If no

---

[2] Compare this to the critique of reason set ninety-eight years after *Meditations on First Philosophy:* "Reason first appears in possession of the throne, prescribing laws, and imposing maxims, with an absolute sway and authority. Her enemy, therefore is obliged to take shelter under her protection, and by making use of rational arguments to prove the fallaciousness and imbecility of reason, produces, in a manner, a patent under her hand and seal. This patent has at first an authority, proportion'd to the present and immediate authority of reason, from which it is deriv'd. But as it is suppos'd to be contradictory to reason, it gradually diminishes the force of that governing power, and its own at the same time; till at last they both vanish away into nothing, by a regular and just diminution." David Hume, *A Treatise of Human Nature*, Book I, Part IV, section 1, "Of Scepticism with Regard to Reason,"125.

unestablished reason is reliable, then Reason is not reliable. Therefore, Reason is not reliable. This preamble from Montaigne is drawn
to suggest that Descartes, too, should have worried, with the skeptics,
over the reliability of reason. Did he?

"I have always thought," says Descartes, in the "Dedicatory Letter to
the Sorbonne," which serves as the opening of the *Meditations on First
Philosophy,*

> that two topics – namely God and the soul – are prime examples of subjects
> where demonstrative proofs ought to be given with the aid of philosophy rather
> than theology. For us who are believers, it is enough to accept on faith that the
> human soul does not die with the body, and that God exists; but in the case of
> unbelievers, it seems that there is no religion, and practically no moral virtue,
> that they can be persuaded to adopt until these two truths are proved to them
> by natural reason.[3] (CSM II, 3; AT VII, 1–2)

Descartes goes on to say that, of course, we must believe in God because it is the cardinal doctrine of the Holy Scriptures, and that we must
believe in the Holy Scriptures because they are a gift of God. The reasoning is circular. For the believers it does not matter; but it is of some
consequence if one wishes to persuade the unbelievers, the skeptics.[4]

What, then, is this thing called *Natural Reason,* and why should an
unbeliever trust it any more than faith or scripture?[5] It is often noted

---

[3] Raymond Sebond put it this way: "It alleges no authority – not even the Bible – for
its end is to confirm what is written in Holy Scripture – and to lay the foundations
on which we can build what is obscurely deduced from them. And so, in our case, it
precedes the Old and New Testament." (M, Appendix 2, xlii–xliii)

[4] Lest I be as guilty as his biographers (R, ix), let me hastily cite the last words of
Maurice of Nassau, who, when admonished by a pastor to "make a kind of profession
of faith," said: "I believe that 2 and 2 are 4 and that 4 and 4 are 8" (R, 62). Descartes
was interested in defending the faith, especially against skeptical mathematicians who
held statements of mathematics to be veridical while doubting the existence of God
(R, 79, 108–109). Among others, Descartes quarreled with Voetius, who found hyperbolic doubt unpalatable and by implication accused Descartes of being an atheist
(R, 147–148, 163–164, 169–170, also 171–173, 206). Descartes "wanted official acknowledgment that he had never been suspected of atheism" (R, 170).

[5] So when Rodis-Lewis claims, "Nevertheless, to avoid all polemic, and because 'natural reason' is in agreement with 'the Christian religion,' which "wants us to believe
in that manner," (R, 102), a skeptic might respond, "*That* still needs to be demonstrated; Descartes must assure us that he is beginning with reason that is neither
Christian, nor of any other religion, in its underpinning. It must be natural *tout court.*
Otherwise, the argument that Descartes was involved in circular reasoning would
stand undiminished."

that Descartes' doubt is not sufficiently sweeping: He doubts his senses, his belief in an external world, mathematics, and other such things, but he never doubts his reason. Why should not reason be just as much subject to serious doubts as anything else? Indeed, the circularity of reasoning, an unbeliever might argue, is no less evident here. To justify reason, one has to produce good, strong reasons. How else can reason be justified? But no matter how strong and good the reasons are in support of Natural Reason, they are first and foremost reasons. So one would have to say that one must believe in reason because there are good and strong reasons in support of it, and conversely that one must believe in these good and strong reasons because they are the deliverances of reason.

Now, of course, the good and strong reasons can be redescribed in such a way that they are no longer described as reasons. But then they are either stronger or weaker than reasons. If weaker, the justification is incomplete; if stronger, then they in turn have to be justified. At this point, the matter is given up. There is a parallel problem in justifying deductive and inductive logic, respectively. Deductive logic can be justified either deductively or inductively; to justify deductive logic deductively is to argue in circles, and to justify it inductively is not to argue strongly enough. Similarly, inductive logic can be justified either inductively or deductively; to justify inductive logic inductively is to argue in circles, and to justify it deductively is to argue too strongly.[6] Nor do I have a way of solving the problem of justifying reason – as against faith, say. But Descartes cannot take that stand, if his initial skepticism is to be comprehensive.

Indeed, Descartes' failure to question his capacity to reason is puzzling, for his manner of doubting his senses would have provided him with a near-exact model for doubting his reason. There are, I shall argue, three degrees of doubt. Descartes could have constructed doubts about his reason that are analogous to the doubts about his senses. His first round of doubt about the senses explains, and justifies, the obvious claim that our senses sometimes deceive us; the second round of doubt justifies a stronger claim, namely, that at any given time we are unable to say whether they deceive us or not; and finally, the third and strongest claim is made, namely, that we (may) have no senses

---

[6] See Susan Haack, "The Justification of Deduction."

at all. Similarly, Descartes could have ventured the following: a first round of doubt about reason, showing how using reason sometimes misleads us; a second round of doubt to show that at any given time we would be unable to tell whether we have reasoned correctly; and finally, a third round of doubt to show that we (may) have no reliable reason at all.

As we have seen, Descartes' view of the ideal seeker evolved quite gradually. It must have been an important problem for him, otherwise his frequent remarks on the issue would be difficult to explain. Consider, then, Descartes' remark in *Discourse on the Method*: "The simple resolution to abandon all the opinions one has hitherto accepted is not an example that everyone ought to follow. The world is largely composed of two types of minds for whom it is quite unsuitable." (CSM I, 118; AT VI, 15) The first type consists of those who think themselves too clever, are precipitate in their judgements, are unable to make an orderly inquiry, and so on; the second type consists of those who have just enough reason to recognize their lack of capacity to distinguish the true from the false. And let us say that there is a third type, composed of those who have just the right disposition, aptitude, and capacity – the type that constitutes the ideal thinker.

Descartes needs some justification for discriminating the first two types from the third. The first two types of people are known to make mistakes in reasoning, plain and plenty. So that even if these individuals occasionally reason correctly, it is best not to trust their reasoning. "It is prudent," someone seeking to justify the use of Natural Reason might say, "never to trust completely those who have deceived us even once." But this issue does not challenge Descartes to produce a justification for using Natural Reason, or for relying on the third type of individuals, who, let us grant, occasionally make errors. Could the demon be deceiving Descartes into thinking that the first two types of individuals would not be good ideal seekers? Could the demon be deceiving Descartes into thinking that the third type would make for a good ideal seeker? How should the demon be answered?

Consider the following famous passage:

[H]ow could it be denied that these hands or this whole body are mine? Unless perhaps I were to liken myself to madmen, whose brains are so damaged by the persistent vapours of melancholia that they firmly maintain they are kings when they are paupers, or say they are dressed in purple when they are naked, or that their heads are made of earthenware, or that they are pumpkins, or made of glass. But such people are insane, and I would be thought equally mad if I took anything from them as a model for myself.[7] (CSM II, 13; AT VII, 18–19)

Let us say that these constitute set₁ of mad beliefs.

But Descartes' doubt had led him to the claim that there is nothing in the world: no sky, no earth, no minds, no bodies, no colors, shapes, or sounds, no hands or eyes, and no flesh and blood. Yet, in the Synopsis he had described these as things "no sane person has ever seriously doubted" (CSM II, 11; AT VII, 16). These, say, constitute set₂ of mad beliefs. How should one distinguish one set of mad beliefs from another set? How are we to distinguish set₁ from set₂? Not, surely, in terms of the *content* of their claims: for any one claim in one set is as false as any claim in the other set. If Descartes is to argue successfully, he has to show us that there is a difference in the manner and structure of their reasoning.

If the physical world is doubted, then the scientific conjecture that the madmen have had their brains deranged by the vapors of melancholia is untenable, or ought to be untenable, to the inquirer. Worse yet, perhaps minds of the third type are infected by the noxious vapors. How can one tell? Perhaps, then, a neutral terminology is required. The first and second types of individuals have mental processes of *X*-kind. Descartes and others belonging to the third type of individuals have mental processes of *Y*-kind. In terms of *what* are the *Y*-kind mental processes to be preferred over the *X*-kind? Once again, why should not the evil demon be persuading Descartes that the *Y*-kind of mental process is to be preferred? Let us suppose that he who thinks that he is a pumpkin, or a king, is at least consistent. That, surely, cannot be ruled out in an a priori way. Of course, consistency is so minimal a demand that it can easily be met by the most absurd collection of statements. This is just the point, though. One should not eliminate the

---

[7] Having just seen, and heard, the three witches, Banquo exclaims:

Were such things here, as we do speak about,
Or have we eaten on the insane root
That takes the reason prisoner?

Macbeth, act 1, scene 3, lines 83–85. See also act 1, scene 3, lines 122–124; and act 1, scene 7, lines 66–68. It is useful to be reminded that Shakespeare wrote *Macbeth* in 1623.

objection by claiming that inconsistency is written into the statements of a lunatic, or of an individual belonging to one of the first two types.

Here is a different problem: How can Descartes tell that he is not, at certain moments, seized by the X-kind of state or process? If that were the case, at any given time Descartes could not tell whether he was, at that moment, in an X-kind or a Y-kind state or process. This problem is analogous to the second degree of doubt with respect to the senses, namely, that for all we know, at any given time, our senses may be deceiving us.

Perhaps this alone might have convinced Descartes that there is, after all, no certainty. He had made room for just that possibility in the opening paragraph of the Second Meditation: "I will proceed in this way until I recognize something certain, or, if nothing else, until I at least recognize for certain that there is no certainty" (CSM II, 16; AT VII, 24). He might have concluded that his reasoning is simply a teaching of nature: "Nature has apparently taught me to think this" (CSM II, 26; AT VII, 38). If Descartes reasoned at all, it was inevitable that he did so, but his reasoning was not therefore reliable. His reasoning would be a spontaneous, blind impulse that leads him to believe certain things (CSM II, 26–27; AT VII, 38–40).

There is a different problem that needs to be addressed, and one that falls within the purview of Descartes. But for all that, he did not raise the question, let alone answer it. This is not a problem of how to justify reason over faith, but rather a problem of how to arbitrate between two doctrines concerning the origin and reliability of reason: reason as a natural property of a person as against reason as a God-given property of a person. At the start, Descartes relies on reason as a natural property of a person: He thinks that he cannot do otherwise, or else he will fail to convince the atheist, the unbeliever, and the skeptic. With the aid of this natural property alone he establishes the existence of God, and then claims that the natural property of a person is really a God-given property of man. Hence, he can rely on it and not err.

By contrast, consider, for example, Saint Augustine's theory of reason as illumination. Augustine argued that the light of God illuminates our mind, and that it is this illumination that enables us to see clearly and distinctly; were it not for this illumination, we would have no reason to believe in what we perceive through the intellect.

There is *no* argument in support of reason as a natural property of man. And, surely, it needs justification. Descartes imagines that it is possible that he was created by "fate or chance or a continuous chain of events, or by some other means." But, he says, the less powerful the cause that brought him to his present state, the more likely it is that he is an imperfect being. This imperfection may be in his sense experiences; perhaps they are defective. The imperfection may also be in his reason; perhaps he errs more often than not when he uses his reason. Perhaps truth is to be acquired through feeling, in a manner after Blake or Wordsworth.

To put the point crudely, but in a more contemporary idiom: Human beings have evolved through natural selection; traits survive that best fit the demands of the environment. Other traits perish. Our reason is one of our traits: Our ability to reason may well have evolved over time, although some think not.[8] If so, our reason is minimally imperfect, even as practiced by the scientists.[9] We may be making lots of mistakes. What reason have we to think that our Natural Reason is powerful enough to yield metaphysical truths of the highest order? Evidently, one must develop some argument in support of the claim that reason as a natural property of a person can be relied upon. Failure to do so would be a fatal omission in the system. Such a defense would be required to sustain all the propositions from the *cogito* on up.

II. "Buy All or Nothing"

In this section, I offer a new Cartesian Circle (paralleling the old one offered by Arnauld). This new Circle has, I think, profound implications for how the *cogito* should be read, whether as an argument or an intuition. The immediately succeeding chapters will use the result obtained in the present section as a significant backdrop against which their own claims are set. That result is my primary concern here, but this new Circle is offered in the context of an argument against Curley, my secondary concern. This bit of demolition, together with the new Circle, will bring out the importance of deciding what precisely lies within the scope of Cartesian doubt, and thus

---

[8] Brian Ellis, *Rational Belief Systems.*
[9] See David Faust, *The Limits of Scientific Reasoning.*

how the famous passage from the Third Meditation should be read. The reading of that passage has an enormous implication for the *cogito.*

Curley concludes his chapter on the *cogito* thus:

We must reverse a very common judgment about Descartes' system. It is often said that Descartes, in his quest for absolute certainty, is able to establish his own existence, but unable to establish the existence of anything else. If what has been argued here is correct, Descartes would hold that even the proposition "I exist" is fully certain only if the rest of the argument of the Meditations goes through. We must buy all or nothing. (C, 95)

Call this Curley's Central Contention.[10]

I want to argue that Curley's Central Contention commits Descartes to an egregious error. This is how my argument goes. Suppose that there is the following argument for "I exist." Call it the *cogito-*argument:

Premises: S_1
               S_2
               S_3 Rules of Inference: $R_1, R_2, \ldots, R_n$
               .
               .
               .
               S_n
               _____
               $\therefore$ *I exist.*

[10] I wonder why Curley needs to make so strong a claim. Wouldn't going up to the Third Meditation, which offers two proofs of the existence of God – or perhaps just one proof, given what Descartes said to Johannes Caterus – suffice? How about up to the Fifth Meditation, which offers the ontological proof? Why is it that we need to rely on the *rest* of the argument of the *Meditations*? What, in particular, does the Sixth Meditation have to add that is of vital concern to the present enterprise?

While I argue against Curley, my argument applies to any other view tending in the same direction. For example, it applies to Stephen Gaukroger, who maintains a Curley-like thesis, thus: "The *cogito* presents us with a paradigmatic case of clarity and distinctness of the kind that Descartes is seeking, but it does not legitimate the use of clarity and distinctness as a criterion. That task rests ultimately with God, whose existence we can deduce [*sic*] from the idea that we have of Him. God then acts as the guarantor of knowledge, although how He acts in this way is not specified here." (G, 320)

Now a skeptic might argue against Curley's Descartes as follows: If Descartes were offering an argument for the *cogito*, as Curley alleges – not a sound argument, not a proof, not a demonstration, not any such thing – that argument minimally would have to be valid.[11] But the validity of the argument is directly dependent upon the soundness of the rules of inference.[12] Since the rules of inference, like the truths of mathematics, could be questioned by postulating a most malignant and powerful demon, the rules of inference cannot be demonstrated, at this stage of the argument anyway (which is all of the First Meditation and into the second paragraph of the Second Meditation). Therefore, even Curley's quite modest proposal seems to be based on the truth of propositions – eternal truths, so-called – that Descartes has left quite scathed by the end of the First Meditation. Curley's *cogito* argument is not even known, nor can it be known, to be valid. Not only Curley's particular version of the nondemonstrative argument, but *no* argument can be offered as a valid one, at this juncture in the *Meditations*, to capture the *cogito*. But I intend to make a much stronger claim.

Curley thinks that the remedy lies in having a proof of the existence of God. Once the argument for the existence of God is in place, then

---

[11] I discuss in detail Curley's way of understanding the *cogito* in the next chapter – see the Fourth View – and so I omit it here.

[12] In his reply to Pierre Bourdin, Descartes says, "Finally, when he is about to deploy syllogisms in his formal presentation, and he extols them as "a method of conducting our reasoning" which is to be contrasted with my own, his apparent intention is to persuade people that I do not approve of syllogistic patterns of argument, and hence that my method is not a rational one. But this is false, as is clear enough from my writings where I have always been prepared to use syllogisms where the occasion required it." (CSM II, 355; AT VII, 522)

Well, what might such an occasion be? "Amongst others, the very syllogism whose matter and form my critic pretends that I repudiate, is one which he copied down from my own writings; for I use it at the end of my Replies in the Second Set of Objections, proposition 1, where I demonstrate the existence of God" (CSM II, 371; AT VII, 544). In his letter to Silhon (March or April 1648), Descartes wrote that intuitive knowledge is quite different from discursive knowledge, and that it is the latter we must engage in perforce when it comes to acquiring knowledge about God. Thus, "to speak more accurately, using the natural (and consequently comparatively rather obscure) knowledge of one attribute of God, to construct an argument leading to another attribute of God. So you must admit that in this life you do not see, in God and by his light, that he is unique; but you deduce it from a proposition you have made about him, and you draw the conclusion by the power of argument, which is a machine which often breaks down." (CSMK, 332; AT V, 138–139) For a more complete background, I beg the reader to consult Chapter 6, pp. 191–2, 203–7.

the *cogito* can be justified, which in turn would be required to get
the proof of the existence of God going (or, at least, one of the three
proofs of the existence of God that Descartes offers in the *Meditations*).
Suppose, then, that there is the following argument for "God exists."
Call it the *God*-argument:

Premises: K_1
                       K_2
                       K_3 Rules of Inference: $L_1, L_2, \ldots, L_n$
                        .
                        .
                        .

                       K_n
                       _____

                       $\therefore$ *God exists.*

   Curley's Central Contention argument cannot go through. Either
the rules of inference, $R_1, R_2, \ldots, R_n$, of the *cogito*-argument are the
same as the rules of inference, $L_1, L_2, \ldots, L_n$, of the *God*-argument, or
they are different. (For the sake of simplicity, I ignore the alternative
in which they partially overlap.) We have this paradox: If they are the
same, then the rules are as much in need of justification in the proof of
the existence of God – that is, in the *God*-argument – as they were when
offered as part and parcel of the first argument, the *cogito*-argument,
which implied the truth of "I exist." This is a simple case of question
begging.
   Alternatively, if the rules of inference are not the same, then the
existence of God may verify the rules of inference, $R_1, R_2, \ldots, R_n$, and
yet not verify the rules of inference, $L_1, L_2, \ldots, L_n$. One cannot say
that if, indeed, God does exist and can verify, by His goodness and
undeceitful nature, the eternal truths (namely, the rules of inference,
$R_1, R_2, \ldots, R_n$), then surely God justifies the rules of inference, L_1,
$L_2, \ldots, L_n$, as well. Of course not. The careful thing to say is that if
Curley is right, then Descartes has simply not given us a proof of the
existence of God. For the rules of inference, $L_1, L_2, \ldots, L_n$, which are
being used in the *God*-argument, are just as much in doubt as were the
earlier rules of inference. The soundness of the rules of inference, L_1,
$L_2, \ldots, L_n$, has to be established *before* they can be used in constructing

the proof, the *God*-argument. This he surely cannot do. This is a simple case of justification failure.[13]

There is an extra puzzle. Curley has said, when arguing against Harry Frankfurt's book *Demons, Dreamers, and Madmen,* that even if the premises were true, they would still not ensure the indubitability of the conclusion (C, 82–84). But if there is no assurance that the premises of an argument are true, *whence* the assurance that the conclusion is true, let alone indubitable? (Was this the insight that compelled Frankfurt to divorce truth and indubitability in his book?) Unless, of course, there is a core supposition whose truth is guaranteed and from which, and from which alone, flows the truth of "I exist"? But Curley is unwilling to be saddled with the epistemic labor of justifying the premises. To go a step further, if the *cogito* provides a crucial starting point for a proof of the existence of God, and the *cogito*-argument is dubious, we should regard the *God*-argument as merely an alleged proof.

There is a line of argument that might be suggested in defense. It might be argued that Curley explicitly draws attention to two types of indubitability, namely, normative as opposed to descriptive indubitability (C, 82–83, 100–101). Until one has a proof of the existence of God, one might have descriptive indubitability for the *cogito*-argument, but after, and only after, that proof can one have normative indubitability for that same *cogito*-argument. Curley says, referring to a passage cited by a critic, "The passage would thus be saying that because I cannot, in fact, doubt the teachings of the natural light (when I attend to them), I must, at least provisionally, treat them as though they ought not to be doubted in examining whether there is a God."[14] Presumably, then, once we have the proof for the existence of God, we would at the same time achieve normative indubitability.

---

[13] There is a parallel here with David Hilbert's claim about proving the consistency of arithmetic. Other branches of mathematics can be shown to be consistent if arithmetic is assumed to be consistent. Hilbert himself has shown, for example, that Euclidean geometry is consistent if arithmetic is. "In geometry and physical theory the proof of consistency is accomplished by reducing it to the consistency of arithmetic. This method obviously fails in the proof of arithmetic itself." Quoted in Morris Kline, *Mathematics: The Loss of Certainty,* 249. Hilbert's claim was that if in proving the consistency of arithmetic one used in the metalanguage (the language in which the proof was carried out) the very rules of inference whose consistency was in question, then, of course, arithmetic could be "demonstrated" to be consistent. But, one would have done so only by begging the question.

[14] This is suggested both in the text and in note 25 (C, 94–95).

I do not see how. We run into the same problem. Once we have the proof – *if* we have it – of the existence of God in hand, the rules of inference, $R_1, R_2, \ldots, R_n$, are now no longer descriptively indubitable, but rather normatively indubitable. Even supposing that were so, this would leave the rules of inference, $L_1, L_2, \ldots, L_n$, without any normative justification. Since these were *used* in the proof of the existence of God, their indubitability was at best descriptive. Of course, the careful thing to say is that if Curley is right, then Descartes has simply not given us a proof of anything. For the rules of inference, $L_1, L_2, \ldots, L_n$, that are being used in the *God*-argument are just as much in doubt as were the previous rules of inference. We do not have a normative proof of the existence of God, only a descriptive proof – if I may be permitted a parallel distinction. Since God is the guarantor of the truth of everything else, according to one reading of a passage I shall presently cite, this spells epistemic doom.

Curley, like several other scholars, reads the following passage from the Third Meditation of Descartes' *Meditations on First Philosophy* as including the *cogito* in its skeptical scope:

I spontaneously declare: let whoever can do so deceive me, he will never bring it about that I am nothing, so long as I continue to think I am something; or make it true at some future time that I have never existed, since it is now true that I exist; or bring it about that two and three added together are more or less than five, or anything of this kind in which I see a manifest contradiction. And since I have no cause to think that there is a deceiving God, and I do not yet even know for sure whether there is a God at all, any reason for doubt which depends simply on this supposition is a very slight and, so to speak, metaphysical one. But in order to remove even this slight reason for doubt, as soon as the opportunity arises I must examine whether there is a God, and, if there is, whether he can be a deceiver. For if I do not know this, it seems that I can never be quite certain about anything else. (CSM II, 25; AT VII, 36)

If the correct reading of this passage is that I cannot be certain about the *cogito*, about the truths of mathematics, and so on, unless I have examined and successfully concluded – unless, that is, I *know* – that there is a God, it would result in the eventual collapse of the normative indubitability of $R_1, R_2, \ldots, R_n$, and with it the collapse of the *cogito*-argument and everything else.[15]

---

[15] On Curley's interpretation, Descartes was remarkably coy about telling us in a forthright manner that his famous conclusion of the Second Meditation was provisional, subject to the success of the enterprise of proving the existence of God, to

Many historians and philosophers are quite bothered by the just-cited passage, and seem to argue, or at least to arrive at the same conclusion, in a manner not unlike Curley's. The astonishing thing is that very rarely, if ever, does one even mention, let alone discuss, a passage that comes in the same meditation just three and a half pages later:

> But what is my conclusion to be? If the objective reality of any of my ideas turns out to be so great that I am sure the same reality does not reside in me, either formally or eminently, and hence that I myself cannot be its cause, it will necessarily follow that I am not alone in the world, but that some other thing which is the cause of this idea also exists. But if no such idea is to be found in me, I shall have no argument to convince me of the existence of anything apart from myself. (CSM II, 29; AT VII, 42)

Descartes is here stating quite explicitly, and in the context of the proof – the first proof – of the existence of God, that even if he had no proof of the existence of God, he would still be *convinced* that he himself existed, only he would have no argument to demonstrate that something besides himself existed as well. He emphatically does not say that because he has no proof of the existence of God, he cannot be reasonably sure that he exists in the world, too.[16]

---

be undertaken in the Third and Fifth Meditations. Not only was he not coy, with Bourdin he was particularly blunt. Here are two passages from his reply to Bourdin, the author of the "Seventh Set of Objections." "Note that my critic here admits that I have made my first step in philosophizing, and for the first [*sic*] time established a proposition as firm, by recognizing my own existence" (CSM II, 323; AT VII, 480). One page later: "Thus I was right to begin by rejecting all my beliefs; and later on, noticing that there was nothing which I could know more certainly or more evidently than that I existed so long as I was thinking, I was right to make this my first [*sic*] assertion." Furthermore, if Curley is right, the order of philosophizing, which Descartes so emphasized, is inexplicable. If the *cogito* and the general epistemic rule are unreliable without the proof of God's existence, and the proof of God's existence can, in principle, go through without the other two, why did the proof of God's existence not directly succeed the metaphysical doubt? Descartes could then have laid down his general rule, then the *cogito*, and then the proof about his essence. Why did not Descartes proceed in that way? I submit that it was not odd for Descartes to do what he did precisely because Descartes fully recognized that without the *cogito* and the general rule, no subsequent part of his philosophy could be carried out. I aver that even if the proof of the existence of a good God fails, the *cogito* would still stand unscathed.

[16] In a letter (June or July 1646), Descartes wrote to Clerselier: "[I]t is very useful indeed to convince oneself first of *the existence of God*, and then of the existence of all creatures, *through the consideration of one's own existence*." In the immediately preceding paragraph, Descartes had identified the first principle [*sic*] as *that our soul exists* (CSMK, 290; AT IV, 444–445).

Curley has seriously underestimated the problem that Descartes would face on his reading. It is not, as Curley thinks, merely a matter of Descartes' not coming up with an adequate proof of the existence of God. If my argument is correct, Curley has made sure that Descartes *could not* come up with such a proof. For any proof must presuppose the soundness of the rules of inference that it uses; *ex hypothesi*, in the absence of a proof of the existence of God, no rules of inference can be demonstrated to be sound. Therefore, there can in principle be no proof of the existence of God. On Curley's reading, Descartes' project is inescapably circular.[17] Descartes' defense of reason is a failure. So there really *is* nothing to buy. *Caveat emptor!* Since there cannot be a proof of the existence of God, in the absence of rules of inference known to be sound, there is no assurance for the *cogito* either. Curley's view of the *cogito* as an inference or an argument leaves Descartes with nothing. So a skeptic might argue.

III. Attempting to Step Out of the Circle

Antoine Arnauld found Descartes guilty of circular reasoning.[18] This is what Arnauld famously wrote to Father Marin Mersenne (1588–1648):

I have one further worry, namely how the author avoids reasoning in a circle when he says that we are sure that what we clearly and distinctly perceive is true only because God exists.

[17] Here is another oddity. In the Fourth Meditation, in the context of explaining the source of his mistakes and the scope of his will, and giving examples to illustrate where and how he makes mistakes and where and how he does not make them, Descartes says: "For example, during these past few days I have been asking whether anything in the world exists, and I have realized that from the very fact of my raising this question it follows quite evidently that I exist. I could not but judge that something which I understood so clearly was true." (CSM II, 41; AT VII, 58) First, there is talk of what exists in the world; second, the *cogito* is offered as a prime example of evident knowledge; third, in this case the will is freest when it assents to the *cogito*; fourth, there is no qualification; and fifth and finally, there is no mention of God.

[18] This is the same Arnauld of whom Descartes wrote to Mersenne on March 4, 1641, after he had received objections from several readers of his *Meditations on First Philosophy*: ". . . M. Arnauld, who has put me greatly in his debt by producing his objections. I think they are the best of all the set of objections, not because they are more telling, but because he, more than anyone else, has entered into the sense of what I wrote." (CSMK, 175; AT III, 331)

It should be noted that while the "Second Set of Objections" was attributed to a nameless set of "theologians and philosophers," the objections were mainly authored by Mersenne. Furthermore, Mersenne gave as crisp a statement of circular reasoning as Arnauld did. (CSM II, 89; AT VII, 124–125)

But we can be sure that God exists only because we clearly and distinctly perceive this. Hence, before we can be sure that God exists, we ought to be able to be sure that whatever we perceive clearly and evidently is true. (CSM II, 150; AT VII, 214)

In the Third Meditation, Descartes had formulated the crucial general rule. It stated that "whatever I perceive very clearly and distinctly is true" (CSM II, 24; AT VII, 35). But the general rule, Arnauld asserted, could not be relied upon until the proof of the existence of God was forthcoming. The proof of the existence of God, on the other hand, could be a proof only if it were very clear and distinct – Descartes had spoken of his proofs for the existence of God and for the distinction between the mind and the body as "quite certain and evident" (CSM II, 5; AT VII, 4). Thus we have a short, inescapable circle. Making it as closely parallel to the circular argument Descartes himself had identified,[19] we can state the Cartesian Circle as follows: "It is of course quite true that we must believe in the existence of a good God because it is a doctrine delivered and endorsed by reliable clear and distinct ideas, and conversely, that we must believe in the reliable clear and distinct ideas because they are endorsed by the existence of a good God; for since faith is the gift of God, He who gives us grace to believe other things can also give us grace to believe that He exists and that we can rely on clear and distinct ideas. But this argument cannot be put to skeptics, because they would judge it to be circular." Is there no escape?

Enter Curley:

Descartes's defense of reason is much stronger than it is generally given credit for being. In particular, I shall argue...that Descartes *is* attempting a rational defense of reason (not something else), and that this defense is neither obviously nor subtly circular, that on a proper understanding of the skeptical opposition, there is no reason in principle why Descartes' defense should not succeed. I shall then argue that, though the defense of reason does fail in the end, it fails because Descartes' arguments for God's existence

---

[19] "It is of course quite true that we must believe in the existence of God because it is a doctrine of Holy Scripture, and conversely, that we must believe Holy Scripture because it comes from God; for since faith is the gift of God, he who gives us grace to believe other things can also give us grace to believe that he exists. But this argument cannot be put to unbelievers because they would judge it to be circular." (CSM II, 3; AT VII, 2)

are not good enough, not because the project itself is inescapably circular. (C, 100)

How does Curley plan and prop his defense? To meet the skeptical challenges laid down in the First Meditation, Descartes must adopt, thinks Curley, "a subjective conception of proof." "Descartes will accept an argument as a proof if, as he is going through it, it compels his assent, and if, at the end of the argument, he finds that he has no valid ground for doubting the conclusion" (C, 115–116). This leads to a peculiarly anti-Cartesian conclusion: A sequence of propositions may well constitute a proof of p, and yet p may not be true. This version renders Descartes no less a proponent of a coherence theory of truth than does the version of Frankfurt in *Demons, Dreamers, and Madmen*. The central function of the subjective conception of proof is less to establish truth than it is to avoid arbitrary rejection, or establishment, of claims. Thus, Curley reads anew not the notion of *truth* in Descartes, but the notion of *proof*.[20]

So the burden of this argument lies in offering an adequate account of *proof*. The central notion in this account is the notion of the *assent-compelling proposition*. Now, where a proposition fails to compel our assent, we have no proof. But compelling our assent is not a sufficient condition. Over and above our assent being compelled, we must have "*no valid or reasonable ground for doubting it.*" The task is to characterize the latter notion. Curley offers this as a preliminary attempt:

(*D*) Someone has a valid ground for doubting a proposition (say p) if and only if he can think of (that is, able to state when requested) some other proposition (say q) such that
  (*i*) q is incompatible with p;
  (*ii*) he can think of no assent-compelling proposition incompatible with q;
  (*iii*) q explains how he might have erroneously thought p. (C, 119)

---

[20] A reader in haste to know at least in outline the central thesis of this book, and how it is arrived at, can skip the rest of this section and the next one for now, and return to them later, without sacrificing too much by way of understanding what is to follow.

The three requirements are justified as follows. Condition (*i*) is fairly plausible, for if we are to doubt the truth of one proposition by another, they must at least be contraries, if not contradictories; in short, they must be incompatible. Condition (*ii*) states a minimal evidential requirement, and the following from Descartes is adduced in support: "A reason may be valid enough to force us to doubt, and nevertheless be doubtful itself, and so not to be retained.... [Such reasons] are indeed valid so long as we have no others which induce certainty by removing doubt." (C, 120) Condition (*iii*) ensures that if a skeptic "does not offer some conjectural explanation of my error, then his attempt to cast doubt on my belief is not likely to be very persuasive" (C, 88).

The criterion for what makes a proposition, *p*, dubious on the strength of another proposition, *q*, is that the negation of the latter proposition should not compel assent. Moreover, it is a virtue of this view that what is doubtful at one stage of the inquiry need not be doubtful at a later stage. For example, while the existence of the physical world is doubted in the First Meditation as well as in all the others through the Fifth Meditation, it is no longer doubted after the Sixth. Likewise, the existence of God might be doubted in the first two meditations, but not after the Third (or at any rate after the Fifth).

But (*D*) is only a first approximation. Let us, then, consider the next approximation.

(*D'*) Someone has a valid ground for doubting a proposition, *p*, if and only if he can think of some other proposition, *q*, such that

   (*i*)   *q* is incompatible with *p*;
   (*ii*)   (*a*) if *p* is not assent-compelling, then he can think of no assent-compelling proposition incompatible with *q*;
           (*b*) if *p* is assent-compelling, then *q* is also assent-compelling,
   (*iii*)   *q* explains how he might have erroneously thought *p*. (C, 120)

Curley deems (*D'*) a bit more satisfactory, particularly because of the addition ensconced in clause (*ii*) (*b*). But first, consider clause (*ii*) (*a*). It is straightforward enough. If I wish to retain *p*, and *p* is not assent-compelling, and q is incompatible with p, then I must find a proposition, j, such that j is assent-compelling and j is incompatible with q.

Now for clause (*ii*) (*b*). Curley claims, rightly, that if we have two propositions, both of which are assent-compelling, it would seem arbitrary to opt for one over the other. We should rightly withhold assent, at best. In the phrasing of Descartes in the First Meditation, "I must withhold my assent from these former beliefs just as carefully as I would from obvious falsehoods" (CSM II, 15). But Curley makes a further claim. He says, "The effect of this change is to make the evidential requirement imposed on a valid ground of doubt vary with the 'evidence' of the proposition to be doubted" (C 120–121).

What change is that? Where a proposition to be doubted is assent-compelling, any proposition incompatible with it, so long as *it* is also assent-compelling, can serve as a ground for doubt. Where a proposition to be doubted is not assent-compelling, any proposition, no matter how improbable, incompatible with it can serve as a ground for doubt (C, 121). That the latter is a sufficient condition is understandable, but it is not a necessary condition. For consider why Descartes rejects the truths of mathematics in the First Meditation. He postulates the existence of an evil genius who tricks him into believing that two plus three is other than five. Now p, two plus three is five, is a proposition of mathematics, so it is safe to say that it is assent-compelling. Proposition q is the hypothesis of an evil genius; being, at most, a contingent proposition, it could scarcely be assent-compelling. So requirement (*ii*) (*b*) clearly goes a-begging. (Perhaps this is just the difficulty that Curley thought sprang from his amendment.)

Curley then proposes to modify (*D'*) by amending not (*ii*), but rather the incompatibility requirement, (*i*). He proposes the following:

(*D"*) Someone has a valid ground for doubting a proposition, p, if and only if he can think of some other proposition, q, such that
   (*i*) q is incompatible with p or with some principle, r, which provides the basis for his assent to p;
   (*ii*) (*a*) if either p or r is not assent-compelling, then he can think of no assent-compelling proposition incompatible with q;
           (*b*) if both p and r are assent-compelling, then so is q.

(*iii*)   *q* explains how he might have erroneously thought *p*. (C 122)

The significant clause added in requirement (*i*) is "or with some principle, *r*, which provides the basis for his assent to *p*." Not only would this include the premises, if there are any, but more significantly, it would include second-order principles used in the subsequent, reflective assessment of arguments. (Might not second-order principles be used in the argument itself – as, for instance, when principles of inference are used?) Thus, if *p* is a "first principle," then *r* could be used to derive *p* from skeptical hypotheses; if *p* is the conclusion of an argument, then *r* could be a principle governing the reliability of that type of argument. This new definition, (*D"*), would enable Descartes to draw a distinction he desired, namely, that an atheistic mathematician cannot have genuine knowledge of mathematics, which a theistic mathematician can have. Thus, an atheistic mathematician would eventually have no grounds for accepting the truth of any mathematical statement, since he can easily learn to doubt some principle, *r* – such as, "If a proposition compels assent whenever considered, or follows by compelling steps from compelling propositions, it is true." If his doubt is weakly justified, as demanded in (*D"*), then he could not claim genuine mathematical knowledge, in view of (*D"*) (*ii*) (*a*). A theistic mathematician, who has grounds for believing both in the truth of a mathematical statement as well as in the principle, *r*, can invalidate this knowledge claim only if he finds *q* to be at least as compelling as *p* and *r*. But given the proof of the existence of God, he will not be able to find any such *q*. This, in some detail, has been Curley's argument.

IV. No Escaping from the Circle

Our task now is to examine its adequacy. First, Descartes might have wondered how Curley could have gotten behind his general rule – "Whatever I perceive very clearly and distinctly is true" – to something more basic. Thus, he would have asked, "Is (*D"*) clear and distinct?" Or, "Is each part of (*D"*) clear and distinct?" If it is, then the final reason for accepting (*D"*) is his general rule. If it is not, then clearly (*D"*) is not good enough. What makes the reason good enough must *eventually* be clear and distinct, and not something else. Or, at the very least, Curley must offer concepts with which he would replace 'clear' and 'distinct'. He does not do so.

Second, can *valid or reasonable grounds for doubting p* be defined in terms of *assent-compelling*? If so, and if no alternative seems clear or forthcoming, then a proposition's capacity to compel our assent is not only a necessary condition, but also a sufficient condition for the concept of proof. Descartes' objection then might well be that Curley's view is too subjective.

This view is at variance with one of Descartes' important distinctions. In the Third Meditation, Descartes had explicitly drawn a distinction between *impulse* and *light*: "blind impulse," "natural impulse," or "spontaneous impulse," on the one hand, and the "natural light" on the other (CSM II, 26–27; AT VII, 38–39). The impulse results from the prompting of Nature, nothing more. Thus, it is uncertain whether the proposition to which we feel compelled to assent as a result of a blind impulse is true. Such can never be the case where we are compelled to assent as a result of what is revealed to us by the natural light. Descartes says, "When I say 'Nature taught me to think this', all I mean is that a spontaneous impulse leads me to believe it, not that its truth has been revealed to me by some natural light" (CSM II, 26–27; AT VII, 38). Even if (*D*") were otherwise correct, it seems to be unfaithful to the text – and to another as well. In the *Principles of Philosophy*, Descartes had drawn a distinction between moral certainty and metaphysical or absolute certainty (CSM I, 289–291; AT VIIIA, 327–329). Perhaps (*D*") might capture moral certainty, and not just psychological certainty; but it does not capture, nor can it, the metaphysical certainty that Descartes so earnestly sought.

Third, I now want to argue that (*D*") could not save for Descartes the principles of inference that he will need for constructing first and further arguments. The first is the argument of the *cogito* (if, indeed, it is an argument); the subsequent arguments concern his essence, the existence of God, the existence of the physical world, and so on. My argument proceeds as follows: Suppose *L* to be a theory of logical inference that Descartes (or Curley) prefers. But we know that Descartes *did* have to contend with other theories of logical inference.[21] Let one of these be labeled *L**. At the very least, neither theory of logical

---

[21] See Curley's brilliant chapter on methods (C, Chapter 2).

inference is compelling. Or if one is compelling, then so is the other. One might easily invoke the hypothesis of the evil genius to convince one of the implausibility of a theory of logical inference.

Now, suppose (D") were adequate. Let us then apply (D") to L^*. The first clause is satisfied: L^* is incompatible with L.[22] The second clause is satisfied: Either both are assent-compelling or neither is, and if the latter, then there is no assent-compelling proposition incompatible with L^*. The third clause is satisfied: Curley himself has done a remarkable job of explaining just that in an earlier chapter. Given the minimal condition that a proposition must satisfy in order to make it cast doubt on another proposition, I take it that L^* satisfies (D") and thus casts doubt on L. At the very least, we must withhold assent from both L and L^*. My argument is sufficiently general. So, what holds for L, holds for *any* other theory of logical inference. If no logical theory can pass muster, there cannot be a proof of the existence of God. With that, the *cogito*-argument collapses, too, since it is Curley's thesis that the latter argument depends on the former. My argument, if correct, is important for this reason: We do not have to wait until a proof of the existence of God is offered, so that we can find a lacuna in the substance of that proof. Curley's (D") assures us, with one of its consequences, that such a proof cannot be forthcoming.

Fourth, I want to demonstrate that (D") collapses when it is applied to itself. Thus it returns to the skeptic the weapons Descartes wants (and Curley wants) to wrench from him. Imagine a rival theory of "valid or reasonable grounds for doubting" a proposition – call it D^* – to be:

(D*) Someone has a valid ground for doubting a proposition (say p) if and only if he can think of (that is, can state when requested) some other proposition (say, q) such that:
q is self-consistent but is inconsistent with p.

One might argue that this is unsatisfactory because the third clause, whereby it explains why the proposition in question errs, does not exist. But I think that it need not exist, and that Curley could have

---

[22] I have skipped the clause referring to r, which serves as a basis for the proposition under consideration; in this discussion, it adds nothing but complexity to the argument.

made his demand less stringent, in accordance with the aim of the enterprise. Let me say a word about that aim.

One can offer a general explanation of the sort that Descartes did offer in the *Principles*. There he considered three astronomical theories, namely, the theories of Ptolemy, Tycho Brahe, and Copernicus (CSM I, 250–251; AT VIIIA, 85). All of these theories, save one, could account for the phenomena. The remaining two were mutually incompatible. One might draw from this consideration a familiar claim: that theories can be underdetermined by data. So if a theory has not been proved – in some strong Cartesian sense, not in the sense of a merely subjective conception of proof – we can rely on the possibility that another incompatible theory could just as well account for the data at hand. This shows, as antirealists say, that while a theory may well be empirically adequate, that does not mean it is true.

Now, consider $(D")$. Substitute (D^*) in place of q, and $(D")$ itself in place of p. Such a substitution roundly defeats $(D")$. For consider: The first clause is satisfied: (D^*) is incompatible with $(D")$. The second clause is satisfied: Neither of them is assent-compelling, and there is no assent-compelling proposition incompatible with (D^*). I take the third clause to be satisfied quite easily, and a plausible story can be told, if a story needs to be told. (I have argued that the third condition is too stringent and should not be required anyway.) Wouldn't this have given Descartes reason to reject $(D")$? This, a skeptic might claim, gives Descartes enough to be skeptical about reason.

Fifth, according to Curley, p is proved if there is no q that satisfies $(D")$. Acceptance of a notion of proof – the subjective conception of proof – would show that Descartes can, contra Curley's own recommendation, wholly dispense with the proof of the existence of God, yet accept the proof of the *cogito*, so that Curley's reading of the Third Meditation becomes untenable. Curley's view is hung on a dilemma. Let me explain this in detail.

Suppose $(D")$ is adequate. Any proposition, p, meets the requirement of certain knowledge provided it successfully resists being dethroned by another proposition, q, that is incompatible with it and that satisfies $(D")$. Now, either the *cogito* is a proposition of which we have certain knowledge or it is not. If the *cogito* is not successfully dethroned by another proposition that satisfies $(D")$, then it is certain knowledge. But then we do not require the proof of the existence of

God. However, we saw that Curley insists that – a central theme of his book – we must have the proof of the existence of God in order to be assured of the proof of the *cogito*, so that in the absence of that proof, the *cogito* is not such a piece of knowledge. We must buy all or nothing, as Curley said. Presumably, the proposition that satisfies (*D"*), and thus dethrones the *cogito*, is the hypothesis of the evil genius.[23] This, as we saw, was Curley's reading of the relevant passage (CSM II, 25; AT VII, 36) in the Third Meditation.

Curley finds Descartes' proofs for the existence of God defective. What is of enormous interest is *how* he finds them defective. He finds them defective on *substantive* grounds. Thus, he finds that the principle of causation, which Descartes presupposes, wanting – or he finds that, at least since Hume, philosophers have found it wanting. He finds that the argument unjustifiably presupposes a first cause, if not of the first member of a series, then of the series of contingent beings. (Curley does not quite ask this question, though we might: If there is nothing wrong in there being an infinite regress, what is wrong in there being an infinite regress in that which created a contingent series?) He finds defective the talk about formal and objective reality, and with it the associated talk of degrees of reality. To be sure, much of this is standard fare among Descartes' critics.

It is worth quoting Curley in full:

[Descartes] admits that indubitability is compatible with falsity. But he is unconcerned about this, not because he is not interested in absolute truth, but because he thinks that rejecting a proposition which is, in his sense, indubitable is a patently arbitrary act. The skeptic does not want to be, and does not think he is, patently arbitrary. Descartes' argument is designed to show that by the skeptic's own standards, the skeptic would be acting arbitrarily if he rejected the argument.

I think Descartes is right. There is no difficulty in principle about Descartes' procedure in the *Meditations*. The really serious objection to his argument is the substantive one that his arguments for the existence of a nondeceiving God are just not compelling. (C, 118)

This, however, misses the most interesting problem or difficulty. *Even if* one could find a proof of the existence of God – say, a version

---

[23] See Appendix A for some connected arguments as they emerge from Jeffrey Tlumak's "Certainty and Cartesian Method."

of the ontological argument, which Curley respects more than other proofs for the existence of God (C, 125) – the truth of the substance of the premises in that argument would not be nearly enough. It would not be enough because besides true premises, we would also require sound rules of inference in order to move from premises to the conclusion. But given (D"), the proof would be impossible. Why? Because (D") could not recognize the soundness of any rules of inference – for reasons given earlier. Thus (D") makes the proof of the existence of God impossible.

Someone might say in Descartes' defense: "Not necessarily, surely. One might be able to come up with a set of rules of inference that do satisfy (D") and a proof for the existence of God that is sound in the light of those rules of inference. Thus far we have just not found any." Suppose, then, this were possible (as I think it is not). If so, those very rules of inference could be used to prove the *cogito*-argument to be sound, without the demonstration of the existence of God. Consequently, we do not have to buy all or nothing.

Finally, and most importantly, has Curley succeeded in showing Descartes the way out of the Circle? Is there a parallel circular argument? Consider the following: "Distinguish between a theist logician and a nontheist logician. Like his counterpart in mathematics, a nontheist logician can never have genuine knowledge, since, in the absence of a proof of God's existence, he can never be sure that the principles on which his science of logic is founded are true. Only the theist logician can be so certain. Thus: It is, of course, quite true that we must believe in the existence of God and the reliability of human reason because they satisfy the doctrine of (D"), and conversely, that we must believe in the doctrine of (D") because it comes from God and is demonstrated by the reliability of human reason." This argument cannot be put to a skeptic, because he would judge it to be circular – rightly, so far.

V. Another Failed Attempt

This section examines a different attempt to show how Descartes might escape from the Cartesian Circle; it is an attempt by James van Cleve, presented in his widely discussed paper "Foundationalism,

Epistemic Principles, and the Cartesian Circle." This attempt, I shall argue, also fails.

Van Cleve argues cogently against Alan Gewirth's "The Cartesian Circle" and Fred Feldman's "Epistemic Appraisal and the Cartesian Circle," both attempts to avoid the Cartesian Circle in their own distinctive ways; Van Cleve then proceeds to offer his own way of exiting from the Circle. Van Cleve distinguishes psychological, practical, and metaphysical certainty.[24] Psychological certainty is merely an irresistible compulsion to believe; practical certainty is the sort of certainty involved in ordinary knowing of the justified-true-belief variety; and metaphysical certainty is an objective affair, implying truth. To answer the question, "How can certainty about God possibly give rise to certainty about clear and distinct perceptions?," Gewirth touted psychological certainty, while Fred Feldman touted practical certainty, such as the kind of certainty we have about God; and from each of these claims, Gewirth and Feldman, respectively, attempted to derive metaphysical certainty about clear and distinct ideas. Van Cleve persuasively demonstrates that from these watered-down concepts of certainty one could not extract metaphysical certainty. Thus far, this is an exercise in Hume.

Van Cleve, however, goes on to offer his own alternative way of escaping from the Circle, one that I find objectionable as well. Following Kenny, van Cleve, in reading the general rule – "Whatever I perceive very clearly and distinctly is true"– draws the following distinction:

(A) For all *P*, if I clearly and distinctly perceive that *P*, then I am certain that *P*.
(B) I am certain that (for all *P*, if I clearly and distinctly perceive that *P*, then *P*). (111)

"The difference," says Van Cleve, "is that (A) says that whenever I clearly and distinctly perceive any proposition, I will be certain of *it* (the proposition in question), whereas (B) says that I am certain of a *general principle* connecting clear and distinct perception with truth. Clearly, (A) could be true even though (B) were false. (B) requires that I have the concept of clear and distinct perception, but (A) does not." (111) "The point I have been insisting upon could be summed

[24] For a very useful discussion of some of these distinctions see Edwin M. Curley, "Certainty: Psychological, Moral, and Metaphysical."

up as follows: (*A*) is not a principle I have to *apply* in order to gain knowledge; I need only *fall under* it." (114)

In the *cogito*-state, I agree that the former doubter cannot know a truth, even the first truth, by seeing that he has applied any principle, because at this stage he *knows* of no principle to apply; he has doubted them all. Even his doubt itself, as we saw, generates that truth. But unless van Cleve's doubter is remarkably un-Cartesian and philosophically lax, it is unfathomable how he could refrain from doing what Kenny urged that he should do – and what van Cleve denied that he need do (113, note 34):

> If every other certainty is to be built upon the certainty afforded by clear and distinct perception, then it is essential, if there is to be any certainty at all of the type Descartes sought, that one should be able to be certain that one is clearly and distinctly perceiving something. Moreover, it must be possible to be certain of this independently of being certain of the truth of what one perceives. For Descartes offers it as the sovereign methodological principle for the avoidance of error never to make a judgment about anything that one does not clearly and distinctly understand. (K, 197)

Kenny distinguishes what we may be uncertain about. (a) We may be uncertain about whether or not our current mental state is clear and distinct, and even if we are certain about that, (b) we may be uncertain about whether or not our current clear and distinct mental state is true. Consider, then, van Cleve's three claims: First, there is a claim about what kind of certainty Descartes sought: "The certainty [Descartes] sought was certainty in a sense entailing both *maximal evidence* and *truth*" (106). Second, there is a claim about what constitutes a reason for doubt: "Reasons to doubt need not be certain; they need only be epistemically possible. . . . I define epistemic possibility as follows: if *P* is a proposition that *S* is considering at *t*, then *P* is *epistemically possible* for *S* at *t* if and only if *S* is not certain at *t* of non-*P*." (108) Let me call this claim *R**. Third, there is a claim about what I need to know in order to become certain of a proposition: "I maintain that, in order to become certain of a proposition, I do not need to know that I am clearly and distinctly perceiving it, nor that whatever I so perceive is either certain or true. It is enough that I *do* clearly and distinctly perceive the proposition. (*A*) *says* that this is enough. . . . It follows that nothing else is necessary." (113)

So much for the claims. Substitute not-(B) – the denial of (B) – for reasons in R^*. Now, obviously, not-(B) is not clearly and distinctly perceived at this stage (past the *cogito*, but before the completion of the proof of the existence of God); in fact, van Cleve allows (B) to be false even if (A) is true (by implication, even if P is true). But for the doubter of the First Meditation, this constitutes a good reason to cast P in doubt: For if (B) is false, he can invest *no* epistemic confidence in any particular proposition, say P, that he may be entertaining at the moment, because he can and should ask, "How can I justify my belief in this proposition, P, which may well be misleading me now, given the epistemic possibility of not-(B)?" Raising and answering such a question is the *only* way to acquire *maximal* evidence for P. The only thing that prevents him from doubting P is his refraining from asking that pertinent question. Consequently, he may well *fall* under the concept, yet not *know* – unless he knows the general principle – *that* he has done so. (As a parallel: The doubter of the First Meditation may fall under the concept of walking, but he surely does not *know* that he falls under it unless he confronts and satisfies the skeptic's scruples.)

How could that doubter falling under a concept convince himself that the mental state he is presently in is not merely the state of psychological certainty rather than the state of metaphysical certainty? Van Cleve says, "Moreover, to say (as I do) that we must be certain at the outset of some clear and distinct perceptions is not to say (as I don't) that we must be certain at the outset of the proposition *some clear and distinct perceptions are true*. Nor is it to say that we must be certain of a more specific proposition of the form *those clear and distinct perceptions that are F* (e.g. bathed in the light of nature) *are true*." (114) Well, let us grant him some sort of certainty. Evidently, it is not metaphysical certainty of the sort that Descartes sought. Let us call it certainty*. With this in hand, van Cleve wishes to proceed to the proof of the existence of God, and thence to the claim that (A) is true (115). Even if van Cleve is right in thinking that this shows that as a starting point (A) was not arbitrarily espoused (115–117), it does not help him out of the Circle. If each premise in the proof of the existence of God is known only with certainty*, then one knows that God exists only with certainty*. Using van Cleve's own form of argument (against Gewirth and Feldman), one might say that whatever follows thereafter

cannot have a certainty that goes beyond certainty*. We can never
free ourselves from the mire of certainty* to arrive at metaphysical
certainty.[25]

VI. How *Not* to Read the *Meditations*: A Skeptic's Reply

There is one challenge that the foregoing must face, a challenge that
can be constructed from the works of Stephen Gaukroger, principally
from his book *Descartes: An Intellectual Biography* and his paper "The
Sources of Descartes's Procedure of Deductive Demonstration in Metaphysics and Natural Philosophy."[26] Let us begin by raising the question,
"What was the method Descartes adopted in his deductive demonstrations in his *Meditations*?" Gaukroger answers that there are three significant alternatives to consider, two of which – the geometrical method
and the humanist-Aristotelian method – in his view present mistaken
ways of reading the *Meditations*; the third, the method of *disputationes* –
his own alternative way of reading – he deems satisfactory. But if this way
of reading is correct, it must have a significant impact on the reading
of the *cogito*, since the *cogito* is thought to be a demonstrative argument.
How might a skeptic respond to Gaukroger's historical conjecture?

Consider the first method: the geometrical method. This method,
says Gaukroger, cannot offer the right way to read the *Meditations*.

---

[25] The discussion on the Cartesian Circle has had a curious history. There are two solutions available, and it is never the case that both views are held in roughly equal
regard. When the fortunes of one view goes up, those of the other decline. And which
solution holds the center of attention among Cartesian scholars depends on other
things, not always of intrinsic value. If the central thesis of this book is correct, then
perhaps the second view will be accorded the pride of place that it richly deserves.

    As is well known, Descartes offered the second view in order to escape from the
Cartesian Circle in the *Meditations* itself. In the Fifth Meditation, he wrote: "Admittedly my nature is such that so long as I perceive something very clearly and distinctly
I cannot but believe it to be true. But my nature is also such that I cannot fix my
mental vision continually on the same thing, so as to keep perceiving it clearly; and
often the memory of a previously made judgement may come back, when I am no
longer attending to the arguments which led me to make it. And so other arguments
can now occur to me which might easily undermine my opinion, if I did not possess
knowledge of God; and I should thus never have true and certain knowledge about
anything, but only shifting and changing opinions." (CSM II, 48; AT VII, 69)

    And it is surely interesting that when Descartes came to reply to his two critics,
Mersenne and Arnauld, the *only* solution he offered as a way out of the Circle (alleged, by his lights) was the second solution (CSM II, 89, 104–105, 150, 171; AT VII,
124–125, 146, 214, 245–246, respectively).

[26] Hereinafter GS.

Juxtapose Euclid's *Elements,* Descartes' *Geometry,* and his *Meditations*
and we find that each differs from the others in significant respects.
Thus, Euclid's work begins with definitions and axioms and derives
theorems, trivial and not-so-trivial, from them. This is the stock deductive model. But Descartes' *Geometry* does no such thing. There the
reader is introduced, in a few pages, to how an arithmetical operation
can be represented geometrically; thereafter he is immediately thrown
into the midst of a serious and difficult problem, namely, Pappus' locus
problem for four or more lines. Descartes' concern in his *Geometry* "is
not deductive demonstration but rather problem solving and the elaboration of techniques for problem solving" (GS, 49). This, however,
says Gaukroger, is not an accidental feature of Descartes' procedure –
he forswears the geometrical method as a matter of *principle.* Why?
Because Descartes had accused the ancients of using this method with
guile: The ancients were insinuating that they had been led to their
discoveries in the way in which they presented their results, and such
false advertising enabled them not only to gain undeserved recognition, but also to conceal their true method. As early as the *Regulae,*[27]
Descartes had admonished thus:

> I have come to think that these writers themselves, with a kind of pernicious
> cunning, later suppressed this mathematics as, notoriously, many inventors
> are known to have done where their own discoveries were concerned. They
> may have feared that their method, just because it was so easy and simple,
> would be depreciated if it were divulged; so to gain our admiration, they may
> have shown us, as the fruits of their method, some barren truths proved by
> clever arguments, instead of teaching us the method itself, which might have
> dispelled our admiration. (CSM I, 19; ATX, 376–377)

Descartes' reasoning is not entirely perspicuous, if he is about what
Gaukroger claims he is about. First, what is "this mathematics" that
the ancients later suppressed? Is it just their method? Second, we can
distinguish between a method of discovery and the results to which it
leads. If all the results were barren, few would have been moved by the
ancient mathematicians; at the very least, this was not true of Descartes.
Consequently, some results must have been fecund and were no less
the fruits of the method of yore. Third, the ancient mathematicians

---

[27] Various parts of this work were composed at different times.

wanted to pass themselves off as clever for the results they were able to discover; so they concealed their easy and simple method for fear of being thought no more ingenious than they in fact were. Consequently, there was a useful method – albeit an easy and simple one. Fourth, there was a powerful desire on Descartes' part in the *Regulae* to make evident a method of proceeding in mathematics and science that would speed up discovery. Descartes is implying that had the ancient mathematicians revealed their methods, we, their successors, might have been led to make similar discoveries after them (otherwise, the analogy with the many inventors makes little sense). They thus failed us, and for this they deserve to be chastised. Fifth and finally, the *Meditations* seems to have far less in common with Descartes' *Geometry* than with the *Elements*. Here the reader is not introduced, in a few pages, to some philosophical preliminaries and thereafter immediately thrown into the midst of a serious and difficult philosophical problem, namely, how can we be sure the external world exists? It would clearly be false to say of the *Meditations* that in it Descartes was not interested in deductive demonstration but rather in philosophical problem solving and the elaboration of techniques for philosophical problem solving. Descartes approvingly cites in the *Meditations* the works of Archimedes, Apollonius, and Pappus, and explicitly makes several comparisons between their geometries and his metaphysics; above all, he speaks repeatedly of "proofs," "demonstrative proofs," and "exact demonstrations" and leaves no doubt that he is doing in his *Meditations* what good mathematicians had done in their own works[28] (CSM II, 4–6; AT VII, 4–6). The lesson to be learned, then, is that Descartes was not so much opposed to the geometrical method as he was, rightly, to moving by guile. His method, he thought, would lead to interesting results in metaphysics no less than in mathematics; but he would not deny to the public, or at least to the able, access to that method.[29]

Consider the next method of discovery: the humanist-Aristotelian method. Peter of Spain and Lambert of Auxerre had defined dialectic,

---

[28] In a letter of July 31, 1640, to Huygens, Descartes wrote: "For I draw a comparison between my work in this area and the demonstrations of Appollonius. Everything in the latter is really very clear and certain." (CSMK, 150; AT III 751) Since it would take too much space to cite long passages from the "Second Set of Replies," I ask the reader to consult CSM II, 110–111; AT VII, 155–157.

[29] These claims are made not only in *Regulae*, but also in the *Discourse on the Method*.

following Aristotle, as "the art of arts, the science of sciences, possessing the path to the principles of all methods" (GS, 50). This need not be a method of discovery, but in the scholastic tradition it was widely recognized as such. "The details," writes Gaukroger, "of how the procedure was to be effected were generally left vague, however, and if one takes this 'dialectic' to be something conducted in a systematic way, starting from first principles, then it is hard to see what it could be other than syllogistic" (GS, 50). But Descartes, in clear anticipation of John Stuart Mill, had roundly rejected the syllogism as a means of discovery. In rule 10 of *Regulae*, he forewarns against logicians' using the syllogism. Such logicians "are unable to devise by their rules any syllogism with a true conclusion unless they already have the whole syllogism, i.e., unless they have already ascertained in advance the very truth deduced in that syllogism." Plainly, it follows that neither the discovery nor the justification of the *cogito* could be a syllogistic argument – and Descartes knew no other.

Ramond Lull (1233–1315) proposed an alternative method, "the art of finding the truth" (*ars inveniendi veritatem*). Lull's aim was to devise a universal language from the axioms of which new truths could be generated, especially ones pertaining to the doctrines of the Trinity and the Incarnation. Henricus Cornelius Agrippa's *De incertitudine et vanitate de scientarium et artum* (1527) shed Lull's religious goals in the devising and use of his method, and exhibited two key, almost Cartesian, features. First, that method is a general and universal science: It advocated starting from absolutely certain principles, armed with an equally certain criterion of knowledge; and second, it offered a way of ordering all knowledge. Gaukroger then argues that Descartes had utterly rejected the Lullian approach by the late 1620s, "and there is no question of it playing a role in, for example, the *Meditations*" (GS, 51). Gaukroger further adduces Descartes' letter to Father Marin Mersenne (November 20, 1629) as evidence. In that letter, Descartes had explicitly rejected the possibility of discovering anything new vis-à-vis a constructed universal language. Such a language could serve only as a vehicle for expressing truths already discovered, not one in or through which new truths could be discovered. However, Agrippa's 1527 treatise with its two features can be easily understood without any reference to a universal language; indeed, it could be understood even if one admitted the impossibility of a universal language. That being the case, to what extent should Agrippa's method be regarded as a way of discovering new truths, and what Cartesian arguments might be offered against such a watered-down enterprise? But let me proceed to the third method, the method of *disputationes*: Gaukroger's own preferred alternative.

In 1513, the Lateran Council, held under Pope Leo X, condemned any reading of Aristotle that led to the conclusion that there was no personal immortality, and admonished philosophers and theologians alike to rise in defense of the contrary claim. As a result, a new genre of commentaries arose, commentaries by Suarez, Fonesca, Toletus, and the Coimbra commentators. Unlike the medieval commentaries on Aristotle that attempted to use Aristotle to provide Christianity with a philosophical foundation, as in the works of Saint Thomas Aquinas, these commentators simply reworked, revised, and rewrote Aristotle.[30] There was an extant body of Aristotle's theory that was to be reconstituted and there was an explicit religious agenda: Any reconstitution that did not yield the required theological conclusion was to be rejected; those that yielded the desired conclusion were to be retained. Descartes was schooled in metaphysics by these commentaries. Gaukroger adverts to three reservations about how this model was to be applied to the *Meditations* (GS, 57–59). The reservations were that the *Meditations* did not read like a textbook, nor did it belong to the genre of devotional manuals; that there was no independently existing metaphysical material that the *Meditations* set out to reconstitute; and finally, that Descartes himself thought he was doing analysis in the *Meditations*. But in the end, Gaukroger sets these reservations aside and concludes that the *disputationes* "explicitly enable one to provide a defense of doctrines whose truth one is already certain of, by showing how such doctrines can be deduced from shared premises. And they do this in a way that makes no reference at all to mathematical demonstration, but which, on the contrary, is designed *specifically* for metaphysical, theological, and natural-philosophical arguments." (GS, 59)

I find this view deeply mistaken. My primary concern is to show that if Descartes did what he is alleged to have done, then his philosophical

---

[30] See Charles H. Lohr, "Jesuit Aristotelianism and Sixteenth Century Metaphysics," "Metaphysics," and "The Sixteenth-Century Transformation of the Aristotelian Division of the Speculative Sciences." See also G, 59–61.

enterprise is quite suspect – he gives the skeptics enough to cavil about. If I am right, perhaps historians of ideas more astute than I will find good reasons why they should confront Gaukroger's historical conjecture head on. There are three reasons for my misgivings. First, a skeptic or an atheist might claim that if the *Meditations* are nothing more than an expression of what follows from shared premises – premises shared by the believers, that is – then Descartes' pleading to the faculty of Sorbonne that with his arguments in the *Meditations* he would convince the most hardened disbeliever was something of a sham. Descartes had offered to convince the skeptics and the atheists (in obedience to the dictates of the Lateran Council) by demonstrative proofs based on natural reason; only then could he demonstrate, as he himself foresaw, that his arguments were noncircular.[31]

There were several interpretations of Aristotle in circulation: "Metaphysics had become an extremely contentious subject by the sixteenth century, not so much because of the proliferation of Platonist and other rivals to Aristotelian philosophy, but because of the proliferation of different and unorthodox interpretations of Aristotle." (GS, 55) Some interpretations were scarcely Christian in orientation, so that, at a minimum, Descartes would have had on his hands the epistemological problem of how to determine the truth of an Aristotelian interpretation of a Christian variety from a non-Christian variety. Moreover, if Descartes was justified in his approach, should the atheists have gone about their business constructing an interpretation of Aristotle based on *their* shared premises? How would the author of the First Meditation have reacted to such an interpretation?

Second, in mathematics Descartes had drawn a sharp distinction between the analytic method and the synthetic method, or the method of exposition. Once Descartes had solved a mathematical problem on a satisfactory basis of analysis, his synthetic demonstration did not particularly worry him; he did this, claims Gaukroger, in his *Geometry* all the time, where he mostly offered an analytic solution to a mathematical problem, and only on occasion the synthetic proof (GS, 54). Perhaps, then, in metaphysics Descartes had in mind a parallel distinction: Analytic problem-solving techniques were to be used in solving a metaphysical problem – for example, does God exist? – and once

---

[31] See the opening page of the *Meditations*, "Dedicatory Letter to the Sorbonne."

he had that solution, he could then offer a synthetic demonstration. But he did not do that, for he thought ill of the synthetic or syllogistic method. Why then did he even occasionally use it in mathematics? Did he even occasionally use the method of *disputationes* in mathematics? Did Descartes have any such problem-solving techniques in metaphysics? If he did, and did not share them with the public, he would have been no less guilty of low cunning than the ancient mathematicians he chided. If he did not have them, and had no genuine analytical solutions to metaphysical problems, his guilt would have been immeasurable.

But what constituted a genuine analytical solution? Imagine: In writing his *Geometry*, Descartes was not concerned about the order in which the theorems were presented. He took whatever important mathematical problems struck his fancy and solved them analytically. Each theorem was presented in the order in which he solved it, there being no particular order in which he solved them. Then, imagine that he wrote another book called *The Philosophical Foundations of Geometry*. In this second book, Descartes took the theorems of the first book and analyzed each of them in order to uncover the basic axioms or principles on which it rested. Next, he collected all of these axioms or principles and attempted to simplify the list. The lot being simplified, he placed them at the start of the book. Finally, he rearranged the entire order of the theorems as they appeared in the first book in such a way that no theorem in the second book came before any theorem it needed for its own demonstration. Question: How was the justification of the theorems in the first book in essence different from the theorems in the second book? How could Descartes have claimed to have made a discovery in the absence of a proof?

Third, in light of Gaukroger's thesis, it might be a very useful exercise to conjecture how Descartes might have persuaded himself about the genuineness of the solutions to the philosophical problems he was engaged upon, and then to compare that conjecture with what we actually find in his *Meditations*. It should not be at all surprising, I submit, to find that the conjectures are very nearly identical. This would be especially true of Descartes' *cogito*. Descartes may well have had an inkling of the truth of the *cogito* – indeed, he had more than an inkling, given its role in the *Discourse*. But the more he thought about the problem and the provisional solution, the better his sense of the *cogito* became, until it was finally embedded in the Second Meditation.

I conclude with a cautionary note. The central claim of this chapter is embedded in section II, wherein the argument for the new Cartesian Circle is presented; some of the other sections treat of the old Cartesian Circle and how to escape from it. The argument for the new Cartesian Circle shows how Descartes' attempt to prove the existence of God is foiled: In order to prove that God exists, Descartes needs to justify the rules of logic; but in order to establish the rules of logic, Descartes needs to establish that God exists. Descartes' system is riddled with this circular argument. The importance of the argument, for the main thesis of this book, lies less in showing why Descartes' proof for the existence of God needs to be amended than in showing that *before* the Third Meditation, the rules of logic have no proper Cartesian anchor; they can be open to serious doubt. Caution: The conclusion of this argument is limited. It is not intended to throw everything reason touches into disrepute; it is only intended to show that whatever else may be reliable as a deliverance of Natural Reason – say, Descartes' intuition – no reliance on the rules of logic has been, or can be, justified, even by the end of the Second Meditation. Naturally, our next task is to show what impact, if any, this has on Descartes' *cogito*.

5

The Five Ways

Often a system of philosophy rests on a central claim. The rest of the system is so tightly interwoven with that central claim that changing it changes the system, challenging it challenges the system. The system is like a spider's web: Touch the spider, and the whole web reverberates. The central claim of the logical positivists of early twentieth-century Vienna, and of their immediate successors, was the principle of verification: A sentence of a language was meaningful if and only if it was either analytically true or empirically verifiable. On the basis of such a central claim, a new philosophy was defined; metaphysics was eliminated; a new critique of ethics and theology was propounded; an alternative account of personal identity was suggested; and a fresh view of the nature of logical and mathematical propositions was touted.[1] With the alteration of the principle of verification, the system was altered. When a final successful assault was launched on said principle, the system as a whole tottered. As a consequence, metaphysics began to flourish again.

In Descartes' philosophy, the *cogito* is the central claim. Consequently, it is quite important to be as clear as possible about the precise nature of this claim. Thus: Is the *cogito* an argument? Why is this problem so important? Why is it necessary to settle the issue of whether or not the *cogito* is an argument? After all, one might argue, we have captured a very interesting truth: What does it matter whether that

---

[1] Still worth reading is A. J. Ayer's *Language, Truth and Logic*, first published in 1936.

truth is encased in an argument (a sequence of appropriately related propositions) or in a single proposition? The reason is that the answer to the question, "Is the *cogito* an argument?", affects our understanding of other issues in Descartes, including Descartes' views on syllogism, discovery, and explanation; his views on the nature and purpose of questioning the truths of logic and mathematics; and his views on the role of memory and will.

In section I, I set up five distinct ways of reading the *cogito* as an argument. To my knowledge, the rest of the ways of reading the *cogito* as an argument are just variations upon these five themes. Then, in the next section, I discuss another way to read the *cogito*, a famous view that reads the *cogito* as a performance. I have two aims in presenting these claims. First, each way illuminates a certain part of this dark and complex problem, even if it eventually fails as a whole. Second, and more importantly, despite their overt differences – different failures, different insights – each way of reading the *cogito* as an argument bears a simple and striking resemblance to the others. This core similarity is defective. The defect is isolated in this chapter, and is shown to be irreparable in the next.

I. The Five Ways...

Reconsider the famous passage in the Second Meditation:

> But there is a deceiver of supreme power and cunning who is deliberately and constantly deceiving me. In that case I too undoubtedly exist, if he is deceiving me; and let him deceive me as much as he can, he will never bring it about that I am nothing so long as I think that I am something. So after considering everything very thoroughly, I must finally conclude that this proposition, *I am, I exist,* is necessarily true whenever it is put forward by me or conceived in my mind. (CSM II, 17; AT VII, 25)

Conspicuous by its absence is the word 'therefore'. Hence, one might assume that Descartes was not offering an argument. But there are at least two considerations that militate against such an assumption. First, there is an equally famous passage in *Discourse on the Method* that serves as a counterpoint:

> But immediately I noticed that while I was trying thus to think everything false, it was necessary that I, who was thinking this, was something. And observing

that this truth, "*I am thinking, therefore I exist*" was so firm and sure that all the most extravagant suppositions of the sceptics were incapable of shaking it, I decided that I could accept it without scruple as the first principle of the philosophy I was seeking. (CSM I, 127; AT VI, 32)

Also, consider the following passage in *The Search for Truth*, which, although posthumously published, was written (probably) in summer of 1641, when Descartes was intensely occupied with the issues raised and discussed in the *Meditations on First Philosophy*. Here it is, in the words of Eudoxus, the mouthpiece of Descartes:

You cannot deny that you have such doubts; rather it is certain that you have them, so certain in fact that you cannot doubt your doubting. Therefore it is also true that you who are doubting exist; this is so true that you can no longer have any doubts about it. (CSM II, 409–410; AT X, 515)

A little later, here is Eudoxus again:

I quite share your view, Epistemon, that we must know what doubt is, what thought is, what existence is, before being convinced of the truth of this inference, "I am doubting, therefore I exist," or what amounts to the same thing, "I am thinking, therefore I exist." (CSM II, 417; AT X, 523)

The many 'therefore's, and at least one use of 'inference', lend support to the claim that Descartes' *cogito* passages had better be construed as an argument.

There is a second reason. Descartes had explicitly regarded the *cogito* passages as an enthymematic argument, a syllogism with a missing general premise, such as, "Whatever thinks, exists."[2] Without it, the argument is invalid. With the general premise supplied, the argument is valid and reads as follows:

[1]   Whatever thinks, exists
[2]   I think
      ———————————
[3]   ∴ I exist

Once such an argument has been set up, philosophers have worried over the following sorts of problems: What is the relationship between

---

[2] Descartes, *Conversation With Burman*, 90–91. For details see the following discussion.

the general proposition and the particular? Which one comes first? Does, as Gottfried Wilhelm Leibniz thought, the general come first, because without it we could not know the particular? Or, as John Locke thought, does the particular come first, from which the general is adduced? But if Leibniz is right, then Descartes has not said anything novel in the conclusion that he has not already said in the premises (WM, 57–58). On the other hand, if Locke is right, the argument is merely inductive, and it is a probable syllogism of the sort Descartes had expressly condemned (CSM I, 11; AT X, 363–364). Another problem that has been raised is: Is existence a predicate? An elegant problem first introduced by Kenny is whether Descartes' *cogito* argument is compatible with his ontological argument (K, Chapters 4 and 7).

Thus we have been led to suppose that the *cogito* is an argument. This approach fails, I think, because it fails to pay attention to what are seemingly harmless elements in most of these passages; it fails to take into account such things as the role, if any, of memories at this stage in the argument in *Meditations on First Philosophy*; and above all, it fails to take into account what was said in the First Meditation. It can be demonstrated that whatever Descartes may have said about the *cogito*, expressly or implicitly, he is philosophically preempted, unless the First Meditation is a sham, from regarding it as an argument.

There is a passage in Willard Van Orman Quine's *Methods of Logic* that nicely summarizes the history of the attempts to capture the *cogito* in the net of an argument.

When we want to analyze and appraise a logical inference which someone has propounded, we have to take such suppressed premises into account. At this point two problems demand solution simultaneously: the problem of filling in details of a logical deduction leading from premises to desired conclusion, and the problem of eking out the premises so that such a deduction can be constructed. Solution of either problem presupposes solution of the other; we cannot set up the deduction without adequate premises, and we cannot know what added premises will be needed until we know how the deduction is to run.[3]

There are, in all, five ways in which the *cogito* has been considered as an argument, with varying premises and with different runs of deduction.

[3] W. V. O. Quine, *Methods of Logic*, 186.

First, it has been regarded as a syllogistic argument. The *cogito* is put in the form of an argument with which Descartes would have been familiar. Second, the *cogito* is considered to be an enthymematic syllogistic argument. "Whatever thinks, exists," or some variant of it, serves implicitly as the major premise in the latter argument, explicitly in the former. These two are, historically speaking, the most common representation of Descartes' view. Third, the *cogito* has been considered to be an enthymematic nonsyllogistic argument, invoking the aid of first-order logic or quantification theory. So considered, the *cogito* consists (usually) of two or more premises, and the missing premises are filled out in various ways. Fourth, the *cogito* is considered to be a one-premise argument, with "Whatever thinks, exists," serving not as a premise but rather as a rule of inference. Fifth and finally, the *cogito* is construed as a particular kind of argument that invokes the notion of presupposition. I shall argue that while each one of these attempts to read the *cogito* as an argument has peculiar problems of its own, each is foiled by a singular, irreparable difficulty.

A. *The First and Second Ways*

I shall consider the first two views together, since they both purport to regard the *cogito* as a syllogism, the uninteresting difference being that one is fully elaborated, the other is enthymematic.[4] The missing implicit major premise of the latter syllogism, "Whatever thinks, exists," or some variant of it, occurs explicitly in the former. Now, suppose that Frans Burman's (1628–1679) report of a conversation

---

[4] Gordon Baker was kind enough to suggest, in conversation, that the central thesis of this book, namely, that the *cogito* is not an argument, is not implausible. But so deep-rooted is the tradition of regarding it is an argument that when one consults the book *Descartes' Dualism*, one finds that the authors, Baker and Morris, repeatedly speak of the *cogito* as if it were an argument. They do not recognize any particular argument pattern that the *cogito* is alleged to be, but they speak of premises, argument, entailment, inference, and validity in connection with the *cogito*. For example, they speak of "admissible premises in the argument schema of the *Cogito*," (34); "Thus, *pace* Hobbes, '*Cogito, ergo sum res cogitans*' is a valid inference," (65); "these reports play a parallel role as the premise for the *Cogito*" (72); and other examples can be found on 76 note 43, 115, and 117. In fairness, their book is on Descartes' famous two-substance doctrine, and it sets out to demolish a different legend about Descartes' philosophy; it is not principally about the *cogito*.

with Descartes is accurate:

> Before this conclusion, *I think, therefore, I am,* one can know the major, *whatever thinks is,* because it is really prior to my conclusion, and my conclusion rests on it. And so in the *Principles* the author says that it is prior, because it is always implicitly presupposed and prior. But I do not on that account always know expressly and explicitly that it is prior, and I do know my conclusion first, because I attend only to what I experience in myself.[5]

This seems unproblematic enough: The major premise is always in the background, even if the conclusion is reached first. In the final analysis, we have a syllogistic argument. There are at least three problems with this. First, if we are searching for the first principle, the first truth, then the *cogito* is arrived at first, the major premise is reckoned next. Note that the *cogito* is regarded as a truth, a first principle, a first item of knowledge, a proposition, an inference, a piece of knowledge, a consequent, and a conclusion, but it is never (?) called an argument. Indeed, Descartes is explicit that the major premise is dependent on establishing the conclusion:

> When someone says "I am thinking, therefore I am, or I exist," he does not deduce existence from thought by means of a syllogism, but recognizes it as something self-evident by a simple intuition of the mind. This is clear from the fact that if he were deducing it by means of a syllogism, he would have to have had previous knowledge of the major premiss "Everything which thinks is, or exists"; yet in fact he learns it from experiencing in his own case that it is impossible that he should think without existing. [6] It is the nature of our mind

---

5 Descartes, *Conversation With Burman,* 90–91. Anyone – such as Kenny, for example – who claims that *cogito ergo sum* is an argument, and that this is shown by the appearance of *"ergo,"* might consider the following: First, few seem to have noticed that even in this passage Descartes is referring to *I think, therefore, I am* as the conclusion! And a conclusion is a single proposition. Second, the most famous *cogito* passage from the *Meditations on First Philosophy* does not contain a conclusion indicator. Kenny acknowledges this, but he claims that the *"cogito"* is also missing. On the contrary, I take it to be not only present in that passage, but elaborately present in the following guise: "whenever it is put forward by me or conceived in my mind."

6 To anyone who, like Kenny, sees this as a clear instance of Descartes' endorsing the view that the *cogito* is a one-premise argument, I reply: First, Descartes does not say – not even implicitly – that it is an argument. He simply remarks on what an individual might learn from his own case, leaving it entirely open whether what he learns, what convinces this individual, is based on a deductive argument or on an intuition of a single proposition. Second, Descartes is insistent that the *cogito* cannot be a syllogism. From this assertion, it will not do to infer that it is a nonsyllogistic argument. Third, Descartes avers that we can know general truths only from particular ones. Fourth, if the *cogito* were an argument, it would leave the general principles of inference entirely

to construct general propositions on the basis of our knowledge of particular ones. (CSM II, 100; AT VII, 140–141)

This, as Bernard Williams rightly points out, is no mere *psychological* observation; it is surely intended as something more. But here we disagree on what that more is. Williams goes on to say that "if we suppose that Descartes believed for one instant that, as a matter of logic, the proposition that everything that thinks exists can be established by *induction* from one's own case – and that he used this as an argument to deny that the *cogito* is a syllogism – we should be obliged to say that he was mistaken." (WC, 91).

Why would we be so obliged? How *else* is the general proposition, "Whatever thinks, exists," to be known? Descartes himself often took the inductive approach, not only in the empirical sciences but also in mathematics: "[S]ay," says Descartes,

I wish to show by enumeration that the area of a circle is greater than the area of any other geometrical figure whose perimeter is the same length as the circle's. I need not review every geometrical figure. If I can demonstrate that this fact holds for some particular figures, I shall be entitled to conclude by induction that the same holds true in all the other cases as well. (CSM I, 27; AT X, 390)

I suggest, then, that it is not at all implausible, but rather quite likely, that Descartes would infer the truth of "Whatever thinks, exists" by relying on the truth of a particular statement, such as "I think, therefore, I exist," even if we regard "Whatever thinks, exists" to be on all fours with a mathematical proposition or an eternal truth.

The truth of a proposition is known either by sense experience or by reason. Sense experience, at this stage, cannot be relied upon; this

undefended. Fifth and finally, Descartes claims, in this very passage, that the *cogito* is an intuition.

To Father Mersenne, Descartes wrote on October 5, 1637, complaining that Fermat had misunderstood him, "He thought that when I said that something was easy to believe, I meant that it was no more than probable; but in this he has altogether mistaken my meaning.... [W]hen I say that something is easy to believe I do not mean that it is only probable, but that it is so clear and so evident that *there is no need for me to stop to prove it.*" (CSMK III, 74; AT I, 450–451; my italics) How might one explain this letter on the view that the *cogito* is a one-premise argument? Might one say that it only goes to show that the *cogito* is not "so clear and so evident" after all, so that it *is* in need of proof? Or might one simply deny that an immediate inference is a proof?

leaves us with reason as the only source of knowledge. *If* reason were to validate that general proposition, *prior* to the *cogito*, then of course the *cogito* would hardly be the first truth that Descartes was looking for. At the very least, there could be other truths, like the general truth, any one of which could serve as the first truth. One way in which the defense has then proceeded is to argue that Descartes was not looking for *any* truth, but rather for an existential truth. Descartes is cited:

And when I said that the proposition *I am thinking, therefore I exist* is the first and most certain of all to occur to anyone who philosophizes in an orderly way, I did not in saying that deny that one must first know what thought, existence and certainty are, and that it is impossible that that which thinks should not exist, and so forth. But because these are very simple notions, and ones which on their own provide us with no knowledge of anything that exists, I did not think they needed to be listed. (CSM I, 196; AT VIIIA, 8)

But Descartes is simply mistaken; either that, or the First Meditation is remarkably deceptive. When Descartes doubts the truths of sense experience or the truths of mathematics (which he does both in *Principles of Philosophy* and in *Discourse on the Method*), he should not invoke the evil genius, or something like it, since mathematical truths, as well as the principles of logic and the rules of inference, do not typically yield any existential truth. If Descartes is searching for an existential truth, why should he doubt the truths that purport to be harmless, nonexistential truths? What is the point in denying these? Contrariwise, if he is searching for any certain and necessary truth, then why should the *cogito*, rather than a host of logical and mathematical truths, be regarded the first truth ?

"I think," says Margaret Wilson,

it is quite possible Descartes simply could not make up his mind. On the one hand he wanted to say that we can know the (necessary) truth of "If I think, I exist," without having heard or thought of any abstract principle such as "Whatever thinks exists." This does seem plausible, and it suggests that (as Locke might say) we know the instance without knowing the principle. On the other hand, he wanted to say that the (necessary) truth of "If I think, I exist," is not strictly independent of the truth of "Whatever thinks exists" or the validity of "if . . . *a*, exists *a*." This seems plausible also, and tends to suggest (as Leibniz might hold) that we must in some sense, explicitly or implicitly, know the first principle. (WM, 57)

Wilson correctly observes that the universal principle is presupposed in the *Principles of Philosophy*, occurs in the *Discourse on the Method* post *cogito*, and is not mentioned at all in the *Meditations on First Philosophy*.

Could Descartes hold the Leibnizian view? Under the circumstances at the end of the First Meditation, I think not. The universal principle is either implicit or explicit. If it is implicit, Descartes cannot rely on it: For there is no reason at all to believe that that universal principle can be relied upon and is not subject to the dictates of the evil one. If it is explicit, then Descartes requires that there be a reason, too, to hold onto it. But this reason can hardly be forthcoming where even the truths of logic and mathematics are not held sacrosanct. It is sufficient to cite Descartes in the Second Meditation: "I do not now admit anything which is not necessarily true." This makes Wilson's following remark puzzling: "One can recognize that the inference is sound prior to achieving *express* recognition of any universal principle" (WM, 57). But how? Shouldn't the ideal seeker say, "This inference *seems* sound. But it relies on a universal principle which I do not, yet, know to be true. How, then, can I hold the inference to be sound? For I do not want a mere sound argument, or for that matter just a valid argument. I want an argument that I *know* to be sound." The question, therefore, of Descartes' admitting, relying, resting on, presupposing, taking for granted, or the like, propositions that are implicitly or explicitly held, but without justification, simply does not arise. There is, given the epistemic enterprise, no alternative for Descartes but to opt for the Lockean view.

Imagine: There is a thinker, *D*, who undergoes methodical doubt; he not only challenges all his explicit and consciously held belief, but also asserts that he should not rely on anything that invokes implicit principles; he abandons everything. At this stage, he also abandons, as a natural outcome of his doubt, the belief that there is any other thinker save himself. Consequently, he prevents himself from making any generalization concerning thought, doubt, or existence about any other thinker besides himself. He commences his procedure of doubt, introducing the evil genius to provide him with a rationale for doubting things that he could not otherwise doubt. As he engages in this methodical doubt, he discovers the *cogito*: Namely, no matter how much the evil one deceives him at *this* moment, t_0, he cannot be deceived into thinking that he, *D*, does not exist, since if *he* is deceived, then assuredly he exists. End of t_0. *This* D regards as a necessary truth about *himself.* In the next moment of time, he reflects that this is surely true of himself as a general truth, namely, that whenever he, D, thinks, he exists. End of t_1. In the next moment, he recognizes (but *how?*) that even though he does not know that any other thinker besides himself exists, it is true that if there were another thinker, he too would inevitably exist whenever he thought. End of t_2.

Suppose, now, that D had died at the end of t_0. Would Descartes have said that there was something missing in the light of which D could not be said to know the *cogito* as the first principle, the first truth? What did D miss? One might say, "Well, he missed the universal principle." Suppose that D dies at the end of t_1. He now has a limited general principle, a general principle true only of him. Would Descartes have argued that that was insufficient, too? In what way is *it* inadequate? One might say once again, "Well, he missed the unrestricted universal principle." Finally, suppose that D dies at the end of t_2. Now, at last, as some of the commentators would have it, Descartes would be satisfied.

At the very least, what this shows is that the limited generalization is based on a particular instance, and that the full generalization is based on the limited generalization. It is difficult to see how, if at all, Descartes could have proceeded correctly to the full generalization without the particular instance or the limited generalization. Leibniz would, of course, counter that at t_0 Descartes had implicit knowledge of the unrestricted general principle, "Whatever thinks, exists," without which he could not be said to have knowledge of the *cogito*. But implicit knowledge, as we have just seen, is simply not sufficient for Descartes to have the kind of knowledge that he is seeking at the end of the First Meditation. If one contemplates what condition has to prevail before Descartes can explicitly know, have justified belief in, the unrestricted universal generalization, it turns out that he must first know the truth of the particular. This imaginary case demonstrates that Descartes has full and correct knowledge of the *cogito* without the general principle. To demand anything more is to put weight on the full general claim that it is quite unable to bear.

The aim of this example is to show that if in this singular case the universal principle is not invoked, and yet a thinker has correct knowledge of the *cogito*, then the universal principle is inessential. Second,

if the thinker does not have knowledge of the first principle, what
in particular is his failure? Third, could he have arrived at the truth
of the universal principle without first recognizing the absolute truth
of its first instance? One might say that the particular instance cannot
demonstrate its *necessity* in a way in which the universal can. But what
makes for the necessity of the universal proposition that leaves the
necessity of the solitary instance in doubt? There is no such additional
element, and the claim that the universal alone would confer necessity
upon the singular instance needs much argument and illustration.

There is a second problem facing this view: Descartes wanted his
premises, in a deduction, to be not only true, but also certain and necessary. His theory of deduction, which I shall consider in detail later, says
so explicitly, and it was strongly implied in his method of analysis. The
axiom of metaphysics cannot be an ordinary, contingent truth. What,
then, is the status of the minor premise, "I think," in the syllogism?
Even if it is conceded that it is "transparently clear," it would be false to
accord it the status of a necessary truth rather than that of a contingent
truth. This flies in the face of Descartes' theory of deduction.

Third, if the *cogito* is a syllogistic argument, then Descartes unjustly
relies on the principles of inference, such as the rule of universal
instantiation and *modus ponens,* which have not been – and at this stage
cannot be – shown to be certain or even reliable. Thus, the inference
should be held suspect.

B. The Third Way

In "*Cogito Ergo Sum*: Inference or Performance?,"[7] Jaakko Hintikka has
argued (without espousing the view) that the *cogito* can be formulated
as an argument in quantification theory or first-order logic, thus:

[1] $Ba \supset (\exists x) (x = a)$
[2] Ba

_____

[3] $\therefore (\exists x)(x = a)$[8]

_____

[7] Hereinafter H.
[8] H,111–114.

In the above argument, Bx = x is a thing that thinks; a refers to 'I,' the thinker – in this case, Descartes. Now,

[4] $Ba \supset (\exists x)((x = a)$ & B$x)$

is a provable formula in first-order theory, and it unproblematically entails [1]. Then, given *modus ponens*, Descartes can conclude [3], namely, "I exist." Hintikka thinks that Descartes' reply to Gassendi, who had maintained that Descartes could just as well have said,"I walk, therefore I am," is "not very clear," partly on the ground that Bx can be any predicate and [4], from which [1] can be derived, will be just as provable. "This already makes the interpretation [1] suspect" (H,112). But Descartes' reasoning is fairly clear. If he is looking for an argument at all, he is not looking for just a valid argument. He is also looking for a sound argument. If so, the premise "I walk" is not certain: Descartes may be dreaming that he is walking while he lies comfortably in bed. But the premise "I think" serves his needs, since to doubt that he thinks, or to be deceived into thinking that he is thinking, are no less veridical instances of thoughts.

But Hintikka thinks that "the gravest objection" against the argument is that it is question-begging. He explains this in the following way: Formula [1] is provable in first-order quantification theory, but at a price. First-order quantification theory makes *existential presuppositions*, namely, that all singular terms (names, pronouns, definite descriptions, and so on), such as a, refer, denote, or designate an existing individual. Consequently, since a cannot fail to refer in the system, and it refers to 'I' (or whoever the thinker happens to be), it follows trivially that "I exist." But if we consider systems that do not make such existential presuppositions, we find that we are unable to draw "I exist" as a conclusion in such a system.

"My point," says Hintikka, "may perhaps be illustrated by means of an example constructed for us by Shakespeare. Hamlet did think a great many things; does it follow that he existed?" (H, 114) The rhetorical question has little force. Consider the following two arguments:

[A]   Hamlet thinks.   [B]   Hamlet thinks.
       ―――――――――   ―――――――――

       ∴ Hamlet exists.   ∴ There is a thought.

Hintikka thinks that [A] is clearly invalid, since, on his view, Hamlet "did think a great many things," but nonetheless Hamlet does not exist. But consider [B]. [B] is invalid, too, on the ground that there is no *actual* thought of Hamlet's in the way in which there have been actual thoughts since Adam. To say that Hamlet's thoughts lie in the same domain as actual human thoughts is, to say the least, obfuscating. Perhaps they lie in the domain of fictional thoughts, where there are also other thoughts such as those of Chichikkov, Hedda Gabler, and Faust. This renders [B] valid; but it takes the sting away from Hintikka's claim, since [A] is no longer invalid. Hamlet thinks and exists in a possible world: the fictional world.

There is a host of examples in the literature of the *cogito* as an argument. I arbitrarily outline one, which is all but stated in Kenny:

[1] Whatever object has a property,   [Metaphysical Premise]
     then that object exists.
[2] Whatever substance in which the   [Universal Instantiation, 1]
     attribute of thought inheres, that
     substance exists.
[3] If I am a substance in which the   [Universal Instantiation, 2]
     attribute of thought inheres, then
     I, a substance, exist.
[4] I, a substance, inhere the attribute   [Premise]
     of thought.

_____   _____

[5] ∴ I, a substance, exist.   [Modus Ponens, 3, 4]

In so many philosophers who have claimed that the *cogito* is an argument, a causal principle, or an *ex nihilo nihil fit* principle, is never stated as one of the premises. Yet if one thinks that the *cogito* is an argument, surely one must at least entertain the possibility that a causal principle might well be one of the premises of the alleged argument. For Descartes explicitly says, "Is there not a God, or whatever I may call him, who puts into me the thoughts I am now having? But why do I think this, since I myself may perhaps be the author of these thoughts?" (CSM II, 16; AT VII, 24) It never occurs to Descartes that thoughts could be produced out of nothing, out of nowhere.

This is a separate claim from the one that both Bertrand Russell and A. J. Ayer were to make later, that there might simply be authorless thoughts. This was essentially the view of Georg Lichtenberg when he criticized Descartes for claiming that the 'I' of "I exist" in the conclusion (for the sake of argument) is unjustifiably assumed in the premise of the *cogito*. Descartes, so goes the litany, was entitled only to the assertion, "There are thoughts." Consequently, that view would challenge the implication of premise [2], and argue that one needs to demonstrate why any attribute needs to inhere in any substance at all. Bernard Williams offers a criticism of such views,[9] but I should like to concentrate on a version offered by Baker and Morris.

Baker and Morris argue that Lichtenberg's is a seriously flawed reading of Descartes, since it ignores Descartes' logic and metaphysics, which prohibit him from making any such move in his language-game. They write,

It invalidates the common criticism that Descartes begged the crucial question in formulating the premise as '*I* think' ('*cogito*') rather than as 'Thinking occurs' ('*cogitatur*'). In his view, there *can* be *no* judgement about thinking (or the occurrence of a thought) whose logical subject is not a substance. To predicate a mode of thinking *of a thinking thing* is the *minimal* move in the language-game. A thought (or an act of thinking) isn't a substance, and there is no such thing as a mode which doesn't inhere in a substance.... Descartes' conception leaves no logical room for contrasting '*cogito*' with '*cogitatur*' (as Lichtenberg did in accusing Descartes of committing a fallacy in drawing the conclusion '*sum*').[10]

As exegesis, this is not only entirely appropriate, but also makes a very plausible case. What makes their view interesting, however, is that Baker and Morris use arguments that are now familiar both in philosophy of language and in philosophy of science and apply them to the history of philosophy, and to Descartes in particular. Thus, their view faces an objection similar to the ones often raised, say, in philosophy of science. Their view blocks the possibility of progress in philosophy.[11]

---

9 See BW, 95–101.
10 Gordon Baker and Katherine J. Morris, *Descartes' Dualism*, 65–66; see also 24, note 1, and 209, as well as note 23.
11 See, in particular, *Descartes' Dualism*, 201–219 for a discussion of a wealth of examples of fundamental concepts.

If one is constrained to speak only in terms of language-games, then *no* view can be fundamentally criticized as being wrong-headed; one is allowed to say only, "*This* move is not permitted in *that* language-game." The modern view of logic and metaphysics should not be allowed to judge the philosophical systems of the past, and, of course, conversely. Consequently, what happens to philosophical progress? Is it simply that one philosophical system replaces another, and we are no more entitled to speak of truth and progress in philosophy than we are in science (say, on Thomas Kuhn's view of science)? When a revisionary metaphysics replaces a descriptive one, shall we say that it is just a replacement, and that we are no closer to the truth about the basic features of the universe than we were before? This is a desperate view, I believe, and must be embraced only as a last resort.

But, if the foregoing is anywhere near right, then Lichtenberg, Russell, and Ayer can assert that they were finding fault at the heart of the metaphysical system that Descartes was offering, not merely offering an interpretation of what Descartes was saying.

As a proper interpretation of the *cogito*, this full version of the argument has the following problem facing it. So far as the ideal seeker knows, *no* metaphysical truths except the *cogito* have been established at this stage in the investigation. If that is the case, Descartes has no reason to rely on an argument one of whose premises – namely, [2], if not also [1] – may be untrue. This would render the argument as yet not known to be sound. Such arguments, formulated by Curley, Hintikka, and Kenny, among others, share the defect of relying on principles of logic that have not yet been shown or proven, at this juncture, to be sound: That is, we have no guarantee that in using them we may not move from true premises to a false conclusion. In the formulated version not only *modus ponens* is involved, but also the rule of universal instantiation, in proving [5] from [1]; and neither rule has been demonstrated to be sound. This is not to say that this version of the argument may not be (indeed, it is) a good explanation[12] – an explanation that comes *long* after the *cogito* – but it is not a correct version of the *cogito*, which comes in the opening paragraphs of the Second Meditation.

---

[12] See Chapter 8, 306.

Several critics, especially Frankfurt, have made much of a remark
of Descartes:

I know a man who once, when falling asleep, heard the clock strike four, and
counted the strokes as 'one, one, one, one'. It then seemed to him that there
was something absurd about this, and he shouted: 'That clock must be going
mad; it has struck one o'clock four times!' Is there really anything so absurd
or irrational that it could not come into the mind of someone who is asleep
or raving? (CSM II, 306; AT VII, 457)

So a skeptic might parody someone who thinks that the *cogito* is an
argument, thus: "I know a man who once, when falling asleep, read
the *cogito* argument having four premises, and counted the premises as
'one, one, one, one'. It then seemed to him that there was something
absurd about this, and he shouted: 'That argument must be mad; it
has repeated the first premise four times.' Is there really anything so
absurd or irrational that it could not come into the mind of someone
who is asleep or raving?" Indeed, a few lines later Descartes says, "There
are no limits to what a dreamer may not 'prove'."

There is a lovely problem facing Descartes. The problem is designed
by Kenny:

Descartes says that his system rests on two principles, his own existence and
God's existence. If my account is right, he cannot have both these principles in
quite the way he wants them. If what does not exist can have properties, then
he can perhaps prove God's existence, but not his own. If what does not exist
cannot have properties, he can perhaps prove his own existence, but he cannot
prove God's existence from God's essence without begging the question. The
cogito and the ontological argument cannot both be valid. (K, 170–171)

Kenny shows their incompatibility in the following brief: Quite like
Alexis Meinong, Descartes maintains not only that that which exists can have a nature, but also that that which is not has a nature,
too. To begin with, God is a datum and has a nature; it is part of
his nature, essence, or property to exist. Therefore, God exists. But
then the 'I' of a thinker can be a possible subject with an essential
nature of thought; such a thinker can subsist without existing. Since
it is not the essence of said thinker to exist, his existence cannot
be proved. My purpose is not to examine the details of Kenny's argument, but simply to focus on its main property: namely, that *both*
the *cogito* and the ontological proof for the existence of God are

arguments, and that both arguments cannot be valid; at most, only one can be.

Now, if my reading of the *cogito* is correct, it shows Descartes a way out of the Kenny dilemma. The occasion that gives rise to the dilemma has been undercut. The *cogito* is not, and cannot be, an argument, while the proof of the existence of God is, and must be, an argument. This, of course, does nothing to show that Descartes' ontological argument is sound, either in Kenny's version or in any other. It only aims to show that the *cogito* and the ontological proof of the existence of God are not obstacles to one another.

C. The Fourth Way

The fourth formulation of the *cogito* as an argument is owed to Edwin M. Curley. The best entry into the discussion is Curley's partial criticism, and partial support, of Frankfurt's view as presented in his book *Demons, Dreamers, and Madmen.* Frankfurt had argued that Descartes' aim was to conclude not that "I exist" is true, but only that it is indubitable.[13] But the notion of "indubitable" is normative, as opposed to descriptive, in this sense: A proposition is normatively indubitable if it could not be reasonably doubted.

We misunderstand Descartes' enterprise, cautions Curley, if we see Descartes as interested in offering a proof: "[T]he *cogito*, while it is inference, is not intended to be a demonstration or proof of *sum.* It is not essential to a valid inference that the premisses of the argument be known with certainty to be true, though this is essential to a proof, or demonstration, of the classical Aristotelian sort." (C, 84) To say that a proposition is proved is to say that the argument constituting a proof eventually *begins* with some proposition in that proof. The premises cannot go back to infinity; they must terminate in a first proposition or propositions. But the skeptics had averred that, ultimately, to rest on a first proposition is to rest on an arbitrary premise. For one could just as well have chosen other premises as starting points. These leave unanswered questions about their justifiability. Couldn't these first

---

[13] I find this to be an extraordinary view, one that cannot be sensibly foisted upon Descartes. Confronted with the claim that a proposition was indubitable and yet not true, Descartes would have been amused. In what is an otherwise extraordinary book, *Sources of the Self,* Charles Taylor reads Descartes in this way, too. I share Bernard Williams' reaction that such a view is "totally implausible historically" (W, 35, note 2). But, for the sake of argument, I am not contesting that view here.

propositions be regarded as self-evident? "Descartes, I suggest," says Curley, "does not want to rely, in his published works (that is, making an exception for the *Regulae*), on the contention that his first principles are self-evident."[14] (C, 85).

Since Descartes does not wish to countenance the skeptic's criticism of arbitrariness, a mere subjective certainty, he offers an argument. This he does by a negative procedure: the famous procedure of doubting. It is important to understand the nature of the doubt. It is not essential that what leads to the doubt be substantiated; we do not have to believe in the veracity of the doubt. This frees us to keep pushing at the limits of what can be doubted; hence, our doubt escalates from being reasonable to being metaphysical, hyperbolic. Yet our standards should not be so high that they cannot, in principle, be met. In short, our task of discovering the first truth must not be an impossible one. What, then, is a reasonable doubt? "The one most relevant to the *cogito* is that a reasonable ground for doubting a proposition must offer some explanation of how it is that we might erroneously believe the proposition even if the explanation is only conjectural" (C, 86).

So Descartes sets up the method of doubt. It is a method informed by a variety of hypotheses: My senses are not trustworthy; I am dreaming; a demon of incredible power is bent on deceiving me. Each of these hypotheses involves the supposition that I am thinking. In short, if each of these hypotheses is to explain how I err, each must involve my thinking. "But that supposition entails my existence. So 'I exist' is inferred from 'I think'" (C, 86). Here Curley lists the two virtues of his view of the *cogito*. First, the proposition "I think" is not a premise of a proof. If it were a proof, one would have demanded how we can know the truth, or be certain, of the proposition "I think." But Descartes need take no epistemic responsibility for ensuring the truth of the premises. Indeed, Curley shows that were Descartes to take responsibility for demonstrating that he is certain that he is now thinking, he would find himself bound to an infinite task.[15] Second, the *cogito* is not question-begging, because "I exist" is not the conclusion of a proof. If it were, then, as the skeptics had argued, and as Curley

---

[14] In the absence of the citation of a single line explicitly denouncing the value or reliability of intuition, this is a fairly strong historical claim.

[15] I have skipped this neat part of the argument, since it is not essential to my enterprise (C, 86–87).

so admirably illustrates, the conclusion would be contained in the premises.[16]

There is, however, this stubborn exegetical fact, thinks Curley, that "Descartes does often suggest that 'I think' is peculiarly certain" (C, 87). This lends credence to the claim that "I exist" is, after all, the conclusion of a proof or demonstration. But if someone were to show that a proof or demonstration is possible, something that Curley himself tries to show, that in itself would not refute Curley's claim. For Curley is not claiming that a proof or demonstration is impossible, only that it is possible to do without it. Here is the crucial passage:

For it seems to me that the claim of "I think" to be a first principle can be defended in the same way that the claim of "I exist" can, that is, a proposition entailing "I think" is a common element in any reasonable skeptical hypothesis which might be invoked as a ground for doubting that I think. Any supposition that explains how my thinking might be erroneous must entail not only that I exist, but also that I think. So "I think" would also survive systematic doubt, and the two propositions are on a par. And if that is so, then we have the making of a demonstration of "I exist." (C, 88)

He then immediately continues:

This is why Descartes sometimes is tempted to treat "I think" as certain and "I exist" as the conclusion of a demonstration. But to Descartes there would be no advantage in using such an argument for the certainty of "I think" to establish the certainty of "I exist." For if the fact that a proposition is immune to reasonable doubt is sufficient to make its acceptance as a first principle rational, then we might as well take "I exist" as a first principle to begin with. (C, 88)

Curley thinks that "I think, therefore I am" is an argument. But, he claims, instead of regarding "Whatever thinks, exists" as a missing premise, we ought to regard it as a rule of inference that permits us to move from "I think" to "I exist." Thus it would appear that in a neat and concise way, he avoids some of the difficulties attendant upon the first two ways of viewing the *cogito* as an argument.

If the *cogito* were a syllogistic argument, then it would be a very special type of syllogism. The major premise would be "Whatever thinks, exists," and this type of premise, says Curley, would require careful attention. Such a premise would be what Descartes called an eternal

---

[16] C, Chapter 2.

truth, a common notion, or a truth that we would normally say is necessary. Add to it the fact that because it is a major premise in an Aristotelian syllogism, it has existential import, and we would have to face some pretty unpalatable consequences. It is a commonplace theorem in modal logic that if p is necessary, and p entails q, then q is necessary. Since "Whatever thinks, exists" is necessary, then via the existential import of that major premise, it would follow that it is necessary that there are thinkers. We would find ourselves saddled with too many necessary existential propositions (C, 34). Furthermore, if we are trying to establish the existence of a thinker via the *cogito*, this will hardly do (WC, 93).

From this Curley concludes that "Whatever thinks, exists" had better be construed as a rule of inference rather than as a statement. Any necessary truth, such as the one under consideration, should be regarded as a rule of inference, so as to avoid the troublesome implication of too many things existing necessarily. This also squares with Descartes' assertion, says Curley, that knowledge of eternal truths does not give us knowledge of any existing thing (C, 34; see also CSM I, 196; AT VIIIA, 8).

Now there is a modal principle that Curley invokes. It is this. If a valid argument has a premise that is necessarily true, that premise can be eliminated without affecting the validity of the argument: If p and q entail r, and p is necessarily true, then q alone entails r. "So if an argument which is not, as it stands, formally valid, were to be rendered formally valid by the addition of a premise which is necessarily true, Descartes would be right to think the exercise an empty one. If the original argument requires only the addition of a necessarily true premise to achieve formal validity, then the original argument was already valid." (C, 34; see also 32) Curley concludes that the major premise is either a necessary truth and hence redundant, or not a necessary truth and hence in need of support.

Here is Curley's overall view in his own words:

The reading of Descartes which seems to me to do the least violence to the texts would run as follows: Yes, there is a general maxim whose correctness is a necessary condition of the validity of the inference from thought to existence; this maxim is a necessary truth, not merely a contingent one; so it is best regarded, not as a suppressed premise, but as a rule of inference; the argument, therefore, need not take the form of a syllogism, and it is artificial to put it in that form, since what comes first in the order of discovery is the realization that the inference is valid in the particular case; but later, reflecting on the inference, we recognize that justifying it requires us to justify the maxim. (C, 91)

So much for the preamble. Let us turn to examine Curley's view. First, among the very common notions or eternal truths is the following, "that it is impossible that that which thinks should not exist." This eternal truth can be reformulated as "Necessarily, whatever thinks, exists." Of these simple notions, Descartes says, there are ones "which on their own provide us with no knowledge of anything that exists" (CSM I, 196; AT VIIIA, 8). Curley claims that we should use such an eternal truth as a rule of inference. But one could use it as a premise, too: For if eternal truths have no existential import, how do we over-populate the ontological slum by using them as premises instead of artificially construing them as rules of inference?

Descartes' texts support the reading that one need not make existential commitments in a general statement of the type serving as a major premise.[17] Descartes had maintained in the Fifth Meditation that from "the fact that I cannot think of a mountain without a valley, it does not follow that a mountain and valley exist anywhere, but simply that a mountain and a valley, whether they exist or not, are mutually insepa-rable" (CSM II, 46; AT VII, 66–67). Likewise, whether triangles exist or not, they have certain properties, such as that the sum of their interior angles is equal to two right angles. Consequently, it would appear that similar things might be said about minds or thinkers, or about exis-tence. Whether thinkers exist or not, so long as there is a thought, there is a thinker. In the Second Meditation, Descartes had convinced him-self "that there is absolutely nothing in the world. . . . no minds . . ." (CSM II, 16; AT VII, 25), no bodies, no earth, no sky, no world. But from that it would not follow that the eternal truth "Whatever thinks, exists," or alternatively, "that it is impossible that that which thinks should not exist," is not true, even necessarily true. One can conclude that one need not fear the consequences of existential import; one could read the major premise in the Aristotelian syllogism as having no existential import.[18] Using eternal truths as premises in such an

---

[17] I find Kenny's reading of this point congenial; see K, 146–151.
[18] Bernard Williams also argues that the *cogito* cannot be a syllogistic argument, in part because of the existential import of the major premise, which would already

argument is more in keeping with Descartes' intentions than using them as rules of inference.

Second, Curley thinks that the *cogito* is an argument, even if that argument is not to serve as a proof or demonstration. But minimally, a skeptic might say, surely the argument must be valid? If so, then it will be subject to the skeptical strictures. It is true that the stricture here is not that Curley has stopped at an arbitrary stopping point, with no more than a subjective conviction at hand. Rather, the stricture is that if the argument is valid, then the truth of the conclusion must be contained or presupposed in the conclusion. Why in this specific case the stricture does not apply, Curley does not say.

Third, the modal principle that Curley invokes is controversial. To repeat the modal principle in question: If p and q entail r, and p is necessarily true, then q alone entails r. The restricted version of the principle, championed by Peter Thomas Geach,[19] reads: If p and q entail r, and p is necessary, and q and r are contingent, then q alone entails r. While the restricted version has been courted by Curley, both versions of the principle have been rejected by Alan Anderson and Nuel Belnap.[20]

How, then, should Curley's argument be re-read? Perhaps as something like the following: The *cogito* is an argument where p (*Whatever thinks, exists*) and q (*I think*) entail r (*I exist*), and since p (*Whatever thinks, exists*) is necessary, and q (*I think*) and r (*I exist*) are contingent, then q (*I think*) entails r (*I exist*). This does not treat the eternal truth "Whatever thinks, exists" as a rule of inference. It is rather treated as a premise in an argument, a premise that can be dispensed with in accordance with the restricted modal principle. Nor is there any gain in

---

presuppose the existence of thinkers. There is, surely, a slip in Williams' remark, "The eternal truth 'In order to think, it is necessary to exist' presupposes no existential proposition; but, by the same token, it cannot play the role of major premise in a syllogism" (WC, 93). Why? There are adequate interpretations of the Aristotelian system of categorical syllogism that make no existential presupposition; such a system has a restricted set of valid schemas. It is worth noting, with Williams, that one can construe the eternal truth as "If one thinks, then one exists," without knowing how that conditional statement is to be taken. For one thing, it presupposes that existence is a predicate. Yet the difficulties that Williams goes on to raise would have been, as Williams himself recognizes, alien to Descartes' thinking.

[19] Geach, *Logic Matters*, 182. Only the letters used for variables have been altered for the sake of uniformity.

[20] Anderson and Belnap, "Enthymemes."

this. The restricted modal principle, like the unrestricted one, would have been construed by Descartes as an eternal truth, and both would be just as much in need of defense as any other eternal truth, such as "Whatever thinks, exists."

Be that as it may, there is a significant step in Geach's proof of the restricted modal principle that Curley fails to relate. It is this: "q entails r if and only if there is an a priori way of getting to know that 'If q then r', which is not a way of getting to know either whether q, or whether r."[21] This is Geach's truth condition of an entailment statement. It follows that "I think" entails "I exist" provided that there is an *a priori* way of getting to know "If 'I think', then 'I exist'," which is not a way of getting to know either whether "I think," or whether "I exist." How could that statement – "If 'I think', then 'I exist'" – be known in a way that would satisfy the Cartesian epistemic strictures? But suppose, *per impossibile*, that it can be known, without knowing whether "I think," or whether "I exist"; where then is the need for using it as a rule of inference? Curley had argued that if "If p, then q" is a necessary statement, then it is not essential for deriving q from p. He invoked Geach's restricted modal principle. But Geach's proof for the restricted version of the modal proof relies on showing that "If p then q" is a necessary truth. We would be back to the original question: How could the statement – "If 'I think', then 'I exist'" – be known to be a necessary truth that would satisfy the Cartesian epistemic strictures? Whatever the accuracy of Geach's theory as a theory of entailment, it is of little aid to Curley.[22]

---

[21] Peter Thomas Geach, *Logic Matters*, 179–180.

[22] Von Wright's theory of entailment, presented in *Logical Studies*, which Geach held in high esteem, reads as follows: "A entails B, if and only if, by means of logic, it is possible to come to know the truth of $A \supset B$ without coming to know the falsehood of A or the truth of B." "By means of logic," says von Wright; "by *a priori* means," says Geach, in *Logic Matters*. There are several inadequacies. As Anderson and Belnap point out, the expression 'come to know' is loose; Strawson, in "Review of von Wright," found a parallel difficulty. Von Wright's response was to say that there were different meanings of 'come to know,' and that, at any rate, the situation was unsatisfactory. Anderson and Belnap also considered the proposal of T. J. Smiley, in "Entailment and Deducibility," but found that that proposal leads to abandoning the transitivity of entailment. My purpose here is not to contest any theory of entailment, or to plead for a particular one. It is rather to show that one ought not to invoke so controversial a principle of entailment to support what is purported to be the first and simple truth – a truth *Polyander* could acknowledge! – that is to serve as a foundation for other truths in the metaphysics of Descartes.

Fourth, consider what I call the problem of justification: "[W]hat comes first in the order of discovery is the realization that the inference is valid in the particular case; but later, reflecting on the inference, we recognize that justifying it requires us to justify the maxim" (C, 91). I do not understand what Curley means by saying that we discover the inference to be valid in the particular case. Surely, there is no recognition of a valid inference in this case, or in any other, *unless* the maxim, or the rule of inference, has been demonstrated to be sound: that is, that it is a rule that never allows a move from true premises to a false conclusion. In short, there is no discovery of the *cogito*, or of any other argument, until the rules of inference are sound, and antecedently known to be such.

Fifth and finally, Curley complains that to cast the *cogito* in the form of a syllogism is artificial; but it is no less artificial to cast "Whatever thinks, exists" in the role of a rule of inference. If anything, it is more so. It is not just our contemporary understanding of rules of inference, such as the *modus ponens*, *modus tollens*, rules of association, and so on, that makes us think that "Whatever thinks, exists" is so different from these other rules of inference. The rules of inference of the Stoics, which the skeptics criticized, and of which Descartes was aware, are also quite different from "Whatever thinks, exists." It bears repeating, with Curley, that Descartes had *no* clear notion of proof. So it is something of a historical problem to decide to what extent Descartes would have espoused talk about rules of inference.[23]

---

[23] Ian Hacking has argued that while it was Leibniz who first gave us the notion of proof as we understand it today, nearly all the elements that go to make up the Leibnizian notion of proof were present in Descartes; see Ian Hacking, "Proof and Eternal Truths: Descartes and Leibniz." If Hacking and Y. Belaval, whose *Leibniz: Critique de Descartes* is the basis of Hacking's interpretation, are right, then the invocation of rules of inference would have greatly puzzled Descartes. This does not undercut my very sympathetic response to Gaukroger's detailed criticism of Hacking's view of the connection between truth and proof in Descartes and the doctrine of eternal truths. Gaukroger's reading would lend further credence to my claim that the *cogito* could not be an argument, at least at this stage of the argument; see Gaukroger, *Cartesian Logic: An Essay on Descartes's Conception of Inference*, 26–31.

Now, one might argue – as did Catherine Wilson – that there is something in Hacking's notion, namely, that Descartes did think of a mathematical proof not formalistically but phenomenologically. Mathematical arguments involve this powerful compulsion to go from step A to step B, even where there is no syllogistic basis for doing so, and no suppressed premise can be supplied. The mathematician just sees where to go. The *cogito* seems to attempt to create just such a compulsion to

D. The Fifth Way

The fifth way of reading the *cogito* as an argument is owed to Bernard Williams. He has argued that the *cogito* is an inference – the proposition inferred is "I exist," and it is said to be inferred from the proposition "I think" – but it is an inference of a special kind, not a syllogistic inference. That there is undoubtedly an inference, Williams thinks, is due to the fact that Descartes, in the relevant passages, uses terms like 'it follows', 'infer', and the like. Moreover, Williams maintains that this way of reading the *cogito* as an argument, based on a special kind of inference, faithfully represents Descartes' own view.

Consider a typical subject–predicate sentence of the form *Fa*, where *F* is a predicate and *a* is a proper name, a pronoun, or a definite description. Now, characteristically, or commonly, *Fa presupposes* that *a* does not fail to refer, or designate: in short, that there *exists* an entity referred to by *a*. The relation of presupposition is quite different from the relation of implication: If *p* implies *q*, then if *q* is false, *p* is false. But if *p* presupposes *q*, then if *q* is false, *p* is neither true nor false. In the language of Sir Peter Strawson, in his *Introduction to Logical Theory*, in such a case no statement has been made. As an example, if I say, "The tenor in my house is fat and wealthy," and there is no tenor in my house, then the subject term, "the tenor in my house," fails to refer or designate any such entity, and the sentence, "The tenor in my house is fat and wealthy," is neither true nor false. In order for the sentence to have a truth-value, at a minimum the subject term must have a reference.

Williams claims that just such a principle of inference, the relation of presupposition, gives us what we need in order to understand why

move, but does so even while holding "mathematics," as a whole body of theory, in suspense.

An adequate response to this proposal will emerge only at the end of the next chapter. Meanwhile, let me raise three questions. First, how is Descartes to distinguish a sound compulsion from an unsound one, even if from a purely phenomenological point of view? Second, at this stage in the *Meditations on First Philosophy*, Descartes has dismissed a simple mathematical truth, namely, $2 + 3 = 5$; how, then, are good compulsions to be distinguished one from another, such that the compulsion induced by the *cogito* underwrites its truth but the other compulsion does not, yet, support a simple mathematical truth? Third, what would be the relationship between the sort of compulsion that guarantees the truth of the *cogito* and the general rule, also guaranteeing truth, that comes only in the Third Meditation? Indeed, why is the general rule even necessary in the presence of said compulsion? See also Gaukroger, *Cartesian Logic*, 50–51.

I The Five Ways...

the *cogito* is an argument and the nature of the inference involved in it. He states that if "'*p* presupposes *q*' means that *q* must be true for *p* to be either true or false, it follows *a fortiori* that *q* must be true for *p* to be true; in other words, if *p* is true, *q* is also true. And this I take to be the principle of the *cogito*." (WC, 96) Williams must mean that the principle of inference in the *cogito*-argument that legitimizes the move from the premise, "I think," to the conclusion, "I exist," is the relation of presupposition. In other words, if the relation of presupposition is a sound principle of inference, then if "I think" is true, the subject term, 'I', cannot fail to have a reference. Consequently, if the *cogito* is asserted, then the relation of presupposition guarantees the truth of the statement "I exist." This is the first principle that Descartes was seeking.

Williams further maintains that "there appears to be a close relation between Descartes' 'eternal truth' or 'maxim' and a rule of language. And language – we should not forget – has at no time been eliminated by doubt: 'Descartes, and even more his reader, begins to meditate in a universe of existing discourse.'" (WC, 97) Presumably, then, there is a close connection between the eternal truth expressed by the relation of presupposition and the rules of language that govern the use of certain kinds of sentences to make statements in that language. Thus, the eternal truth, expressed in the relation of presupposition, guarantees the truth of the proposition "I exist," when the sentence "I think" is correctly used in ordinary language.

There are several difficulties in understanding the *cogito* along the lines recommended by Williams. First, there is no way to determine the truth of *Fa* without first determining whether or not *a* refers or designates. To expand on the point: Let us suppose that there is a logical relation between the sentence *Fa* and the sentence, "There exists something referred to, or designated by, *a*." It still would not follow that we can extract from it a principle of inference, namely, an inference that enables us to come to *know* on the basis of our knowing *p*. For it is written into the relation of presupposition that to know that *Fa* is true is already to know the truth of the sentence, "There exists something referred to, or designated by, *a*."

Williams thinks that this objection trades on a simple confusion: the confusion of two distinct principles, namely a principle of logic, which is what he is offering, and a principle of epistemology, which is what his critic demands. "It is extremely useful in logic," says Williams,

to be able to say, for instance, that there is a principle allowing us to infer "p" from "p and q" even on the assumption that it is in fact impossible to know the truth of "p and q" without first knowing the truth of "p". I do not see why we should not also be justified in considering the relation of presupposition between "I think" and "I exist" as the basis of a principle of inference and hence of the *cogito* itself in so far as it is an inference – not, of course, in the sense of a syllogism with a suppressed major premise. (WC, 97)

This underestimates the objection. Consider the following from Strawson:

Suppose someone says "All John's children are asleep". Obviously, he will not normally, or properly, say this, unless he believes that John has children (who are asleep). If John has no children, then the sentence, "All John's children are asleep," does not have a truth-value, although it is perfectly meaningful. But to say that the man who uses the sentence in our imagined case fails to say anything either true or false, is not to say that the sentence he pronounces is meaningless. Nor is it to deny that he makes a mistake. Of course, it is incorrect (or deceitful) for him to use this sentence unless (a) he thinks he is referring to some children whom he thinks to be asleep; (b) he thinks that John has children; (c) he thinks that the children he is referring to are John's. We might say that in using the sentence he *commits himself* to the existence of children of John's.[24]

So, too, we might say the following: "The man who says, 'I think', and is using that sentence to make a statement, and not to test his voice, for example, is incorrect or (deceitful) unless (a) he thinks that 'I' is referring to himself; (b) he thinks that he is acquainted with a thought; and (c) he thinks that the particular thought in question with which he is acquainted when he says, 'I think', does belong to him. If these conditions are not satisfied by anyone saying, 'I think', then he has failed to make a statement; he has said something which has no truth-value, even though the sentence he speaks is meaningful." But Williams' critic can now point out that if condition (a) is satisfied, the relation of presupposition can be safely dispensed with; it will not add anything to what we can know.

One must of course insist on Williams' distinction between the principles of logic and the principles of epistemology, but one must equally

---

[24] P. F. Strawson, *Introduction to Logical Theory*, 175.

insist that what is at stake, in Descartes, is the principle of epistemology. After all, the primary epistemological problem is, what can I know for certain? And Williams' critic can make his point thus. Consider the following argument, he might say:

I think and I exist.

Therefore, I exist.

This instantiates the principle of logic that Williams referred to, namely, the "principle allowing us to infer '*p*' from '*p* and *q*'." No one need dispute the validity of this argument, nor the soundness of the principle of inference. But it would be a poor thing if it were offered as a reason for accepting the conclusion, since what is asserted in the conclusion is already asserted in the premises. Descartes could not claim to know with certainty that he exists on the basis of the premises, since, in this case, the conclusion is blatantly contained in the premises.

For an exactly parallel reason, the critic is unsatisfied with the relation of presupposition, not because it is not a correct principle of inference, but rather because it adds nothing to our knowledge. Descartes must offer us a reason for accepting the conclusion, if the *cogito* is an argument, such that that reason does not already presuppose the truth of the conclusion. But that is exactly what the principle of presupposition does in this case. *Step 1*: Establish that "I think" is true. *Step 2*: State, in this case, an instance of the relation of presupposition, namely, "If 'I think' is true or false, then the subject term, 'I', must have a reference; in other words, 'I exist' must be true." *Step 3*: Conclude that "I exist." The critic's point is not to question the correctness of Step 2, but rather to point out that Step 1 simply cannot be carried out without first establishing the truth of Step 3.

The second objection: There is no need to be certain of the premise, "I think." Descartes could just as well have said, I am walking, or I am breathing, and that would have been enough. That sentence has a truth-value: It could be true, if Descartes was indeed walking or breathing, or false, if he was dreaming and lying in bed, in the one case, or if he did not have physical body, in the other. In either case, he would be using the sentence to make a statement, and that, via the relation of presupposition, would presuppose the existence of the individual denoted by 'I'. But Descartes explicitly wanted a true premise, and argued against claims that meant the premises could be false. Williams' view turns a crucial part of the text into a puzzle.

Thus, consider the following passage from a letter that Descartes wrote to Reneri for Pollot in April or May 1638: "When someone says 'I am breathing, therefore I exist,' if he wants to prove he exists from the fact that there cannot be breathing without existence, he proves nothing, because he would have to prove first that it is true that he is breathing, which is impossible unless he has also proved that he exists" (CSMK, 98; AT II, 37–38). This makes it difficult to sustain the claim that Williams' view was also Descartes' view. First, insofar as someone is making the statement that "I am breathing, therefore I am," and not just uttering a sentence to test his voice, then the falsity of the claim means nothing, since in making the statement the speaker has guaranteed the referent of 'I'. Second, Descartes himself would object, in a manner similar to Williams' critic, by saying that "unless he has [first] also proved that he exists," his claim means nothing.

The third objection is, of course, the most fundamental. It is that Williams makes Descartes presuppose an eternal truth at a stage in the discussion when *no* truth of mathematics, or of logic, is accepted. They are all under the cloud of doubt. Whether rightly or wrongly, Descartes would not have linked the truths of language as intimately to the truths of logic as Williams has him do. Descartes never questioned the truths of language: For him, these truths amounted to no more than our knowing or understanding the meaning of words. On the other hand, he at least attempted to seriously question the truths of mathematics and logic, or the so-called eternal truths.[25] If there was

---

[25] It will clearly not do to say that Descartes does not call all the truths of logic into doubt when he calls the truths of mathematics into doubt. Even if God can make contradictories true together, that doesn't mean that we can doubt the truth of the principle of noncontradiction. At most he can raise a second-order doubt about logical principles. There is much evidence, especially in the letters, for the second sentence in the foregoing remark (CSMK, 23; AT I, 145–146; CSMK, 25; AT I, 152; CSMK, 235; AT IV, 118; CSMK, 358–359; AT V, 224). But from the point of view of the critic, there are severe problems facing Descartes. First, one might easily argue that the same could be said to be true of mathematical principles; yet Descartes did not prevent himself from doubting those in the First Meditation (*pace* Frankfurt). Second, second-order doubt about logical principles is of no help to Descartes; it is not as if having doubted them at the second-order level, he could then safely use the logical principles in his first-order reasoning. The sweep and power of the hyperbolic doubt in the First Meditation ensures that however minuscule the doubt, at whatever level, and of whatever

a link in Descartes' mind between these truths, it needs explaining why he never thought he had reason to doubt the truths of language, when he had provided himself with reasons to doubt the eternal truths.

The fourth objection: There are a variety of ways of understanding a certain class of subject–predicate sentences, not all of which involve the relation of presupposition. There is, of course, Bertrand Russell's theory of definite descriptions; there is David Kaplan's reading of Russell; and finally there is van Fraassen's and Lambert's view of presupposition. So long as this is controversial, Williams' principle of presupposition will not support the *cogito* as well as Descartes might have thought. It would not be difficult for the evil genius to persuade Descartes that, given the rival logical theories of subject–predicate sentences, there is no conclusive reason to settle for Williams' relation of presupposition over other theories. It should best be left untouched, at least initially, while Descartes is searching for a first principle of which he is absolutely certain; that principle cannot be tainted by the possibility that it relies on something less than absolutely certain, like the relation of presupposition. For example, Russell's theory would make the statement, "I think," false when 'I' fails to have a referent, rather than neither true nor false, as on Strawson's or Williams' view.

There is a fifth and final objection (which affects not only Williams but also Hintikka and Curley). It lies in Descartes' explicit hypothesis about the ideal seeker. Descartes repeatedly says that the first principle can be understood by an ordinary person, guided by the natural light of reason. Such an individual is represented by Polyander, who has little, if any, knowledge of logic and mathematics. But on Williams' view, as well as on Hintikka's and Curley's, Descartes' ideal seeker has to be a pretty sophisticated thinker in order to make the inferences that he is supposed to make. And yet, it was Williams who wrote:

Descartes does not suppose that his right to claim a reader's attention lies in any sacramental, traditional or professional position. His authority to show us how to think lies only in this, that he has himself, as he supposes, uncovered

nature, it undermines the proposition in question. So let me suggest a dilemma for anyone who would claim that Descartes treated principles of logic separately from principles of mathematics: If logic stays unquestioned, so should mathematics; and if so, a significant part of the First Meditation remains quite inexplicable. On the other hand, if mathematics is questioned, so should logic be questioned; if so, the validity of the *cogito* argument would be impossible to determine.

methods of simple, clear-headed and rational inquiry which all reasonable people can conduct if they clear their minds of prejudice and address themselves in a straightforward way to the questions. No special training, no religious discipline, no knowledge of texts or of history is needed in order to do this. He was disposed to think, in fact, that such things could be an actual obstacle.[26]

Question: Could an ideal thinker be one ignorant of the theory of presupposition and the laws of logic and inference? He could not, says Williams. This seems to me to be quite contrary to Descartes' own avowed aim of making the *cogito* clear "even to women."[27] My aim is not to parade Descartes' male chauvinism, a seventeenth-century commonplace. It is rather to insist that Descartes' enterprise not be lost sight of. He was offering a claim that he frequently felt could be understood by the least sophisticated. Perhaps Descartes was wrong in this: But then we need a separate argument to show this, and until such an argument is forthcoming, we must not dismiss the notion of the ideal seeker that was a central part of his epistemic view.

II. ... Plus One

Written nearly thirty years ago, Jaakko Hintikka's "*Cogito, Ergo Sum:* Inference or Performance?" argues that the *cogito* is a performance, a denial of which leads to existential inconsistency. Both terms, *performance* and *existential inconsistency*, need to be defined. But first, I begin with an intuitive idea of what Hintikka famously offers.

He asks us to consider sentences such as, "De Gaulle does not exist," "Descartes does not exist," and "Homer does not exist." When uttered by De Gaulle, Descartes, and Homer, respectively, each of these sentences is self-defeating. It is self-defeating in the sense that the utterance of that sentence leads the listener (who may be the speaker himself) to a belief exactly the opposite of that which the speaker intends to convey. By contrast, when uttered by a third party these

---

[26] Bernard Williams, "Introduction," ix.

[27] Here is the context: "The certainty and evidence of my kind of argument for the existence of God cannot really be known without distinctly recalling the arguments which display the uncertainty of all our knowledge of material things; and these thoughts did not seem to me suitable for inclusion in a book [*Discourse on the Method*] which I wished to be intelligible in part even to women while providing matter for thought for the finest minds" (CSMK 86; AT I, 560).

sentences do not have that failing. Thus, De Gaulle's saying, "De Gaulle does not exist," is odd, absurd, inconsistent; my uttering the same sentence, even in the presence of De Gaulle, is not. It is the purpose of ordinary discourse that when one utters a declarative sentence one intends to convey a piece of information. But that purpose is defeated or destroyed in certain special cases, such as the case of De Gaulle. Now, in order to convey information to others, I have to do something that is heard, seen, or felt by others; but in my own case, I do not have to do any such thing: A thought is sufficient.

Hintikka claims that the *cogito*-sentence, "I think, therefore I am," is just such a proposition, a piece of information. It is a declarative sentence; when its negation is uttered by a speaker, say, by Descartes, it defeats its very purpose. In ordinary circumstances to an ordinary listener, the denial of the *cogito*-sentence would convey that Descartes exists, rather than what Descartes intends to convey, namely, that Descartes does not exist. "This transition from 'public' speech-acts to 'private' thought-acts, however, does not affect the essential features of their logic" (H, 119).

It is time to define terms. First, *existentially inconsistent*:

The notion of existential inconsistency may be defined as follows; let *p* be a sentence and *a* a singular term (e.g., a name, a pronoun, or a definite description). We shall say that *p* is *existentially inconsistent* for the person referred to by *a* to utter if and only if the longer sentence

  p; and *a* exists

is inconsistent (in the ordinary sense of the word). (H, 116)

Second, to elucidate *performance*:

The inconsistency (absurdity) of an existentially inconsistent statement can in a sense be said to be of *performatory* (performative) character. It depends on an act or "performance," namely on a certain person's act of uttering a sentence (or of otherwise making a statement); it does not depend solely on the means used for the purpose, that is, on the sentence which is being uttered. (H, 118)

Third, consider *statement*. The notion of existential inconsistency applies to a statement, and not to a sentence. A statement is more than a sentence: A sentence is a grammatical entity; in order to characterize a statement, on the other hand, we need to specify at least three things, namely, the speaker, the sentence he utters, and the context or circumstance in which he utters it. Thus, "De Gaulle does not exist" is a perfectly good sentence, but it is not existentially inconsistent or even ordinarily inconsistent. However, if we specify that the speaker is De Gaulle, that the sentence is "De Gaulle does not exist," and that the circumstances are ordinary ones in which De Gaulle wishes to convey a piece of information, then we can say that we have an existential inconsistency on our hands. In the case of the *cogito*, Descartes is the speaker; the sentence is "Descartes does not exist"; and Descartes is his own audience, intending to convey to himself the truth of the sentence. In this, of course, he fails.

"We may now appreciate," says Hintikka,

the function of the word *cogito* in Descartes's sentence as well as his motives in employing it. It serves to express the performatory character of Descartes's insight; it refers to the "performance" (to the act of thinking) through which the sentence "I exist" may be said to verify itself. For this reason, it has a most important function in Descartes's sentence. It cannot be replaced by any arbitrary verb. (H, 123)

Let us examine Hintikka's interpretation of the *cogito*. First, a minor point: I simply see no existential inconsistency, or at least Descartes should not, in De Gaulle's claiming that "De Gaulle does not exist," as Hintikka maintains, as opposed to De Gaulle's saying, "I do not exist." The reason is simple enough: If De Gaulle, like Descartes, were searching for a certainty and was at the moment in the throes of doubt, he could genuinely doubt that *he* was De Gaulle. It is implied that De Gaulle knows that he is De Gaulle, and that when De Gaulle says, "De Gaulle does not exist," he does so in full knowledge of who he is. But that, at least, is not certain at the end of the First Meditation.

But I want to go a step further. Not only is there no inconsistency in De Gaulle's claiming, "De Gaulle does not exist," there is also none in his saying, "I do not exist." I think it is possible for someone to genuinely assert, "I do not exist." Imagine someone who has gone through the First Meditation, its arguments deeply impressed upon him. He comes to genuinely doubt everything he knows; at the very end of that meditation (and not knowing what is to come shortly thereafter) he wonders if *he* exists, and he can find no reason to allay his doubt. A thinker in the throes of doubt need not have discovered the route to the *cogito*. He could have become permanently embedded in doubt (or, Hume-like, he would have dismissed those doubts as soon as he went out of his study). It is only after he reads the Second Meditation and reflects upon it, invokes the demon argument, and so on, that the thinker is relieved to learn that his existence can be demonstrated.[28]

Imagine: Someone doubts the existence of the external world. There is a satisfactory "proof" of the existence of the external world, but no one has yet made that philosophical discovery. What does he do in the meantime? Well, he either takes its existence for granted and asks for a proper analysis of sentences referring to the external world, much as G. E. Moore did; or he continues to search for the proof; or he ignores the problem. Similarly, someone doubts his own existence. There is a satisfactory "proof" of the existence of the self, but no one has yet made that philosophical discovery. What does he do in the meantime? Once again, he either takes its existence for granted and asks for a proper analysis of sentences referring to the self; or he continues to search for the proof; or he ignores the problem.

For someone who thinks that the problem of whether or not he exists is a genuine philosophical problem, it is not implausible to contend that, for all he knows, he does not exist. If you find this puzzling, it is because you already have a philosophical theory mitigating your doubt. Hintikka is worth quoting on this: "It is not strictly true to say that an inconsistency arises from Descartes's attempt to *think* that he does not exist or to doubt that he does. Someone else may think so; why not Descartes himself?" So far, so good. But immediately Hintikka continues: "He can certainly think so in the sense of contemplating a 'mere possibility.' What he cannot do is to *persuade* anybody (including himself) that he does not exist; wherefore he cannot try to *profess* (to others or to himself) that he does not exist without defeating his own attempt." (H, 123, note 26) This is so unlike Descartes. It is, surely, enough that Descartes can envisage a "mere possibility"; that is enough to make him doubt his existence. Descartes doubts the existence of the physical world on just this "mere possibility"; why not doubt his own existence? In fact, if he can envisage the possibility of his nonexistence, how can he take the knowledge of his existence for granted?

---

[28] For an elegant telling of this point, see Jorge Louis Borges, "Borges and I" and "The Circular Ruins."

Let me turn to the second objection. For all the talk about performance, there is an "inference" after all. Were Descartes to enlist Hintikka's view, Descartes would have to maintain the following argument, without which he would have no reason to believe that he exists:

[1]   If I, as both speaker and listener, in the ordinary circumstances, intending to convey a piece of information, were to claim, *S*, "I do not exist," then I must make a statement that is existentially inconsistent (that is, necessarily false).

[2]   But if a statement, *S*, entails a necessary falsehood, then not-*S* is necessarily true.

[3]   I *do* claim that "I do not exist."

---

[4]   ∴ Not-*S* is necessarily true. That is, "I exist" is necessarily true.

The foregoing is an argument making use of several principles of logic and inference. Descartes cannot reach the conclusion without premise [3], a premise that I have just argued is in need of justification. Moreover, will an attempt to understand and justify [3] return us to Hintikka's thesis, thus forcing us to argue in circles?

Third, if uttering or saying to myself, "I do not exist," is existentially inconsistent when the intention is to convey a piece of information, then uttering its negation, "I exist," is surely existentially tautologous in character. But then, what is to be gained from that statement, which could count as the first truth? Why is an existentially tautologous statement, preferred over any other simple tautologous statement, such as, "Either I exist, or I do not exist"?

Fourth, Hintikka's definition of existential inconsistency does not serve his purpose, much less Descartes'. The definition is too broad. Consider the following statements uttered by me:

[1]   I cannot speak a word of English.
[2]   I am a liar.
[3]   I wish for nothing.
[4]   I cannot think a thought.
[5]   I cannot utter a sentence.

When each of these statements, *p*, is uttered by me, *a*, it, strictly speaking, satisfies Hintikka's definition of existential inconsistency: "*p*;

and *a* exists" is ordinarily inconsistent. In these cases, "*a* exists" is not necessary, for there is something about each statement which, when uttered to perform a speech act, renders it "absurd." This shows that Hintikka needs to put certain restrictions on what is to count as *p*. Otherwise, on Hintikka's view of Descartes, Descartes could have uttered any sentence [1] through [5], and there would have been an ordinary inconsistency, but not the existential inconsistency that Hintikka needs to establish. As nearly as I can tell, *p* can only be the statement, "*a* does not exist." But then,

p; and *a* exists

reduces to

a does not exist; *a* exists

Surely, that is trivial.

Fifth, Hintikka had tried to show that the *cogito* is an argument: Hamlet has many thoughts, but assuredly Hamlet does not exist. So Descartes' having many thoughts would not entail that Descartes exists, unless his existence is presupposed. Or consider the following argument, said Hintikka: Homer was a Greek, or he was a barbarian (non-Greek). If he was a Greek, then he existed; if he was a barbarian (non-Greek), then he existed. Therefore, Homer existed. This, Hintikka had argued, is a poor argument, since it, too, blatantly assumes the existence of the very thing that the argument purports to prove. "The celebrated Homeric question cannot be solved on paper" (H, 115). Alternatively, one can see that the case of Hamlet shows the inference to be fallacious. Thus, either Hamlet is the prince of Denmark, or he is not. If he is the prince of Denmark, then he exists; if he is not the prince of Denmark, then he exists. Therefore, Hamlet exists.[29] So far, Hintikka.

Imagine that Hamlet had the thought, "I do not exist," and that Shakespeare had made Hamlet, in a different soliloquy, go through Hintikka's philosophical argument that leads Hamlet to the thought that he does exist after all. It would be a poor inference from this to conclude that, therefore, Hamlet exists. Hintikka needs existential presuppositions just as much as those he argues against. He is not

[29] See Appendix B.

defended by the following: "If Hamlet exists, and Hamlet says, 'I do not exist', then, and only then, is an existential inconsistency committed when Hamlet makes that statement." But this is only a conditional statement, and it is on all fours with the statement, "If I exist, and I say, 'I do not exist', then, and only then, is an existential inconsistency committed by me when I make that statement." Those statements are uncontroversially true. If the antecedent is false, then the conditional is trivially true; if the antecedent is true, then the consequent is true. The problem, of course, is to establish the truth of the antecedent, "I exist, and I say, 'I do not exist'." This cannot be established in Hintikka's way.

Sixth, Hintikka says:

> It seems to me that the most interesting interpretation one can give to [the *cogito*] is to say that Descartes realized, however dimly, the existential inconsistency of the sentence "I don't exist" and therefore the existential self-verifiability of "I exist." *Cogito, ergo sum* is only one possible way of expressing this insight. Another way actually employed by Descartes is to say that the sentence *ego sum* is intuitively self-evident. (H, 121)

In the next paragraph he says that the *cogito*

> cannot be a logical inference in the ordinary sense of the word. . . . In Descartes's argument the relation of *cogito* to *sum* is not that of a premise to a conclusion. Their relation is rather comparable with that of a *process* to its *product*. The indubitability of my own existence results from my thinking of it almost as the sound of music results from playing it. (H, 121–122)

This will not do. The 'therefore' is puzzling: The opposite of existential inconsistency is existential tautology, hardly existential self-verifiability. One is a logical notion, the other an epistemic one. Next, as I have just tried to show in reconstructing Hintikka's claims, the individual thinker can scarcely do with a single intuition, but needs an entire argument. Finally, this leaves no room for doubt to play a role in Descartes' argument. The doubting, or the possibility of deception, is not essential. The deceiving demon could be set aside as so much color, an insubstantial aspect of Descartes' doctrine of the *cogito*. One could simply have begun with, "I don't exist," and reached the conclusion that one did exist. To this extent, Hintikka's suggestions are quite out of harmony with Descartes' actual enterprise.

Seventh and finally, Hintikka has claimed that the *cogito* is so singular that it will permit no generalization from it. But here is the proposition from *Meditations on First Philosophy*: "This proposition, *I am, I exist* is necessarily true whenever it is put forward by me or conceived in my mind." This lends itself to a simple generalization from which the quoted sentence can be derived. Thus: "For any individual, this proposition, *I am, I exist* is necessarily true whenever it is put forward by the individual or conceived in the mind of the individual." Perhaps this is the right representation of the compact proposition, "Whatever thinks, exists." "In a sense, therefore," says Hintikka, "Descartes' insight is not generalizable. This is of course due to its performatory character." (H, 127) This is to confuse the epistemic problem of how one can know the truth of the *cogito* with the logical problem. Regardless of whether the *cogito* is a performance, one could generalize, and Descartes was right to think that he could do so.

Each of these five plus one ways of understanding the *cogito* as an argument is riddled by several difficulties. But there is one difficulty so deep and so irreparable that we had better conclude that the *cogito* is not an argument. This brings me to the heart of my thesis.

6

Cogito: Not an Argument

Perhaps nowhere in this book is the Sulmo principle more steadfastly used than here. The principle states that "a philosopher's system must not be reconstructed and judged until after his death."[1] In order to reconstruct his system, we may bring together elements that the philosopher himself did not bring together – for lack of time, or insight, or whatever. Such a reconstruction is permissible so long as it is consistent with his major views. Only such a picture is worthy of being examined.

I have brought together theses that Descartes maintained at various periods, and none of which – at the very least, no central thesis – he recanted. For example, I have brought to bear on the *cogito* Descartes' theory of deduction. The theory was cast in *Rules for the Direction of the Mind*, written as early as 1628, perhaps even earlier, never discussed in detail again, and never published during Descartes' life. Even before it was finally published in 1684 in a Dutch translation,[2] it had already profoundly influenced *Logic or The Art of Thinking*, famously known as *Port-Royal Logic*, first published anonymously in 1662.[3] The problem I

---

[1] See the Preface.
[2] A Latin version appeared in 1701, a better version than the Dutch version in scholarly opinion, and it is that version that sits in AT. For the backdrop to *Port-Royal Logic*, see Appendix C.
[3] "In setting out their philosophical foundations, the authors borrow whole arguments from Descartes' *Rules for the Direction of the Mind, Discourse on the Method,* and *Meditations,* occasionally acknowledging their source." Buroker, "Introduction," xx.

have set myself is to determine the truth-value of a counterfactual. It goes something like this: If Descartes had given us in the first meditation (or in the first three parts of *Discourse on the Method*) his theory of deduction, his metaphysical doubts, the doctrine of the creation of eternal truths, and the theory about memory, could Descartes have regarded the *cogito* as an argument? Not just anywhere, but at the right place: Could he have, for example, regarded the *cogito* as an argument at the end of the third paragraph in the Second Meditation? Or at the end of the fourth paragraph in Part IV of *Discourse on the Method*?

In section I, I delineate the preliminaries. In section II, I provide the core argument, the general defense of my central claim about the *cogito*. Then, in section III, I prove – I hope I am not overstating my case by using that word – that Descartes could not claim, and assuredly ought not to have claimed, that the *cogito* is an argument. Finally, in section IV, I offer Descartes' theory of deduction, and the skeptical background, to further support this claim.

I. The Preliminaries

Let me begin, then, by noting several things as preliminaries to establishing the thesis, namely, that the *cogito* in not an argument. There are, in all, seven prefatory remarks. First, in the very paragraph before the one that contains the *cogito* passage in the *Meditations on First Philosophy*, Descartes says, "I will suppose then, that everything I see is spurious. I will believe that my memory tells me lies, and that none of the things that it reports ever happened." (CSM II, 16; AT VII, 24) So memory cannot be trusted, and the *cogito* claim, if an argument, cannot essentially rely on memory.

Second, having just finished the First Meditation (recall that the *cogito* passage in the Second Meditation is less than four paragraphs away), "the malicious demon of the utmost power and cunning" is uppermost in Descartes' mind. The *cogito* passages are burdened with it. Thus, the passage from the *Meditations on First Philosophy* explicitly mentions "a deceiver of supreme power and cunning"; and the passage from *Discourse on the Method* refers to "the most extravagant suppositions of the skeptics."

Consequently, third, we need to be clear about the task to which the malicious demon of utmost power, cunning, and deception was set to perform in the First Meditation. For the sake of accuracy, it must be noted that the malicious demon hypothesis is introduced only in the final paragraph of that meditation; the earlier supposition was that an omnipotent God was engaging in an act of deception. But here the demon hypothesis is substituted for the hypothesis of God, because God is all-good and cannot deceive; and so the demon is made to perform the tasks once assigned to the deceiving God. Thus, the malicious demon is to deceive Descartes into thinking that all of the sciences that study composite things – physics, astronomy, medicine, and all other such disciplines – are false; he will deceive Descartes into thinking that there is a sky, earth, air, colors, shapes, extended things, size, place, and sound; that he, Descartes, has hands, eyes, flesh, blood, and senses, when, in fact, he has none of these things at all, nor do any objects exist. Descartes may have moral certainty (CSM I, 130; AT VI, 37–38) about these things; what he does not have, yet, is metaphysical certainty.

"What is more, since I sometimes believe that others go astray in cases where they think they have the most perfect knowledge, may I not similarly go wrong every time I add two and three or count the sides of a square, or in some even simpler matter, if that is imaginable?" (CSM II, 14; AT VII, 21) More significant for our purpose, one of the principal tasks of the malicious demon is to make Descartes doubt the truths, even the simple truths, of mathematics – so pervasive is his hyperbolic doubt. But if the truths of mathematics are to be doubted, the doubting of the truths of logic cannot be far behind. And it was notorious that Descartes was very impatient with scholastic Aristotelian logic.[4] At the very least, Descartes' doubt would have been, at best, an incomplete doubt if the laws of logic and the principles of inference were not included in the scope of his doubt.

Fourth, consider this:

Where knowledge of things is concerned, only two factors need to be considered: ourselves, the knowing subjects, and the things which are the objects of knowledge. As for ourselves, there are only four faculties which we can use for this purpose, *viz.* intellect, imagination, sense-perception, and memory. It is of course only the intellect that is capable of perceiving the truth, but it has to be assisted by imagination, sense-perception and memory if we are not to

4 See the last chapter, section II.

omit anything which lies within our power. (CSM I, 39; AT X, 411; see also, CSM I, 32; AT X, 398–399)

The assistance of imagination and sense perception cannot be wholly relied upon, since they "botch things" up. Thus, at the start, unless there are arguments to the contrary, one should rely only on the intellect and memory.

Fifth, in brief, consider Descartes' account of intuition and deduction.

By 'intuition' I do not mean the fluctuating testimony of the senses or the deceptive judgement of the imagination as it botches things together, but the conception of a clear and attentive mind, which is so easy and distinct that there can be no room for doubt about what we are understanding. Alternatively, and this comes to the same thing, intuition is the indubitable conception of a clear and attentive mind which proceeds solely from the light of reason. Because it is simpler, it is more certain than deduction, though deduction, as we noted above, is not something a man can perform wrongly. (CSM I, 14; AT X, 368)

Now consider, in brief, Descartes' account of deduction: "deduction, by which we mean the inference of something as following necessarily from some other propositions which are known with certainty" (CSM I, 15; AT X, 369). Descartes' use of the notion of deduction is different from ours. We can have a legitimate deductive inference from false premises; not so for Descartes. For him, the premises have to be known with certainty. However, there is this in Descartes: "Now none of the conclusions deduced from a principle which is not evident can themselves be evident, even though they may be deduced from the principle in an evident manner" (CSM I, 183; AT IXB, 8). This seems to hint at the possibility of an inference from false premises; but its central point is to focus on the unreliability of the conclusion if the premises are untrue or uncertain.

Descartes' "method cannot go so far as to teach us how to perform the actual operations of intuition and deduction, since these are the simplest of all and quite basic. If our intellect were not already able to perform them, it would not comprehend any of the rules of the method, however easy they might be." (CSM I, 16; AT X, 372) This cannot mean that deduction is not analyzable. For when Descartes speaks of the chain of deduction or inference, he must presuppose an understanding of intuition without which deduction could not get off the ground. But no understanding of deduction is presupposed in the understanding of intuition.

Sixth, in an utterly crucial passage in the *Rules for the Direction of the Mind*, written in 1628, thirteen years before *Meditations on First Philosophy*, Descartes says that it is necessary to distinguish between intuition and deduction:

> There may be some doubt here about our reason for suggesting another mode of knowing in addition to intuition, *viz.* deduction, by which we mean the inference of something as following necessarily from some other propositions which are known with certainty. But this distinction had to be made, since very many facts which are not self-evident are known with certainty, provided they are inferred from true and known principles through a continuous and uninterrupted movement of thought in which each individual proposition is clearly intuited. This is similar to the way in which we know that the last link in a long chain is connected to the first: even if we cannot take in at one glance all the intermediate links on which the connection depends, we can have the knowledge of the connection provided we survey the links one after the other, and keep in mind that each link from first to last is attached to its neighbour. Hence we are distinguishing mental intuition from certain deduction on the grounds that we are aware of a movement or a sort of sequence in the latter but not in the former, and also because immediate self-evidence is not required for deduction, as it is for intuition; deduction in a sense gets its certainty from memory.[5] (CSM I, 15; AT X, 369–370)

And again:

> As we have said, conclusions which embrace more than we can grasp in a single intuition depend for their certainty on memory, and since memory is weak and unstable, it must be refreshed and strengthened through this continuous and repeated movement of thought. (CSM I, 38; AT X, 408)

In a deduction, more than one proposition is involved. Hence, there is a passage or a movement from one proposition to the next; the greater the number of propositions, the longer the movement. Where movement is involved, a thinker must inevitably rely on his memory to hold the links that bind the propositions together in his mind. But in an intuition, there is no movement; there is no link; hence, there is no

---

[5] Elsewhere, Descartes speaks of a number of "separate inferences" "between the conclusion and the primary and supremely simple proposition" and of the difficulty of keeping in view "all the connections together" (CSM I, 22–23; AT X, 383–384).

memory involved. If memory is unreliable, as just noted in the fourth preliminary point, then deduction can scarcely be relied upon.

Seventh and finally, Descartes was explicitly searching for, and claimed to have found, a single, solitary, and self-evident principle, which would serve as the *foundation* of his philosophy. Here are examples of such a claim: From the *Principles of Philosophy*: "Accordingly, this piece of knowledge ["... this inference" – French version] – *I am thinking, therefore I exist* – is the first and most certain of all to occur to anyone who philosophizes in an orderly way"[6] (CSM I, 195; AT VIIIA, 7). From the *Discourse on the Method*: "And observing that this truth '*I am thinking, therefore I exist*,' was so firm and sure that all the most extravagant suppositions of the sceptics were incapable of shaking it, I decided that I could accept it without scruple as the first principle of the philosophy I was seeking" (CSM I, 127; AT VI, 32). Unquestionably, Descartes is seeking the *first* indubitable proposition from which the rest would follow.[7] Nowhere in Descartes is the geometrical model more evident. In short, he claims to have discovered *the* philosophical axiom. With this, I bring the seven prefatory remarks to a close.

II. The Core of the Claim

Together, these Cartesian claims make it indisputable that the *cogito* cannot be construed as an argument. Why? *If* the *cogito* is an argument, then it should have several elements. In the case of the *cogito*, there must, in some versions, be at least three propositions – two premises and a conclusion – and two links: a link between the premises, and a link between them and the conclusion. There must be an uninterrupted movement of thought from the premises to the conclusion, a movement where each proposition is clearly intuited. Self-evidence is not required, but the conclusion must follow necessarily from some other propositions that are known with certainty. In the case of the

[6] Arnauld's *Port-Royal Logic* offers this clarification: "Wishing to abbreviate their speech, people created an infinity of words all signifying both an affirmation, that is, what is signified by the substantive verb, and in addition a certain attribute to be affirmed. All verbs besides the substantive are like this, such as 'God exists,' that is, 'is existent,' 'God loves humanity,' that is, 'God is a lover of humanity.' When the substantive verb stands alone, for example when I say, 'I think, therefore I am,' it ceases to be purely substantive, because then it is united with the most general attribute, namely being. For 'I am' means 'I am a being,' 'I am a thing.'" (AN, 83)

[7] Again, keeping in mind Chapter 1, section III.

cogito, this means that "Whatever thinks, exists" and "I think" are principles that are true and known with certainty, and that "I exist," the inferred proposition, if known certainly, is known only derivatively. Finally and most importantly, one has to *remember* the various propositions and their links: "[E]ven if we cannot take in at one glance all the intermediate links on which the connection depends, we can have the knowledge of the connection provided we survey the links one after the other, and keep in mind that each link from first to last is attached to its neighbour." This we must do because "deduction in a sense gets its certainty from memory." But at this stage of the argument in the *Meditations on First Philosophy*, memory is held to be *explicitly* unreliable, and therefore we cannot trust our memories of various links and connections. *Any* argument would be essentially unreliable; at the very least, it could not be known to be valid.

But isn't the *cogito* argument simple enough? Cannot all of it be held in the mind simultaneously? Isn't each proposition sufficiently self-evident to warrant confidence in the validity of the argument? The answer is no. Descartes gives as an example a simpler argument that he considers to be an inference. "The self-evidence and certainty of intuition," he says, "is required not only for apprehending single propositions, but also for any train of reasoning whatever. Take for example, the inference that 2 plus 2 equals 3 plus 1; not only must we intuitively perceive that 2 plus 2 make 4, and that 3 plus 1 make 4, but also that the original proposition follows necessarily from the other two." (CSM I, 14–15; AT X, 369) (Does not this rely on some general principle – for example, that two things that are equal to a third are equal to one another? Is not such a proposition a correlative of "Whatever thinks, exists"?) But where there is inference, there is movement of thought; if there is movement of thought, then there must be reliance on memory, and since memory is in doubt, the correctness of the inference is in doubt.[8]

The foregoing passage also makes it clear that there is a deductive chain of knowledge. In that chain or hierarchy, certain propositions

---

[8] One can, of course, blandly deny that where there is an inference, there is memory. One would make such an assertion, because it is the *only* way to have it both ways: namely, to maintain that the *cogito* is an argument and that the inference to the conclusion does not rely on memory. However, we have Descartes' own words quoted earlier: "deduction in a sense gets its certainty from memory." There is *no* evidence that 'deduction' here refers only to mediate inference, and not to immediate inference as well.

are self-evident; other propositions rely on these as theorems do on axioms. If Descartes' explicit aim is to arrive at a certainty from which, Archimedes-like, he can move his entire philosophical system, then the *cogito* understood as an argument can hardly serve that aim. Something else – say, the general proposition, "Whatever thinks, exists," or the singular proposition, "I think" – must serve as the axiom, and the *cogito* as the theorem. There is no warrant in the texts for attributing such a view to Descartes. Indeed, as we saw from passages in the *Meditations on First Philosophy* and the *Discourse on the Method*, Descartes' explicit aim is to find the first principle. Whereas on the view that the *cogito* is an argument, the *cogito* is a philosophical theorem, not a philosophical axiom.

In any event, Descartes himself settles this point in his "Appendix to the Fifth Set of Objections and Replies":

The author of the *Counter-Objections* claims that when I say "I am thinking, therefore I exist" I presuppose the major premiss "Whatever thinks exists," and hence I have already adopted a preconceived opinion. Here he once more misuses the term "preconceived opinion." For although we can apply the term to the proposition in question when it is put forward without attention and believed to be true only because we remember that we judged it to be true previously, we cannot say that it is always a preconceived opinion. For when we examine it, it appears so evident to the understanding that we cannot but believe it, even though this may be the first time in our life that we have thought of it – in which case we would have no preconceived opinion about it. But the most important mistake our critic makes here is the supposition that knowledge of particular propositions must always be deduced from universal ones, following the same order as that of a syllogism in Dialectic. Here he shows how little he knows of the way in which we should search for truth. (CSM II, 271; AT IX A, 205–206)

The passages representing the *cogito* are, in fact, far too complex to be represented in the way in which they have been represented. Thus, in the syllogism just cited,

[1]   Whatever thinks exists.
[2]   I am thinking.
_____
[3]   ∴ I exist.

the representation skips the important qualifier. The qualifier occurs in various forms. For instance, in the *Discourse on the Method* it occurs in this way: "I noticed that while I was trying thus to think everything false . . ." In the *Meditations on First Philosophy*, it occurs as follows: "*I am, I exist*, is necessarily true whenever it is put forward by me or conceived in my mind."

The syllogism, if one is to be constructed, must take into account these propositional attitudes. The syllogism would then read:

[1a] Whenever I think, or put forward, or utter, or conceive in my mind, "*I am, I exist*," it is necessarily true.

[2] I am thinking.

_____

[3] ∴ I exist.

This argument is plainly a non sequitur. Since the proposition, "I am, I exist," occurs in [1a] in the context of a propositional attitude, [3] does not follow from [1a] via [2].

The word 'thought' in Descartes covers a multitude of mental states. It is, in most of its uses – and in the *cogito* passages especially – elliptical. It stands for "I think *x*." Here is a passage from *Principles of Philosophy*, Part I:

9. *What is meant by 'thought'*. By the term 'thought', I understand everything which we are aware of as happening within us, in so far as we have awareness of it. Hence, *thinking* is to be identified here not merely with understanding, willing, and imagining, but also with sensory awareness. For if I say "I am seeing, or I am walking, therefore I exist," and take this as applying to vision or walking as bodily activities, then the conclusion is not absolutely certain. This is because, as often happens during sleep, it is possible for me to think I am seeing or walking, though my eyes are closed and I am not moving about; such thoughts might even be possible if I had no body at all. But if I take 'seeing' or 'walking' to apply to the actual sense or awareness of seeing or walking, then the conclusion is quite certain, since it relates to the mind, which alone has the sensation or thought that it is seeing or walking. (CSM I, 195; AT VIIIA, 7–8)

Thus, whenever "I think" occurs, it is elliptical; it stands for "I think I am walking," "I think I am breathing," "I think I am seeing a tree," and so on. The syllogism with premise [1] is thus incompletely stated. Premise [1] is elliptical; it stands for statements such as "Whatever thinks it is walking, exists" or "Whatever thinks it is seeing a tree, exists." As nearly as I can determine, there cannot be just a thought; it has to be a thought of something or other.

In rule 3 in *Rules for the Direction of the Mind*, Descartes said, "[L]et us now review all the actions of the intellect by means of which we are able to arrive at a knowledge of things with no fear of being mistaken. We recognize only two: intuition and deduction." (CSM I, 14; AT X, 368) If all our acquisition of knowledge can be explained in terms of intuition and deduction, and the *cogito* is unquestionably knowledge, then how was it acquired? Was it acquired by intuition or by deduction?

We may consider a different perspective by reconsidering the following from an earlier chapter:

Case 4. Second-order mental state

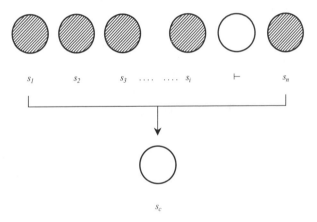

Case 5. Second-order mental state

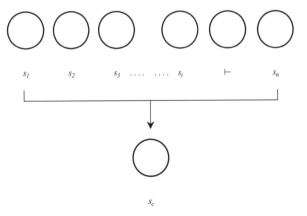

Now evidently, as Descartes is engaged in the method of doubt, he cannot be certain of any proposition that he entertains prior to his establishing the *cogito*. But granting that the *cogito* is an argument, one must also admit that such an argument not only must be valid, but also must be sound – that is, its premises must be true. If so, Case 4 scarcely represents the mental process of the thinker. The only alternative left is Case 5. But here there is an obstacle. Since the *cogito* is the *end* result of the argument, it simply cannot serve as the *first item of knowledge* that Descartes had clearly and repeatedly said it was. That privilege must now be accorded to s_1 or s_2 or s_3 or . . . , but emphatically not to s_c. This is in clear violation of the first criterion that the absolutely certain truth must satisfy.[9]

Quite clearly, the *cogito* cannot be listed as a deduction. It must be an intuition, something simple, alongside a host of mathematical things that we clearly and self-evidently see.

III. The Proof

The simplest, strongest, most conclusive argument in favor of my view that the *cogito* cannot, and ought not, be construed as an argument, I have saved for this section. Here is the proof. Descartes' alleged argument, when made explicit, runs in at least one common version as follows:

[1]	Whatever thinks, exists.	Premise
[2]	I think.	Premise
[3]	If I think, I exist.	1, Universal Instantiation
[4]	∴ I exist.	2, 3, Modus Ponens

Note that [1] explicitly occurs in Descartes in the *Principles of Philosophy* and is formulated in this way: "*He who thinks cannot but exist while he thinks.*" Such a principle is labeled by Descartes as a common notion, an axiom, an eternal truth (CSM I, 209; AT VIIIA, 24). I grant that the argument is valid; I overlook the problem that *existence* is treated as a predicate; and I dismiss, as did Descartes, questions concerning how we can know the meaning of words. The question is, how can Descartes

---

[9] See Chapter 2, section III.

know that this argument is valid? At this point in his philosophical investigations, he cannot know this.

At this juncture in the Second Meditation in *Meditations on First Philosophy*, the demon has not relented. The existence of the external world, the deliverance of his senses, whether he has a body, the principles of mathematics, *and* by parity of reasoning the principles of logic and inference are all in doubt. *Ergo*, Descartes has *no* principle of inference to rely on to show that his alleged *cogito*-argument is valid. It is of no avail to say: While men may make mistakes, "none of the errors to which men – men, I say, not the brutes – are liable is ever due to faulty inference; they are due only to the fact that men take for granted certain poorly understood observations, or lay down rash and groundless judgements" (CSM I, 12; AT X, 365). For all that Descartes knows at this stage of the inquiry, the rule of universal instantiation and the rule of *modus ponens* are *false* or "rash and groundless judgements." The demon may well be deceiving him into thinking that these principles of inference, like the cognate principles of mathematics, are true when in fact they are not.

Quite simply, knowing that an argument is valid presupposes knowledge of the principles of inference; so if one cannot be sure that one is not being deceived about the veracity of certain principles of logic and inference (which show the argument under consideration to be valid), one cannot know that the argument is valid. If it is true that an argument "is a machine which often breaks down," as Descartes wrote, probably to Silhon, in March or April 1648 (CSMK, 332; AT V,139) – a passage rarely, if ever, cited in the literature – then in this situation the thinker has every reason to suspect the validity of the argument, let alone its soundness. It is indeed the case that Descartes could not, at this stage of the argument, settle for even that much-despised probable syllogism (CSM I, 11; AT X, 363–364) – watering down his aim to mere probable belief rather than knowing – for even the correctness of a probable syllogism must presuppose principles of inductive inference in virtue of which some arguments are more probable than others.

It is worth noting the context in which Descartes spoke of the machine of deduction breaking down. Silhon is interested in the nature of knowledge about God. He distinguishes the nature of that knowledge in beatific vision from our present knowledge of God. The latter,

Silhon claims, is intuitive knowledge. Descartes *denies* this. Descartes writes:

Intuitive knowledge is an illumination of the mind. ... Whatever we can know of God in this life, short of a miracle, is the result of reasoning and discursive inquiry. It is deduced from the principles of faith, which is obscure, or it comes from the natural ideas and notions we have, which even at their clearest are only gross and confused on so sublime a topic. Consequently, whatever knowledge we have or acquire by way of reason is as dark as the principles from which it is derived, and is moreover infected with the uncertainty we find in all our reasoning. (CSMK, 331; AT V, 136–137)

As if this were not enough, Descartes continues in the next paragraph thus: "You will surely admit that you are less certain of the presence of the objects you see than of the truth of the proposition 'I am thinking, therefore I exist.' Now this knowledge is not the work of your reasoning...; it is something your mind sees, feels, and handles." Clearly, then, Descartes knows that when it comes to the *cogito* he cannot, should not, rely on principles of logic or reasoning; intuitive knowledge must suffice. When it comes to God, intuitive knowledge cannot suffice.[10]

Consider, next, an extraordinarily strange passage from *The Search for Truth*, where he says,

For is there anything in what you have said which is not exact, which is not validly argued, which is not correctly deduced from what has gone before? All these points have been stated and worked out not by means of logic, or a rule or pattern of argument, but simply by the light of reason and good sense. When this light operates on its own, it is less liable to go wrong than when it anxiously strives to follow the numerous different rules, the inventions of human ingenuity and idleness, which serves more to corrupt it than render it more perfect. (CSM II, 415; AT X, 521)

He had expressed similar reservations earlier in the *Discourse on the Method*, Part II. "When I was younger," he says there,

my philosophical studies had included some logic. ... But on further examination I observed with regard to logic that syllogisms and most of its other techniques are of less use for learning things than for explaining to others the

---

[10] To avoid undue repetition, I urge the reader to consult Chapter 4, note 12, for the other aspect of the background under consideration here.

things one already knows or even, as in the art of Lully, for speaking without judgement about matters of which one is ignorant. And although logic does contain many excellent and true precepts, these are mixed up with so many others which are harmful or superfluous that it is almost as difficult to distinguish them as it is to carve a Diana or a Minerva from an unhewn block of marble.[11] (CSM I, 119; AT VI, 17)

In Part IV of *Discourse on the Method*, he is even more explicit. Here is a statement that comes just one sentence before the statement of the *cogito*. "And since there are men who make mistakes in reasoning, committing logical fallacies concerning the simplest questions in geometry, and because I judged that I was as prone to error as anyone else, I rejected as unsound all the arguments I had previously taken as demonstrative proofs" (CSM I, 127; AT VI, 32). Given the systematic doubt he was engaged in, it would clearly be essential to his enterprise to discard all of these principles of logic, so that the bad ones did not stay inadvertently in the good lot and contaminate his reasoning. And so he decided that "in place of the large number of rules that make up logic" (CSM I, 120; AT VI, 18), he would follow his famous four rules of philosophical procedure. But these four rules, as we have seen, are rules of the method of analysis and synthesis, not rules of inference.

---

[11] The history of traditional logic as it was practiced between 1350 and 1600 is interesting in its own right. It becomes more interesting when viewed from the vantage point of the topic under discussion. For example, E. J. Ashworth argues that among the questions raised by logicians during this period were those concerning "the relation of the theory of consequences to syllogistic"; these questions were about "the status of conversion, the status of consequences in syllogistic reduction and the status of the syllogism itself" ("Traditional Logic," 169). For example, (i) Johannes Dolz, pursuing the standard procedure of the Parisian treatise on syllogism, had offered an apparent counterexample in his treatment of *Barbara* (164); (ii) for second and third figures, in trying to state the rules of conversion the threat of circularity posed itself (169); (iii) the status of the fourth figure was "the most burning issue" (170); (iv) the discussion of insolubles slowly dwindled, in part because the logicians of this day thought them to be merely puzzles. "Although they wrote a great deal about them," Ashworth is quoting Spade, "there is no hint that they thought the paradoxes were crucial test cases against which their whole logic and semantics might fall" (165, note 145). Finally, (v) conflicting views about the paradoxes of material implication appeared (168–169). Ashworth's final lines are worth quoting: "Moreover, many textbooks simply adopted a position without enquiring whether it could be given a logical justification. Syllogistic may have been regarded as central to logic, but it was not always handled well" (172). Assuredly, Descartes could have detailed more powerful reasons for doubting the system of logic he was familiar with than he did for doubting the simple truths of arithmetic in the First Meditation.

This point gains further credence when connected to the famous doctrine about the creation of eternal truths. This doctrine was designed to answer the question, can any limitation be put on the powers of God? The answer: No, God can do anything, including alter the laws of logic and mathematics. To his longtime friend Father Mersenne, Descartes wrote on April 15, 1630:

> The mathematical truths which you call eternal have been laid down by God and depend on him entirely no less than the rest of his creatures. Indeed to say that these truths are independent of God is to talk of Him as if he were Jupiter or Saturn and to subject Him to the Styx and the Fates. Please do not hesitate to assert and proclaim everywhere that it is God who has laid down these laws in nature just as a king lays down laws in his kingdom. (CSMK, 23; AT X, 145)

Solon, the lawgiver, laid down one sort of laws, just and humane, that bound and governed the Athenian community. But quite conceivably he could have changed or altered those laws. He could have given them a different set of laws, in which, as in the laws of Draco before, enslavement was permitted for debt, and death was the penalty for almost all criminal offenses. Now, God is a giver of laws, too. Descartes is maintaining not merely the more plausible doctrine that God is a giver of natural, empirical laws that he could change at will. For example, God might have laid down that force, *mass × acceleration*, is instead *mass × velocity²* (as Leibniz had conjectured *vis viva* to be). He is rather maintaining the doctrine that God is also a giver of mathematical laws, eternal truths, which he could also alter at will. For example, God might have laid down that the area of a circle, πr^2, is $\pi\sqrt{i}$, where i is the imaginary number, $\sqrt{-1}$. His will is absolutely free and is not subject to anything, let alone to the Styx or the Fates.

In a letter of May 2, 1644, probably to Father Mesland, Descartes wrote:

> I turn to the difficulty of conceiving how God would have been acting freely and indifferently if he had made it false that the three angles of a triangle were equal to two right angles, or in general that contradictories could not be true together. It is easy to dispel this difficulty by considering that the power of God cannot have any limits, and that our mind is finite and so created as to be able to conceive as possible the things which God has wished to be in fact possible, but not be able to conceive as possible things which God could have

made possible, but which he has nevertheless wished to make impossible. The first consideration shows us that God cannot have been determined to make it true that contradictories cannot be true together, and therefore that He could have done the opposite. The second consideration assures us that even if this be true, we should not try to comprehend it, since our nature is incapable of doing so. (CSMK, 235; AT IV, 118; see also CSMK, 23; AT I, 145–146; and CSMK, 25; AT I, 152)

More straightforwardly, in a letter of July 29, 1648, probably to Arnauld, he wrote:

But I do not think that we should ever say of anything that it cannot be brought about by God. For since every basis of truth and goodness depends on his omnipotence, I would not dare to say that God cannot make a mountain without a valley, or bring it about that 1 and 2 are not 3. I merely say that he has given me such a mind that I cannot conceive a mountain without a valley, or a sum of 1 and 2 which is not 3; that such things involve a contradiction in my conception. (CSMK 358–359; AT V, 224)

If limits are to be placed, therefore, they are to be placed not on the power of God but rather on the powers of the human mind, which cannot conceive how 2 and 3 can add up to anything other than 5.[12]

Pierre Bourdin had objected that even if Descartes could make him doubt many things, he could not bring Bourdin to doubt the validity of *Barbara*. *Barbara* is a valid syllogism of the form "All M is P; all S is M; therefore, all S is P." Says Bourdin:

Even if you give me every possible reassurance I shall still be very afraid of overdoing my distrustful attitude if I renounce and forswear as false such long-standing and virtually innate beliefs as "A syllogism in Barbara has a valid conclusion." (CSM II, 317; AT VII, 471–472)

Far from repudiating any such doubts, or invoking the idea that it is possible for God to alter the laws of syllogistic logic, Descartes claims that Bourdin is simply fearful of the maxim to doubt, and fear does not constitute an argument against the maxim. If anything,

---

[12] Rodis-Lewis puts the point thus: "According to Descartes, a mathematics different from Euclidean geometry is conceivable for God but not for man" (R 104). A note of caution: Non-Euclidean geometry is at least consistent, whether conceivable by man or not, in a way in which $2 + 3 = 13$ is not. Descartes, clearly, was after a much stronger point: namely, that what is inconsistent, and not just inconceivable for man, is conceivable for God.

it counts in favor of the maxim, since one has no reason, except one's inexplicable fear, to rely on the syllogism in question. Indeed, Descartes cites Bourdin's own example back at him: "But a man who adds two and three together can be deceived by such a demon, as is shown by the example my critic himself has produced concerning the man who counted one o'clock four times" (CSM II, 320; AT VII, 476).

Note that there was nothing unusual about challenging the truths of logic and mathematics. So strong was the skeptical atmosphere with respect to mathematics in the early part of the seventeenth century that a demand for the defense of the alleged "queen of the sciences" seemed natural. Wilhelm Languis wrote *De Veritatibus Geometricis* in 1656, defending the truths of geometry against the sceptics Sextus Empiricus and Marcum Meibornium. Marin Mersenne devoted most of his *Verite des Sciences* to demonstrating the considerable number and variety of mathematical truths, as the best means of "overthrowing Pyrrhonism."[13]

This is not to say that Descartes is wholly against the syllogistic form of reasoning.[14] As we shall see, the occasion for using the syllogism is *after* the discovery of the *cogito* has been made and not *before*. Thus, Descartes did not want to be seen as relying on the principles of logic at the time when he was doubting and was in the process of discovering the *cogito*.

Next, consider the following fairly self-explanatory passage:

And when we become aware that we are thinking things, this is a primary notion which is not derived by means of any syllogism. When someone says "I am thinking, therefore I am, or I exist," he does not deduce existence from thought by means of a syllogism, but recognizes it as something self-evident by a simple intuition of the mind. This is clear from the fact that if he were deducing it by means of a syllogism, he would have to have had previous knowledge of the major premiss "Everything which thinks is, or exists"; yet in fact he learns it from experiencing in his own case that it is impossible that he should think without existing. It is in the nature of our mind to construct general propositions on the basis of our knowledge of particular ones. (CSM II, 100; AT VII, 140–141; see also CSMK, 330–332; AT V, 135–139)

---

[13] Popkin, *The History of Scepticism: From Erasmus to Descartes*, 87.

[14] CSM II, 355; AT VII, 522. See Chapter 4, note 12, where Descartes' remark is quoted in full.

Descartes is saying that [1] cannot be justified unless the truth of the *cogito* is already recognized. That is, "I think I exist" must first be perceived clearly and distinctly in the *cogito*-state for it to serve as a support for [1]. The critics then point out that Descartes is involved in a clear case of *petitio principii*. This would be true, as Descartes himself foresaw, *if* one were offering an argument. So this is another reason why the *cogito* should not be considered an argument. Descartes' view is in fact much stronger. His view is that it is of our nature, our essence, that we cannot know any generalization unless we begin with instances. We cannot know any general proposition without knowledge of particular ones. Since [1] is a generalization, then essentially it must appear to us later than, at least, one of its instances.

One final argument: Having established the truth of the *cogito*, Descartes asked himself what, if anything, he could believe, given the *cogito*-state. His answer was the powerful general rule, namely, that whatever appears to him as clear and distinct is true. This rule was to be his epistemic guide; it would provide him the indispensable insignia of truth. By implication, Descartes was saying that he would not accept anything as true that was not clear and distinct. Descartes' procedure would force him to measure each premise of the argument by using the general rule as the yardstick, *as well as* using that rule to determine if each inference was sound. If the measure provided by the general rule is satisfactory, the *cogito*-argument is satisfactory; if not, then not.

But here is the rub. If the *cogito* were an argument, then the general rule could not be used to determine its validity, because the general rule emerges *from* the *cogito*; the correctness of the general rule becomes evident when one sees the correctness of the *cogito*. Therefore, without substantiating the general rule and becoming certain that it is correct, the rules of inference cannot be determined to be sound. If the rules of inference cannot be determined to be sound, the validity and soundness of no argument can be determined; *ergo*, the validity and soundness of the *cogito*-argument cannot be determined. Consequently, either Descartes has no grounds for accepting the *cogito* as even a valid argument, let alone a sound one; or Descartes did not intend the *cogito* to be an argument at all.

It is easy to see the difficulty in which Descartes is placed if he is construed in the *cogito* passages as offering an argument. The existence of God, let alone the goodness of God, has not yet been demonstrated in the Second Meditation. That will be demonstrated in the Third Meditation. Then, given the doctrine of the creation of eternal truths, God could have created the laws of logic such that in them the principle of universal instantiation and the principle of *modus ponens* are *false*. If they are, then no matter what Descartes' finite mind can conceive or not conceive, he cannot be assured of having found even a valid argument.

If Descartes had been confronted with the foregoing objections, he would have granted them. But he would have insisted that his *cogito* principle was still indubitably true. He would have said something like this: "Imagine as strange a logical and mathematical world as you wish, a world in which the laws of logic and mathematics are vastly different and inconceivable to the human mind. Even in this strange world, where the malicious, powerful demon is deceiving me about the truths of logic and mathematics, he cannot deceive me unless I exist. That deception, or any similar deception, in any possible (or impossible?) world, would guarantee my existence. This is what the *cogito* aims to show; the argument that casts doubt on the principles of logic and mathematics makes it even more evident." It is only against a background such as this that we can make sense of Descartes' otherwise rather puzzling, and repeated, remark that the *cogito* is *more* certain than the truths of logic and mathematics.

But there is a dilemma facing Descartes that I am unable to resolve. Either memory plays a role in the *cogito*-state of a thinker, or it does not. If memory plays a role, then of course the certainty of the *cogito* is spurious, because memory, at the present stage in the investigation, is not yet known to be reliable. On the other hand, if memory does not play a role, then in the *cogito*-state the thinker cannot reliably remember the earlier skeptical arguments against relying on the truths of mathematics or the deliverances of sense experience.[15] But the failure

---

[15] One might argue that the "state" that is produced by this long process requires of the thinker that he remember – that he "include" somehow in the present state – the past experiences he has been through. Must he not remember what the extraordinary doubt has shown to be doubtful? In short, does not certainty in the present require, for its possibility, that it include a faithful memory of what has failed to pass muster in the past and is now seen to be quite different from the present "truth"? But if memory is doubtful, we are left hanging. I should add to my answer that follows in

to remember the skeptical arguments entails that in the *cogito*-state the thinker has, at best, reason only to acknowledge the *cogito* as *a* truth – but hardly as *the* truth, the first truth, or the truth on which everything else should rest. On February 22, 1638, Descartes wrote to Vatier: "The certainty and evidence of my kind of argument for the existence of God cannot really be known without distinctly recalling the arguments which display the uncertainty of all our knowledge of material things" (CSMK, 86; AT I, 560). One might well ask, "Could the certainty and evidence of the *cogito* as the *first* truth really be known without a distinct memory of the arguments that display the uncertainty of mathematics and of all our knowledge of material things?" Hardly.

IV. Skepticism and the Theory of Deduction

With an aim to show that it cannot ultimately be done, I wish to construct a case for reading the *cogito both* as an intuition and as an argument. The case rests on one way of reading Descartes' theory of deduction. The governing point is that Descartes allows whole deductions to be intuited. If the *cogito* is an argument, then nothing prevents its being intuited in one fell intellectual swoop.[16] First, we consider the type of case in which principles of inference are involved, then the type of case in which they are not. The case then can be supported in the following way. A deduction consists of a sequence of steps plus principles of inference. The final step is the conclusion; the others are premises. Now, memory is involved as we move from one step to the next. Since memory is unreliable, we keep repeating, slowly and carefully, the steps. And if we keep repeating the steps in our minds, we shall eventually be able to dispense with our memory and see the whole argument in one intellectual intuition.

the next sentence that (a) at best this concern would show that our not remembering what the extraordinary doubt has shown to be doubtful would not enable us to claim that the *cogito* is the *first* truth that we have chanced upon; (b) perhaps that Descartes should have drawn a distinction between a memory that he cannot rely upon as being veridical and a state in which he has *no* memory at all; the latter state would be rather difficult to handle, but a case in which he was not entirely sure of his memory – in which his memory was merely apparent – would not rob him of knowing of *this* certainty in the present; and (c) a lot more needs to be said in order to demonstrate that certainty in the present requires, *even for its possibility*, a veridical memory of what has failed to pass muster in the past.

[16] Kenny assures me that this represents his position exactly.

Thus, reconsider the following argument:

[1]   Whatever thinks, exists.   Premise (Intuition 1)
[2]   I think.   Premise (Intuition 2)
[3]   If I think, I exist.   1, Universal Instantiation
                                         (Intuitions 3, 4, and 5)

_____

[4]   ∴ I exist.   2, 3, Modus Ponens (Intuitions 6,
                                         7, and 8)

The argument for the case is that, in accordance with Descartes, we intuit several things: Specifically, we intuit the first proposition (Intuition 1); the second proposition (Intuition 2); the third proposition (Intuition 3); the first rule of inference, namely, the rule of universal instantiation (Intuition 4); the application of that rule of inference to this argument (Intuition 5); the second rule of inference, namely, the rule of *modus ponens* (Intuition 6); and the application of the second rule of inference in this argument, resulting in the fourth proposition (Intuition 7). Finally, we intuit the conclusion of the argument (Intuition 8). We need to run over these steps again and again, until memory plays virtually no part and we can finally see the entire argument in a single intellectual intuition.[17]

This procedure is valid even if, as has been contended, Descartes' theory of deduction does not involve (the second type of case) any explicit or implicit principle of inference. One simply intuits that the conclusion follows from the premises. Reconsider the following passage: "Take for example, the inference that 2 plus 2 equals 3 plus 1: not only must we intuitively perceive that 2 plus 2 make 4, and that 3 plus 1 make 4, but also that the original proposition follows necessarily from the other two" (CSM I, 15; AT X, 369). To set it up formally:

[1]   2 plus 2 make 4.   (Intuition 1)
[2]   3 plus 1 make 4.   (Intuition 2)

_____

[3]   ∴ 2 plus 2 equals 3 plus 1.   (Intuition 3, and then Intuition
                                         4, namely, that the conclusion
                                         follows from the two premises)

---

[17] See Stephen Gaukroger's *Cartesian Logic: An Essay on Descartes's Conception of Inference*, 50.

Somewhere, Descartes recognizes the law that two things equal to a third thing are equal to one another, and consequently that law ought to figure in the foregoing deduction.

What lies in parentheses are justifications: Notice that they contain nothing beyond intuitions. There are no principles of logic or inference that occur therein. One goes over these premises and conclusions again and again until one can grasp the entire argument in one single intuition. Thus, one might conclude from considering the two types of cases that the kind of skepticism that I am suggesting does not apply to Descartes after all. If my argument were to question the reliability of intuition, then of course the claim of this case would collapse;[18] but then the *cogito* would collapse as well. The significant thing to note is that the *cogito* can now be seen as an argument without falling prey to the kind of objection that I have leveled against the traditional interpretation. The latter could be set up formally as follows:

[1] Whatever thinks, exists.   (Intuition 1)
[2] I think.   (Intuition 2)
[3] If I think, I exist.[19]   (Intuition 3 that [3] follows
                                         from [1])
     ─────────────
[4] ∴ I exist.   (Intuition 4, and Intuition 5,
                                         namely, that the conclusion
                                         follows from the two premises)

This case seems to undercut nicely my argument against the traditional interpretation. If there are no rules of inference, there is nothing, save intuitions, to be skeptical about. Being skeptical about intuition is not only utterly un-Cartesian, it is ruinous for *any*

---

[18] Descartes must suppose, I am claiming, that intuition in particular cases is in fact reliable. But must he also suppose that all intuitions are reliable (that he knows a general principle) without which intuition in particular cases cannot be reliable? Descartes, I surmise, would answer as follows: Let us suppose that the meditator knows the general rule and only on the basis of it makes the claim that this particular intuition is reliable. "How, then," Descartes would ask, "would the meditator demonstrate that the general rule (at this stage in the *Meditations*) is reliable? Either intuitively or deductively. To demonstrate deductively would be to push the justification a step back; one would have to justify the premises in that argument. To do so intuitively would be to beg the question."

[19] Descartes would have contended – as did *Port-Royal Logic* (AN, 99–101) – that conditional statements in a deduction or demonstration would have to be necessary truths. For their relevance and importance to the argument here, see Appendix C.

interpretation of the *cogito*. This interpretation seems to be lent further support by Descartes:

> But when we think of the process of deduction as we did in Rule Three, it does not seem to take place all at once: inferring one thing from another involves a kind of movement of our mind. In that passage, then, we were justified in distinguishing intuition from deduction. But if we look on deduction as a completed process, as we did in Rule Seven, then it no longer signifies a movement but rather the completion of a movement. That is why we are supposing that the deduction is made through intuition when it is simple and transparent, but not when it is complex and involved. (CSM I, 37; AT X, 407–408)

One might say that the *cogito*-argument is not complex or involved, but rather simple and transparent, and that, given what Descartes has just said, it can be known through intuition rather than deduction; it is not necessarily to be known by a deduction,[20] and it does not rely on memory.[21]

This objection must be met if my claim is to survive.[22] To that end, first, let us distinguish, as Descartes could have but did not, between

---

[20] "But the deduction seems in all important respects to be simply an intuition, albeit an intuition whose content is a relation between other intuitions" (G, 117). A page later, Gaukroger adds that Descartes "seems concerned above all to restrict intuition to an absolutely instantaneous act, so that if there is any temporal sequence of any kind, no matter how brief, we are dealing with deduction rather than intuition."

[21] "Memory, in any genuine sense," writes Gaukroger, "would seem to play no real role in the deduction from $2 + 2 = 4$ and $3 + 1 = 4$ that $2 + 2 = 3 + 1$. And why does he specify that *remote* consequences are known only through deduction? Could it be that the consequence in the example, which is far from being remote, is known not by deduction but by intuition? No: it is the example that Descartes himself gives of a deduction, and the only example at that." (G, 117–118) If one reads 'remote' as literally as does Gaukroger, it raises an insolvable difficulty. But if one simply reads 'remote' as being 'away from' the first principles – which is exactly how it is juxtaposed in the passage – the difficulty evaporates. Only first principles are known by intuitions; other propositions derived from these first principles, i.e., those propositions that are away or 'remote' from first principles, are known by deduction. Otherwise, one has to make plausible the claim that Descartes, while claiming intuition and deduction to be of paramount importance, did not bother to ask the obvious question, "Where do I place the boundary line that demarcates remote consequences from consequences that are near?"

[22] It may appear that the objection developed here against my view is indeed the one that Descartes gave to Burman, or something quite similar to it. (CSMK, 334–335; AT V, 148–149). This is only an appearance. A more perceptive reader will immediately focus on the following: "And as for as long as he does pay attention to [the axioms in the proof of God], he is certain that he is not being deceived, and he is compelled

primary intuition and secondary intuition. Consider any of the preceding arguments. Each is analyzable into several parts, and each part
is known through an intuition. Thus, there are at least four intuitions
involved. These four intuitions must then be coalesced into a single
intuition: The argument as a whole, in accordance with Descartes'
method of analysis, is analyzable into distinct propositions, where each
of the steps of the argument (with or without the rules of inference)
is not further analyzable. The knowing by intuition of atomic propositions (that is, propositions not analyzable into further propositions)[23]
I shall call *primary intuition.* By contrast, any other intuition I shall refer
to as *secondary intuition.*[24]

to give his assent to them." This claims effectively that each axiom is assured of its
indubitability – *without* the proof of the existence of God – so long as the axiom is
being carefully attended to. What assures the truth of these axioms is, of course, the
general rule, namely, whatever is clear and distinct is necessarily true. This rule is
dependent entirely on the *cogito,* and not on God. For if it were dependent on God,
the circularity objection would be unavoidable (*vide* Chapter 4, section II).

[23] To be a bit more precise: First, I am not denying that atomic propositions can be
analyzed, only that they are not analyzable into further propositions as compound
propositions can be so analyzed. The last formal argument in the text, for example,
can be thought of as a compound proposition, and it is clearly analyzable into four
other propositions, each of which is to be known independently by an intuition. The
cogito claim, by contrast, is not such a compound proposition. It may have parts – a
subject and a predicate – or it may simply be a concatenation of names, à la Wittgenstein, but it does not have as parts other propositions. Second, Descartes has no
theory about what is an atomic or elementary proposition and why it is unanalyzable into other propositions. Bertrand Russell says somewhere that when he pressed
Wittgenstein to give him an example of an atomic proposition, the latter replied that
he was not interested in merely empirical matters! Max Black argued that "[w]e can
produce no elementary propositions and would not recognize them if we had them"
(*A Companion to Wittgenstein's Tractatus,* 11). Descartes, on the other hand, claimed
that there was an elementary proposition in his system. It was unanalyzable, and it was
recognizable: That proposition was the *cogito.* So I shall rest with this. If there can be
only propositions that are analyzable into other propositions, then the *cogito* cannot
be rescued as an argument, because the *cogito* argument could not ever be stated in
full; each premise of that *cogito* argument would have to be further analyzable into
other propositions, which in turn. . . . Descartes' Tree of Philosophy would have to be
uprooted. Third and finally, there might be a persistent worry that Descartes' intuitions are not sufficiently clearly individuated. Notice: Such a difficulty would plague
not only the account of the *cogito* offered in this book, but *any* account (since all
accounts must at a minimum invoke intuitions). But insofar as Descartes maintains
that there are atomic propositions (whether he has a theory about them or not),
one might claim that primary intuitions can, indeed, be individuated: In Descartes,
primary intuitions are intuitions about atomic propositions.

[24] "Notice, however, that as well as consisting in a grasp of a necessary connection between two limiting terms, which is what deduction reduces to, intuition can also

Second, Descartes draws a distinction between the process of deduction and the completed process of deduction. This is a significant distinction for our purposes, and it seems to me to coincide with the divide between the method of analysis and the method of synthesis.

consist in a grasp of a single proposition. Later in the same paragraph, Gaukroger adds: "Although *intuitus* disappears from Descartes' vocabulary in his later writings, this general conception does not, and indeed its crowning achievement is the *cogito*. The *cogito* is effectively an intuition of a basic premiss which, because of its indubitability and self-evidence, can be grasped independently of anything else, including rules of inference. It forms the starting point for knowledge and the paradigm for knowledge in that . . . *it is a grasp of a single proposition*." (*Cartesian Logic: An Essay on Descartes's Conception of Inference*, 50–51; my emphasis) The *cogito* would be a primitive intuition, on my view.

Judging from the just-quoted passage, one might think that Gaukroger was also peddling the view that the *cogito* is not, and cannot be, an argument. But one would be wrong. Here is the central passage from his later book: "Many commentators have been misled into thinking that Descartes is maintaining here that the *cogito* is not an inference. Quite the contrary, . . . *intuitus* is the paradigm form of inference. If the *cogito* is an *intuitus*, then it is necessarily an inferential judgment of some kind. And what makes the *cogito* so important is that it is the paradigm form of *intuitus*, which is in turn the paradigm form of inference." (G, 341) A bit later, Gaukroger removes any residual doubt: "There is a widespread view that Descartes thought that awareness of one's own mental states was in fact constitutive of the uniqueness of the human cognition, and this view has been reinforced by an interpretation of the *cogito* whereby my grasp of my own existence is an instantaneous act of self-consciousness, rather than an inference or judgement. We have seen that such an interpretation is mistaken: The *cogito* does involve inference and judgment." (G, 349)

Returning to the earlier work, Gaukroger says, "In construing deduction in terms of intuition rather than rules of inference, one thing that Descartes is doing is ruling out any attempt at analyzing inferential steps: in the limiting case, there are no such steps. Inference cannot be analyzed on Descartes's view because it is simple and primitive." (*Cartesian Logic: An Essay on Descartes's Conception of Inference*, 51.) One might then construe inference as being reliable for the following reasons: First, it is unanalyzable; second, it is known through intuition. One might then think that such a deduction might be used to construct the *cogito* as an argument. This, in my view, would be a mistake. First, let us grant that some particular deduction is primitive, not derivable from any other. But to come to know that deduction intuitively, one would antecedently have to know its correct application in at least one instance (for Descartes, though not for us). However, in that instance, one would have to come to know at least one true proposition that serves as a premise and from which, using that deduction, a true conclusion is derived. Thus, knowing intuitively that deduction would be an instance of a secondary intuition.

Second, suppose that we could know the soundness of the deduction prior to any application. Why, then, should it, and not the *cogito*, be treated as the first truth? After all, if the *cogito* is an argument, we must *first* be intuitively assured of the deduction on which the *cogito* is based. But the deduction cannot be treated as the first truth unless we assume that Descartes distinguished between eternal truths: Some (such as mathematical propositions) he doubted; some (such as rules of inference) he did not.

One offers a synthesis once the analysis is complete; that synthesis reflects the completed process of deduction. Here there is no movement of the mind, and intuition and deduction can collapse into one. But insofar as one is doing the analysis, there is a movement of the mind; memory plays an essential role,[25] and we must draw a distinction between intuition and deduction.

The application of this distinction to the *cogito* is clear. Insofar as Descartes has made the discovery of the first truth, analysis is complete; he can now offer it as an argument, reflecting a completed process of deduction, and such an argument might be intuited. By contrast, so long as Descartes is searching for the first truth, analysis is not complete; there still remains the distinction between intuition and deduction. Thus, the discovery of the *cogito* can only be an intuition, not a deduction.

The key question to be faced, then, is, must the *cogito* be known only by a primary intuition? Or, can it, at least, be known by a secondary intuition? The answer must be that it cannot be known by a secondary intuition. There is a world of difference between knowing the full

[25] I take the following to be strongly supportive: "Scholastic thought generally treated being *conscius of* something as a *time-relative* cognitive capacity. Descartes clearly held this view. He defended this principle: *at the time of* thinking something, I must be *conscius* of so thinking, but I may later forget what I was thinking earlier and thereby lose this *conscientia*. Given that *conscientia* is a form of knowledge and that knowledge of any kind is a capacity to make judgements, this principle can be rephrased: *at the time of* thinking something, I must have the capacity to say what I am thinking, but I may subsequently, sooner or later, lose this particular cognitive capacity through lapse of memory." (Gordon Baker and Katherine J. Morris, *Descartes' Dualism*, 109–110) Explicating a phrase in this passage, Baker and Morris state in note 134, "Arguably Descartes conceived the present moment to be temporally extended and to be differentiated from the past by virtue of the fact that our knowledge of what is present is independent of memory."

Consider the *cogito* to be an argument. Let us say that it is conceived in the present moment, *t*, which is temporally extended. Are there parts of that argument about which similar things can be said? For example, could we say that a premise or a rule of inference of that argument was conceived in the present moment, *t′*, which is temporally extended too? (Never mind that the notion of "the present moment" becomes rather vague, given that *t′* is a subset of *t*, and yet both are present moments!) If so, is it – the premise or the rule of inference – liable to be lost through lapse of memory or to become something about which we may be uncertain, given the unreliability of the memory? What if the *cogito* were a nonargument, a statement, conceived in the present moment, *t″*, which is also temporally extended? In which present moment, *t* or *t″*, does a subject run greater epistemic risk? If the answer is that he does so in *t* – in that moment, he has more to remember – then Descartes is better off not making the *cogito* something that can be conceived only in *t*.

argument intuitively *after* each of the propositions (including principles of inference, if any) have been known intuitively, and knowing it
before knowing any of its constituent propositions intuitively. But then
the secondary intuitions *presuppose* primary intuitions.[26] When that
much is granted, we run into an intractable problem for the traditional
interpretation, namely, which of the several intuitions is to be regarded
as the first truth? By the nature of the case, they are all *equally* good con-
tenders for that position! So even if Descartes would have applauded
G. H. Hardy's remark – proofs are "gas, rhetorical flourishes designed
to affect psychology . . . devices to stimulate the imagination of pupils" –
this would still not be innocuous for the *cogito*-argument.

My third argument against this approach is its reliance on an unar-
gued premise that the *cogito*-argument is simple and not what Descartes
calls "complex and involved." Immediately following the last quoted
passage, Descartes says that when the argument is complex and involved, "we call it 'enumeration' or 'induction', since the intellect
cannot simultaneously grasp it as a whole, and its certainty in a sense
depends on memory, which must retain the judgments we have made
on the individual parts of the enumeration if we are to derive a single

---

[26] Consider Descartes' own example of deduction, the deduction of $2 + 2 = 3 + 1$ from
$2 + 2 = 4$ and $3 + 1 = 4$. In order to intuit the first truth, he must clearly first intuit
the truth of $2 + 2 = 4$ as well as the truth of $3 + 1 = 4$. The latter two would be
examples of primary intuitions, the first would be an example of a secondary intuition.
The inference itself would be a secondary intuition inasmuch as it relies on intuiting
some other truths, not necessarily intuiting some other rules of inference.

For the point in question, among others, perhaps the letter that Descartes wrote
to Huygens on July 31, 1640, is worth close scrutiny: "For I draw a comparison between
my work in this area and the demonstrations of Apollonius. Everything in the latter
is really very clear and certain, when each point is considered separately; but because
the proofs are rather long, and one cannot see the necessity of the conclusion unless
one remembers exactly everything that has gone before, you will hardly find a single
person in an entire country who is capable of understanding them. Nevertheless,
because those few who do understand them vouch for their truth, everyone believes
them. Similarly, I think that I have fully demonstrated the existence of God and
the non-material nature of the human soul; but this depends on several successive
arguments, and forgetting the smallest element will make it impossible to understand
the conclusion." (CSMK, 150; AT III, 751–752) First, the proofs for the existence of
God and for the immateriality of the human soul are long; second, therefore, the
reliance on memory – which is presently in doubt – is indispensable in Descartes'
two proofs; and third, Descartes explicitly avows that those proofs are dependent on
several successive arguments. This dependence clearly necessitates the drawing of
the distinction between primary and secondary intuitions.

conclusion from them taken as a whole" (CSM I, 37; AT X, 408). Now, admittedly, Descartes is referring here to induction, and to the kind of complexity it begets, rather than to the complexity of an argument with a fairly complex structure. But I think the substance of the claim should remain unaffected. If so, there would be a loss of certainty, since, together with other things, "the intellect cannot simultaneously grasp it as a whole."[27]

Fourth, if any argument can be intuited, there is the problem of why the *cogito* should be regarded as the "first truth." For example, with the *cogito* providing an essential step in the argument, Descartes is led to prove the existence of God. Why should not this entire argument be intuited as well, and be regarded as the first truth? Indeed, some have thought that we have no truth in the meditations until such time as the existence of a good and nondeceiving God has been proved[28] (C, 95).

What bearing, if any, does the history of logic have on the problem of interpreting the *cogito*? Is there, for example, a real historical background against which we can make our conjecture – that the *cogito* should not be regarded as an argument – more plausible? Why is it that Descartes does not rely, or ought not to have relied, on proof or principles of inference? There is such a historical background. There were two skeptical texts that had been widely known since the sixteenth century, namely, Cicero's *Academica* and Sextus Empiricus's *Outlines of Pyrrhonism* and *Against Mathematicians*. We may, therefore, assume that Descartes was familiar with them or had encountered them in some form, particularly since he wished to be the scourge of skepticism. Descartes had already argued, in conformity with the traditional criticisms, that the syllogism was question-begging – see, for example, rules 10 and 13 of *Rules for the Direction of the Mind*. What I wish to do here, briefly, is to set up the skeptical challenge, translate it into the context of the *cogito*, and then claim that Descartes could not

---

[27] Can we save the day by distinguishing, with A. K. Stout, between retentive memory and reminiscing memory? (See "The Basis of Knowledge in Descartes," 185.) I do not think so, because none of Stout's arguments undercuts my fundamental contention that there is an important and irrevocable distinction between intuition and deduction in Descartes. The essential difference lies in the following: Memory is indispensable in deduction; it is not so in intuition.

[28] See my argument against Curley in Chapter 5, section II.

adequately have responded to it with the resources available to him in the Second Meditation at the point where he had established the *cogito.*

In *Outlines of Pyrrhonism*, in his attack on the Stoic conditional argument, Sextus asks us to consider the following two arguments,[29] Argument [A] and Argument [B]:

Argument [A]:	**Argument [B]:**
[1*a*] If it is day, it is light.	[1*b*] It is day.
[2*a*] It is day.	
———————	———————
[3*a*] It is light.	[2*b*] It is light.

Argument [A] is the proof for the inference made in Argument [B]. Now, says Sextus, either "It is light" follows from "It is day," as in Argument [B], or it does not. If it does, then the first premise, [1*a*], of Argument [A] is redundant. Since redundancy is involved, then by the light of Stoic logic, the inference is invalid. If "It is light" does not follow from "It is day," then the first premise, [1*a*], of Argument [A] is false. Thus, the alleged proof will be invalid or will contain a false premise.

Sextus then goes on to apply similar arguments against the Aristotelian categorical syllogism. He argues in this way:

> [I]n the argument – "The just is fair, but the fair is good, therefore the just is good," either it is agreed and pre-evident that the fair is good, or it is disputed and is non-evident. But if it is non-evident, it will not be granted in the process of deduction, and consequently the syllogism will not be conclusive; while if it is pre-evident that whatsoever is fair is also without exception good, at the moment of stating that this particular thing is fair the fact that it is good is likewise implied, so that it is enough to put the argument in the form "The just is fair, therefore the just is good," and the other premiss, in which it was stated that the "fair is good" is redundant.[30]

The skeptical argument, against Stoic or Aristotelian logic, is aimed at undercutting the possibility of proof.

---

[29] Sextus Empiricus, *Outlines of Pyrrhonism*, II, para. 159. In what follows I am indebted to Stephen Gaukroger's *Cartesian Logic: An Essay on Descartes's Conception of Inference*, especially 11–18; and C, 30–31. I refer the interested reader to the very useful bibliography on ancient skepticism regarding inference supplied by Gaukroger.
[30] Sextus Empiricus, *Outlines of Pyrrhonism*, II, para. 163.

It does not require much effort to apply Sextus' argument to the case of the *cogito*:

Argument [C]:   **Argument [D]:**
[1*c*] If I think, then I exist.   [1*d*] I think.
[2*c*] I think.

_____   _____

[3*c*] I exist.   [2*d*] I exist.

Argument [C] is offered as a proof of the inference made in Argument [D]. So, Sextus might say, either "I exist" follows from "I think," as in Argument [D], or it does not. If it does, then the first premise, [1*c*], of Argument [C] is redundant. Since redundancy is involved, then by the light of Stoic logic, the inference is invalid. If "I exist" does not follow from "I think," then the first premise, [1*c*], of Argument [C] is false. But there is no interpretation I know that maintains that Argument [D] is valid.[31] Thus, the alleged proof will be invalid or will contain a false premise.[32]

Or, if the *cogito* were cast in the mold of Aristotelian logic, Sextus might have said:

In the argument – "I think, but whatever thinks exists, therefore I exist," either it is agreed and pre-evident that whatever thinks exists, or it is disputed and is nonevident. But if it is nonevident, it will not be granted in the process of deduction, and consequently the syllogism will not be conclusive; while if it is pre-evident that whatever thinks also without exception exists, at

_____

[31] A Kenny-like counterposition would go as follows: "*Cogito ergo sum* is an argument, but it is an argument that does not require the use of memory; the following of *sum* from *cogito* is an object of immediate intuition." Anyone purchasing the just-mentioned argument from Sextus Empiricus ought to find the foregoing defense puzzling. First, the validity of the said argument has not been, and cannot at this stage be, assured. Second, there is no justification for the claim that there is no use of memory, in contrast to Descartes, who alleges that there is, and must be, the use of memory in such an argument. Third, nowhere does Descartes distinguish between "deduction *with* memory" and "deduction *without* memory" (without a *caveat*, such as "completed process"), let alone provide a justification for the latter. If there were such a justification, it would clearly be trumped by "self-evidence is not required for deduction, as it is for intuition; deduction in a sense gets its certainty from memory" (CSM I, 15; AT X, 369–370); or we would be saddled with the task of explaining away the inconsistency. Finally, it is difficult to fathom the precise difference, if any, between the immediate intuition of the Kenny-like argument and the immediate intuition of a single proposition. See also Appendix C.

[32] See also Lisa Jardine, 'Humanistic Logic,' 180, as well as the next note.

the moment of stating that this particular thing thinks the fact that it exists is likewise implied, so that it is enough to put the argument in the form, "I think, therefore I exist," and the other premise, in which it was stated that "whatever thinks exists," is redundant.

It is to be borne in mind that Descartes had discarded the syllogism as a tool of discovery; perhaps it was satisfactory as a vehicle for explaining things, but it was worse than useless in enabling us to make new and fresh discoveries in science or in philosophy. Consequently, Descartes could not have used the syllogistic approach in his discovery of the *cogito*.[33]

It is not quite to the point that Descartes did not, if he did not, subscribe to the conditional logic of the Stoics, or the Aristotelian

---

[33] Some social historians might argue that mathematics was actually viewed as very problematic and doubtful by seventeenth-century skeptics. For instance, it was associated with magic and cabalism and was "obscure"; to some people who casually picked up a book, its formulas would resemble weird incantations and magic signs, not to mention the fact that it was associated with demonic machines. Making mathematics a paradigm of transparency was a social task. Descartes seems preeminently to contribute to this task, though this involves at the same time discovering truths that are "more certain" than those of mathematics and even logic. He makes mathematics nonoccult, one might say, with the help of this theory of intuition and his rejection of other forms of learning. Now I am no social historian of logic and mathematics, but given that bit of social history, Descartes would have had even more reason for doubting the principles of logic than I have indicated.

Let me turn to a historian of logic to support that claim, (that Descartes would have had even more reason for doubting the principles of logic), this time from the side of internal history, not social history. "A humanist treatment of logic," writes Lisa Jardine, "... takes the view, therefore, that any significant study of argument (the subject-matter of logic/dialectic) must concern itself equally with argument (strictly, argumentation) which is compelling but not amenable to analysis within traditional formal logic. It is this fundamental difference of opinion over what is meant by 'compelling' argument which accounts for the dogmatic insistence (on ideological grounds) of the scholastic (and of the historian of scholasticism) that the humanist is a 'grammarian' or a 'rhetorician'." ("Humanistic Logic," 175–176) Or consider this: "As long as distinguished thinkers like Valla proposed a radically different approach to reasoning, namely a sceptical acknowledgement that an argument must always fall short of certainty, and that greater or lesser degrees of likelihood were the object of the logician's attention, they could hold their own against their scholastic adversaries" ("Humanistic Logic," 192).

The point is that these humanist logicians, with their concern for *oratio* and exegesis, need not be right, but that Descartes was required to take these as possible objections against his favored ideas about logic, consequence, and validity, at least in the First Meditation, so that by the time he got to the Second Meditation to display the truth of the *cogito*, he could not rely, or ought not have relied, on the tools of logic (which, of course, on my view, he did not).

logic. The point is that Descartes should have entertained the skeptical arguments on logic very seriously. These arguments did not simply invoke the evil demon, as Descartes was wont to do with respect to mathematics. Rather, they were offered as a serious skeptical challenge to anyone who would invoke the laws of logic or the principles of inference. At the end of the First Meditation and at the point in the Second Meditation where he had established the *cogito*, Descartes had simply no resources with which to answer the skeptic. Thus, any use he made of the principles of inference would have been dubious, at best.

I conclude that the traditional interpretation of the *cogito* as an argument leaves quite baffling how Descartes could have overlooked so simple a challenge to his first truth presented as an argument – or, if he was aware of it, why he insisted on regarding the *cogito* as an argument.

There is an interesting conjecture by Harry Frankfurt. The 'I' of the First Meditation, he argues in *Demons, Dreamers, and Madmen*, is a naive realist, not our ideal thinker. Consequently, when Descartes challenges the truths of logic and mathematics in that meditation, he is challenging those claims as expressed by a naive realist. One might add they are the claims of a crude empiricist who confuses "$2 + 2 = 4$" with an empirical claim, such as "2 apples plus 2 apples are equal to 4 apples." Frankfurt thinks that Descartes never seriously challenged the truths of logic and mathematics, because they are clear and distinct ideas, and such ideas are never challenged by Descartes.

With that as a backdrop, Frankfurt then proceeds to offer one of the several arguments that can be construed as the *cogito*-argument. One can no more doubt the rules of inference, so one might argue with Frankfurt, than one could doubt the truths of mathematics. This is the *cogito*-argument that Frankfurt presents.

There are at least four things wrong with Frankfurt's view. First, the truths of mathematics have been challenged everywhere, as a sort of a prolegomena to the *cogito*: for example, in the *Discourse on the Method*, *The Search for Truth*, and in Descartes' letters. Descartes repeatedly claims that he wishes to establish a truth that is more certain than the truths of mathematics. Second, the general rule of accepting clear and distinct ideas as true is not established until the Third Meditation, hence one cannot invoke *that* principle anytime earlier than the Third Meditation. Third, it follows as a corollary that the 'I' of the First

Meditation is not a crude empiricist, any more than the 'I' of the Sixth Meditation is. Indeed, the conceptual questioning of time, place, and so on leaves little room to doubt that the kind of thinker that Descartes has invoked is sufficiently sophisticated to challenge well-established truths. Fourth and finally, and by far most significant, the principles of inference are nowhere near established at the time when the *cogito* is presented in the Second Meditation. That being the case, the naive realist has every reason to be skeptical of the truths of logic and the principles of inference here, for they are no more than rules of thumb, as in the First Meditation.

I conclude with a small, but not insignificant, textual clue. The first few pages of the *Meditations on First Philosophy* consist of the Dedicatory Letter to the Sorbonne, the Preface to the Reader, and the Synopsis. A careful examination of these pages reveal that when Descartes speaks of "demonstrative proofs," "exact demonstration," "proof by natural reason," "demonstrated by reasoning" – or of truths "proved" or "demonstrated"[34] – he speaks of proofs of only five truths: proof of the existence of God, proof of the immortality of the soul, proof of the distinction of the human mind from the body, proof that the external world exists, and finally, proof that humans have a body. None of these phrases referring to proofs is *ever* used for the *cogito*. Nor is this notion of proof in metaphysics isolated from the notion of proof in mathematics, for twice in the course of these pages Descartes explicitly draws a parallel between these metaphysical proofs and proofs in geometry, and once he draws a parallel between his work and the geometrical writings of Archimedes, Apollonius, Pappus, and others. The *cogito* is mentioned precisely once. And then Descartes refers to it as an "exercise" (CSM II, 9; AT VII, 12), not as a proof. No sooner is that done than he reverts in the very next sentence to talking about proofs and compares his method explicitly to that of the geometers: "Hence the only order which I could follow was that normally employed by geometers, namely to set out all the premises on which a desired proposition depends, before drawing any conclusions about it" (CSM II, 9; AT VII, 13). So the *cogito* cannot be an argument; it has to be a proposition. Or, in the language of the geometers – or of seventeenth-century logicians – the *cogito* is not a theorem; it is an axiom.

---

34 For instance, see CSM II, 3, 4, 5, 12; AT VII, 2, 3–4, 12–13.

7

The Content of the *Cogito*

The strength of an interpretation lies not only in the interpretation of a core idea, but also in how well it coheres with Descartes' other central theses and ideas. The more that these – interpretation, conjectures, and consequences – dovetail with one another, make other texts more plausible, make surprising connections with other issues in other texts and the claims of contemporary philosophers, make cogent the analysis of the source of errors, make plausible the solution of philosophical problems, the greater is the strength of that interpretation. This is what I aim to do in this chapter and the next. I make conjectures, offer variant readings of Cartesian texts, and draw consequences from claims thus far developed, in the hope of showing that my interpretation of the *cogito* preserves not only much of what Descartes said about the *cogito*, but also what he explicitly maintained on other matters.

In section I, I pad up the proof of the core claim, namely, that the *cogito* is not an argument, by conjecturing what might have led some to think that it was. Section II provides, as a follow-up, the outline of a solution to the problem of the content of the *cogito*. Finally, section III attempts to explain why the 'I' is elusive – it is because one is seeking the content of the 'I' in the wrong place.

I. A Source of the Mistake

Let me venture a guess about what has perhaps gone wrong when philosophers have insisted that the *cogito* is an argument.

Someone might have said: Consider the stream of consciousness of a thinking being. Let us divide this stream into his thoughts: $T_1, T_2, T_3, \ldots, T_g, \ldots, T_t, \ldots, T_e, \ldots, T_n$. The Ts are the thoughts; in particular, T_g is the thought, "Whatever thinks, exists"; T_t is the thought, "I think"; and, T_e is the thought, "I exist." We delineate the thoughts in this way so that we can give a one-to-one correspondence between the three propositions, P_1 (*Whatever thinks, exists*), P_2 (*I think*), and P_3 (*I exist*) in the *cogito* argument and the three thoughts, T_g, T_t, and T_e, respectively. More generally, we map the various thoughts onto the various propositions that express the content of the thoughts. Then we get the situation in which we see a movement of thought in that thinking being: namely, from T_t to T_e, or from T_g to T_e via T_t. Thus, we see a movement in thought in the mind of the thinking being corresponding to the inference of the argument that we see on paper. Thus:

T_g	is the thought	Whatever thinks, exists.
T_t	is the thought	I think.
T_e	is the thought	I exist.

This entire mode of representing the *cogito*, by no means explicit, is wrong. First, this picture is mistaken since it forces the thinking being to rely on his memory: He must remember not only his thoughts, T_g and T_t, but also the links between them, in order to ensure that he has carried out the movement of thoughts correctly to the thought T_e.

Second, there is *no* thought in *isolation* that corresponds to the proposition T_e, "I exist." Take the famous wax example. There is a piece of wax before Descartes. It has a certain taste, scent, color, shape, and size; it is hard and cold to the touch, and when knocked it makes a sound. Descartes puts it by the fire and the wax alters radically: the taste disappears, as do the scent, color, shape, and size. It is no longer hard and cold; it does not make any sound when knocked. It is nevertheless the same piece of wax. Clearly, Descartes does not *know* this on the basis of his senses or by the faculty of his imagination, but "by the intellect alone" (CSM II, 22; AT VII, 34).

If we were to represent this in terms of the foregoing, we would begin by enumerating a sequence of properties, something like the following: P_1 (*This piece of wax has a pleasant taste*), P_2 (*This piece of wax has the scent of the flowers*), P_3 (*This piece of wax has an off-white color*), and so on up to P_n. Then there will be the familiar corresponding thoughts. Thus, T_1 would correspond to P_1; T_2 would correspond to P_2; and so on. *Nowhere* is there just a thought, C_w, corresponding to the proposition P_w (*This is a piece of wax*), where *no* property of the wax that the mind perceives with the help of the senses or the imagination is present. There is always "This is a piece of wax that is white," or "This is a piece of wax that is cold," or "This is a piece of wax that is hard," and so on.

Similarly, there is no thought, T_e, in the mind of the thinker corresponding to the proposition P_3 (*I exist*). "I regard," wrote Descartes (quite likely to Mesland) on May 2, 1644, "the difference between the soul and its ideas as the same as that between a piece of wax and the various shapes it can take. Just as it is not an activity but a passivity in the wax to take various shapes, so, it seems to me, it is a passivity in the soul to receive one or other idea, and only its volitions are activities"[1] (CSMK, 232; AT IV, 113–114). Descartes is getting us to see that the 'I' already exists in the thought; it could not be otherwise. Properly reformulated, the suggestion would go as follows:

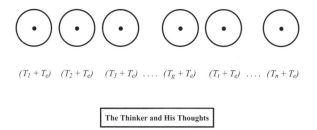

$(T_1 + T_e)$ $(T_2 + T_e)$ $(T_3 + T_e)$ .... $(T_g + T_e)$ $(T_1 + T_e)$ .... $(T_n + T_e)$

The Thinker and His Thoughts

Each circle represents the thought in question, the point or the dot in the circle, •, the thinker of that thought. There is a major difference, of course, between the wax case and the *cogito* case. T_w (*This is a piece of wax*) can be associated only with other *T*s that are about other aspects

---

[1] A nice argument could be developed out of a passage in a letter to Mesland, written on February 9, 1645; but it is too involved to develop here (CSMK, 241–244; AT IV, 166). Descartes is speaking of the conditions under which the body of a person is "*numerically the same* body, so long as it remains joined and substantially united with the same soul" (CSMK, 243; AT IV, 166). This would raise the question of the conditions under which the soul of a person is numerically the same soul. The answer to that question would be something akin to what now follows.

of the wax pertaining to its color, shape, size, taste, fragrance, and so on. It cannot be made a necessary part of every thought. By contrast, T_e is a part of every thought, but it is not given to the mind by the senses or the faculty of the imagination, any more than is the wax. T_e cannot be isolated in pristine purity.

Here Descartes would have agreed with Hume: When he introspects his mind, he cannot see himself stumbling over a thought that is his pure self, however hard he might try.

For my part, when I enter most intimately into what I call *myself*, I always stumble on some particular perceptions or other, of heat or cold, light or shade, love or hatred, pain or pleasure. I never catch *myself* at any time without a perception, and never can observe anything but the perception. When my perceptions are remov'd for any time, as by sound sleep; so long am I sensible of *myself*, and may truly be said not to exist.[2]

Hume's mistake, Descartes would have said, was to assimilate the entity, 'I' to the entities observable by sense experience. In fact, the 'I' is cognized "by the intellect alone." Here is Descartes' formulation:

For even if all the accidents of the mind change, so that it has different objects of the understanding and different desires and sensations, it does not on that account become a different mind; whereas a human body loses its identity merely as a result of a change in the shape of some of its parts. And it follows from this that while the body can very easily perish, the mind ["or the soul of man, for I make no distinction between them" – added in the French version] is immortal by its very nature. (CSM II, 10; AT VII, 14)

One need not nurture the claim about immortality, as Descartes himself did not in the book, in order to maintain the more modest thesis of the singleness of the mind that persists so long as the body persists.

Thus, in a telling passage in a letter to Mersenne of July 1641, Descartes wrote:

In the case of the soul the matter is even clearer. As I have shown, the soul is nothing but a thing which thinks, and so it is impossible for us ever to think of anything without at the same time having the idea of our soul as a thing capable of thinking of whatever we think of. It is true that a thing of such a nature

---

[2] David Hume, *A Treatise of Human Nature*, 165. It is not frequently enough noticed that Hume was not entirely pleased with his own views on personal identity: See the Appendix to the *Treatise*, paras. 20–21.

cannot be imagined, that is, cannot be represented by a corporeal image. But that is not surprising, because our imagination is capable of representing only objects of sense-perception; and since our soul has no colour or smell or taste, or anything which belongs to the body, it is not possible to imagine it or form an image of it. But that does not make it any less conceivable; on the contrary, since it is by means of it that we conceive all other things, it is itself more conceivable than all other things put together. (CSMK, 186; AT III, 394; see also CSMK, 357; AT V, 221)

When Gassendi had objected that Descartes was carrying too much unnecessary baggage, that he could have done what he wanted to do by assuming any of his actions, Descartes had replied, "When you say that I 'could have made the same inference from any one of my other actions' you are far from the truth, since I am not wholly certain of any of my actions, with the sole exception of thought. ... I may not, for example, make the inference, 'I am walking, therefore I exist' except in so far as the awareness of walking is a thought." (CSM II, 244; AT VII, 352) In a letter to Reneri for Pollot (April or May 1638), he had said something quite similar:

When someone says, "I am breathing, therefore I exist" if he wants to prove he exists from the fact that there cannot be breathing without existence, he proves nothing, because he would have to prove first that it is true that he is breathing, which is impossible unless he has also proved that he exists. But if he wants to prove his existence from the feeling or the belief that he has that he is breathing, so that he judges that even if the opinion were untrue he could not have it if he did not exist, then his proof is sound. For in such a case the thought of breathing is present to our mind before the thought of our existing, and we cannot doubt that we have it while we have it. To say, "I am breathing, therefore I exist," in this sense, is simply to say, "I am thinking, therefore I exist." (CSMK, 98; AT II, 37–38)

Thus, the ego cannot be asserted to exist in isolation; it can exist only in the context of a particular thought.

But then: Assume *any* thought of a general proposition, T_x, and any thought of a particular proposition, T_y, which, in conjunction with the general proposition, t_x, is used to derive the *cogito* argument. Deny these thoughts. Assume thoughts about *any* laws of logic and principles of inference, such as universal instantiation and *modus ponens*, T_z (both required for the *cogito*-argument). Deny them, as assuredly one can, on the still operating demon hypothesis and in conformity with the doctrine of the creation of eternal truths. One could, I believe, *still* arrive at the truth of the *cogito*. In short, "I think that '*Not* T_x and *Not* T_y' and '*Not* T_z', therefore I exist," is as good a *cogito* proposition as can be formulated.

Even such a proposition as that would necessarily have been true; it would have been the simplest; its discovery would not have required much skill or intelligence; it would have been indubitable; and it would have served Descartes as a starting point for the rest. But had he offered an *argument*, then Descartes would have been guilty of having "built upon sand instead of digging further down to find hard rock or clay" (CSM II, 408; AT X, 513).

II. The Content of the *Cogito*

The point or dot, '•', in the diagram, representing the 'I', is convenient and picturesque, but it is a poor substitute for a philosophical argument. Gassendi, the author of the "Fifth Set of Objections," wrote: "Moreover, when you think you somehow perceive this underlying 'something', how, may I ask, do you do so? Do you not perceive it as something spread out and extended? For you do not conceive of it as a point." (CSM II, 190; AT VII, 272) Descartes' *cogito* has raised the problem of the content of the *cogito* (WC, 103, and for details, 103–107). What, exactly, does the 'I' refer to, and what does "I exist" assert? The 'I' seems to be a descriptionless referent. The statement "I exist" seems to be a typically empty proposition, devoid of content. If that is the case, it is argued, since only analytic statements are thought to be empty or devoid of content, it is unavoidable that "I exist" is an analytic statement, and hence cannot be an informative statement serving as the first truth from which other informative truths would follow.

Contemporary metaphysics may provide a clue or two toward a better understanding of the content of the *cogito*. There are two things that we need to consider: first, the notion of *primitive thisness* as an indispensable metaphysical category, and second, the property of *self-ascription*. When someone raises the question of the content of the *cogito*, he is inevitably working within the Leibnizian framework. Leibniz held that in the final analysis everything can be defined, without residue, in terms of basic qualities, or primitive *suchnesses*. From God's point of view, every individual in the universe has a certain set of properties such that it, and only it, possesses these qualities. By contrast, it has been recently proposed that the notion of primitive thisness might be indispensable, too.

The individual thinker, as he examines the sense content of his mind, cannot identify himself with any of that sense content. He has doubts about a myriad of things, but the one thing that he cannot doubt, while in that mode of doubt, is that he exists. I suggest that Descartes would have approved of the idea that the 'I' cannot be defined in terms of a set of qualities, characteristics, properties, and so forth, but can only be denoted, referred to, or designated by the thinker, and that this relation is to be captured by a primitive thisness. The point is pithily put in *Discourse on the Method,* thus: "this "I" – that is, the soul by which I am what I am –" (CSM I, 127; AT VI, 33). The 'I' in the *cogito*-state in *Meditations on First Philosophy* frames it in this way:

> I know that I exist; the question is, what is this 'I' that I know? If the 'I' is understood strictly as we have been taking it, then it is quite certain that knowledge of it does not depend on things of whose existence I am as yet unaware; so it cannot depend on any of the things which I invent in my imagination. (CSM II, 18–19; AT VII, 27–28)

The 'I' is captured by a thisness, on which qualities can then be pegged.

The argument of this section, I believe, entirely squares with one of the principal theses of Baker and Morris about Descartes' two-substance theory and the Aristotelian logical theory that comes attached to it, and it dovetails as well with Descartes' view of *conscientia*.[3] Quite briefly, the authors argue that the basic logico-metaphysical structure of Descartes' philosophical system involves a substance (designated by the subject term of the Aristotelian categorical proposition) and a mode (designated by the predicate term of that proposition). All judgments are of subject–predicate form; singular judgments differ from both particular and universal judgments; and each judgment must be uniquely analyzable into subject and predicate.

What I am attempting to discover, in particular, is this: What is this Cartesian substance designated by "I" in the singular proposition "I am a being"? Descartes, alas, says very little about it. Let me put my point

---

[3] Baker and Morris, *Descartes' Dualism,* especially 59–69, 100–112.

in terms of *conscientia*. *Conscientia* is possessing knowledge (*scientia*) of
the soul and its operations (*operationes*). My concern is not with how
one acquires *conscientia* about the operations of the soul – operations
such as, borrowing from Saint Thomas Aquinas, voluntary actions,
acknowledging what we have done, judging what we are to do, making
judgments about our moral character; or, borrowing from John Locke,
operations such as compounding, comparing, and abstracting ideas –
as it is with how one acquires *conscientia* about the soul. "*Conscientia*
is knowledge *of the soul* and its attributes (or its operations)," write
Baker and Morris. "It is *self*-knowledge, and it is confined to attributes
of the soul (as opposed to properties of the body). Consequently, it
must be manifested in making true singular judgments about the soul's
operations."[4] This, of course, cannot be read literally. Descartes cannot
maintain that having full and complete knowledge even of *all* the
operations of the soul would be equivalent to having knowledge of
the soul. His metaphysics, as Baker and Morris might say, would not
permit him to make that move in the language-game. For one thing,
the notion of substance would become redundant. It would be safer to
say that there are two types of knowledge: first, knowledge of the soul,
and second, knowledge of the operations of the soul. I am interested
in the first type of knowledge.

This much is clear: 'I' is a mental substance, independent of any
other substance, but God-dependent. This should at least partially ac-
commodate Robert Merrihew Adams' reservations, to be listed later.[5]
But these are general characteristics, possessed by all rational beings –
given the absolute use of *conscientia*[6] – and, therefore, would not distinguish Descartes from any of us.

"In Descartes' thinking, this agent-centred aspect of *conscientia* is
given a more rigid form. Given that modes must inhere in substances,
and given that any singular judgement must have a substance as its
logical subject, the logical form of any judgement that exhibits my
conscientia must be that *I* (the soul) have a mode of thinking." Having
listed several instances of *conscientia*, the authors continue, "I can't
make a true judgement about any mode of thinking 'that I find within

4 Ibid., 110.
5 See p. 218, this volume.
6 Baker and Morris, *Descartes' Dualism*, 105–106.

me' unless I think that this mode of thinking is a property of myself (i.e. my soul). For this reason, I–thoughts must be the minimal moves in the language-game of exhibiting *conscientia.*"[7]

Why is this a problem in discussing the *cogito?* Here is why. In the *cogito*-state, the 'I' has *no* knowledge of *any* of its operations; the only thing that the 'I' claims to know, in that instant, is that "I exist." Existing does not seem very much like an activity of the soul – on a par, say, with making a promise, dreaming, judging, wishing, and so on. If the 'I', therefore, has no content, it would be very difficult to explicate the content of the *cogito.* The 'I' that is the soul of one person (using the term in its ordinary sense, not in the Strawsonian sense) is surely different from the 'I' of another person. (Furthermore, since both are existing, even if existence were a predicate, it would not distinguish between these two persons). If one could specify the difference between two 'I's in the *cogito* state, then one could give content to the 'I,' and thence to the proposition "I exist." But, surely, not otherwise.

Nevertheless, there is an 'I' – "this puzzling 'I' which cannot be pictured in the imagination" (CSM II, 20; AT VII, 29) – a qualityless, descriptionless 'I,' referred to by a thisness. Gassendi objected that Descartes had told them only what this 'I' is *not,* and not what it *is,* and demanded that Descartes give them "a kind of chemical investigation" in terms of spirits, tartar, the distillate, and other ingredients, which would manufacture this 'I,' what this 'I' really was that had the property to think (CSM II, 192–193; AT VII, 276). Descartes rejoined that it was the wrong kind of question to ask. It was wrong because it was asking for a description: something like the proportion of salt, sulphur, and mercury that went into the making of this 'I.' Descartes was, however, careful enough to point out that "the more attributes of a given substance we know, the more perfectly we understand its nature" (CSM II, 249; AT VII, 360). That knowledge of attributes is necessary, for the knowledge of a substance does not mean that the substance is not something different and distinct from its attributes. It *is* different, and that is Descartes' view. It was to this that A. J. Ayer objected: "But when I tell myself that I exist, I do not identify myself by any description: I do not identify myself at all. . . . There is nothing more to me than

7 Ibid., 110–111.

what can be discovered by listing the totality of the descriptions which I satisfy."[8] Contemporary metaphysics is more on the side of Descartes than, understandably, was Ayer.

It does not follow, nor do our intuitions allow, that once we have divested primitive thisness from primitive suchness, then any suchness, quality, or characteristic can be pinned to a primitive thisness.

The conclusion, that there cannot be any purely qualitative necessary condition for the possession of any given thisness, is absurd, however. It implies that you and I, for example, could have been individuals of any sort whatever – plutonium atoms, noises, football games, places, or times, if those are all individuals. If we cannot trust our intuition that we could not have been any of those things, then it is probably a waste of time to study *de re* modalities at all. If there are any transworld identities and non-identities, there are necessary connections between thisness and some suchnesses.[9]

Whatever may be the case otherwise, we know that Descartes would have acknowledged this. He would not have claimed that you and I could be any of those things just listed: At a minimum, we have to be thinking beings. In Descartes' view, there *is* a necessary connection between the 'I' denoted by a thisness and a set of suchnesses, in particular, thought. "But what then am I? A thing that thinks. What is that? A thing that doubts, understands, affirms, denies, is willing, is unwilling, and also imagines and has sensory perceptions." (CSM II, 19; AT VII, 28) These are all suchnesses, and no amount of specifying them in detail would succeed in getting at Descartes' 'I,' any more than it would succeed in getting at the 'I' of you or me. Descartes in his doubt captures his 'I' by a primitive thisness (a thisness that cannot be defined in terms of suchnesses). He can later peg the various suchnesses onto this 'I': A necessary condition of his being this 'I' is that he must possess the property of thinking. So when someone insists that we give content to the *cogito*, we answer that the 'I' cannot be defined away in terms of primitive suchnesses, which is essentially what that demand amounts to. So it is contentless in the strict sense that it has not been defined in terms of suchnesses, but this does not warrant the conclusion that the *cogito* is therefore without content.

[8] A. J. Ayer, "I Think, Therefore I Am," 85.
[9] Robert Merrihew Adams, "Primitive Thisness and Primitive Identity," 24. See note 5 to this chapter.

Let me try a different path. Consider the following from John Perry:

An amnesiac, Rudolf Lingens, is lost in the Stanford Library. He reads a number of things in the library, including a biography of himself, and a detailed account of the library in which he is lost. . . . He still won't know who he is, and where he is, no matter how much knowledge he piles up, until that moment when he is ready to say, "*This* place is aisle five, floor six, of Main Library, Stanford. *I* am Rudolf Lingens."[10]

The point is that Rudolf Lingens can acquire much by way of knowledge, but at some point *self*-ascription has to take place; Lingens has to self-ascribe the property of being in a certain perceptual situation.

David Lewis proposes a more difficult case:

Consider the case of two gods. They inhabit a certain possible world, and they know exactly which world it is. Therefore they know every proposition that is true at their world. Insofar as knowledge is a propositional attitude, they are omniscient. Still I can imagine them to suffer ignorance: neither one knows which of the two he is. They are not exactly alike. One lives on the top of the tallest mountain and throws down manna; the other lives on the top of the coldest mountain and throws down thunderbolts. Neither one knows whether he lives on the tallest mountain or on the coldest mountain; nor whether he throws manna or thunderbolts.

Surely their predicament is possible. (The trouble might perhaps be that they have an equally perfect view of every part of their world, and hence cannot identify the perspectives from which they view it.) But if it is possible to lack knowledge and not lack any propositional knowledge, then the lacked knowledge must not be propositional. If the gods came to know which was which, they would know more than they do. But they wouldn't know more propositions. There are no more to know. Rather, they would self-ascribe more of the properties they possess.[11]

Lewis concludes that "[s]ome belief and some knowledge cannot be understood as propositional, but can be understood as self-ascription of properties." To apply this insight to the case of the *cogito*: At first sight, one is likely to dismiss it out of hand as being not only implausible, but also simply false when applied to Descartes. Descartes was looking for *propositional* knowledge, and if Lewis is right, then what Descartes has is

---

[10] John Perry, "Frege on Demonstratives," 474–497.
[11] David Lewis, *Philosophical Papers*, Volume 1, 139.

knowledge of a self-ascription, which is nonpropositional knowledge – not a first truth.

There are two steps that for a long time, in no small measure owing to Descartes himself, have been fused as one. There is, first, the non-propositional knowledge of self-ascription of the property of existing. Second, and only then, there is the formulation of the proposition that is to serve as the first truth – namely, "I am thinking, therefore I exist" is articulated. With only a minor modification, the Lewisian argument can be made to apply in the case of the *cogito*. Let us suppose there are two persons, D and D', in a possible world, w. They know every proposition that is true in w. Insofar as knowledge is a propositional attitude, they are omniscient. Still, I can imagine them to suffer ignorance: Neither one knows which of the two he is. They are not exactly alike. Unlike the Lewisian case, in which the two gods are vastly different and do vastly different things, the two persons in w are very similar and do very similar things. Indeed, they differ in exactly *one* thing. Aside from every other similarity, each of them has engaged in Cartesian doubt (by the very same route, by the very same reasoning), but only one of them – say, D – has arrived at the *cogito*, "I am thinking, therefore I exist"; the other has not. After the *cogito*, they once again do similar things (consequently, in w neither D nor D' has proceeded beyond the stage described in the third paragraph of the Second Meditation). Neither of them knows who it is that has arrived at the *cogito*-proposition, although each of them knows that one and only one of them has. Until there is *self*-ascription, there is not, as Descartes himself had intended, the knowledge of that first truth. This argument is a much weaker version of Lewis' argument, and so it must be correct if Lewis' argument is sound. Once that first step has been carried out, the first truth can then be trumpeted out, and the game of deduction begins – but not until then.

The 'I' of Descartes cannot be defined by the essential property of his mind, namely, thought, for that essential property defines the mind of, say, Spinoza, as well. The 'I' of Descartes could not be the 'I' of Spinoza, even if Descartes and Spinoza had in common every suchness. Imagine a possible world, w_0, in which there are two men, D and D'. Whatever suchness D possesses, D' possesses, and vice versa. Imagine a possible world, w, which is an extension of w_0, in which only D exists but not D' and another possible world, w' in which D' exists but not *D*. Surely, so the argument goes, *w* is different from *w'*: for in one, *D* exists but not *D'*, and in the other, *D'* exists but not *D*. Yet, *ex hypothesi*, *w* is identical to *w'* in terms of suchnesses. Two things can be different without that difference being a difference in suchnesses. Such is the way in which the Leibnizian principle of the identity of indiscernible is defeated. It is the thisness that would capture the 'I' of Descartes, as it would the 'I' of Spinoza; and so to demand that I be defined in terms of suchnesses is to work implicitly with a disjunction: Either the 'I' in the *cogito* can be defined in terms of suchnesses, or the 'I' in the *cogito* is without content. There is reason not to accept that disjunction.[12]

---

[12] Pertaining to the arguments of the last several pages, John Compton wrote: "My concern would be better put in terms of 'what' it is that the *cogito*, as an intuition, reveals. For, as a matter of experiential fact, I can certainly coincide with my activity of thinking and have the experience of self-existence." (Quoted remarks of John Compton in this chapter are from a private communication of June 1, 1999.) I fear that Descartes did not say much about what that ego is – and given his view, I surmise, he could not have said more about it – whose existence the *cogito* is supposed to have established. But I am reasonably confident that Descartes would have vehemently denied the possibility that Compton speaks of when he says, "I can certainly coincide with my activity of thinking," for reasons very much of the sort Baker and Morris have advanced. "We cannot," Compton continues, "leave the matter in the hands of John Perry and David Lewis – there must be more than a self-ascription or a 'thisness' to give content to the proposition 'I am thinking, therefore I exist.' We are after 'propositional knowledge' after all." Otherwise, Compton concludes, we seem to be left "with an unanalyzed 'subject' and an unanalyzed process of 'thinking'." I take Perry's and Lewis's argument to demonstrate that there is a difference between the two gods, and that that difference cannot be stated in terms of a description. There is no propositional knowledge of that difference to be had. I surmise that Descartes would have accepted that the propositional knowledge he begins with is not a proposition about the nature of that 'I' it is rather about the existence of that 'I'.

"'Thisness' just is not enough here," says Compton. "No doubt the individuality of the existent self cannot be defined by 'suchnesses'. But defining is one thing and characterizing or 'pointing' to what we experience as our individual existence is another. There must be some way of characterizing this 'I' experientially... 'intuitively,' and without using an appeal to the senses,... Husserl tried to characterize the ego experientially as the 'pole' of conscious 'intentional' activity and describes its 'self-constitution' through time. What might have Descartes said about this?"

One might reply as follows: (a) *Pointing* and *thisness* are quite intimately linked; with pointing one might capture the thisness of the object, although capturing the thisness of the object need not always involve pointing. But *characterizing* an object is quite different from pointing to it and seems prima facie to be not different from describing or listing its suchnesses. Once Compton concedes that individuality may not be defined by suchnesses, how might suchnesses characterize an object in a way that enables us to get at what Perry and Lewis want to get at, namely, the individual?

There are two other, and separate, consequences that I wish to explore. The first is the issue of the identity of the 'I' over an interval of time;[13] the second is the importance of the *cogito* to the general rule via the case of the wax. Let us begin with the first issue. "But what then am I?" (CSM II, 19; AT VII, 28) asks Descartes. He answers that the 'I' is that which thinks, and to think is to affirm or deny, to doubt or understand, to will or otherwise, to imagine or have sensory perceptions, to love or hate. These are all quite different activities of the 'I' and could not be performed simultaneously: For instance, the 'I' could not both affirm and doubt at the same time. Thus, an interval of time is required for the performance of these distinct activities. For example, the 'I' may affirm the *cogito* at one instant, doubt that it has a body in the next, will to solve a mathematical problem a moment after that, understand its solution in the next few moments, and so on. That 'I' is the "one and the same I"[14] (CSM II, 19; AT VII, 28). By what argument or criterion is Descartes able to judge that it is one and the same 'I'?

In the "Sixth Set of Objections," compiled by Father Mersenne, we have this: "[W]hen you say you are thinking and that you exist, someone might maintain that you are mistaken, and are not thinking but are merely in motion, and that you are nothing else but corporeal motion" (CSM II, 278; AT VII, 413). But the idea, replies Descartes, of corporeal motion is essentially different from the idea of thought, and therefore the two cannot be one and the same. If we are to regard

---

(b) What is the Husserlian "pole" of conscious intentional activity that is not captured by the Cartesian ego engaged in thinking, understanding, willing, affirming, denying, doubting, and so on, which are paradigmatically intentional activities? The parallel question to ask of Husserl would be, how might one characterize the individuality of *this* pole experientially, intuitively, without using an appeal to the senses? Or, for that matter, the self-constitution of that pole through time? I hope the last section will go a small way toward further answering some of Compton's concerns discussed in this chapter.

[13] Descartes had not much to say on the issue of the identity of the 'I' over time. At least since Locke, that question has been of considerable interest. While it is clearly a deficiency in Descartes not to have raised and answered that question, I am not sure I would go so far as some who maintain that what Descartes *does* establish is consequently not quite important – not to mention the importance of the *way* in which he establishes the claim of existence.

[14] I agree with Bernard Williams and Margaret Wilson that one needs to distinguish the autobiographical 'I' of the respondent to the objections to *Meditations on First Philosophy* (he is Descartes) from the 'I' of the investigator in *Meditations on First Philosophy* (he could be any investigator).

them as one and the same thing, we may do so "either in virtue of the unity or identity of their nature, or else merely in respect of unity of composition" (CSM II, 285; AT VII, 423). For example, the idea of shape is not the same as the idea of motion, but we perceive clearly that the same substance that is capable of taking shape is capable of motion. The idea of volition is not the same as the idea of understanding, but we perceive clearly that the same substance is capable of both volition and understanding. This is possible in virtue of the unity of nature. By contrast, the idea of flesh is different from the idea of bone, and they are found in the same animal, the same substance, in virtue of the unity of composition. Such, then, is the case with respect to corporeal motion and thought, we have different and distinct ideas of them, and they belong to the same substance, not in virtue of the unity of nature, but rather in virtue of the unity of composition. Finally, says Descartes, "it is self-contradictory to suppose that things we clearly understand as different and independent could not be separated, at least by God" (CSM II, 287; AT VII, 425).

Has Descartes then successfully shown that it is one and the same 'I' that underlies the activities of volition, affirmation, denial, understanding, perceiving, and so on? I begin with Descartes' last claim first. At this stage, the existence of God, let alone of a good God, has not been proved, and so God cannot be effectively marshaled in the argument. Thus, for all we know, God could have, but did not, separate what we perceive to be clearly different and distinct.[15] But Descartes' distinction between the unity of nature and the unity of composition does not answer the kind of question I am raising, even if we accept his answer to his critic.

---

[15] Compton suggests an interesting route that the argument might take: "Perhaps it is that certainty of this identity awaits the certainty of the existence of God. For, Descartes does hold that God is necessary to sustain each being in its existence from moment to moment." Two qualifiers before following this suggestion: First, the issue is not epistemological in nature; we are not asking how we can know the identity for certain; it is rather an ontological question about the nature of identity. Second, while it is true that God preserves or creates (Descartes does not distinguish these concepts in this context [CSM II, 33; AT VII, 49], each creature must already have an identity that God preserves or creates. Might Compton then suggest that the question of the identity of the individual is only settled at that individual's creation by God, and in no other way? What then would it be for God to create *this* individual, or to re-create this individual from one moment to the next, rather than some other?

Look at it from the point of view of an infant. "I do not doubt that the mind begins to think as soon as it is implanted in the body of an infant, and that it is immediately aware of its thoughts, even though it does not remember this afterwards because the impressions of these thoughts do not remain in the memory" (CSM II, 171–172; AT VII, 246). As yet, no argument has been established to justify reliance on memory, so memory cannot tie in a single knot the various activities, and then hook it onto the 'I'. What, then? Perhaps, at each moment in the womb, a distinct infant, housed in the same body, perceives this 'I', which is himself. Could there then be different 'I's for different moments, a fresh mind supplied, at each fresh instant, to the same body? Why is that an incoherent claim?[16]

To turn to the second issue: The *cogito*, as I have argued before, provides the first and sole support for the much-needed general rule, namely, that whatever is clearly and distinctly perceived is true. If any subsequent claim must have the general rule's insignia, in order to be regarded as true, that insignia will bear marks of the *cogito*. This is further supported by Descartes' view of the content of the *cogito* via the wax case. While the wax case is not essential, it is nevertheless crucial. For with it, Descartes is enabled to make a comparative case. Thus, the wax that was before cold, hard, white in color, and tasted of honey, no longer has those properties when placed near the fire; it is, instead, the wax without the same color, taste, smell, and feel. But the properties of white color, sweet taste, honey smell, hardness, and so on are known through sense perception or imagination. If he were to rely on them, Descartes would have concluded that the wax has changed. But, of course, it has not; it is "the same wax." Descartes concludes: "I must therefore admit that the nature of this piece of wax is in no way revealed by my imagination, but is perceived by the mind alone" (CSM II, 21; AT VII, 31).

But with this argument, Descartes wished to establish not just that human perception requires the human mind, but also this: "Surely my awareness of my own self is not merely much truer and more certain than my awareness of the wax, but also much more distinct

---

[16] See Chapter 3, section IV: the argument against Descartes based on his claims about the Eucharist.

and evident"[17] (CSM II, 22; AT VII, 33). The general rule claims that whatever is clear and distinct is true; according to Descartes' argument, the *cogito*-state is more clear and distinct than the perception of the wax, which is clear and distinct enough; at the very least, he implies that nothing else is as clear and distinct at this stage. What degree of clarity and distinctness is required, then, before the general rule is applied? It is, or ought to be, the highest degree of clarity and distinctness, the degree noticed in the *cogito*-state. This, I shall argue much later, leads to the undoing of Descartes.

Finally, there is a curious bit in the Second Meditation. When Descartes begins to consider the wax case, he says: "Let us consider the things which people commonly think they understand most distinctly of all; that is, the bodies which we touch and see. I do not mean bodies in general – for general perceptions are apt to be somewhat more confused – but one particular body. Let us take, for example, this piece of wax." (CSM II, 20; AT VII, 30) Not bodies in general, but *this* particular body. Not pieces of wax in general, but *this* piece of wax, says Descartes. The crucial assumption is that, at this stage of the inquiry, a perception of a general body, a general piece of wax, is apt to be confusing, and so one ought not to rely on it. But this has implications for general perceptions generally. For note that Descartes speaks of general perceptions generally as being confusing, and not just of

---

[17] "What could be meant here," says Compton, "is that not only the existence and nature of our own minds (as thinking things) is 'much truer and more certain' than the existence and nature of the piece of wax, but that the *unity* of our own minds across time is even more certain than the *unity* of that piece of wax. For it is unity across time, precisely, that is at stake in the case of the wax. And similarly, one could hazard that it is what is at stake for the mind.

"If this were the argument, we would have something akin to Kant's argument in the transcendental deduction, namely, that in order for there to be 'objects' for us – i.e., 'unities' of the manifold – there is presupposed the unity (and unifying activity) of our transcendental 'I'. And it is precisely, for Kant, the unity across time that is centrally at issue. Descartes' argument would be a 'psychological' or 'existential' version of Kant's 'transcendental' one....

"I do not see how Descartes could do without a very strong sense of mental 'substance,' a change-independent substrate, intuitively given with the cogito...." First, Descartes rarely, if ever, speaks about the identity of anything over an interval of time. Second, were Descartes to follow Kant, he would have termed his view "metaphysical" – much to Kant's chagrin – rather than "psychological" or "existential." Third, Compton, Baker, and Morris are agreed: Substance is an indispensable metaphysical category in Descartes.

general perceptions about bodies being confusing. "When I reflect on the *cogito*," Descartes might have said, "my focus of attention is solely on this *I*. It is not on thinkers and doubters generally, for general perceptions, at this stage of the inquiry, are apt to be confusing. What I see most evidently is that '*I* am', '*I* exist', is necessarily true whenever it is put forward by *me* or conceived in *my* mind. (CSM II, 17; AT VII, 25) There is no reference here to thinkers and doubters generally, nor to what would happen to *them* if *they* put forward something before *themselves* or conceived something in *their* minds."[18] If this is not an unfair way of speaking on Descartes' behalf, it is difficult to see how a general statement, "Whatever thinks, exists" – the central premise in the *cogito*-argument – can find support at this stage of the inquiry.

III. Ryle and the Elusive 'I'

There are three and a half puzzling pages in Gilbert Ryle's *The Concept of Mind* (Chapter 6, "Self-Knowledge") entitled "The Systematic Elusiveness of 'I'" (186–189). Ryle claims to explain therein why the notion of 'I' is systematically elusive, and why there is a partial nonparallelism between that notion and the notions of 'you' and 'he'. My interest in Ryle is limited: It aims only at showing that, given Descartes' argument for the *cogito*, the 'I' *is* elusive in a significant way that Ryle fails to notice. If my arguments are sound, it will follow that they also defeat Ryle's second claim about the partial nonparallelism between the direct indexical word 'I', on the one hand, and indirect indexical words 'you' and 'he', on the other. But I shall not labor to argue for that separately here.

Let me outline Ryle's central thesis by beginning with his examples.[19] A singing-master criticizes the accents or notes of a pupil; he does so by exaggerating each word the pupil sings. Had the pupil sung slowly, the master could have parodied each word the pupil sang before the next came to be sung. Then, humbly, the singing-master

---

[18] Gaukroger offers some very interesting reflections on the nature of the self, which is "a unified locus of subjectivity." Consult, in particular, the first three of his five points (G, 346–352).

[19] There are at least twenty such examples in the last two sections of this chapter alone, each example making roughly the same point. The examples I take are ones that Ryle has discussed in detail.

criticizes his own singing in a similar way; even more, he mimics with exaggerations each word that he utters, including those that he utters in parody of his own singing. Needless to add, the singing-master can demonstrate a parody of a parody of a parody of a parody of . . . his own singing. Two things are clear, says Ryle. First, the singing-master can never get beyond the very earliest word of his song; second, at any given moment he has uttered one note that has yet to be mimicked. "He can, in principle, never catch more than the coat-tails of the object of his pursuit, since a word cannot be a parody of itself." (187).

Similarly – the second example – one may criticize a book in a review; someone else may review that first review in turn and criticize it, but the second review is not a criticism of itself. It can only be criticized by a third review: "any review of any order could be published, though at no stage would all the reviews have received critical notices" (187). The last review, in any series of reviews, is, *ex hypothesi*, exempt from review; ineluctably, there is always such a review.[20]

It is not hard to mimic how the argument would go for showing the systematic elusiveness of 'I'. Let us describe a situation in which a person in a soliloquy (silent or verbal, public or private) is engaged in the task of self-commentary.[21] At one time, he makes several comments about himself. He says to himself, say, that he was boorish to a friend. A little later, that criticism is itself an object of appraisal: He thinks the boorishness was in part playacting, because he (the friend) needed to be taught a lesson (nor was there any other way to help him stiffen his spine), and thus the person mitigates his self-condemnation. Still later, this appraisal is itself appraised: He thinks that the animus with which the act was performed revealed an old, harbored hurt, thus recognizing the real cause of his action from the apparent one; and so on. As the soliloquy proceeds, it leads the person to better understand him*self*. But what a person knows (in this limited way) about himself can

---

[20] Burman, in his conversations with Descartes, had asked him something astonishingly similar: "But how can [the mind] be aware, since to be aware is itself to think? In order to have the thought that you are aware, you must move on to another thought; but if you do this, you can no longer be thinking of the thing you were thinking of a moment ago. It follows that you cannot be aware that you *are* thinking, but only that you *were* thinking." (CSMK 315; AT V, 149)

[21] Or self-suasion, self-dissuasion, self-reporting, self-exhortation, self-commiseration, self-ridicule, self-admonition – all Rylean terms.

in principle be known by anyone else. Just imagine what a person says of himself, then imagine the other person saying something similar. Thus, "You were boorish," "You only meant to teach him to take a clear stand," or "You wished to avenge an old, but grievous, insult."

Now, at no point is the understanding of a person about himself complete, says Ryle, because the vantage point from which the last critical appraisal was made is itself not appraised, examined. Of course, *it* can in principle be examined, but only from the perspective of *another* view, which will remain at that moment unexamined. "A higher order action cannot be the action upon which it is performed. So my commentary on my performance must always be silent about one performance, namely itself, and this performance can be the target only of another commentary. Self-commentary, self-ridicule, and self-admonition are logically condemned to eternal penultimacy." (186) Each of us – no matter how morally perfect, intellectually brilliant, and psychologically astute – will forever fall short of fulfilling, if only by one step, the Socratic maxim, "know thyself." "This, I think, explains the feeling that my last year's self, or my yesterday's self, could in principle be exhaustively described and accounted for, and that your past or present self could be exhaustively described and accounted for by me, but that my today's self perpetually slips out of any hold of it that I try to take" (187). One is thus logically prevented by this permanent penultimacy from knowing oneself; it is not merely something very difficult to perform or execute. This explains, thinks Ryle, not only the systematic elusiveness of the 'I' but also the nonparallelism between 'I', on the one hand, and 'you' and 'he', on the other. Thus far, Ryle.

Would – or should? – Descartes have been moved? Take the review example. The book under review has content, and, in principle, a reviewer can latch onto that content and criticize it. Likewise for the second, third, fourth, . . . n[th] reviews. Each review has specific content, and it is open to criticism. But the 'I', Descartes would have said, has no content that can, in principle, be described. It is not the case that the individual has caught a partial description, which then gets focused on to reveal some additional descriptions missed in the first round of descriptions, and then the third round gets even more, has greater verisimilitude, and so on. Descartes would have claimed (and I take it that David Lewis would, too) that the 'I' is remarkably different from the *sorts* of things Ryle has focused his attention on: namely, words, notes, songs, reviews, and so on.

Put in a Rylean way, Descartes' point would go something like this. I, who am engaged in self-commentary, self-ridicule, or self-admonition, encounter an 'I', my I, "this 'I' – that is, the soul by which I am what I am –" (CSM I, 127; AT VI, 33) *plus* some description. This 'I' – "this puzzling 'I' which cannot be pictured in the imagination" (CSM II, 20; AT VII, 29) – a qualityless, descriptionless 'I', referred to by a thisness,[22] is spewing out the description in an attempt at self-knowledge. That description is open to examination, criticism, and commentary, which in turn is subject to examination, criticism, and commentary, which in turn... and so on. This is entirely susceptible to Rylean analysis. What never gets captured in the net is the elusive 'I'. The 'I' casts the net, and the fish that is caught is a thought (which *can* be described); never does the 'I' cast a net and catch itself. It cannot, in principle, do that. "Should I, or should I not, put my knowing self down on my list of the sorts of things that I can have knowledge of? If I say 'no', it seems to reduce my knowing self to a theoretically infertile mystery, yet if I say 'yes', it seems to reduce the fishing-net to one of the fishes which it itself catches." (178) To the "yes" part, Descartes would have readily assented; to the "no" part, he would have expressed his puzzlement thus: "It is only a theoretically infertile mystery if you take away what you acknowledged in the 'yes' part: A net is not a fish. The 'I' is simply not that which can be captured in any description beginning with the first description and ending with the last description."

Talking in terms of levels (see Figure 7.1), at each level there is a description, if only a description of an earlier description; no two descriptions are identical. Specifically, $Review_n$ is about $(\uparrow)Review_{n-1}$ which is about $Review_{n-2}$, and so on; at each level there is a review, if only a review of an earlier review; no two reviews are identical. Likewise, $Thought_n$ is about $Thought_{n-1}$, which is about $Thought_{n-2}$, and so on; at each level there is a thought, if only a thought about an

---

[22] Says Ryle, "philosophers have speculated whether 'I' denotes a peculiar separate substance and in what consists my indivisible and continuing identity" (177). It is precisely this mistaken search that leads to "a family of enigmas" from which Ryle's theory is supposed to free us.

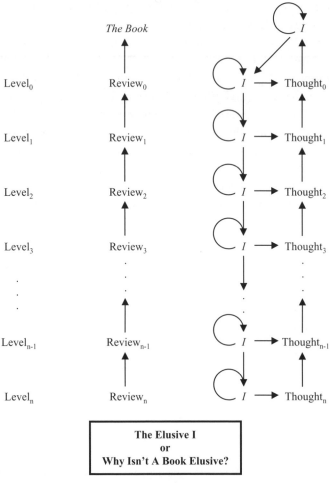

FIGURE 7.1.

earlier thought; and no two thoughts are identical. Comparing the two columns, one finds that the only constant at each level is the 'I', which is the numerically same 'I' at any other level, $\downarrow$ indicating the same 'I' perpetuating from one level to the next. The 'I' referring to itself is indicated by $\circlearrowright$. Only if we identify the 'I' with some description in a manner after Hume, as Ryle does, does Ryle have any force against Descartes' argument (but then Ryle's view has some enigmas of its own to face, as we shall see) and make the 'I' column in the chart disappear. Descartes attempted to show that to make any such identification – even a partial identification – is to look in the wrong place, to make an error about the content of that 'I'.

Look at it this way. The 'I' and the book are remarkably different – for one thing, no one speaks of the book as elusive; and so what Ryle says about the book and its reviews cannot apply to the 'I' without qualification. Consider: Each review of the book is a different and distinct entity; it is assuredly not a continuous – indeed, not even a discrete – part of the book, whereas the book provides the nucleus that assures continuity over reviews about reviews about reviews . . . of this book. By contrast, consider: Each December 31, a person reviews his old self; and he does this, say, over a ten-year period. Each such "review" is not only about himself but also a critical "review" of his earlier "reviews" of himself. But these "reviews" – unlike the reviews of the book – are not about distinct persons (each "review" representing a different person), for no other than a good Rylean reason:

As if an ordinary person is really some sort of committee or team of persons, all laced together inside one skin; as if the thinking and vetoing 'I' were one person, and the greedy or lazy 'I' were another. But this sort of picture is obviously of no use. . . . So the suggested reduction of a person to a team of persons would merely multiply the number of persons without explaining how it is that one and the same person can be both narrator and auditor, or both vigilant and dreamy, both scorched and amazed at being scorched. (181)

But if there is no 'I' that assures continuity between these "reviews" spread out over a ten-year period, *what* does?

Reexamine this crucial passage: "This, I think, explains the feeling that my last year's self, or my yesterday's self, could in principle be exhaustively described and accounted for, and that your past or present self could be exhaustively described and accounted for by me, but that my today's self perpetually slips out of any hold of it that I try to take" (187). Thus: I can know my past self in its entirety, but never my present self in its entirety; on the other hand, I can know your past self in its entirety *and* your present self in its entirety; and vice versa. At any given moment, I am always partially inscrutable to myself; you are never, in principle, inscrutable to me. To me, therefore, you are like a book; unto myself I am no such thing.

The Rylean view has force only because it denies that 'I' is different from the set of descriptions one might give of that 'I' or self; this is precisely why I am able to know the whole of you without remainder but fail in the attempt to know the whole of me. Why? Because any attempt on my part to know that 'I' changes the very 'I' that I am attempting to know. The knower and the known are never identical in my case. For obvious reasons, too, this would render each 'I' at each level a different 'I'. Because the 'I' at one level – say, level$_3$ – investigating what the 'I' is at level$_2$ already has a thought that the 'I' at level$_2$ does not possess. If the time interval between these levels – between thoughts and thoughts about thoughts – is shortened, the problem becomes extremely acute: We have a series of 'I's rapidly coming-into and going-out-of existence. But there is simply *no* reason to think that the two 'I's, in so short an interval of time, are numerically different and distinct (while granting that the descriptions that the two 'I's spew out may be remarkably so). This is Heraclitean flux with a vengeance. Without wishing to be a paradox monger, could ever an 'I' witness such a flux?

If the foregoing argument is correct, then other enigmas follow. First, there is no reason to think that *I* can capture in terms of a description *your* puzzling 'I', any more than I can capture my own.

What is more, second, I know what it is for *me* to have a privileged access to this 'I' that is *mine*, but I have no access to what *you* would indexically designate as the 'I' that is *yours*. This should undermine Ryle's claim that

[n]o metaphysical Iron Curtain exists compelling us to be for ever absolute strangers to one another, though ordinary circumstances, together with some deliberate management, serve to maintain a reasonable aloofness. Similarly no metaphysical looking-glass exists compelling us to be for ever completely disclosed and explained to ourselves, though from the everyday conduct of our sociable and unsociable lives we learn to be reasonably conversant with ourselves. (173)

I have direct access to that 'I' of mine, to which you have none, and vice versa; to this extent, if no more, we are absolute strangers.

Third, given the fallibility of first-person reporting, no less than of third-person, Ryle concludes that self-consciousness does not have the role that Cartesians attach to it. "Self-consciousness," says Ryle, "must not be described on the hallowed para-optical model, as a torch that illuminates itself by beams of its own light reflected from a mirror in its own insides" (186). This is just mockery. Descartes allowed for the possibility, *even* in the case where the *cogito* is established, that a thinker may well be mistaken in his particular thought. Quite simply, the evil genius can deceive me about what I am currently thinking. There is not a solitary passage in Descartes suggesting that we are like metaphysical looking glasses unto ourselves, forever completely disclosed and explained to ourselves. He would have insisted only that, given the proper thought experiment, I cannot be mistaken in the belief that I exist while I am thinking an admittedly fallible thought. Perhaps, then, *self*-consciousness – as the word indicates, or as $\circlearrowright$ symbolizes – may be required only to demonstrate the existence of the self, and nothing more. That is, it is not required to serve as a surety, a guarantor, an underwriter for the veracity of any thought that it is currently casting its light on.

Fourth, the 'I', the thinker, has a property of self-consciousness not possessed by its thoughts: *I* am aware of having a thought, my *thought* is not aware of my having this thought or any other; it is just a thought. There is nothing more to a book than the information encoded in its inscriptions; the book itself has no capacity for self-reference; it cannot behold its contents. One can, of course, imagine a book replete with self-referential sentences and sentences that refer to other sentences; it may even have a humorous self-referential title, such as the title of Raymond M. Smullyan's book, *What is the Name of This Book?* But one cannot, *per impossible*, imagine a book that itself has any such property as self-consciousness. On the other hand, the qualityless 'I' that Descartes speaks of has just that property; and nothing else in the universe – save a thinking thing – has that property.

The fifth and final argument: Ryle says, "For any performance of any order, it is always *possible* that there should be performed a variety of higher order actions about it" (185). The emphasis is mine, for I wish to indicate that it is not *necessary* that one perform a higher-order action. Let us, then, suppose that a person, say Gilbert Ryle, wishes to understand himself. He goes through reviews upon reviews of himself (reviews of his own making about himself), and finally he comes to a halt at some stage. Let us call this the Ground State. Here is the crucial step: Either it is possible that the Ground State is transparent to Ryle, or it is not possible. To say that a state is transparent is to make an epistemic claim, but not a claim about epistemic infallibility. It is a state in which a person, say Ryle, sees no epistemic need to evaluate, rate, rank, weigh, classify, pigeonhole, codify, catalog, measure, reflect upon, expound upon, comment upon, define, explain, or criticize the state; he understands the state, he thinks, perspicuously. Of course, he could be mistaken. On the other hand, when in the *cogito*-state he is making the *cogito*-claim; he is in an infallible state and knows himself to be in such a state, but he need not be in the *cogito*-state to be in what he thinks to be a transparent state.

Now consider the *first* alternative: If the Ground State is transparent to Ryle, it would circumvent any need on Ryle's part to move to a higher stage, the better to know himself. As we saw, it is not necessary that Ryle perform a higher-order action. Ryle could, in principle, know all of the states of Ryle that in their totality constitute what can be described about Ryle, including the Ground State, which is transparent to him, and no state would remain unknown (*ex hypothesi*, there being no state *to* know, in particular none from which alone the Ground State can be known, evaluated, measured, and so on). If this is possible, Ryle has failed to explain the elusiveness of 'I'. It is false for him to say: "This, I think, explains the feeling that my last year's self, or my yesterday's self, could in principle be exhaustively described and accounted for, . . . but that my today's self perpetually slips out of any hold of it that I try to take" (187).

No sooner is this said than the reader will instinctively revert to the book-and-reviews case just presented and protest that there cannot be, on Ryle's view, such a transparent Ground State. Let us, then, consider the *second* alternative. If there cannot be a transparent Ground State, then Ryle is mistaken when he says that "your past or present self could be exhaustively described and accounted for by me" (187). And the reason is this. Consider the case in which it is not Ryle who is trying to know Ryle, but I who am trying to know Ryle. Surely, in order to exhaustively describe Ryle as Ryle says that I could – "your past or present self could be exhaustively described and accounted for by me" – I would have to be in some Provisionally Basic State, a state in which I could describe, among his other states, Ryle's own Provisionally Basic State. Now, if that Provisionally Basic State of mine is not transparent to me, I will never be epistemically sure whether I have really understood Ryle, and I will push further to evaluate my own state of understanding of Ryle's states; and each such state of understanding of Ryle's states being fallible, it will push me to perform higher-order actions. But if I cannot be in a transparent state, *ex hypothesi*, then surely I can no more know Ryle than he can know himself. There is more symmetry between 'I' and 'he' than Ryle acknowledges.

In conclusion: Either I can know myself, rendering the 'I' nonelusive in cases where Ryle himself thinks that it is and ought to be elusive, or I cannot know myself, for the same reasons that you cannot know me either, thus making the 'I' elusive even in those cases where Ryle thinks that it is not. The Rylean way ineluctably keeps us from seeking the content of the 'I' in the right place.

8

Memory, Explanation, and Will

The aim stated in the last chapter is pursued further in this final chapter. That aim is to demonstrate how interpretations of various philosophical theories of Descartes cohere with the core interpretation that the *cogito* is not an argument. Three additional such philosophical theories of Descartes are examined here, theories that have no overt connection with one another – namely, his theories about memory, logic and explanation, and will. I trust that their mutual independence (something akin to independent testability) will strengthen my interpretation of the *cogito*.

In section I, Descartes' distinction between two types of memory is drawn; this distinction is then examined, and it is shown how it lends added support to the core argument. Now, Descartes had interesting things to say about the nature and logic of discovery and explanation, and he prided himself on differing from the traditional study of logic. When we take this aspect of Descartes' thought into consideration – section II is designed for that purpose – it further strengthens the central thesis. Finally, in section III, I analyze Descartes' theory of the will – not all aspects of it, but just that aspect that contributes to the central thesis of this book.

I. The Role of Memory

There are two types of memory, according to Descartes. I shall call them *physical memory* and *intellectual memory*, respectively. In the terminology of Descartes' posthumously published *Treatise of Man*, "the seat of memory" lies in the internal part of the brain. After leaving a gland, the spirits pass through the tubes and into the pores of the filaments that compose the solid part of the brain. Depending on the force of the spirits and the degree of openness of the tubes, the spirits will expand, bend, and rearrange the filaments they encounter. At first, the passage of the spirits will be difficult; but with time, intensity, frequency, and repetition of the encounters, the passage will become increasingly easier. They will then leave a *pattern* – an *imprint*, a *trace*, a *crease* – in the brain that cannot be easily erased and that can easily be activated without the presence of the relevant corresponding object. "And it is in this that *memory* consists."[1] Now, oddly enough, Descartes thinks that memory is located not only in the brain, but outside of it as well: "[W]hat people call Local Memory is outside of us."[2] For example, a lute player has a part of his memory in his hands; some of our recollection of a book is not in our heads but "on the paper of the copy which we have read" (CSMK, 146; AT II, 48). This is physical memory.

"But," says Descartes, "besides this memory, which depends on the body, I believe there is also another one, entirely intellectual, which depends on the soul alone"[3] (CSMK, 146; AT II, 48). This is intellectual memory.

Descartes often bemoans the weakness and unreliability of memory. If the *cogito* were an argument, then the mind would have to traverse the various premises to the conclusion, and see *and remember* the several premises and the conclusion and the links between various propositions in the argument. Let me quote at length:

[D]eduction sometimes requires such a long chain of inferences that when we arrive at such a truth it is not easy to recall the entire route which led us to it.

[1] Descartes, *Treatise of Man*, 87–88. Also see CSMK, 143; AT III, 19–20; and CSMK, 233; AT IV, 114.

[2] Descartes, *Treatise of Man*, 71.

[3] Curiously, Descartes maintains in a letter, dated June 4, 1648 probably written to Arnuald that intellectual memory "was not in use in the womb" (CSMK, 354–355; AT V, 193). I should point out that the original translation in Kenny is much stronger; it reads: "intellectual memory, which was not possible in the womb." But the infant in the womb has thoughts, and so it has a soul. Intellectual memory, we were just told, depends on the soul alone, and the soul has all the innate ideas even then. So it would follow that something more would be required for intellectual memory in the womb to commence operating. What, then, is it? Is one to infer that the infant in the womb cannot engage in the *cogito*? See also CSMK, 356–357; AT V, 220–221.

That is why we say that a continuous movement of thought is needed to make good any weakness of memory. If, for example, by way of separate operations, I have come to know first what the relation between magnitudes A and B is, and then between B and C, and between C and D, and finally between D and E, that does not entail my seeing what the relation is between A and E; and I cannot grasp what the relation is just from those I already know, unless I recall all of them. So I shall run through them several times in a continuous movement of the imagination, simultaneously intuiting one relation and passing on to the next, until I have learnt to pass from the first to the last so swiftly that memory is left with practically no role to play, and I seem to intuit the whole thing at once. In this way our memory is relieved, the sluggishness of our intelligence redressed, and its capacity in some way enlarged. (CSM I, 25; AT X, 387–388)

The central question is, which, (if either) of the two memories – physical memory or intellectual memory (or both) – can the thinker rely on while he is in the process of getting to the *cogito* through the method of doubt? Self-evidently, it cannot be physical memory, either internal or external, since this kind of memory *presupposes* the existence of physical objects, such as the brain of the thinker, the hands of a lute player, and the pages of a book. If the thinker doubts the existence of physical objects, as he does in his hyperbolic doubt, then he has little reason to believe in the existence of physical memory, and even less to rely on its alleged dicta.[4]

But intellectual memory cannot be relied upon either, for *it* pre-supposes the existence of the soul, which is only established simul-taneously with, or subsequent to, the *cogito*. So if the *cogito* were an argument, the thinker at this stage in his inquiry would have *no* reason to rely on intellectual memory.[5] Therefore, the thinker cannot rely on

---

4   "But memory is no different from imagination – at least the memory which is corporeal and similar to the one which animals possess. So we can conclude with certainty that when the intellect is concerned with matters in which there is nothing corporeal or similar to the corporeal, it cannot receive any help from those faculties." (CSM I, 43; AT X, 416) Imagination is notoriously unreliable, therefore physical memory is unreliable.

5   Nor will the following defense do: Intellectual memory is a function of conscious-ness, and remains so whether one answers the ontological question of the ground of memory. And as a function of consciousness, it is certainly available to be used by the mediator in bringing together the various steps of an argument. The reliability of memory is an epistemological question, and justifying its ontological ground in the existence of the soul is irrelevant to deciding whether it is reliable and available to be used by consciousness in its reasonings. There are two responses: First and foremost, intellectual memory is notoriously unreliable, and so Descartes questioned relying on

memory, and hence cannot judge even the validity of the argument, since that would presuppose the memory of the premises and the rules of inference that have been invoked. I conclude that intuition, and not deduction, is the only thing that Descartes can rely on at this stage of the inquiry. Consequently, the *cogito* is a simple proposition and not an argument.

"This overlooks the fact," someone might protest, "that Descartes, in the passage just cited, does in fact speak of the possibility of a deduction being intuited, if one went over it several times. There is an analogy that one can draw from vision. When I look out from my study window, I can see, at a single glance, the white mailbox, the road, the lawn, the red-brick house across the street, the lamppost, and the massive oak tree. I do not look, as a matter fact, at each of these objects one at a time and then put the whole thing together. Rather, I take in the whole scene at once. Similarly, if by repeated practice and learning I could take in the whole deduction at once, and not in stages, I would not have to look at one proposition at a time, at each rule of inference at a time, and then slowly and carefully put the whole argument together. I could take in the entire *cogito*-argument at a single intellectual glance, in what Descartes calls intuition. Thus, even if memory is unreliable, it is quite dispensable. The *cogito* could be an argument, and the argument could be intuited." So someone might say.

There are several responses. First, the role of memory cannot be got rid of in principle. One can reduce its role, but one cannot eliminate it. As Descartes himself says, only after "I have learnt to pass from the first to the last . . . swiftly," is "memory . . . left with practically no role to play." But practically no role to play is not the same thing as no role to play. There is an implied lemma in the foregoing: Memory has no role to play in an act of intuition.

Second, the analogy with ordinary vision would not sit very well with Descartes:

We can best learn how mental intuition is to be employed by comparing it with ordinary vision. If one tries to look at many objects at one glance, one sees none of them distinctly. Likewise, if one is inclined to attend to many things

it even in the opening paragraph of the Second Meditation. Second – and admittedly this is bold – if the fundamental root (the soul) of the thing (intellectual memory) can be held suspect, or if its nonexistence is seen as a distinct possibility, that should cast doubt even on the existence of that thing, with whatever nature it is alleged to possess.

at the same time in a single act of thought, one does so with a confused mind. Yet craftsmen who engage in delicate operations, and are used to fixing their eyes on a single point, acquire through practice the ability to make perfect distinctions between things, however minute and delicate. The same is true of those who never let their thinking be distracted by many different objects at the same time, but always devote their whole attention to the simplest and easiest of matters: they become perspicacious. (CSM I, 33; AT X, 400–401)

Descartes is maintaining that one ought *not* to "be distracted by many different objects at the same time, but always devote [one's] whole attention to the simplest and easiest of matters." This advice is not just for craftsmen, but for knowledge seekers as well. Correspondingly, Descartes would maintain that one ought not to be distracted by many different propositions at the same time, but instead should always devote one's whole attention to the simplest and easiest proposition. At least, one should do this at the beginning. "[T]wo things are required," says Descartes, "for mental intuition: first, the proposition intuited must be clear and distinct; second, the whole proposition must be understood all at once, and not bit by bit" (CSM I, 37; AT X, 407). But if one were attempting to intuit the whole argument, one would at some point in the beginning inevitably consider it bit by bit, proposition by proposition, in order to ascertain the argument's validity and soundness.

But, third, there is a more interesting reason why the analogy fails. When I look out of my study window and see the various objects, they do not *depend* on one another. If the oak tree were cut down, the house would still remain; if the house were completely remodeled, the mailbox would still remain; if the mailbox were painted brown, this would have no effect on the red-brick house across the street. But the propositions in the *cogito*-argument are essentially linked with respect to their content, structure, and truth-value. If any of these latter characteristics of the premises were to change, the argument might no longer be valid or sound.

II. Discovery, Explanation, and the New Logic

This section is not simply a very terse note on the history of logic. It is also meant to show the implications of Descartes' view of logic, explanation, and discovery for the *cogito*.

Descartes outlined a new logic; or, at least, he believed that he had one. Antoine Arnauld and Pierre Nicole, the joint authors of *La Logique, ou L'Art de Penser*, famously known as *The Port-Royal Logic*, agreed. The old scholastic logic concentrated on a theory of communication of settled knowledge. It was designed to *explain* known truths. The new logic aimed at providing a means for guiding reason in the acquisition of knowledge. It was designed to *discover* new truths. The *cogito*, construed as an argument, is patterned after the old way; the *cogito*, construed as a nonargument, is in harmony with Descartes' new way. Or so I shall argue.

Pierre de la Ramee, known as Peter Ramus, proposed in his master's inaugural thesis in 1536 a bold thesis: *Quaecumque ab Aristotle Dicta Essent, Commentitia Esse*. This meant: "Whatever Aristotle Has Said Is a Fabrication." Logic needed to be refurbished. First, it was to be a logic of learned disputation; that is, logic was to be devised to assist in disputes, on the assumption that such disputation is a better means of discovering the truth than anything else. Second, logic was to be instrumental in a theory of communication. "The logic of the scholastics and the Ramists had been formulated as an instrument for the transfer of knowledge from expert to expert."[6] But in communication, in transferring the old wisdom to the next generation, order and systematization are of great importance; and so the Ramists proposed, in proper scholastic fashion, the order to be followed: the most general statement should come first, the next-most-general statement second, and so on. Third and finally, logic was for a theory of speculative sciences, and not for mere practical things.

Descartes was vehemently opposed to this. He thought that the old logic was perhaps a satisfactory tool to explain what was already known and established, but that it was useless for discovering new truths.[7]

---

[6] Wilbur Samuel Howell, *Logic and Rhetoric in England, 1500–1700*, 347.

[7] Thus: "I observed with regard to logic that syllogisms and most of its other techniques are of less use for learning things than for explaining to others the things one already knows or even, as in the art of Lully, for speaking without judgement about matters of which one is ignorant" (CSM I, 119; AT VII, 17). And: "I do not mean the logic of the Schools, for this is strictly speaking nothing but a dialectic which teaches ways of expounding to others what one already knows or even of holding forth without judgement about things one does not know. Such logic corrupts good sense rather than increasing it. I mean instead the kind of logic which teaches us to direct our reason with a view to discovering the truths of which we are ignorant." (CSM I, 186; AT IXB, 13–14)

Evidently, then, Descartes was explicitly opposed to the syllogism as a tool of discovery. Syllogisms may enable one, at best, to explain to others what one already knows, or, at worst, to hold forth on matters about which one is ignorant. Such a logic, and its techniques, corrupts the mind. It does not guide it in the direction of truth. Descartes subtitled his *Discourse on the Method* as follows: *of rightly conducting one's reason and seeking the truth in the sciences.* He would never have subtitled it, as did Ralph Lever his 1573 treatise on logic, *The Arte of Reason,* as: *rightly termed, Witcraft, teaching a perfect way to argue and dispute.* He was not interested in arguing or disputing, in communicating settled knowledge or explaining it; he was interested in discovering what had hitherto been unknown. *That* called for a fresh logic.[8]

Descartes' logic was a logic of discovery, and the logic of the scholastics was the logic of explanation. Descartes' logic was meant to be an aid in making inquiries into nature, to discovering in a systematic way the truth about things. The old logic was meant to explain what had already been discovered. Essentially, the distinction between the order of discovery and the order of explanation is the distinction between epistemology and ontology. The first is about what and how we can know and, in Descartes' case, what and how we can know with certainty; the second is about what is the case regardless of what and how we know. "[W]hen we consider things in the order that corresponds to our knowledge of them, our view of them must be different from what it would be if we were speaking of them in accordance with how they exist in reality" (CSM I, 44; AT X, 418).

If we had a complete system of knowledge that reflected the order in which we came to know the things in the universe – the order of discovery (*ordo cognoscendi*) – and we set it beside a complete system of knowledge that reflected the causal order of things in the universe – the order of explanation (*ordo ascendendi*) – then each complete system of knowledge would appear as a tree that is the inverse (loosely speaking) of the other.[9] (See Figure 8.1.)

---

[8] See Chapter 1, sections III and IV.

[9] To Morin on July 13, 1638, Descartes wrote: "You say also that there is a vicious circle in proving effects from a cause, and then proving the cause by the same effects. I agree: but I do not agree that it is circular to explain effects by a cause, and then prove the cause by the effects; because there is a big difference between *proving* and *explaining.*" (CSMK, 106; AT II, 197–198)

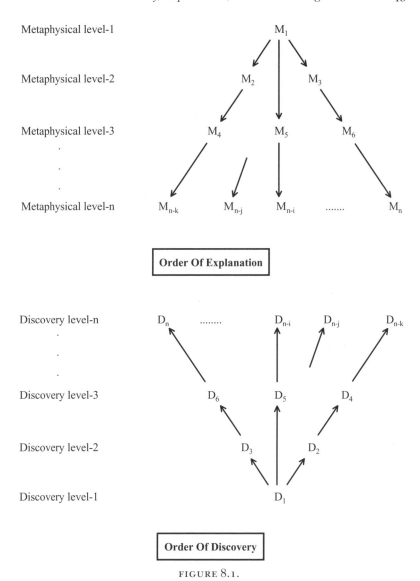

FIGURE 8.1.

To explain. If we had a complete system of knowledge that reflected the order in which we came to know the things in the universe (*ordo cognoscendi*), the cardinal proposition would be the *cogito*. (This would be D_1 in the order of discovery.) From this proposition, propositions about other things, such as God and the external world, would be known. (It would be very useful to compare the tree of the order of discovery to Descartes' Tree of Philosophy.)[10] If we had a complete system of knowledge that reflected the causal order of things in the universe (*ordo ascendendi*), the cardinal proposition would be that God exists (M_1 in the order of explanation), from which the truth about other things in the universe would follow. It does not follow, of course, that what comes first in one system comes last in the other, and so on. For example, the proposition that God exists does not come first in the order of knowledge; it comes second. However, in the causal order that proposition comes first, not next-to-last.

Eudoxus, playing Descartes in *The Search for Truth*, has just succeeded in demonstrating to Polyander the truth of the *cogito*. He wants to move to the next step, and he says to Polyander, "But what are you – you who have doubts about everything but cannot doubt that you yourself exist?" Polyander replies, "The answer to that is not at all difficult, . . . I shall say I am a *man*" (CSM II, 410; AT X, 515). I quote at length Eudoxus chiding Polyander:

> You are not paying attention to my question, and the reply you give me, however simple it may seem to you, would plunge you into very difficult and complicated problems, were I to press you even a little. If, for example, I were to ask even Epistemon himself what a man is, and he gave the stock reply of the scholastics, that a man is a "rational animal," and if, in order to explain these two terms (which are just as obscure as the former), he were to take us further, through all the levels which are called "metaphysical," we should be dragged into a maze from which it would be impossible to escape. For two other questions arise from this one. First, what is an *animal*? Second, what is *rational*? If, in order to explain what an animal is, he were to reply that it is a "living and sentient being," that a living being is an "animate body," and that a body is a "corporeal substance," you see immediately that the questions, like the branches of a family tree, would rapidly increase and multiply. Quite clearly, the results of all these admirable questions would be pure verbiage, which would elucidate nothing and leave us in our original state of ignorance. (CSM II, 410; AT X, 515–516)

The scholastic approach is no good: It sprouts endless definitions. In defining one term, we use two others; in defining those two, we use four more; in defining those four, and so on, down to a plethora

---

[10] See Chapter 1, section III.

of definitions. Thus, Descartes gives by way of illustration what would happen if one attempted to define one of the terms, namely, *animal.* But the same problem would arise if we attempted to define the other term, namely, *rational.* Indeed, here we may well have a conflict of definitions. For example, when Ramus claimed that a person was rational, he meant that it was his innate capacity to reason syllogistically; Descartes thought otherwise; Aristotle might have had still a third view. Ramus' definition of *rational* would then lead us to define *syllogism,* among other things. The result of all this, says Descartes, "would be pure verbiage, which would elucidate nothing and leave us in our original state of ignorance."[11]

Epistemon, the scholastic, is quite offended:

> I am sorry you despise the tree of Porphyry . . . which has long been universally accepted in the Schools. To this day no better or more appropriate way has been found for explaining what we are than displaying all the levels which make up our whole nature, for in this way, by passing up and down through all these levels, we can learn what our nature has in common with the natures of all the other things, and in what respects it differs from them. And this is the highest point to which our knowledge can reach. (CSM II, 410–411; AT X, 516)

Porphyry of Tyre (third century A.D.), successor to Plotinus, had proposed a method of classification. Each object or thing was to be explained in terms of a genus and a species. When the whole tree, a system of knowledge, was complete, there would be the highest genus (*summum genus*) and the lowest species (*species infima*). Below the *species infima* would be individuals. To explain something is to appropriately place it on one of these metaphysical levels: In short, it is to define it. "[I]n order to know what these are, we have to rack our brains trying to find the 'proximate genus' and the 'essential differentia' which go to make up their true definition" (CSM II, 417; AT X, 523). And retracing those levels, we discover what we share in common with others and wherein they differ from us. Consider, for example, the question, what is a thinking substance? Bourdin replies with a diagram (Figure 8.2) of a partial tree of Porphyry (CSM II, 344; AT VII, 506).

---

[11] Rudolph Agricola, writes Lisa Jardine, with his applied dialectic handbook, "exclusively concerned with practical argument strategies at the expense of the study of formal inference, . . . prepared the way for the most notorious of the advocates of 'loose' reasoning, Petrus Ramus." ("Humanistic Logic," 184)

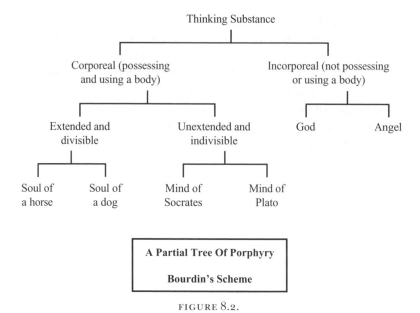

FIGURE 8.2.

What Epistemon was recommending – and what Descartes, in the person of Eudoxus, was vigorously opposing – was that Polyander should reply in the manner of the scholastics to Descartes' question, "But what are you – you who have doubts about everything but cannot doubt that you yourself exist?" Part of Eudoxus' objection is to the metaphysical levels.

> Indeed, whatever Epistemon may say, it strikes me that there is a great deal of obscurity in these metaphysical levels. If, for example, we say that a body is a "corporeal substance," without making clear what a corporeal substance is, these two words do not tell us any more than does the word "body." In the same way, if we assert that to be living is to be an "animate body," without first explaining what a body is and what it is to be animate – and likewise with all the other metaphysical levels – we are uttering words and putting them as it were in a certain order, but we are not really saying anything. (CSM II, 411; AT X, 517)

But I do not see the scholastic logic and Descartes' new logic as being incompatible. The new logic takes the investigator from one discovery level to the next in a way in which the old logic could not. But once a truth has been discovered, one has to explain that truth.

The explanation of a truth has to follow a certain pattern: the most general statement coming first, the next-most-general statement coming second, and so on. It is here that the old logic is used. Such a logic would presumably take us from one metaphysical level to the next. This is precisely what Descartes must have meant, since he has Eudoxus say: "I have never had any intention of condemning *the method of explanation* ordinarily employed in the Schools" (CSM II, 411; AT X, 516; my emphasis).

Now reconsider the following *cogito*-argument:[12]

Metaphysical level-4	[1]	Whatever object has a property, then that object exists.
Metaphysical level-3	[2]	Whatever substance in which the attribute of thought inheres, that substance exists.
Metaphysical level-2	[3]	I am a substance in which the attribute of thought inheres.
Metaphysical level-1	[4]	∴ I, a substance, exist.

This is an argument following the order of explanation. It is clearly scholastic, in the sense that as a purported explanation it begins with the most general claim and then descends to less and less general claims. Metaphysical level-4 is of the highest generality: It uses terms like 'object' and 'property', which can take under their umbrella, or subsume, a host of distinct metaphysical categories. For example, in metaphysical level-3, 'object' and 'property' are replaced by the more specific metaphysical categories 'substance' and 'attribute', respectively; and, the general relation 'has' has been replaced by the more specific metaphysical relation 'inherence'. In metaphysical level-2, 'I' is substituted for 'substance', and 'attribute of thought' for 'attribute'. 'Exists' remains univocal throughout.

The foregoing can also be cast in terms of 'proximate genus' and 'essential differentia'. A partial tree of Porphyry might look like Figure 8.3.

How would Descartes have responded? No differently, I suspect, from the way he responded earlier, and it might have gone

---

[12] It was outlined in Chapter 5, p. 150. One step is omitted here.

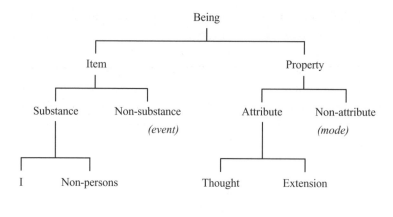

A Partial Tree Of Porphyry

FIGURE 8.3.

thus: "Whatever these modern philosophers may say, it strikes me that there is a great deal of obscurity in the metaphysical levels in this partial tree of Porphyry. If, for example, we say that whatever has an attribute of thought, the subject of thought exists, without making clear what, for example, 'substance', 'attribute', and 'inherence' are, the proposition does not tell us much – and likewise with all the other metaphysical levels. Thus we are uttering words and putting them, as it were, in a certain order, but we are not really saying anything."

If Descartes were pursuing the old scholastic logic, his approach in the *Meditations on First Philosophy* and the *Discourse on the Method* could scarcely be more unsatisfactory. Descartes should have begun with the highest truth, the widest generality. He should have begun with God rather than himself, since God is the cause of everything, including Descartes' existence. The old logic, following Aristotle, traced out the causal lineage. But in fact, Descartes begins with a particular, namely, I (Descartes) exist. He does not begin with the general statement, "Whatever thinks, exists," let alone with the existence of God.[13]

---

[13] See Appendix C, which deals with Francis Bacon's relationship to Descartes on some of the issues treated in this section.

III. Will, *Cogito*, and the Purposes of God

The will plays an important role in Descartes' epistemology, notwithstanding the fact that what he said on the nature and function of the will is disproportionately little.[14] It is fundamental to his theory of error. I shall argue that it is also fundamental to the *cogito.* What needs to be argued is how Descartes can be certain that, in the light of his theory of error, he cannot in the *cogito*-state err. I shall eventually argue that his theory of error is mistaken, or at best insufficient; but even if his theory of error is inadequate, the *cogito* is consistent with Descartes' larger aims, and the latter would be frustrated if the *cogito* were an argument.

[W]hen I look more closely at myself and inquire into the nature of my errors (for these are the only evidence of some imperfection in me), I notice that they depend on two concurrent causes, namely on the faculty of knowledge which is in me, and on the faculty of choice or freedom of the will; that is, they depend on both the intellect and the will simultaneously.[15] (CSM II, 39; AT VII, 56)

Now, both the faculty of knowledge or intellect (*facultas cognoscendi*) and the faculty of will (*facultas eligendi*) are endowed by God. Indeed, so much so that Descartes claims that he knows by experience that his will is "not restricted in any way,"[16] that his will is so ample that "the possibility of a further increase" is beyond his understanding, and finally, that it is in virtue of his will that he understands himself "to bear in some way the image and likeness of God" (CSM II, 39–40; AT VII, 56–57). But clearly this raises a problem. Since the existence of God has been proved, and God is all-good and all-perfect, God, the supreme Craftsman, cannot make anything defective. Whatever He creates is perfect. But if Descartes is perfect, that is, endowed with a faultless intellect and will, whence his error? This is the problem that Descartes sets himself to solve in the Fourth Meditation.

[14] "Our volitions," said Descartes in *The Passions of the Soul,* "are of two sorts. One consists of the actions of the soul which terminate in the soul itself, as when we will to love God or, generally speaking, to apply our mind to some object which is not material. The other consists of actions which terminate in our body, as when our merely willing to walk has the consequence that our legs move and we walk." (CSM I, 335; AT XI, 343) In what follows, I am primarily concerned with the first sort of will.

[15] See Appendix E, section I.

[16] See especially Descartes' reply to Gassendi concerning both his (Descartes') experience of freedom as well what anyone else can experience (CSM II, 259–260; AT VII, 377–378).

The source of error is not to be found in the intellect, even though Descartes' intellect is finite rather than infinite. Finite does not automatically mean defective; it only means that it is not as comprehensive as God's intellect. Imagine a student who is very astute in plane geometry. Set him any solvable problem in the plane geometry of Euclid, and he can solve that problem. Then we would say, and correctly, that in the domain of plane geometry his knowledge is as perfect as it is possible for a human mind's to be.[17] This student is unable, however, to solve problems in spherical or hyperbolic geometry. These domains lie outside his sphere of competence. By contrast, of course, God can solve any genuine problem, in any domain of mathematics, discovered, discoverable, or otherwise – and then some. Analogously, God has given a person a finite intellect that is fashioned to be adequate for whatever knowledge of the universe a person can in principle acquire. These domains lie within his sphere of competence. But his intellect is neither appropriate nor equal to the task of discovering any knowledge of the final causes or the purposes of God about any aspect of the universe.[18] That is God's preserve. These domains of the universe are to him what spherical and hyperbolic geometry are to the student. In short, man's intellect is perfect, but limited to appropriate domains or spheres; God's intellect is perfect, infinite, and not limited to this sphere or that.

But if my mind is limited to knowing only about n domains or aspects of the universe, could not God have created my mind so that I could know about $(n + 1)$ domains? And if He could have created such a mind, then why could He not have created one that could have

[17] On October 8, 1628, Isaac Beeckman made the following entry in his journal on the occasion of Descartes' visit: "He told me that insofar as arithmetic and geometry were concerned, he had nothing more to discover, for in these branches during the past nine years he had made as much progress as was possible for the human mind. He gave me decisive proofs of this affirmation and promised to send me shortly his *Algebra*, which he said was finished and by which not only had he arrived at a perfect knowledge of geometry but also he claimed to embrace the whole of human knowledge." (V, 78)

[18] "...all the purposes of God are hidden from us.... We think of God as a sort of superman, who thinks up such-and-such a scheme, and tries to realize it by such-and-such a means. This is clearly quite unworthy of God...." (CSMK, 341; AT V, 158) Just what is unworthy of God? Is it unworthy of Him to have any schemes at all? Or is it unworthy of Him to try to realize the scheme by particular means? Clearly, the first alternative will not do: It would preempt God from having any purposes at all. But what is intended by the second alternative? That God can accomplish His purposes without employing *any* means? This, surely, needs some defense.

understood $(n+2)$ domains, or $(n+3)$ domains, and so on?[19] The objection is not that He should have created my mind to be as good as His, that He should have made my mind "immense, incomprehensible and infinite" (CSM II, 39; AT VII, 55). But it is rather, why did He make my mind so that I could comprehend only thus and so domains, and no more?

To this, Descartes would have replied, "I cannot produce any reason to prove that God ought to have given me a greater faculty of knowledge than he did" (CSM II, 39; AT VII, 56). To produce such a reason, one would have to look at the whole universe from a God's-eye view. One would have to do this because "what would perhaps rightly appear very imperfect if it existed on its own is quite perfect when its function as a part of the universe is considered" (CSM II, 39; AT VII, 55–56). This surely is not unreasonable. For a long time, for instance, the valves of the heart (the tricuspid and bicuspid valves, respectively) appeared to be insignificant and without function, until William Harvey discovered the circulation of the blood; then all of a sudden the significance and function of the valves became abundantly clear. The valves were there to ensure that the blood flowed only in one direction, from the auricles to the ventricles. To understand the function of the cog, one has to understand the function of the wheel.

Similarly, Descartes might have argued, the human mind considered in itself may appear to be a pretty insignificant piece of – and to have no deeper function in – the universe. If one wanted to know why it has limited powers, having access only to finite domains, one would have to have a larger picture of the universe. *Then* the reason for its limited nature would become abundantly clear. But, alas, in the case of the mind, discovering a larger picture is not like discovering the circulation of the blood. Descartes argued, specifically against the Aristoteleans, that even if we could know all the basic physical principles of the entire universe, we still would not know the final causes. Only the final causes – the purposes of God – would explain what the mind is *for* and *why* the mind is limited. But the purposes of God are

[19] George Schlesinger raises a parallel objection in the context of answering the question, Why did God create a world, including the evil in it? (and infers that there is no such thing as the best of all possible worlds): see his 'The Problem of Evil and the Problem of Suffering' and *Religion and Scientific Method*; see also Robert Nozick's discussion of Schlesinger in *An Examined Life*, 224–226.

inscrutable; hence, the larger picture will forever escape us, and we shall not be able to understand why the nature of the human mind is limited.[20]

Now, if his intellect is not the culprit in what causes Descartes to err, then it can only be his will. The will, strictly considered in itself and as endowed by God, "is both extremely ample and also perfect of its kind" (CSM II, 40; AT VII, 58). Indeed, it is so much so that it is in his will that a person is most Godlike. The function of the will is to affirm or deny, to pursue or avoid. Judgment, which is what can go wrong – and Descartes is providing a theory of why this happens – is dependent on both the intellect and the will in the following way. The intellect proposes a proposition, and the will accepts or denies it.[21]

---

[20] Gassendi had argued that Descartes had failed to notice the difference between the private and public purposes of God, and that knowing the purposes of God that are on "public display" would lead us to bestow great praises on God (CSM II, 215–216; AT VII, 310). Descartes responded that Gassendi's arguments are best construed not as a defense of purposes – for all of God's purposes "are equally hidden in the inscrutable abyss of his wisdom" – but rather as a defense of efficient causes, for example, those pertaining to the functioning of the various parts of plants and animals. These efficient causes mortals *can* know. Then, Descartes goes on to say something interesting: "In ethics, then, where we may often legitimately employ conjectures, it may admittedly be pious on occasion to try to guess what purpose God may have had in mind in his direction of the universe" (CSM II, 258; AT VII 374–375). In August 1641, the same year in which the *Meditations* were published, Descartes wrote to Hyperaspistes, "It is self-evident that we cannot know God's purposes unless God reveals them. From the human point of view adopted in ethics, it is true that everything was made for the glory of God, in the sense that we must praise God for all his works." (CSMK, 195; AT III, 431)

This is a bit puzzling. If we can adopt a conjecture about God's purpose – strictly as a heuristic device – as we go about solving our ethical problem, might we not adopt a similar conjecture (again, strictly as a heuristic device) as we go about solving our scientific problem? In conversation with Burman, in April 1648, Descartes had said that "the knowledge of a thing's purpose never leads us to knowledge of the thing itself" (CSMK, 341; AT V 158). If conjecturing a thing's purpose – "Aristotle's greatest fault" – is inefficacious, misleading, or "futile," what makes the adoption of a similar conjecture in ethics less so? Would knowledge of a thing's purpose lead us to the knowledge about how we should morally deal with that thing? Indeed, would it not be more dangerous to adopt such conjectures in ethics than in science? It is clearly insufficient to say, as Descartes did to Burman, that ethical purposes are ones that are "known through revelation" (CSMK, 341; AT V 158). If the only purposes of God postulated in ethics were those revealed by Him, they would not be *conjectures* any more. They would be God's decrees. Therefore, if conjectures ought not to be allowed in science, they should be made impermissible in ethics as well.

[21] Some recent commentators have claimed that for Descartes, propositions in themselves are neither true nor false, and that therefore error cannot be attributed to

Until the will affirms or denies a proposition, there is no judgment. And it is a judgment – in contrast, say, to desire – which can be true or false.[22]

"So what then is the source of my mistakes?" asks Descartes. He answers, "[T]he scope of the will is wider than that of the intellect; but instead of restricting it to the same limits, I extend its use to matters which

them; error is possible only when propositions are judged – affirmed, denied, and so on (Losonsky, *Enlightenment and Action From Descartes to Kant: Passionate Thought,* 15–16). Presumably, the support for this view comes from the two paragraphs out of the third meditation wherein Descartes says that he wants to classify his thoughts and "ask which of them can properly be said to be the bearers of truth value" (CSM II, 25; AT VII 36–37). They cannot be ideas in themselves; neither can they be will or emotions; and thus Descartes concludes, so goes the claim, that they can only be judgments.

My interpretation differs from this. Descartes would claim that the truth-value that a proposition possesses is an ontological matter – it possess a truth-value whether anyone judges it or not; it becomes an epistemic matter – error becomes possible – when and only when a proposition is judged. My reasons for suggesting this interpretation are three. First, consider "images of things," such as a goat or a chimera; it is only for these cases, says Descartes, that "the term 'idea' is strictly appropriate." And ideas, so long as one does not refer them to anything else, "cannot strictly speaking be false." Then Descartes goes on to say, "for whether it is a goat or a chimera that I am imagining, it is just as true that I imagine the former as the latter." This would be odd if propositions did not have truth-value in themselves: I imagine a goat, but do not refer it to anything else; it is just an image, an idea. Now, I have not entertained the proposition "I am imagining a goat," let alone affirmed it. Nevertheless, says Descartes, "I am imagining a goat" is true.

Second, Descartes is more concerned about how to avoid making a mistake in judgment, an epistemic matter, than he is about claiming that propositions in themselves are neither true nor false, an ontological matter. Descartes says, "Thus the only remaining thoughts where I must be on my guard against making a mistake are judgments. And the chief and most common mistake which is to be found here consists in my judging that the ideas which are in me resemble, or conform to, things located outside me." (CSM II, 26; AT VII 37) Consider the proposition, "The sun is several times larger than the earth." If I refrain from judging it, then I have not in principle run any risk of making a mistake; but surely the proposition has a truth-value nevertheless. Indeed, if I refrain from judging it, because I have not yet come up with any reason or evidence that tilts me one way or another, the proposition must have a truth-value – after all, I am trying to *discover* its truth-value. What Descartes wants to do in this part of the Third Meditation is to demonstrate what kind of mistakes I make when judging a proposition (I might hasten to judgment based on "natural impulse," "blind impulse" or "spontaneous impulse") and how I might avoid acting in a precipitous manner (by relying solely on "natural light").

Third and finally, God is the creator of eternal truths, such as $2 + 3 = 5$, and surely said proposition is true regardless of whether any seeker inquires after or judges its truth.

[22] See Appendix E, section II.

I do not understand" (CSM II, 40; AT VII, 58). To explain: Descartes' intellect offers for consideration by the will, say, the statement *S*, "The earth goes around the sun." Here, as anywhere else, "the intellect should always precede the determination of the will" (CSM II, 41; AT VII, 60; see also CSMK, 195; AT III, 432). If the will affirms that *S* is true, but does not know it to be so, it goes beyond the limit set by the intellect. That is, if *S* is true, Descartes knows it only accidentally. If *S* is false, then surely Descartes does not know *S*.

What is it, precisely, for the will to go beyond the limits or to restrict itself to these same limits? Descartes must mean something like this. The intellect in offering a proposition to the will also defines the limits of the proposition. These limits are set by all the other propositions linked to the one currently entertained by the will. Thus, *S*, "The earth goes around the sun," is limited by the propositions connected to it. To know *S* would be to know these other propositions (presumably, propositions of astronomy) and its links or connections with them. The will is precisely at that limit if it knows these other propositions and the various links. By contrast, it is not exactly at that limit (is within it) if the will affirms *S*, but in the absence of the knowledge of at least some of these other propositions, or if it mistakenly believes that the links are weaker than they in fact are. It is outside that limit if it mistakenly enlarges the set of propositions to which it is linked, or mistakenly strengthens the links, or if it affirms *S* when *S* is false.

If this analysis is correct, then ultimately there must be at least one proposition whose *limit is defined by itself.* Otherwise, there would be an infinite regress, and there would be no possibility of knowledge. Consider, then, the alleged argument of the *cogito*:

[1]	Whatever thinks, exists.	Premise
[2]	I think.	Premise
[3]	<u>If I think, I exist.</u>	1, Universal Instantiation
[4]	∴ I exist.	2,3, Modus Ponens

The first premise cannot be known to be true, for it is surely inductively dependent on the *cogito*. At this point, for Descartes to affirm the first premise is for him to extend the use of his will to matters that he does not yet understand. Once again, to know that the argument is valid, let alone that the argument is sound, the will has to affirm the rules of inference of universal instantiation and *modus ponens*. If the will were to acknowledge the argument to be valid in the absence of the knowledge of the rules of inference, then its acknowledgment would be correct, but only accidentally so. On the other hand, if it correctly acknowledges the argument to be valid by staying within proper limits, that is, if it knows the other propositions to be true, then the *cogito*-argument is hardly the centerpiece of his philosophy. For that, we would have to look elsewhere. By proper contrast, the *cogito* claim, "I am thinking, therefore I exist," sets its own limit. The will, to acknowledge it, does not have to look elsewhere. Indeed, this is precisely what Descartes affirms.

The will is freest when it is powerfully and ineluctably inclined "in one direction." "[T]he more I incline," he writes in the Fourth Meditation, "in one direction – either because I clearly understand that reasons of truth and goodness point that way, or because of a divinely produced disposition of my inmost thoughts – the freer is my choice. Neither divine grace nor natural knowledge ever diminishes freedom; on the contrary, they increase and strengthen it." (CSM II, 40; AT VII, 57–58) Indifference, far from being a sign of freedom, is an indication of bondage. In such cases, the will "turns aside from what is true and good, and this is the source of my error and sin" (CSM II, 41; AT VII, 58).

It is here that Descartes explicitly returns to the *cogito* by way of an illustration of the freedom of the will and its inclination to accept the *cogito*.

> I have been asking whether anything in the world exists, and I have realized that from the very fact of my raising this question it follows quite evidently that I exist. I could not but judge that something which I understood so clearly was true; but this was not because I was compelled so to judge by any external force, but because a great light in the intellect was followed by a great inclination in the will, and thus the spontaneity and freedom of my belief was all the greater in proportion to my lack of indifference. (CSM II, 41; AT VII, 58–59; see also CSMK, 233–234; AT IV, 115–116)

One might argue that for all that Descartes has said thus far, the *cogito* might just as well be an argument. The argument is so clear that Descartes' will is inclined in the direction of affirming it; he could not but judge it to be sound, and in so affirming, his will exhibits freedom. This, I think, would be hasty. Before he has proved the existence of God in the Third Meditation, Descartes says, "In this first item of knowledge [the *cogito*] there is simply a clear and distinct perception of what I am asserting; this would not be enough to make me certain of the truth of the matter if it could ever turn out that something which I perceived with such clarity and distinctness was false." He concludes, as we saw, with an extraordinarily important general rule: "So I now seem to be able to lay it down as a general rule that whatever I perceive very clearly and distinctly is true" (CSM II, 24; AT VII, 35).

Descartes' ideal seeker ought to be armed not only by a perfect, if finite, intellect, but also by a proper will – a will that will not exceed its limits. But the will initially learns the limits that it must recognize only at the foot of the *cogito*; it is there that it learns the insignia of truth. It is in the state of the *cogito* that the will learns what it means to be ineluctably inclined toward affirming a proposition, and what it is to be free.[23] That is the first instance. Only *then* does it provide itself with a general rule and decide henceforth to be guided by that rule. Take away the *cogito*, and the reason for accepting that rule disappears. Take away the rule, and the entire enterprise past the *cogito* collapses. For example, the proofs of the existence of God and material things centrally depend on the general rule. The rule determines whether or not any given proposition, or any idea, bears the appropriate insignia allowing it to be entered in the knowledge log.

Our task, then, is to determine if it could be the *cogito*, construed as an argument, that could serve as that first instance from which the general rule arose. One might claim that the *cogito* argument was so powerfully clear that the will could not help but assent to it. The argument ineluctably bent the will in that "one direction." From this experience, the ego first learned the veracity of the general rule, and the will accepted it. But such cannot be the case, because the argument already presupposes the correct application of the general rule at various places in the *cogito*-argument. The argument experience cannot be the first experience from which the general rule arose. In fact, we can generalize: *No* argument experience can be the first instance in which the veracity of the general rule is acknowledged.

---

[23] This is one of the key points of this section, and I greatly value Kenny's support of it; see also Kenny's "Descartes on the Will," especially 148–149.

On the other hand, the truth of any subsequent idea or proposition is in question if it fails to satisfy the general rule. Thus, to construe Descartes' *cogito* as an argument is to defeat Descartes' strategy and larger aims.

It is time to raise some questions about Descartes' view of the will; in particular, I shall raise three. My first objection will raise the issue of whether Descartes' solution of how and why humans err invokes God's inscrutable purposes, an invocation of the very purposes he had condemned in physics. "I consider the customary search for final causes to be totally useless in physics" (CSM II, 39; AT VII, 55). The second objection will raise the question of whether, in the ultimate analysis, Descartes has a solution at all. The third objection will raise concerns about the precise relation between the intellect and the will, and about which one has primacy over the other.

The first objection: Consider three clear cases. *Case 1*: God has an infinite intellect and an infinite, perfect will. His will is supremely benevolent. "God's will is incomparably greater than mine, both in virtue of the knowledge and power that accompany it and make it more firm and efficacious, and also in virtue of its object, in that it ranges over a greater number of items" (CSM II, 40; AT VII, 57). Thus, He knows everything, takes no incorrect actions, performs all good ones, and makes no mistakes of thought or deed. "In God willing and knowing are a single thing" (CSMK, 24; AT I, 149); "in God *seeing* and *willing* are one and the same thing" (CSMK, 235; AT IV, 119). This is the ideal that no one else can reach.

Case 2: A person has a finite, but perfect, intellect. His will is good and is such that it never transgresses the limits set by the intellect. Let us divide all propositions that the intellect offers the will into three categories. First is the proposition that is its own limit; when it is understood, the will is powerfully inclined to affirm it as being true. Second are the propositions of logic and mathematics; and third are empirical propositions that can be affirmed or denied only with a certain degree of probability. The ideal seeker never denies propositions in the first two categories, and affirms them whenever he encounters them.

Descartes maintains that the will may encounter a proposition – such as, "My essence is corporeal" – and neither affirm nor deny it because he does not as yet have sufficient reasons for doing so. Here he becomes indifferent. As he puts it,

> [M]y intellect has not yet come upon any persuasive reason in favour of one alternative rather than the other. This obviously implies that I am indifferent as to whether I should assert or deny either alternative, or indeed refrain from making any judgment on the matter. What is more, this indifference does not merely apply to cases where the intellect is wholly ignorant, but extends in general to every case where the intellect does not have sufficiently clear knowledge at the time when the will deliberates. For although probable conjectures may pull me in one direction, the mere knowledge that they are simply conjectures, and not certain and indubitable reasons, is itself quite enough to push my assent the other way. (CSM II, 41; AT VII, 59)

The point is well taken. Here I am imagining that the ideal seeker assigns precisely that probability to the propositions in the third category that should be assigned to them, neither more nor less. In short, the ideal seeker will be pulled in the direction of the probable conjecture exactly to the extent that he should be so pulled. This ideal seeker can in principle know the entire knowable universe. At no stage in his investigations will he ever affirm a proposition that transgresses the limits.

Descartes himself envisages two ways in which God could have created a person so that he did not err. "God could easily have brought it about that without losing my freedom, and despite the limitations in my knowledge, I should nonetheless never make a mistake." "The first way": "He could, for example, have endowed my intellect with a clear and distinct perception of everything about which I was ever likely to deliberate; or he could simply have impressed it unforgettably on my memory that I should never make a judgement about anything which I did not clearly and distinctly understand" (CSM II, 42; AT VII, 61). "The second way": "I can avoid error in the second way, which depends merely on my remembering to withhold judgement on any occasion when the truth of the matter is not clear"[24] (CSM II, 43; AT VII, 62).

Case 3: A person has a finite, but perfect, intellect, and a will. The will, however, because it is ample, often transgresses the limits and makes mistakes. These mistakes may reside in the will's affirming (or denying) a proposition when there is not sufficient warrant

---

[24] For lack of space, I am unable to analyze these two ways and to show how Descartes' ways presuppose God's inscrutable purposes.

for such an affirmation (or denial). Or it may reside in the will's affirming a proposition with a higher degree of probability, when only a smaller probability should be affirmed. The will may sometimes understate the probability with which a proposition can be affirmed. Perhaps in time it will correct its mistakes and move forward. But it does make mistakes. This is simply and correctly the view of a human.

The question that arises is this. Why did not God create a finite person on the model of Case 2 rather than on the model of Case 3? The model seems simple and consistent enough. What is more, the model is in harmony with the view of God as the supremely perfect Craftsman and of a person as finite. He is a perfect Craftsman, so His artifact cannot be defective; hence, His artifact, the ideal seeker, does not make mistakes. The artifact, being a mere artifact, need not be infinite – which, as a matter of fact, he is not. Notice that this does not question why God did not give a finite person more knowledge – say, of $(n + 1)$ domains – rather than what He in fact gave him (knowledge of n domains). Granted that we require God's purposes or the God's-eye view of final causes to answer that question, the issue raised here is a different one. Assuming we can know only n spheres – for reasons knowable only to God – why did God not make a person along the model of Case 2? Whatever the limits on his knowledge, a person could acquire it piecemeal, but without making any mistakes.

One might say: If we had the God's-eye view, then we would be able to see clearly why Case 3 is better than Case 2. Lacking such insight or knowledge, we have no grounds to complain. There is a difficulty in this reply. If the valves of the heart appeared insignificant and functionless *before* the discovery of the circulation of the blood, they do perspicuously appear significant and useful *after* the discovery. But we will hardly similarly conclude – for there is no analogy here – that *before* having the God's-eye view, we would see some of our epistemic states as being mistakes, but *after* acquiring the God's-eye view (hypothetically speaking), we would see those epistemic states as being only apparent, and not real, mistakes. Were we to so conclude, we would effectively be pronouncing the death of epistemology. Consequently, on Descartes' view, it must be intrinsically important – something we fail to see now – that we make mistakes, real and genuine mistakes, through the transgression of our will. And why making mistakes is important can be seen only from the God's-eye view.

> But I cannot therefore deny that there may in some way be more perfection in the universe as a whole because some of its parts are not immune from error, while others are immune, than there would be if all parts were exactly alike.[25] And I have no right to complain that the role God wished me to undertake in the world is not the principal one or the most perfect of all. (CSM II, 42–43; AT VII, 61)

    This is an unsatisfactory reply. The critic's complaint is not that in Descartes' solution to the problem of why humans err, God has not assigned Descartes a role that is the most perfect of all. His complaint rather is that Descartes' solution to the problem of why humans err vehemently assumes final causes or the inscrutable purposes of God – namely, that a universe in which humans make mistakes is more perfect than a universe in which they do not make mistakes, and that it is the purpose of God to make the most perfect universe. An Aristotelian might rebut Descartes by saying that if some explanations in metaphysics are incomplete without resorting to final causes, so also are some explanations in physics; on the other hand, if invoking final causes in physics is "totally useless" (CSM II, 39; AT VII, 55), what makes them any different in metaphysics? Indeed, it would still not follow that a universe in which a person makes mistakes is more perfect than one in which he does not – at least not without some pretty powerful arguments. But Descartes provides none. He blandly assumes that the present universe, mistakes and all, accomplishes God's purposes.[26]

    To turn to the second objection: In one sense, Descartes has no theory of error at all. A theory of error must, in part, explain why it is that the ego commits error. Well, it lets the will transgress the limits. But *why* does the will transgress the limits? There are several possible causes. The transgressions may be caused by the emotions – emotions

---

[25] This is a slip: Descartes intends something much stronger than merely "if all parts were exactly alike." After all, if each part were fallible, then all parts would be exactly alike; what Descartes intends, of course, is that each part is but alike in being immune from error.

[26] There is also this: If I am essentially prone to error, and not just accidentally so, it is difficult to see how I can know and correct my mistakes.

such as anxiety, jealousy, confidence, and despair. In *The Passions of the Soul,* Descartes says,

We are prompted to desire the acquisition of a good or the avoidance of an evil simply if we think it possible to acquire the good or avoid the evil. But when we go beyond this and consider whether there is much or little prospect of our getting what we desire, then whatever points to the former excites hope in us, and whatever points to the latter excites anxiety (of which jealousy is one variety). (CSM I, 350–351; AT XI, 375)

Consequently, one conjecture is that the will errs because the emotions, such as jealousy and anxiety, divert the will onto the wrong path. Or the will may transgress because it harbors false beliefs, such as, "The sun goes around the earth." Holding onto such beliefs causes the will to err.

Some such reply would restore Descartes' view against the objection that asks why God did not model a person along the lines of Case 2. Descartes could argue that both the intellect and the will, when unhampered, function faultlessly in the limited domains. What causes the will to make the mistakes is extraneous causes, such as bad emotions and false beliefs. Understandably, Descartes did not take this option, since it only shifts the problem to accounting for the source of the false beliefs and the assenting to propositions under the influence of bad emotions. Hence the purging of all prior beliefs.

The ideal seeker engages in methodical doubt; he doubts everything under the sun. He doubts all of his beliefs, no matter how well settled and deeply entrenched. He rejects as false his cosmology and geography, his history and language, his morals and theology, his fables and mathematics, his medicine and jurisprudence – or so he is made to do in *Discourse on the Method.* "[I]t is good," says Descartes, "to have examined all these subjects, even those full of superstition and falsehood, in order to know their true value and guard against being deceived by them" (CSM I, 113; AT VI, 6). What surprises me is that he does not take the same stand against his emotions when engaging in his methodical doubt. If the beliefs can deceive, the passions or the emotions can deceive no less. No one was more aware of that than Descartes. These passions or emotions may incline us toward affirming (or denying) a proposition that we should deny (affirm), or at least toward abstaining from affirming (denying) it. Thus, an ideal seeker should be purged not only of all false beliefs, but also of all bad emotions that would turn the will "aside from what is true and good." The ideal seeker,before he starts his inquiry, now has an intellect purged of all false beliefs and a will free from the influence of all bad emotions. Let us call this *the pristine state* of the ideal seeker. And in this pristine state he collects and stores true propositions, as and when they are recognized. The first to be recognized is the *cogito*, then the general rule, then the proof of the existence of God, and so on.

Now, in such a pristine state how can the will make mistakes? It seems to me that it cannot. Yet Descartes maintains that the will can make mistakes even in this state, since it is ample and perfect and so may well transgress the limits. But what is the cause of such transgressions? There is no answer; the will just simply plumps itself beyond the limit. It just simply does so, and there is nothing else that can be said.[27] What Descartes does say is puzzling: "In this incorrect use of free will may be found the privation which constitutes the essence of error. The privation, I say, lies in the operation of the will in so far as it proceeds from me, but not in the faculty of will which I received from God, nor even in its operation, in so far as it depends on him." (CSM II, 41; AT VII, 60)

Descartes seems to come very close to maintaining with respect to the will what he has said about the intellect. The finite intellect is a God-given instrument and cannot be defective in the domain of inquiry for which it was intended. The will is a God-given instrument, too, and cannot be erroneous in any way, either. The defect lies in the *operator* of the will, not in the will itself. So, presumably, there is a will* that operates the will. (If you find this paradoxical, replace will* by 'operator.') When the first automobiles had to be started, one had to crank them with a handle. Nothing need be wrong with the car, but the handle or the cranking could be wrong. If this reading is correct, it simply shifts the problem one step backward. What is the reason for the will* operating sometimes without mistakes, and sometimes mistakenly? There seems to be no apparent reason for any of its actions. Thus, I maintain that when we properly understand the ideal seeker, Descartes' theory of error does not seem to amount to

---

[27] There is clearly a tension in Descartes' theory. As will be noted, Descartes also wants to vehemently deny that the will can transgress when in the pristine state.

much. For he really offers no explanation of the causes that incline the will away from the true and straight path.

The will of a person endowed by God must be essentially good. Otherwise, even in this pure case, there is no guarantee that the will will not make mistakes. Indeed, if it is evil it will not be able to help making mistakes,

The third and final objection pertains to the relation between the intellect and the will. Which one has supremacy? The precise relation between the intellect and the will is unclear. On the one hand, it seems that both are autonomous; on the other hand, only the intellect is autonomous. Thus the primacy goes to the intellect – morally speaking, as Descartes would say. The intellect offers the will propositions for the will to affirm or deny. The will seems to be autonomous in the sense that it is free to affirm or deny and is not constrained by the intellect. But the issue is not that simple. For instance, Descartes says that when in the state of the *cogito,* he affirmed its truth, he was not "compelled so to judge by any external force, but because a great light in the intellect was followed by a great inclination in the will" (CSM II, 41; AT VII, 59).

Thomas Hobbes complained that the

phrase "a great light in the intellect" is metaphorical, and so has no force in the argument. Moreover, anyone who is free from doubt claims he has such "great light" and has no less strong a propensity of the will to affirm what he has no doubt about than someone who possesses real knowledge. Hence this "light" can explain why someone obstinately defends or holds on to a given opinion, but it cannot explain his knowledge of its truth. (CSM II, 134; AT VII, 191–192)

For Hobbes, knowing, believing, and giving assent are independent of the will. When a valid argument is presented, or something credible is reported, we often believe against our will. Affirmation and denial, says Hobbes, are acts of will. He then continues, "but it does not follow that our inner assent depends on the will" (CSM II, 134; AT VII, 192). What is puzzling in Hobbes is how affirmation is dependent on the will, and yet our so-called inner assent is not dependent on it. What is it dependent on? It cannot be the intellect, since Hobbes seems to agree with Descartes that the role of the intellect does not extend to affirming or denying propositions.

The great light in the intellect forces the will to follow ineluctably. What is this great light? Is it that the proposition is true? No, because a proposition is true if it corresponds with the state of affairs, and that says nothing about a natural light. Furthermore, the function of the intellect is not to judge propositions to be true or false, it is simply to offer propositions to the will to affirm or deny. When "a great light in the intellect [is] followed by a great inclination in the will," what connects the intellect and the will? Is it a causal connection, such that when the intellect exhibits a great light it necessarily causes the will to affirm the proposition in question? But then the will can scarcely be called free. If it is not a causal connection, then what connection is it, such that the will cannot help assenting to the proposition in that state? Perhaps the will is taught by nature, in the language of the Third and Sixth Meditations, to assent; yet nature has not designed a causal nexus – it has designed something else – between the intellect and the will. However, is this something else any less determinative?[28]

Is it possible – just possible – for the will to deny the *cogito* while in the *cogito*-state? If it is possible, then someone can consistently deny that the *cogito* is certain. Not to deny its certainty would be for him to transgress the limits. But here is what Descartes says in a letter, probably to Mesland, written on February 9, 1645:

[W]hen a very evident reason moves us in one direction, although morally speaking we can hardly move in a contrary direction, absolutely we can. For it is always open to us to hold back from pursuing a clearly known good, or from admitting a clearly perceived truth, provided we consider it a good thing to demonstrate the freedom of our will by so doing.[29] (CSMK, 245; AT IV, 173)

Judged by this passage, it is difficult to tell whether we can move in a contrary direction. In one sense we can, provided we wish to demonstrate the freedom of the will. But the purpose is not to deny a truth we clearly perceive; it is something else, namely, to express and exalt the freedom of the will. In other words, we can vigorously shake our heads and loudly mouth sentences to the contrary – in order to exhibit

---

[28] See Appendix E, section III.

[29] See Kenny, "Descartes on the Will," especially 151–159, for a brilliant analysis of this letter and a refutation of M. Alquié's thesis that the letter demonstrates that Descartes "allows the possibility of rejecting the evident and the good in full knowledge of the cause."

our freedom – but we would be utterly incapable of a genuine dissent within ourselves to a truth we clearly perceive.

Finally, there is an interesting way to show the primacy of the intellect over the will *and* the sheer beauty of the *cogito*. In the *cogito*-state, the intellect – provider of "a great light" – elicits a response from the will. In that state, the will *must* assent; not to do so would be a mark of its bondage or unfreedom – "the more I incline in one direction . . . because I clearly understand the reasons of truth . . . the freer is my choice" (CSM II, 40; AT VII, 57–58). Generally speaking, the will can err by overreaching or by understating. In the case at hand, the will can err if it claims more or less than what is warranted by the *cogito*-statement. It understates it if it claims less than what is warranted by the *cogito*-statement. But what is it for the will to understate in this case? Perhaps one has such a timid will, a will so lacking in trust and confidence in itself, that it always hedges: It gives assent to watered-down claims such as, "Probably, I exist." On the other hand, what is it for the will to overreach in the *cogito* state? It is very hard to imagine. Perhaps something like, "I always existed."[30]

These cases of understating and overstating while in the *cogito*-state are not sustainable alternatives. As argued earlier, the will is not absolutely and unconditionally free; the alleged freedom to deny anything under any circumstances is not freedom but bondage. For example, it cannot deny what it perceives clearly and distinctly; it can only pretend to deny it in order to exhibit its freedom. Let us look more closely at the case of the timid will. Suppose that while in the *cogito*-state, that will affirms only the proposition, "Probably, I exist." But it must have *some* countervailing evidence in order to rationally make only a watered-down claim; if there is no such evidence, – "where the intellect does not have sufficiently clear knowledge at the time when the will deliberates"(CSM II, 41; AT VII, 59) – the assertion "Probably, I exist" is irrational. One cannot argue that it is

---

[30] Replying to Pierre Gassendi's "Fifth Set of Objections," Descartes wrote: "You here ask me to say briefly whether the will can extend to anything that escapes the intellect. The answer is that this occurs whenever we happen to go wrong. . . . Again, we never understand anything in a bad fashion; when we are said to 'understand in a bad fashion,' all that happens is that we judge that our understanding is more extensive than it in fact is." (CSM II, 259; AT VII, 376–377)

the *nature* of a timid will only to assent diffidently to a circumspect proposition.

Let us recall at the end what we said in the beginning about Descartes on the ideal seeker. Among other things, such a seeker must have a quick wit, ample and prompt memory, and the strongest ability to reason; he must be skilled at ordering his thoughts, troubled by no cares or passions, and capable of seeing clearly into his own actions; he must not be precipitate in his judgments. But the timid will is prey to the very cares and passions that Descartes had warned against. In short, the timid will is not "of a fairly robust intellect" (CSM II, 320; AT VII, 475). It follows, therefore, that in the very act of either understating or overreaching, the will will inevitably be compelled to acknowledge the truth of the *cogito*.[31] Why? "Because," as Descartes says, "a great light in the intellect [is] followed by a great inclination in the will" (CSM II, 41; AT VII, 59). This is just as well, because otherwise I do not see how the *cogito* could serve as the foundation. Descartes' entire structure would collapse.[32]

---

[31] Here is a firm denial: "Since I understand falsity to be merely a privation of the truth, I am convinced that there would be a total contradiction involved in the intellect's apprehending falsity under the guise of truth; but this would have to be the case if the intellect were ever to determine the will to embrace what is false" (CSM II, 260; AT VII, 378). One might argue that this passage prohibits the intellect only from determining as true what is in fact false, but that it does not prohibit the timid will from, say, determining a watered-down proposition to be true. Admittedly so, but an interesting defense of Descartes can be set up. If there were *no* countervailing evidence that would justify the assertion of a watered-down proposition, then a timid will no less than an ideal seeker would be in a bit of quandary: He would not know which proposition to assert, the proposition or the watered-down proposition! He would feel indifference as to which path he should take, and "the indifference [he] feels[s] when there is no reason pushing [him] in one direction rather than another is the lowest grade of freedom" (CSM II, 40; AT VII, 58). See also the following note.

[32] Nor would an objection based on the following do: "Unlike Descartes, [recent commentators] do not take seriously enough the cognitive lives of those who suffer from doubt and anxiety about their own capacity to fix their beliefs (even if it is to fix on withholding judgment on some topic). . . . Cases of cognitive irresolution that fit the dysfunctional pattern Descartes describes [in *The Passions of the Soul* under the heading "Irresolution"(CSM I, 390–391; AT XI, 459–460)] are ones in which noncognitive factors undermine cognitive processes. Excessive fear of making mistakes can keep one from settling on a belief in certain circumstances even when there are no competing hypotheses and all the evidence – which is good even if it is not clear and distinct – supports a proposition." (Losonsky, *Enlightenment and Action From Descartes to Kant: Passionate Thought*, 16, 18) Consequently, the objection would run, anyone

This has been a long book, not only in pages; allow me, then, to confine its conclusion to a couple of paragraphs. The heart of this book lies in the thesis that Descartes' *cogito* is not an argument, but an intuition. If it were an argument, it would have to be either an immediate inference or a mediate inference. If an immediate inference, it would have to begin with a proposition known to be certain, from which an inference is drawn to another proposition, the latter also known to be certain. But if the former proposition is already known to be certain before any inference is drawn, the ideal seeker has already arrived at the Archimedean point, and he need look no further. Clearly, then, the *cogito* cannot be an immediate inference. But the *cogito* cannot be a mediate inference (decidedly a dogma in Cartesian studies) either. If it is a mediate inference, then the inference would have to be governed by the rules of inference or the principles of logic. However, the principles of logic, no less than the statements of mathematics, are subject to doubt, courtesy of Descartes' demon. There is no historical evidence, and even less philosophical argument in Descartes, to suggest that the principles of logic are immune from doubt when the statements of mathematics are not so exempt. What is more, Descartes' view would have to face a new Cartesian Circle, more devastating than the old one: Prior to the proof of the existence of God, no principles of logic can be certified to be true or reliable. Without true or reliable

who is cognitively irresolute could deny the truth of the *cogito* because even in the *cogito*-state he suffers from doubt and anxiety about his own capacity to fix his beliefs. Lacking that capacity, he either understates his belief or anxiously overstates it.

First, to someone who is cognitively irresolute, Descartes' advice is to make a decision – rightly or wrongly – and to stick with it (CSM I, 390–391; AT XI, 460). Notice that Descartes is offering this advice as a remedy for someone who is constitutionally indecisive, hardly an epistemic criterion. Descartes urges this remedy in the hope of curing the individual of his indecisiveness, not to suggest that whatever decision such an individual made would be the right or rational decision. At best, it is advice as to what the individual should do if he desires to embark upon the journey of becoming an ideal knowledge seeker. Far from being an ideal seeker, such an individual cannot be in the pristine state (described earlier). As Descartes says, "an excess of irresolution results from too great a desire to do well and from a weakness of the intellect, which contains only a lot of confused notions, and none that are clear and distinct" (CSM I, 390–391; AT XI, 460). Not being in the pristine state – a state in which there are no confused notions, as what notions do inform the state are clear and distinct – he who is cognitively irresolute cannot be a counterexample to Descartes' claim that no one in the *cogito* state can deny the truth of the *cogito*.

principles of logic, Descartes could not execute the proof of the existence of God. There is also this: If the *cogito* were an argument, the ideal seeker would perforce have to rely on memory as he moved from the premises to the conclusion. Now, Descartes drew a distinction between two types of memory: physical memory and intellectual memory. There is no question about relying on physical memory, since at this stage in the *Meditations on First Philosophy* Descartes is unsure whether he even has a body. Nor will intellectual memory do: Memory is unreliable, says Descartes, immediately after the First Meditation. *Ergo*, the *cogito* cannot be an argument, since it rests on memory.

On the constructive side, the *cogito* is an intuition; in order to see *that*, one has to conduct a thought experiment. One has to engage in the process of doubt; and in that process, one must notice oneself. What one will notice when in the utmost state of doubt engineered by a most powerful, malicious demon is that one nevertheless exists. Whatever the breadth or depth of the doubt, at least one proposition escapes from it in virtue of the very process of engaging in doubt. This also enables us to understand the content of the *cogito* and why (*pace* Ryle) the 'I' is so elusive. Finally, Descartes' theory of the will makes it impossible for an ideal seeker to deny, while in the *cogito*-state, the truth of the proposition of the *cogito*, while allowing the ideal seeker to doubt even the validity, let alone the soundness, of the *cogito*-argument. Undoubtedly, then, Descartes' *cogito* cannot be other than an intuition.

Appendix A

Comments on Jeffrey Tlumak's "Certainty and Cartesian Method"

Jeffrey Tlumak, in "Certainty and Cartesian Method,"[1] argues that three important concepts, namely, *irrevisability*, *maximal warrant*, and *unmistakability*, which are often read as entailing one another, are nevertheless quite different and distinct concepts. I shall argue that, far from being independent, they are closely interlinked, and that if Tlumak were right these concepts could have a devastating effect on Descartes' *cogito*. These concepts, together with the claim about their independence, are also utilized by Tlumak to show how to escape from the Circle; but having supplied the groundwork, I shall leave that as an exercise for the reader.

Let us begin with Tlumak's definitions:

(I)   *h* is *irrevisable* for *S* at *t* if and only if *(i)* on the basis of some (possibly empty) set of evidential propositions, *e*, *S* is justified in believing *h* at *t*; and *(ii)* there is no *t'* and possible *e'* such that *t'* is later than *t*, *e* is a subset of *e'*, and *e'* fails to justify *S* in believing *h* at *t'*, where *not-h* is not a member of *e'* (T, 46).

(M) *h* is *maximally warranted* for *S* if and only if *S* is warranted in believing *h* at *t*, and it is inconceivable that there is an *h'*, a *t'* (where there are no restrictions on the choice of *t'*), an *S'* (which may or may not be restricted to *S*) and an *e'*, such that *e'* confers greater warrant on *h'* for *S'*, at *t'* than *h* has for *S* at *t* (T, 50).

(U) [C]ertainties are beliefs which cannot be mistaken (T, 45).

---

[1] Hereinafter T.

At the outset, Tlumak lists six conditions for adequacy of analysis of the concept of certainty. He is careful to say that these are not intended to be jointly exhaustive conditions; however, any analysis that does not square with them should not be regarded as adequate. It is not my purpose to offer, and analyze, that list here; it would take me far outside the scope of this book. I simply wish to grant these conditions to Tlumak and to raise an objection or two. Tlumak says: "(M) fulfills all adequacy criteria. So unless it turns out to be too strict, ruling out indubitable knowledge of the superstructure of Descartes' reconstructed science, (M) seems a worthy contender." (T, 50) He proclaims his real concern to be the following: "I want to show that when viewed abstractly, and not in the context of other Cartesian doctrines, irrevisability, maximal warrant, and unmistakability are logically distinct notions" (T, 51). I will argue that these are not logically distinct notions, and that if they were distinct and were imported into the Cartesian system, they would wreak havoc on it, especially on the *cogito.*

Tlumak claims that maximal warrant entails irrevisability, but the converse is not true. Let us grant the former. For the latter claim, he offer this argument:

> For suppose that no evidence over and above that which supports h for S at t could conceivably overturn h. Even if this required that h have maximally good evidence bearing on *it*... other propositions of other kinds, for which other kinds of evidence are relevant, could conceivably have still more impressive credentials. Constant rational acceptance of h is compatible with greener pastures in an entirely different ball park. (T, 52)

Let us suppose that there are two domains of inquiry, D_1, and D_2; h_1 is entertained in D_1, and h_2 in D_2. One way of understanding Tlumak is to suppose that the maximal warrant that any hypothesis in D_1 can have is .8, whereas the maximal warrant of a hypothesis in D_2 can rise as high as .9. Thus, constant rational acceptance of h_1 is compatible with h_2 having still more impressive credentials. But this will not do: Assigning .8 shows we are not confident that no new evidence will overturn h; we suppose that there is a .2 probability of new evidence surfacing that will overturn h_1. On the contrary, we are assured "that *no* evidence over and above that which supports h for S at t *could* conceivably overturn h" (my emphases). In that case, assigning any probability less than 1 is utterly inexplicable, inexplicably cautious.

On the other hand, if both hypotheses in their respective domains enjoy a probability of 1 (maximal warrant), it is difficult to tell which enjoys the greener pasture, or why.

The relationship between maximal warrant and irrevisability thus understood would have a devastating effect on the *cogito*. The doubter in the Second Meditation, having arrived at the *cogito*, would be left in a quandary: "Well," he might say, "I have produced maximal evidence for the *cogito* and it is irrevisable; but that is not enough. For all I know, there are other propositions in other domains with greater warrant than the *cogito*. Why, then, is it rational for me, in view of such a possibility, to stick with the *cogito* as my starting point – especially when I claim that there is no certainty with greater warrant than the *cogito*?"

Consider next Tlumak's argument in support of the claim that unmistakability does not entail irrevisability (T, 52). Here is what he says: "All necessary truths are unmistakable. Some necessary truths are revisable. One can readily imagine a persuasive argument coming along warranting suspension of judgment on a necessary truth. Therefore, some revisable truths are unmistakable, so that unmistakability does not entail irrevisability." (T, 52) The doubter in the Second Meditation, having arrived at the *cogito*, might think: "Well, I think the *cogito* is a necessary truth; but that is not enough. Some necessary truths are revisable because 'a persuasive argument [might come] along warranting suspension of judgment on a necessary truth'. Consequently, for all I know, the *cogito* may be just such a necessary, but revisable, truth." Is it not far more plausible to think that when Tlumak says, "Some necessary truths are revisable," he simply means, "What *appear* to be necessary truths (but are not) are revisable"?

Tlumak might respond thus:

The argument rests on the assumption that for any proposition whatsoever, it is possible warrantedly to withhold it if it is false, and possible warrantedly to believe it if it is true. But this assumption falsely rules out the possibility of unconfirmable truths [as well as the possibility of unfalsifiable falsehoods?]. Generalizing, since truth conditions, justification conditions, and belief conditions are not invariably correlated, one may say that irrevisability (a concept of privileged evidentiary status) does not entail unmistakability (a concept of privileged doxastic status). (T, 52–53)

The doubter in the Second Meditation, having arrived at the *cogito*, might think: "Well, I believe the *cogito* to be irrevisable; but that is not enough. I might well be guilty of falsely ruling out the possibility of it being an unfalsifiable falsehood. Consequently, for all I know, since truth conditions, justification conditions, and belief conditions are not invariably correlated, I may not have privileged evidentiary status for the *cogito*, merely privileged doxastic status. In short, I had better abandon claims to knowledge – even in the case of the *cogito*."

There is also this concern: *Irrevisability*, Tlumak claims, is an epistemic concept (a concept of privileged evidentiary status), in contrast to *mistakability*, which he says is a doxastic concept. If this were true, one could see how the former does not entail the latter. But it is difficult to see irrevisability, as defined, as an epistemic concept: It uses the notion of 'justified in believing h', not the notion of 'knows h'. The latter entails that h is true, the former does not. But *suppose* that irrevisability were an epistemic notion. Then Tlumak's argument in favor of the claim that irrevisability does not entail maximal warrant collapses. For if h is irrevisable, and hence true, there could *not* be any fresh evidence, e', to justify *not-h*, or to withhold assent from h; h would be maximally warranted.

"Of the three" notions, says Tlumak, "perhaps unmistakability fares least well, largely because it lacks an evidentiary component relativizing certainty to persons in epistemic situations" (T, 53). As it stands, this is true. However, there is an interesting exit: We can analyze the notion of certainty employed by [U] in terms of [M]. We have already seen that [M] entails [I]; consequently, [U] would entail [I] as well. [M] and [I], according to Tlumak, are epistemic concepts; the whole purpose of offering [M] and [I] is that any analysis of metaphysical certainty must satisfy them; perhaps other things might be required in the ultimate analysis. But this will at least insure that [U] has "evidentiary component relativizing certainty to persons in epistemic situations," and that it need not, therefore, fare least well.

Appendix B

Comments on Robert Nozick's "Fiction"

In "Fiction,"[1] Robert Nozick suggests the possibility that he, Nozick, is a fictional character and so is everyone else, except for the one who is the author of the piece. My aim here is not to argue with "Fiction" as a whole, but only with aspects of it that are central to Descartes. Nozick says:

"What!" you say, "we don't really undergo suffering? Why it's as real to us as Oedipus' is to him." Precisely as real. "But can't you *prove* that you really exist?" If Shakespeare had Hamlet say "I think therefore I am," would that prove to us that Hamlet exists? Should it prove that to Hamlet? And if so what is such a proof worth? Could not *any* proof be written into a work of fiction and be presented by one of the characters, perhaps one named "Descartes"? (Such a character should worry less that he's dreaming, more that he's dreamed.) (N, 462)

Nozick starts with the assumption that Hamlet is a fictional character. Then, of course, no matter what speech Shakespeare puts into Hamlet's mouth, including any proof of Hamlet's existence, it is not going to prove that Hamlet exists. *Ex hypothesi*, it could not prove to Hamlet that he exists. By analogy, then – so Nozick seems to suggest – if *we*, like Hamlet, are fictional, no proof of our existence that we can mouth will confirm us in our existence. Recall how in former years philosophers used to prove the existence of "other minds." When we are in a certain mental state (say, pain), these philosophers said, we

[1] Hereinafter N.

273

exhibit a typical physical reaction (say, wincing). Our mental state is unobservable to the rest of the world; not so our physical reaction, but the two are causally connected. One can thus infer the cause (mental state) from the effect (physical reaction). By analogy, then, we infer that someone is in pain (mental state) when we observe that person wincing (a typical physical reaction). Nozick presents the flip side of such an argument. Hamlet is fictional, and could "prove" his existence by any philosophical proof that could be put into his mouth; but such a proof is worthless. *Ergo*, our proof – the *cogito* – of *our* existence may be worth just as much.

Will this do against Descartes? Let us see. We do engage in thinking, and this does not require a formal proof so much as being engaged in thinking. If there is a "proof" of our existence, it comes later. We know that Hamlet cannot engage in thinking – that is what being fictional means. It is not enough that Nozick merely *stipulates* that Hamlet thinks or is engaged in thinking. Nozick might retort, "Aren't you just begging the question? You are assuming that you are real and Hamlet fictional." Descartes might rejoin that Nozick just assumes that Hamlet is fictional; Nozick must first distinguish between a fictional character and a real character. Descartes would distinguish them (so long as we were talking only about characters) as those that lack the capacity to think (fictional) and those that posses it (nonfictional). One might go a step further and say: If Nozick does not draw an initial distinction, his conclusion can actually go in the other direction. It is not that both Hamlet and I are fictional – we are *both* real; and that reality is proved by our both being engaged in the *cogito*.

Nozick's response might simply be that he need only demonstrate the possibility of the *cogito* failing to demonstrate the existence of the 'I' engaged in thinking, not deny the possibility that what we had hitherto thought to be fictional characters are not really fictional. Such a possibility injects doubt into the heart of the Cartesian enterprise. I construct the Cartesian response as follows: When Nozick says, "If Shakespeare had Hamlet say 'I think therefore I am,' would that prove to *us* that Hamlet exists?" (N, 462, my emphasis), Descartes would deny that it proves any such thing to *us*, any more than it would prove to us that the mechanical robot (lacking the property to think) exists if it says, "I am thinking, therefore I am." The *cogito* is not, nor is it intended to be, an abstract, detached, formal proof; it requires a thinking thing as a starting point – a thinking thing that could say to another (perhaps to its author), or even to itself: "Attempt to persuade me that I am fictional: if you fail, then of course I am not fictional; on the other hand, if you succeed in persuading me, it would be a pyrrhic victory: for you have convinced *me*. Therefore, I am not fictional."

Let us say, thinking$_F$ is the thinking of a fictional entity, and thinking$_R$ is the thinking of a real entity. The first step is to deny that the two types of thinking are the same. Thinking$_F$ cannot, from a Cartesian perspective, conduct the *cogito* thought experiment; only thinking$_R$ can do so. An author might create a fictional character and make that fictional character say that he (the fictional character) is undergoing the *cogito* thought experiment, but in reality he is doing no such thing; it is merely the author's projection. Thinking$_R$ is required for such a projection.[2]

Does anything that is a thinking$_R$ thing even understand what it is to be a thinking$_F$ thing? This is not analogous to the question, what is it like to be a bat? That bats have experiences is assumed; what is in question is the accessibility of such experiences. The question before us is a shade deeper. There is the question, what is it like for us to have experiences of fictional entities? But before that is the question, what is it like for fictional entities to have fictional experiences? And this question follows on the heels of the primary question, can fictional entities have experiences? If they do, are these experiences like those of humans, or not? Are we imprisoned in our own mode of thinking$_R$ in a way in which thinking$_F$ things are not imprisoned in their mode? How then do *they* distinguish between the two modes of thinking? Descartes would aver that anyone who can persuade himself that he is a thinking$_F$ thing has deluded himself; in the very act of persuading himself that he is a thinking$_F$ thing, he has demonstrated that he is a thinking$_R$ thing. What is quite lacking in Nozick's proposal is an account of the genuine difference – or an account of why we are mistaken in claiming that there is a difference – between thinking$_F$ and thinking$_R$, such that "I am thinking$_R$, therefore I exist" is acceptable, but "I am thinking$_F$, therefore I exist" is not. What is acceptable, at best, is only the innocuous "I am thinking$_F$, therefore I exist$_F$" (where *exist$_F$* stands for exists in a fictional world – a roundabout way of saying *nonexistent*).

---

[2] Or is it? See the arguments following the next paragraph.

Finally, let us suppose the author of the fictional world to which Hamlet belongs is S. Could S be fictional? Yes, he could be, says Nozick, provided that he had been created in turn by another author, S'; S' could be fictional, provided that he had been created in turn by author, S'', and so on. "*Must* there be a top-floor somewhere, a world that itself is not created in someone else's fiction. Or can the hierarchy go on infinitely?" (N, 463) Clearly, such a hierarchy of fictional worlds could not go on indefinitely. Why? To begin with, notice that this is not analogous to asking if there is a first cause when there is a series of causes, each cause in the series being real and producing the next cause. The issue is not about the reality of the first cause; the question is only if there is an ultimate, first, noncaused cause. Can there be a series of fictional causes, each cause in the series being *produced* by an earlier cause? Can there be an ultimate, first, fictional cause, one not produced by an existing, real entity? Or, at the other extreme, can a fictional cause produce a real (that is, nonfictional) effect? Why not, given that Nozick seems to place no plausible restriction on what is to serve as a cause?

Let us say that there are three types of worlds – the actual world, possible worlds, and fictional worlds;[3] and there is the possibility that there is nothing. Why is there something rather than nothing? If there were only fictional worlds, it would prompt a similar question: Why are there fictional worlds rather than nothing? An answer to the latter question would be even more puzzling than Nozick's own puzzling answer to the former question.[4] If there were at least one real world with a thinker in it, the existence of the fictional world could easily be accounted for in terms of the thoughts of that thinker. If not, how could a fictional world spring up from nothing?[5]

---

3 For my purposes, an intuitive distinction between possible worlds and fictional worlds, allowing for overlap, is more than enough.

4 Nozick attempts to answer this question in the intricate Chapter 2, "Why Is There Something rather than Nothing?" in his *Philosophical Explanations*. For my arguments against Nozick's theory, see "Something, Nothing, and Explanation."

5 This might raise some interesting questions about the type and nature of causation, because Nozick entertains not only the possibility that something could come from nothing, but also the possibility "that a character of one world creates another fictional world wherein a character creates the first world" (N, 463). In the latter case, which, if any, came first?

Descartes says, in the paragraph containing the *cogito* claim in *Meditations on First Philosophy*, "Is there not a God, or whatever I may call him, who puts into me ["puts into my mind" – French version] the thoughts I am now having? But why do I think this, since I myself may perhaps be the author of these thoughts?" (CSM II, 16; AT VII, 24) So, if I were the only existing being in the universe – if there were no one but me to author my thoughts – the very thought that I *might* be a fictional entity, let alone the thought that I *am* a fictional entity, would assure me of my reality. No matter how fictional, how varied the universe is, no matter what its genre – "tragedy, farce, or theater-of-the-absurd" (N, 463) – the evil genius, or Nozick, cannot persuade me, if indeed it is *I* who am persuaded, that I am fictional.[6] This is not something that Hamlet can do or claim, surely.

---

[6] "Our author, we know, is outside our realm, yet he may not be free of our problems. Does he wonder too whether *he* is a character in a work of fiction, whether his writing our universe is a play within a play? Does he have me write this work and especially this very paragraph in order to express his own concerns?" (N, 463) It is the burden of the present argument to demonstrate that the concerns of such an author are ill-founded.

Appendix C

Cogito and the *Port-Royal Logic*

The principal author of *Logic or The Art of Thinking*,[1] famously known as the *Port-Royal Logic*, was Antoine Arnauld, although there is some indication that parts of it may have been written by Pierre Nicole (1625–1695) as well as by the *Messieurs* of Port Royal. Arnauld got his hands on the original manuscript of Descartes, *Rules for the Direction of the Mind* (also found in the remnant possessions of Leibniz) – long before it was published – through the good graces of one of Descartes' ardent supporters, Claude Clerselier. Consequently, when he came to compose *Port-Royal Logic*, Arnauld was heavily influenced by Descartes' work, which Arnauld duly and explicitly acknowledged.[2] Incidentally, *Port-Royal Logic* was written for a young nobleman whose father, *Duc du Luynes*, had translated Descartes' *Meditationes de Prima Philosophiae* into French, a translation that Descartes had approved. It is surely, then, worth considering whether the authors of *Port-Royal Logic* would have construed the *cogito* as an argument or as an intuition. This will have to be a historical conjecture, since the *Port-Royal Logic* does not treat this issue explicitly.

---

[1] Hereinafter AN.
[2] Buroker, in her Introduction to *Logic or The Art of Thinking*, writes: "Rene Descartes was the true philosophical father of the *Port-Royal Logic*. . . . Arnauld and Nicole wholeheartedly embraced Descartes' rationalism. In fact, the Port-Royal theory of knowledge is taken almost verbatim from Descartes." (AN, xx) For Descartes' huge influence on *Port-Royal Logic*, see also AN, xx–xxiii. I am indebted as well to the Introduction in the *Port-Royal Logic* edited by James Dickoff, Patricia James, and Charles W. Hendel.

In "Fourth Part of the Logic" of *Port-Royal Logic*, Chapter 6 begins with a Rule, thus: "Rules concerning axioms, that is, propositions which are clear and evident in themselves..." (AN, 246). There are two cardinal rules. First is the rule that no axioms require demonstration, that is, proof, although some axioms may require explanation. The rule is stated thus:

In order to show clearly that an attribute applies to a subject – for example, to see that being larger than its part applies to the whole – whenever we need only to consider the two ideas of the subject and the attribute with moderate attention, so that we cannot do it without recognizing that the idea of the attribute is truly included in the idea of the subject, then we have the right to take this proposition for an axiom, not needing to be demonstrated. This is because it has in itself all the evidence that could be given in a demonstration, for a demonstration could do nothing more than show that this attribute applies to the subject by using a third idea to show this connection, which is already seen without the aid of a third idea. (AN, 248)

The second is the rule that what is not an axiom must be demonstrated. It is stated as follows:

When the mere consideration of the ideas of the subject and attribute is not enough to show clearly that the attribute applies to the subject, the proposition that affirms it should not be taken for an axiom. (AN, 249)

The text immediately goes on to say: "*But it must be demonstrated, by using some other ideas to show the connection...*" (AN, 249).

Prior to the statement of the two rules, *Port-Royal Logic* illustrates and comments on what is an axiom as follows:

We should not fear that there are people who seriously agree with the conclusion that we do not know what is true or false about anything in itself. For some things are so simple and evident – such as: "I think, therefore I am"; "the whole is greater than its part" – that it is impossible to doubt seriously whether they are in themselves the way we conceive them to be. The reason is that we could not doubt them without thinking of them, and we could not think of them without believing them to be true, and consequently we could not doubt them.[3] (AN, 248)

It concludes: "When we only need to consider the idea, the proposition can be taken for an axiom, especially if this consideration requires

---

[3] See also AN, 228–229, where *Port-Royal Logic* briefly refers to the *cogito* against the background of the skepticism of the New Academicians and the Pyrrhonists.

only the moderate attention of which all ordinary minds are capable" (AN, 248). *Port-Royal Logic* takes the *cogito* to be a crystal clear example of an axiom, not a demonstration. It is in no need of a proof, although it might be in need of an *explanation* (AN, 249). This is heavy testimony, in my view, that Arnauld – a preeminent metaphysician and theologian, writing a book on logic and epistemology, conversant with Descartes' views, in close contact with Descartes and the Cartesians – should have held the *cogito not* to be an argument.[4] Surely, this should take us a step toward settling the exegetical issue, even if it leaves open the philosophical question.

"If I want to know," says the *Port-Royal Logic*,

> whether the soul is spiritual, suppose that, not getting to the bottom of it right away, I choose the idea of thinking to clarify the matter. It is clear that it will be useless to compare the thinking with the soul if I do not conceive any connection between thinking and the attribute spiritual by which to judge whether it does or does not apply to the soul. I can easily say, for example, that the soul thinks, but I could not infer from this, therefore it is spiritual, unless I conceive some connection between the terms "to think" and "spiritual." (AN, 135–136)

Quite clearly, the last sentence is attempting to supply the missing premise without which the argument would be invalid. Confronted with the obviously parallel argument in which I wish to know whether "I exist," is true, *Port-Royal Logic* would not regard "I think" as a sufficient premise (as Kenny contends) from which to extract "I exist." It would enjoin supplying the missing premise (without which it would deem the argument invalid).

A careful, detailed study would have to address at least the following issues. First, according to the *Port-Royal Logic*, how is a judgment, especially a simple judgment – in particular, the *cogito* – to be formed?

Second, there is a rather serious objection against those who, like Kenny, maintain that the *cogito* is an immediate inference. Consequently, it will need to be asked, what immediate inferences did *Port-Royal Logic* recognize? It seems to have recognized only the standard Aristotelian ones. For example, in the "Second Part of the Logic,"

---

4 "The authors [Arnauld and Nicole] also cite Descartes' famous *cogito* argument [*sic*] ('I think, therefore I am') as the primary example of knowledge by intellectual intuition." Buroker, "Introduction," xxi.

Chapters 17–19 (AN, 129–134) deal with conversion; therein seven axioms and three rules are stated to justify the conversions from A (by limitation), E, and I, propositions, none being converted from O. Skipping the stock difficulty of how these axioms and rules are to be justified at the end of the First Meditation, let us ask which, if any, immediate inference in the guise of conversion would be relevant here. It turns out that none are relevant. E and I clearly will not do; A can be converted only by limitation, which means that A would have to be known to be true before I can be demonstrated to be true. At the very least, then, three things will need to be shown: (1) that the *cogito* is an immediate inference, (2) the type of immediate inference it is, and (3) how the axiom or rule justifying the *cogito* as an immediate inference is in turn justified from within the framework of *Port-Royal Logic* in such a way that it does not run afoul of the First Meditation.

Third, *Port-Royal Logic*'s account of conditional statements has troublesome implications for their use in the *cogito*-argument, either as a premise or as a rule of inference. Conditional statements in a deduction or demonstration, Descartes would have contended, have to be necessary truths. If so, these conditional statements in a deduction would themselves raise the question of how they are to be justified. *Port-Royal Logic*'s account of a conditional statement (AN, 99–101), reflecting the Cartesian account, is vastly different from ours. For one thing, in ours it is a material implication; in *Port-Royal Logic*'s account, it is an inference. *Port-Royal Logic* says,

Conditionals are propositions made up of two parts connected by the condition *if*. The first part, which contains the condition, is called the antecedent, and the other part is called the consequent: "if the soul is spiritual" – this is the antecedent – "it is immortal" – this is the consequent.

This inference is sometimes mediate and sometimes immediate. It is only mediate when there is nothing in the terms of either part that links them, as for instance:

> If the earth is immovable, the sun revolves.
> If God is just, the wicked will be punished.

These inferences are quite valid, but they are not immediate because the two parts, lacking a common term, are connected only by what one has in mind, which is not expressed. . . .

To determine the truth of [immediate inferences] we consider only the truth of the inference. For even if both parts are false, if the inference from one to the other is valid, the proposition insofar as it is conditional is true.

If a creature's will can obstruct the absolute will of God, God is not omnipotent. (AN, 99–100)

It is quite evident that it would not be enough to maintain that the *cogito* is an immediate inference. "I exist" is not logically linked to "I think," because there is nothing in the terms of either part that links them, and hence it is prima facie only a mediate inference. Construed as a conditional, it could still be true, while the antecedent is false; therefore, the truth of the antecedent would have to be justified independently. But if the truth of the antecedent is justified first and independently, Descartes need look no further for the first truth. If the *cogito* is justified on the basis of a conditional rule, we would run into the same problem.

Fourth, how precisely should the relationship between the *cogito* and the two rules governing axioms be explicated? Fifth, *Port-Royal Logic* recognizes principally two sorts of truths. The first sort of truth relates to the nature of things and their immutable essences. These statements are deemed necessary truths, if true. The second sort of truth relates to existing things, especially contingent events, both past and future contingent events (AN, 263). Among the questions to be answered are: Does the *cogito*-statement *obviously* fit into one of the two types of statements? If so, how would *Port-Royal Logic* have classified it?

Finally, *Port-Royal Logic* says that

even if it is necessary to have the subject matter in order to organize it, it is not, however, necessary to learn how to find the subject matter before learning how to organize it. In order to learn how to organize the subject matter, it is sufficient to have some general subjects to use as examples.... It is true, then, that we must have some subject matter in order to apply the rules of arguments to it, but it is false that this matter has to be found by the method of topics. (AN, 181)

Port-Royal Logic is here quarreling with Peter Ramus, who held exactly the opposite view. Aristotle and the schoolmen discussed the topics – the logic of discovery or invention – after enunciating the rules for valid reasoning – the logic of justification or explanation. Ramus contended that we need to discover the *content* of our argument first, before we can put its premises and conclusion in proper order. If the *cogito* is an argument, shouldn't Descartes go along at least part of the way with Ramus? For without knowing or discovering the content of the *cogito*, I could not determine its form; and if I could not determine its form – because whatever rules determine the form of a statement or an argument may be open to doubt in the First Meditation – I could not determine its validity. If it is doubted that in order to find the content of the *cogito*, the method of topics (or, for that matter, any rule or method) is necessary, then the enunciation of the rules of valid reasoning ought to come only *after* the content of the *cogito* has been established.

Appendix D

Bacon and Descartes

Descartes is remarkably united with Sir Francis Bacon in his logic of discovery. They both doubted and rejected the ancient systems of knowledge and the unexamined evidence of the senses. The human mind, said Bacon in *The New Organon*,[1] is beset by idols of four kinds: Idols of the Tribe, Idols of the Cave, Idols of the Marketplace, and Idols of the Theater. The Idols of the Tribe represent general human failings in virtue of humanity's mental make-up; Idols of the Cave represent failure owing to the peculiarities of the individual; Idols of the Marketplace reflect the poor choice of language that obstructs the understanding; and finally, Idols of the Theater represent the various outmoded ancient and modern philosophical systems. The mind had to be purged of these idols in order that true inquiry could begin.

But one also has to cast out the old logic:

As the sciences which we now have do not help us in finding out new works, so neither does the logic which we now have help us in finding out new sciences. (B, 41)

Again:

The logic now in use serves rather to fix and give stability to the errors which have their foundation in commonly received notions than to help the search after truth. So it does more harm than good. (B, 41)

---

[1] Hereinafter B.

So learned disputations had to be replaced by experiments. Experiments must be performed that are of "no use in themselves but simply serve to discover causes and axioms" (B, 96). These experiments are called *Experimenta lucifera*, experiments of light, which are to be distinguished from *Experimenta fructifera*, experiments of fruit. The experiments of light will give us a collection of the first particulars; however, "the understanding must not . . . be allowed to jump and fly from particulars to axioms" (B 98). It should move cautiously and carefully.

But then, and then only, may we hope well of the sciences when in a just scale of ascent, and by successive steps not interrupted or broken, we rise from particulars to lesser axioms, and then to middle axioms, one above the other; and last of all the most general. (B,98)

Both Bacon and Descartes wanted to create a new system of knowledge on well-founded truths: Bacon began with simple, careful observations and experiments, Descartes with simple, powerful intuitions. The generalizations and higher generalizations came later, emphatically not before. What role did the syllogism play in Bacon's logic of discovery? Not much.

The syllogism is not applied to the first principles of science, and is applied in vain to intermediate axioms, being no match for the subtlety of nature. It commands assent therefore to the proposition, but does not take hold of the thing. (B, Aphorism 13, p.41)

The syllogism consists of propositions, propositions consist of words, words are symbols of notions. Therefore if the notions themselves (which is the root of the matter) are confused and over hastily abstracted from the facts, there can be no firmness in the superstructure. Our only hope therefore lies in a true induction. (B, Aphorism 14, p. 41)

What we find in Bacon is remarkably parallel to what we find in Descartes. The first principle – in Descartes' terminology, the first item of knowledge – is not to be founded on a syllogism. To "take hold of the thing," one needs to directly experience it. To rely on a syllogism is ultimately to rely on words, and words are often confusing, whence the Idols of the Marketplace. On such a foundation one cannot erect a superstructure of knowledge. Bacon concluded that the way to search for and discover truth is to "derive axioms from the senses and particulars, rising by a gradual and unbroken ascent, so that it arrives at the most general axioms last of all. This is the true way, but as yet untried." (B, 43) Descartes concluded likewise: "It is certain that if we are to discover the truth we must always begin with particular notions in order to arrive at general ones later on" (CSM II, 271; AT VII, 206). There is simply too much similarity in the structure of their respective enterprises. Perhaps, then, these are powerful historical reasons to conclude that the *cogito* was not intended by Descartes to be an argument. If it were, then it would not be the first item of knowledge.

Appendix E

Comments on Anthony Kenny's "Descartes on the Will"

Kenny's paper "Descartes on the Will"[1] is the *locus classicus* on Descartes' theory of will, error, and judgment. Since much of what Kenny says in his paper has no direct bearing on the core thesis of this book, I confine myself to making an observation or two on aspects of his paper that bear more directly on Chapter 8.

I

There is first a purely historical issue. Kenny is keen to establish that Descartes' theory of the will in the *Regulae* – published only posthumously, composed as early as 1628, if not earlier – is sharply different from the one he offered in later works such as the *Principles of Philosophy* and *Meditations on First Philosophy*. Consequently, when Leslie Beck, in his *The Method of Descartes* (17), cites a passage from the *Regulae* that smacks of what Descartes was alleged to have claimed only later, Kenny responds thus:

When he wrote the *Regulae*, Descartes still held the orthodox Thomist view.... There is, it is true, one passage which Leslie Beck sees as presupposing the later view "that judgement whether in its pure or practical use is an assent or dissent, an act of will." But the passage is most naturally interpreted as applying only to practical matters. Descartes exhorts us, in studying, "to think solely of increasing the natural light of reason, not with a view to solving

---

[1] Hereinafter KW.

this or that scholastic problem but in order that in all the happenings of our life, our intellect may show our will what alternative to choose." [CSM I, 10; AT X, 361] In this passage it is choice, and not judgement, not even practical judgement, which is attributed to the will. (KW, 135)

I shall argue that Beck's view is defensible. The passage that Beck cites comes from the very first rule of the *Regulae*. First, while it is true that Descartes speaks of choice, he explicitly speaks of judgment as well in this rule, and judgment not only in the practical context, but also in the pure – arguably theoretical (that is, scientific or metaphysical) – context. Indeed, the theoretical context is Descartes' predominant concern in this rule. Descartes wants men to pursue several sciences, not just one or two, on the grounds that this is the only way to attain the most "respectable and commendable ends" – "good sense," "universal wisdom" – namely, "contemplating the truth": "For every other science is to be valued not so much for its own sake as for its contribution to universal wisdom." (I am slightly overreaching when I speak not of *a* but of *the* most commendable aim; I have in mind the final paragraph of the Third Meditation, which dovetails nicely with what Descartes refers to as the aim that produces happiness.)

Second, Descartes wants to enable us to make judgements "in *all* the happenings of our life" (my emphasis).

Third, I added the emphasis to indicate that the context of the first rule is of cardinal importance. Its caption reads: "*The aim of our studies should be to direct the mind with a view to forming true and sound judgements about whatever comes before it*" (CSM I, 9; AT X, 359). In this first rule, Descartes is bent on persuading us that people often reason erroneously about scientific studies because they rely on a mistaken analogy. In practical matters, they say, a person cannot do everything: "[O]ne man cannot turn his hand to both farming and harp-playing." From this, says Descartes, they incorrectly conclude that "the same must be true of the sciences as well." Hence, they advocate studying the sciences separately; presumably thinking along the lines of one man, one science. But the practical arts require some "bodily aptitude and practice," and so prove restrictive; whereas knowledge is acquired by the mind: "[T]here is no need to impose any restriction on our mental powers; for the knowledge of one truth does not, like skill in one art, hinder us from discovering another" (CSM I, 9; AT X, 359–360).

Indeed, the passage that Kenny cites from the first rule in defense of his interpretation, namely, that Descartes was primarily concerned with choice in practical matters, continues thus: "He will soon be surprised to find that he has made far greater progress than those who devote themselves to particular studies, and that he has achieved not only everything that the specialists aim at but also goals far beyond any they can hope to reach" (CSM I, 10; AT X, 361). 'He' refers to someone who seriously wishes to investigate the truth, not, or not only, to someone interested in making practical choices. 'Particular studies' refers to particular scientific disciplines. Finally, in what immediately precedes the passage that Kenny cites, Descartes says that "the sciences are so closely interconnected that it is much easier to learn them all together than to separate one from the other. If, therefore, someone seriously wishes to investigate the truth of things, he ought not to select one science in particular.... He should, rather, consider simply how to increase the natural light of his reason...." The notion of the natural light of reason is used far more in the context of science and metaphysics, as in the Third Meditation, than in the practical context.

I conclude: There is far greater continuity between Descartes' earlier work and his later work than Kenny would have us believe.

II

"Now as far as ideas are concerned," says Descartes,

provided they are considered solely in themselves and I do not refer them to anything else, they cannot strictly speaking be false; for whether it is a goat or a chimera that I am imagining, it is just as true that I imagine the former as the latter. As for the will and emotions, here too one need not worry about falsity; for even if the things which I may desire are wicked or even nonexistent, that does not make it any less true that I desire them. Thus the only remaining thoughts where I must be on my guard against making a mistake are judgements. (CSM II, 26; AT VII, 37)

Kenny finds this argument "strange." "One could," says he, "as well argue that judgements in themselves could not be false, on the grounds that whether what I judge is true or false, it is none the less true that I judge" (KW, 145).

What is Descartes' justification for lumping desires with judgments? Kenny supplies an answer – an answer, he thinks, that Descartes *should* have given. "If we take together all those mental activities which can have rightness or wrongness ascribed to them, we will find that they include all those activities which Descartes ascribed to the will and exclude those which he ascribed to the intellect" (KW, 144). However, this is open to the objection that "[t]he right, we might say grandly, is a genus of which the species are the true and the good; and Descartes' classification emphasizes the unity of the genus at the cost of ignoring the diversity of the species" (KW, 144). But, says Kenny, according to Descartes a mind properly used is infallible, and hence every erroneous judgment is a moral failure. "What theologian or philosopher," asks Descartes – Kenny's translation is quite different from CSM II, 105 – "or indeed what rational man has ever denied that we are in less danger of error the more clearly we understand something before assenting to it, and that it is a sin to make a judgment before the case is known?" (KW, 144–145) Furthermore, the truth-value of a judgment is dependent on what is asserted, and not on the assertion. What is asserted (*phrastic*) is on a par with the content of the desire; the assertion is on a par with the desire (*neustic*).

This raises a question or two. First, suppose that I judge or assert the proposition, "The sun goes around the earth." The phrastic "The sun goes around the earth" is false; the judgment (containing the assertion) is false, too. It is true that I have also sinned. It may also be the case that I have made an inelegant, injudicious, implausible, even funny, claim. But my sinning – or any of these other things – is parasitic upon my making an erroneous judgment. With desires it is different. Suppose I desire that everyone stop smoking. The phrastic "Everyone stop smoking" – let us assume it to be so, without further argument – is false; on the other hand, my desire may be right or wrong, cruel or kind, serious or laughable, but not true or false – regardless of the truth-value of the phrastic. Consequently, the neustic of a judgment and the neustic of a desire yield essentially different outcomes.

Second, "The point Descartes has missed is what we may call – to adapt an expression of J. L. Austin's – 'the onus of match'"[2] (KW, 145–146). Consider the assertion of a simple declarative sentence, "The sun

---

[2] J. L. Austin, "How to Talk," in his *Philosophical Papers*, 190.

goes around the earth." The judgment is false, because the state of affairs that obtains is one in which it is the earth that goes around the sun. What shall we blame? Shall we blame the assertion or the state of affairs? Well, if it is a map of a street, the onus is on the map to precisely depict the street as it actually is; if it is an architectural plan of how the street should have been laid out in the first place, then the onus is on the street to match the plan. "Descartes, in lumping together affirmation and desire, negation and aversion, confounds the different onus of match involved in the two different kinds of assent and dissent. This, it seems to me, is the fundamental defect in his theory of judgement as an act of the will." (KW, 146) Thus, Kenny.

It is difficult to come up with an example of an assertion in which the onus of match is on the state of affairs. Consequently, I am going to assume, pending examples and arguments from Kenny, that in the case of assertions the onus of match is always on the phrastic component of the assertion, and the aim of the neustic is always to get that match right. Now, consider the following. A pious Christian astronomer, in the days after Galileo, says, "I desire that the sun goes around the earth." Is it obvious that the onus of match is on the state of affairs? Is it obvious that the onus of match is on the astronomer to bring his desires in line with physical reality? If so, it would obliterate the difference between an assertion and a desire. (Notice: Crazy desires are no less desires; and in the case of this example, if the astronomer believes that his theory of the solar system would be enormously simplified if indeed the sun went around the earth, it is not even clear that the desire is *that* crazy.) Or suppose that I said, "I desire that everyone stop smoking." Is the onus of match on me? Must I now think, act, and do things in order to bring about that state of affairs? And if I said, "I desire that extraterrestrial beings descend on earth," would I similarly have an onus to do things that would bring about that state of affairs? What would I have to do? The point is this: Desires do not always, or necessarily, come attached with onuses; judgments never fail to have an onus attached to them.

Third and finally, Kenny considers only desires and judgments as lumped together, but they are not the only ones put together in one class. Will, emotions, and chimeras belong in that class, as well as any ideas that "are considered solely in themselves and I do not refer them to anything else." It is not clear how Kenny's analysis could apply to all of them. For example, consider chimeras. Here Descartes is simply entertaining an idea, not making a judgment. It is not a desire. Let us even grant that there is a phrastic involved, for the sake of argument. What is its neustic? Nonetheless, it is not obvious that we should speak of the idea of chimeras as being true, if accidentally the alleged chimeras do exist. The argument is so much stronger if the idea is false. Even if the notion of rightness ties together judgment and desire, it is not evident how rightness could tie in ideas like chimeras as well.

Descartes' theory of will and judgment is decidedly not adequate for several reasons, not least of which are reasons that Kenny himself has devised (see especially KW, 156–159). But on the present score, Descartes is not guilty of Kenny's charges.

III

Let us follow Kenny following David Hume on the nature of human free will. There is the liberty of spontaneity and there is the liberty of indifference (*A Treatise of Human Nature*, 262–265). The liberty of spontaneity is defined in terms of wanting, and goes thus: "[W]e are free in doing something if and only if we do it because we want to do it." The liberty of indifference is defined in terms of power: "[W]e are free in doing something if and only if it is in our power not to do it" (KW, 146). What follows is a masterly account of how, like most philosophers, Descartes attempted to combine the two forms of liberty in his account of human free will. I have always found Hume's account unsatisfactory. The liberty of spontaneity dispenses with a crucial step, and it does so without much justification. It is the step that answers the question, "Are not the wants *themselves* determined?" If our wants themselves are determined, that is, if we do not enjoy the liberty of indifference with respect to our wants, then it is *never* in our power not to want what we want. I grant that Descartes has a right to stipulate how he is going to use the words 'free' and 'voluntary'. "Descartes was willing to call an act voluntary," says Kenny, "if it was in accordance with the agent's desires, whether or not it was unavoidable; indeed, unlike most scholastics, he was prepared to call an unavoidable, but welcome, action 'free' as well as 'voluntary'" (KW, 139). I contend only that he has provided no philosophical justification for this. One need read no further than Kant.

Descartes' view about where the credit lies when we act correctly can now be seen as equally puzzling. In *Principles of Philosophy*, Descartes says, "[W]hen we embrace the truth, our doing so voluntarily is much more to our credit than would be the case if we could not do otherwise" (CSM I, 205; AT VIIIA,19). Surely, here Descartes is invoking the liberty of spontaneity. Kenny comments on this passage as follows: "At first sight this appears to mean that when we embrace truth clearly seen, we are free not to embrace it; but from the sequel it is clear that this is not so. Perhaps Descartes means that in such a case the credit goes not to us but to the author of our nature, as the credit for the precise operation of a machine goes to its maker." (KW, 149, note 51) I suspect that Kenny had in mind a passage that comes just six paragraphs later: "[T]he minds of all of us have been so moulded by nature that whenever we perceive something clearly, we spontaneously give our assent to it and are *quite unable* to doubt its truth" (CSM I, 207; AT VIIIA, 21; my emphasis). Undoubtedly, what we lack, according to this passage, is the liberty of indifference. What ineluctably follows is that we deserve credit about as much as the machine.

Bibliography

Abbott, Edwin A. *Francis Bacon: An Account of his Life and Works.* London: Macmillan, 1885.

Adams, Robert M. "Primitive Thisness and Primitive Identity." *The Journal of Philosophy,* Volume 76, No. 1 (January 1979), 5–26.

Anderson, Alan, and Belnap, Nuel. "Enthymemes." *The Journal of Philosophy,* Volume 58 (1961), 713–723.

Arnauld, Antoine, and Nicole, Pierre. *Logic or the Art of Thinking.* Translated and edited by Jill Vance Buroker. Cambridge: Cambridge University Press, 1996.

Ashworth, E. J. "Traditional Logic." In Quentin Skinner, Eckhard Kessler, and Jill Kraye, editors. *The Cambridge History of Renaissance Philosophy.* New York: Cambridge University Press, 1988, pp. 143–172.

Augustine. *On the Free Choice of the Will.* Translated with an introduction by Thomas Williams. Indianapolis: Hackett, 1993.

Austin, J. L. "How to Talk." *Philosophical Papers.* New York: Oxford University Press, 1961,

Ayer, Alfred J. "I Think, Therefore I Am." In Willis Doney, editor. *Descartes: A Collection of Critical Essays.* London: Macmillan, 1968, pp. 80–87.

Ayer, Alfred J. *Language, Truth, and Logic.* London: Victor Gollancz, 1964.

Bacon, Francis. *The New Organon and Related Writings.* New York: Bobbs-Merrill, 1960.

Baker, Gordon, and Morris, Katherine J. *Descartes' Dualism.* New York: Routledge, 1996.

Beck, L. J. *The Method of Descartes: A Study of the Regulae.* Oxford: Oxford University Press, 1970.

Belaval, Y. *Leibniz: Critique de Descartes.* Paris: 1960.

Black, Max. *A Companion to Wittgenstein's* Tractatus. Ithaca, N.Y.: Cornell University Press, 1970.

Borges, Jorge Louis. "Borges and I." In Douglas R. Hofstadter and Daniel C. Dennett, editors. *The Mind's I: Fantasies and Reflections on Self and Soul.* New York: Bantam, 1982, pp. 19–20.

"The Circular Ruins." In Douglas R. Hofstadter and Daniel C. Dennett, editors. *The Mind's I: Fantasies and Reflections on Self and Soul.* New York: Bantam, 1982, pp. 344–348.

Buchdahl, Gerd. *Metaphysics and the Philosophy of Science. The Classical Origins: Descartes to Kant.* Cambridge, Mass.: MIT Press, 1969.

Buroker, Jill Vance. "Introduction." In Antoine Arnauld and Pierre Nicole, *Logic or The Art of Thinking.* Translated and edited by Jill Vance Buroker. Cambridge: Cambridge University Press, 1996, pp. ix–xxvi.

Chadwick, Henry. *Augustine.* New York: Oxford University Press, 1986.

Curley, Edwin M. "Certainty: Psychological, Moral, and Metaphysical." In Stephen Voss, editor. *Essays on the Philosophy and Science of Rene Descartes.* New York: Oxford University Press, 1993, pp. 11–30.

Descartes against the Skeptics. Cambridge, Mass.: Harvard University Press, 1978.

Descartes, Rene. *The Philosophical Writings of Descartes*, Volume 3, *The Correspondence.* Translated by John Cottingham, Robert Stoothoff, Dugald Murdoch, and Anthony Kenny. Cambridge: Cambridge University Press, 1991.

The Philosophical Writings of Descartes, Volumes 1 and 2. Translated by John Cottingham, Robert Stoothoff, and Dugald Murdoch. Cambridge: Cambridge University Press, 1984.

Descartes' Conversation with Burman. Translated with an introduction and commentary by John Cottingham. Oxford: Oxford University Press, 1976.

Treatise of Man. Translation and commentary by Thomas Steele Hall. Cambridge: Harvard University Press, 1972.

Dickoff, James, James, Patricia, and Hendel, Charles W. "Introduction." In Antoine Arnauld and Pierre Nicole, *Logic or The Art of Thinking: Port-Royal Logic.* Translated and edited by James Dickoff, Patricia James, and Charles W. Hendel. New York: Bobbs-Merrill, 1964, pp. xxvi–xli.

Ellis, Brian David. *Rational Belief Systems.* Lanham, Md.: Rowman and Littlefield, 1979.

Faust, David. *The Limits of Scientific Reasoning.* Minneapolis: University of Minnesota Press, 1984.

Feldman, Fred. "Epistemic Appraisal and the Cartesian Circle." *Philosophical Studies,* Volume 27 (1975), 37–55.

Frankfurt, Harry G. *Demons, Dreamers, and Madmen: The Defense of Reason in Descartes' Meditations.* Indianapolis, Ind.: Bobbs-Merril, 1970.

Gaukroger, Stephen. *Descartes: An Intellectual Biography.* New York: Oxford University Press, 1995.

"The Sources of Descartes's Procedure of Deductive Demonstration in Metaphysics and Natural Philosophy." In John Cottingham, editor. *Reason, Will, and Sensation: Studies in Descartes's Metaphysics.* New York: Oxford University Press, 1994, pp. 47–60.

Cartesian Logic: An Essay on Descartes's Conception of Inference. New York: Oxford University Press, 1989.

Geach, Peter T. *Logic Matters*. Berkeley: University of California Press, 1980.

Gewirth, Alan. "The Cartesian Circle." *Philosophical Review*, Volume 50 (1941), 368–395.

Haack, Susan. "The Justification of Deduction." *Mind*, Volume 85 (1976), 112–119.

Hacking, Ian. "Leibniz and Descartes: Proof and Eternal Truths," *Proceedings of the British Academy*, Volume 59 (1973), 1–16.

Haldane, Elizabeth S. *Descartes: His Life and Times*. London: John Murray, 1905.

Hintikka, Jaakko. "*Cogito, Ergo Sum*: Inference or Performance?" In Willis Doney, editor. *Descartes: A Collection of Critical Essays*. London: Macmillan, 1968, pp. 108–139.

Howell, Wilbur S. *Logic and Rhetoric in England, 1500–1700*. Princeton, N.J.: Princeton University Press, 1956.

Hume, David. *A Treatise of Human Nature*. David Fate Norton and Mary J. Norton, editors. New York: Oxford University Press, 2000.

Jardine, Lisa. "Humanistic Logic." In Quentin Skinner, Eckhard Kessler, and Jill Kraye, editors. *The Cambridge History of Renaissance Philosophy*. New York: Cambridge University Press, 1988, pp. 173–198.

Joy, Lynn Sumida. *Gassendi the Atomist: Advocate of History in an Age of Science*. New York: Cambridge University Press, 1989.

Kant, Immanuel. *Critique of Pure Reason*. Translated and edited by Paul Guyer and Allen W. Wood. New York: Cambridge University Press, 1998.

Kenny, Anthony. "Descartes on the Will." In John Cottingham, editor. *Descartes: Oxford Readings in Philosophy*. New York: Oxford University Press, 1998, pp. 132–159.

Descartes: A Study of His Philosophy. New York: Random House, 1968.

Kline, Morris. *Mathematics: The Loss of Certainty*. New York: Oxford University Press, 1980.

Kneale, William, and Kneale, Martha. *The Development of Logic*. Oxford: Clarendon Press, 1964.

Leibniz, Gottfried W. *Die Philosophischen Schriften von G. W. Leibniz*. Edited by C. I. Gerhardt. Hildesheim: Georg Olms Verlagsbuchhandlung, 1960.

Lewis, David. *On the Plurality of Worlds*. New York: Oxford University Press, 1986.

Philosophical Papers, Volume 1. New York: Oxford University Press, 1983.

Locke, John. *An Essay Concerning Human Understanding*, Volume 2. Annotated by Alexander Campbell Fraser. New York: Dover, 1959.

Lohr, Charles H. "The Sixteenth-Century Transformation of the Aristotelian Division of the Speculative Sciences." In D. R. Kelley and R. H. Popkin, editors. *The Shape of Knowledge from the Renaissance to the English Enlightenment*. Norwell, Mass.: Kluwer, 1991, pp. 49–58.

"Jesuit Aristotelianism and Sixteenth Century Metaphysics." In G. Fletcher and M. B. Scheute, editors. *Paradosis*. New York: Fordham University Press, 1976, pp. 203–220.

Losonsky, Michael. *Enlightenment and Action From Descartes to Kant: Passionate Thought.* New York: Cambridge University Press, 2001.

Menn, Stephen. *Descartes and Augustine.* New York: Cambridge University Press, 1998.

Montaigne, Michael de. *An Apology for Raymond Sebond.* Translated and edited by M. A. Screech. New York: Penguin, 1987.

Nozick, Robert. *An Examined Life.* New York: Simon and Schuster, 1989.

"Fiction." In Douglas R. Hofstadter and Daniel C. Dennett, editors. *The Mind's I: Fantasies and Reflections on Self and Soul.* New York: Bantam, 1982, pp. 461–464.

Philosophical Explanations. Cambridge, Mass.: Harvard University Press, 1981.

O'Neill, Onora. *Constructions of Reason: Explorations of Kant's Practical Philosophy.* New York: Cambridge University Press, 1989.

Perry, John. "Frege on Demonstratives." *Philosophical Review,* Volume 86 (1977), 474–497.

Popkin, Richard H. *The History of Scepticism: From Erasmus to Descartes.* Revised edition. New York: Harper Torchbooks, 1964.

Popper, Karl. *Conjectures and Refutations: The Growth of Scientific Knowledge.* New York: Harper Torchbooks, 1965.

Prichard, H. A. "Descartes's Meditations." In Willis Doney, editor. *Descartes: A Collection of Critical Essays.* London: Macmillan, 1968, pp. 140–168.

Quine, W. V. O. *Methods of Logic.* Revised edition. New York: Holt, Reinhart and Winston, 1959.

Rodis-Lewis, Genevieve. *Descartes: His Life and Thought.* Translated by Jane Marie Todd. Ithaca, N.Y.: Cornell University Press, 1999.

Rorty, Amelie O., editor. *Essays on Descartes'* Meditations. Berkeley: University of California Press, 1986.

Ryle, Gilbert. *The Concept of Mind.* New York: Penguin, 1966.

Sarkar, Husain. "Something, Nothing, and Explanation." *Southwest Philosophy Review,* Volume 9, No. 1 (January 1993), 151–161.

Schlesinger, George. *Religion and Scientific Method.* Dordrecht: D. Reidl, 1977.

"The Problem of Evil and the Problem of Suffering." *American Philosophical Quarterly,* Volume 1 (1964), 244–247.

Sextus Empiricus. *Outlines of Pyrrohnism.* The Loeb Classical Library. Translated by Rev. R. G. Bury. New York: Putnam's Sons, 1933–44.

Shakespeare, William. *Macbeth.* The Arden Shakespeare. Edited by Kenneth Muir. London: Methuen, 1962.

Smiley, T. J. "Entailment and Deducibility." *Proceedings of the Aristotelian Society,* n.s., Volume 59 (1959), 233–254.

Smullyan, Raymond M. *What Is the Name of This Book?* New York: Prentice Hall, 1978.

Spinoza, Benedict de. *The Chief Works of Benedict de Spinoza,* Volume 2. New York: Dover, 1951.

Stout, A. K. "The Basis of Knowledge in Descartes." In Willis Doney, editor. *Descartes: A Collection of Critical Essays.* London: Macmillan, 1968, pp. 169–191.

Strawson, Peter. *Introduction to Logical Theory.* London: Methuen, 1967.

"Review of von Wright." *The Philosophical Quarterly,* Volume 8 (1958), 372–376.

Taylor, Charles. *Sources of the Self: The Making of the Modern Identity.* Cambridge, Mass.: Harvard University Press, 1989.

Tlumak, Jeffrey. "Certainty and Cartesian Method." In Michael Hooker, editor. *Descartes: Critical and Interpretive Essays.* Baltimore: Johns Hopkins University Press, 1978, pp. 40–73.

van Cleve, James. "Foundationalism, Epistemic Principles, and the Cartesian Circle." In John Cottingham, editor. *Descartes: Oxford Readings in Philosophy.* New York: Oxford University Press, 1998, pp. 101–131.

von Wright, Georg H. *Logical Studies.* London: Routledge and Kegan Paul, 1957.

Vrooman, Jack R. *Rene Descartes: A Biography.* New York: G. P. Putnam's Sons, 1970.

Williams, Bernard. "Introduction." In John Cottingham, editor and translator. *Meditations on First Philosophy by Rene Descartes. With Selections from Objections and Replies.* New York: Cambridge University Press, 1986, pp. vii–xvii.

Descartes: The Project of Pure Inquiry. New York: Penguin, 1978.

"The Certainty of the *Cogito.*" In Willis Doney, editor. *Descartes: A Collection of Critical Essays.* London: Macmillan, 1968, pp. 88–107.

Wilson, Margaret D. *Descartes.* New York: Routledge and Kegan Paul, 1986.

Wittgenstein, Ludwig. *On Certainty.* New York: Harper and Row, 1969.

Tractatus Logico-Philosophicus. London: Routledge and Kegan Paul, 1961.

Name Index

Subject Index